WOMEN IN LAW AND LAWMAKING IN NINETEENTH AND TWENTIETH-CENTURY EUROPE

Women in Law and Lawmaking in Nineteenth and Twentieth-Century Europe

EVA SCHANDEVYL
Vrije Universiteit Brussel, Belgium

Routledge
Taylor & Francis Group
LONDON AND NEW YORK

First published 2014 by Ashgate Publishing

2 Park Square, Milton Park, Abingdon, Oxon OX14 4RN
711 Third Avenue, New York, NY 10017, USA

Routledge is an imprint of the Taylor & Francis Group, an informa business

First issued in paperback 2016

British Library Cataloguing in Publication Data
A catalogue record for this book is available from the British Library.

The Library of Congress has cataloged the printed edition as follows:
Women in law and lawmaking in nineteenth and twentieth-century Europe / edited by Eva Schandevyl.
pages cm
Includes bibliographical references and index.
ISBN 978-1-4094-4873-0 (hardcover)
1. Women lawyers--Europe--History. 2. Practice of law--Europe--History.
I. Schandevyl, Eva, 1974- editor of compilation.
KJC3770.W66 2014
340.082'094--dc23

2014002735

ISBN 978-1-4094-4873-0 (hbk)
ISBN 978-1-138-71097-9 (pbk)

Contents

List of Tables

Notes on Contributors

Maria Rita Bartolomei is a lawyer and a legal mediator with a PhD in Sociology of Legal and Political Institutions. She is presently working as adjunct professor of Cultural Anthropology (University of Macerata) and Sociology of Law (University of Messina). She has conducted anthropological fieldwork in Italy as well as in India (Kerala) and in Africa (Ivory Coast, Tanzania and Zambia). Her fields of interest are traditional institutions in black Africa; migration and legal adaptation; and, especially, the role of women jurists in changing legal cultures and empowering women's and children's (human) rights.

Nadezda Belyakova holds a PhD in History (2009) from the Moscow State Lomonosov University on church–state relations in Belarus, Ukraine and the Baltic Republics. She is currently a researcher at the Centre for Religion and Church History of the Institute of World History (Russian Academy of Science). She has contributed to monographs on women in Russian Canon law, and church and society in Central and Eastern European countries.

Taisiya Belyakova is a PhD candidate at the Johannes Gutenberg University (Mainz), and scholarship holder at the Max Planck Institute for European Legal History (Frankfurt am Main). She is currently a researcher at the Institute of World History and is specializing in the influence of Byzantine law on the Slavic legal tradition; medieval history of the Balkans; and especially women in medieval Serbia and Byzantium.

Mathieu Brûlé is a PhD candidate in the Department of History at York University in Toronto. His research interests include Canadian and French labour history, particularly the relationship between class, gender and sexuality. His current research explores the relationship between the gay and lesbian movements and organized labour in Ontario during the second half of the twentieth century.

Dave De ruysscher is a legal historian and lawyer. He specializes in themes regarding the history of commercial and private law. The focus of his research has thus far been on early modern commercial law, in particular on bills of exchange, partnership and bankruptcy, and also on contract law of that period (assignment, capacity to contract). He has written two substantial books, several peer-reviewed articles and book chapters. He is currently working at the

Department of Interdisciplinary Legal Studies of the Vrije Universiteit Brussel, and as a postdoctoral researcher of the Fund of Scientific Research – Flanders, at the University of Antwerp.

Evdoxios Doxiadis completed his PhD at the University of California, Berkeley, in 2007. He then was the Ted and Elaine Athanassiades postdoctoral fellow at Princeton University, and has since worked at the International Center for Hellenic and Mediterranean Studies in Athens and at San Francisco State University. He is a lecturer at Simon Fraser University in Vancouver, Canada. His research focus is on Greek, Balkan and Mediterranean history, with a particular interest in questions of gender, law, state formation and minorities. He has published the book *The Shackles of Modernity: Women, Property, and the Transition from the Ottoman Empire to the Modern Greek State 1750–1850* (Cambridge, 2012) and several book chapters and journal articles (*Past and Present*, *Byzantine and Modern Greek Studies*, *Journal of Modern Greek Studies*).

Aurore François is assistant professor at the Université Catholique de Louvain (History) and researcher and assistant professor at the Université de Liège (Political Science). She received her PhD in History from the Université catholique de Louvain, with a dissertation on juvenile delinquency – *Guerres et délinquance juvénile (1912–1950). Un demi-siècle de pratiques judiciaires et institutionnelles envers des mineurs en difficulté* (Die Keure, 2011). Her main research interests include juvenile delinquency (data, discourses, practices); institutions for juvenile delinquents; and methodological developments in social science research.

Sara L. Kimble (PhD, University of Iowa) is a historian and assistant professor at DePaul University in Chicago, Illinois. She is also affiliated as a scholar-in-residence at the Newberry Library. As a scholar of modern European history, her research focuses on the intersection of law, gender and socio-political reform in the nineteenth and twentieth centuries. Her current book project, *Women, Feminism, and the Law in Modern France: Justice Redressed*, investigates the role of feminist lawyers in the campaign to expand the definition of the Rights of Man. She has published articles in *French Historical Studies* and *French Colonial History*, and has also written book reviews for *Gender and History*, *Women in Judaism: A Multidisciplinary Journal* and *H-France Review*.

Christine Machiels is a historian and, since 2010, has been director of the Centre d'Animation et de Recherche en Histoire Ouvrière et Populaire (CARHOP). She received her PhD in History from the Université Catholique de Louvain and the Université d'Angers, with a dissertation on feminism and prostitution in Belgium, France and Switzerland (*Les féminismes face à* *la prostitution en Belgique, France, Suisse, XIXe–XXe siècles*, 2011). Her main research interests include feminism, social control and labour history.

Mary Jane Mossman is professor of Law at Osgoode Hall Law School, York University, in Toronto. She has been involved in teaching property and family law, and gender equality. Her research and publications encompass these areas as well as access to justice and the history of women lawyers. She published *The First Women Lawyers: A Comparative Study of Gender, Law and the Legal Professions* (Hart, 2006), and has contributed articles and book reviews about early women lawyers to several journals. Mary Jane Mossman has been the recipient of a number of research and teaching awards in Canada, and was awarded an honorary doctorate by the Law Society of Upper Canada in 2004. She also was director of Osgoode's Institute for Feminist Legal Studies from 2002 to 2010.

Marion Röwekamp is a historian (PhD, University of Munich) and lawyer. After various stays in the United States (Columbia University, Mount Holyoke College, Harvard University) and Mexico (Colegio de México, CIESAS, Universidad Nacional Autónoma de México) as a Feodor Lynen Fellow of the Alexander von Humboldt Foundation, she is now working at the Institute for Latin American Studies of the Freie Universität in Berlin. Her research focuses on the intersections of gender and legal history. She has published the books *Juristinnen. Lexikon zu Leben und Werk* (Baden-Baden: Nomos, 2005) and *Die ersten deutschen Juristinnen. Eine Geschichte ihr*er *Professionalisierung und Emanzipation (1900–1945)* (Böhlau, 2011) as well as various articles.

Eva Schandevyl is a part-time research professor at the Vrije Universiteit Brussel, where she has teached modern Belgian and European history. She received her PhD in History from this university in 2003. She researches themes regarding intellectual history; and the social and political history of justice administration. The focus of her current research lies in particular in gender and legal history. She has written *Tussen revolutie en conformisme. Het engagement en de netwerken van linkse intellectuelen in België, 1918–1956* (ASP, 2011), co-edited *In haar recht? Vrouwe Justitia feministisch bekeken* (ASP, 2009) and published many book chapters and journal articles (in *European Review of History*, *Journal of Belgian History*, *National Identities*, *Historica*, *Revue Belge de Philologie et d'Histoire*, *Cahiers d'histoire du temps présent*, *Res Publica*, *Tijdschrift voor Geschiedenis* and *European Journal of Cross-Cultural Competence and Management*). She is affiliated to the RHEA-Research Centre for Gender and Diversity and the Department of Interdisciplinary Legal Studies, both at the Vrije Universiteit Brussel.

Acknowledgements

First of all I wish to thank the contributors for embarking on this project with me. Contributing a chapter to an edited book is a bit like setting out on a journey with the end destination partly unknown. I am grateful for their continued trust; it has contributed in making this collaboration a pleasant and successful undertaking.

A special thanks to Tom Gray and his colleagues at Ashgate for supporting the project, for their patience and for helping me through the publication process.

In Belgium I thank the Fund for Scientific Research – Flanders, and at the Vrije Universiteit Brussel the RHEA-Research Centre for Gender and Diversity for their financial support.

As always my family has been very supportive, morally and practically, at the right moments and whenever needed. Little Sara has been ever so present in the making of this book. She still has to make her history. It is to her and her generation of future women that this book is dedicated.

An Introduction to Women in Law and Lawmaking in Nineteenth- and Twentieth-century Europe

Eva Schandevyl

This book features the insights of scholars from seven different countries, who analyse barriers to gender equality in various domains of European legal history in the nineteenth and twentieth centuries. Several contributions focus on women's access to the legal profession and their position therein. Other contributions discuss the inequality in relation to what is reflected on the level of jurisprudence. The outlook here moves to gender-based structures within the law and how these had an impact on women's legal status, for instance in property rights, contracting rights and labour rights. Together, the different chapters provide elements of answers to questions that hitherto have been largely ignored by humanities and social science research, but also to questions that are the object of much debate. Does gender make a difference to the way the judiciary and lawyers work or should work?[1] How did nineteenth-century law reforms affect married women's rights in mixed or transitional legal regimes, notably those on the outskirts of Europe? How have reforms affected women's confidence in the ability of law institutions to deliver justice? How, in sum, did women's interaction with the law shape the fields of legal history and gender history?

The subjects broached remain relevant today. The constitutions of nineteenth-century nation states reserved the right to equality for only one sex, men. From there on it took until the twentieth century for women in Europe to see gender justice formally achieved. Yet barriers to actual equality still exist. In most European countries, for example, there is a more or less pronounced glass ceiling to women's judicial careers.[2] It is therefore meaningful and necessary to uncover the very roots of gender stereotype reasoning and discourses (that sometimes persist until today) and to look at the origins of rules of law that have hindered women in their rights. This book aims to do so.

---

[1] This question has recently and comprehensively been explored in: Ulrike Schultz and Gisela Shaw (ed.), *Gender and Judging* (Oxford, 2013).

[2] Ulrike Schultz and Gisela Shaw, 'Introduction: Gender and Judging: Overview and Synthesis', in Schultz and Shaw, *Gender and Judging*, p. 7.

Despite the undisputable growing interest in the field of gender and law and the rapid but relatively recent feminisation of the judicial world, relatively few studies have attempted to sort out the relationship between gender and law in modern Europe. It is surprising that legal historians have largely ignored the issue of women in law and lawmaking in nineteenth- and twentieth-century Europe. As Rosemary Auchmuty pointed out, it is a fact that conventional legal scholarship has mostly been inward looking, recognising only the validity of its own (legal) sources. Thus in an era before women had any role in lawmaking, they were inevitably absent from the story. Notwithstanding the fact that today women represent half of the entrants into the legal profession and well over half of law students in most European universities, their heritage has been overlooked, ignored, suppressed or distorted for a very long time.[3] Moreover, gender as an analytical category has seldom been analysed according to its actual impact on society and social relations in the area of the law, although its application is most obvious: a gender approach to law unravels the mechanisms by which law and its institutions participate in the construction, the persistence or the transformation of gender patterns. Law is indeed not gender-neutral. Discrimination is evident, as illustrated by the contributions in this book.

The feminist movement played a crucial role in uncovering the suppressing mechanisms of the law and in the decision-making bodies of public institutions. Several contributions in this volume demonstrate that women lawyers' activism had certainly, since the nineteenth century, an impact on the politics and institutions of Europe. The year 1865 marks the first feminist protests against the Civil code in France. From the picture that is drawn in this volume, women emerge as being far from powerless and voiceless.

This book thus fills a gap and nuances existing literature by engaging scholars trained in history as well as legal specialists with a broad European comparative focus. The chapters cover all quadrants of Europe – Northern, Southern, Eastern and Western. This volume highlights exciting new research by a number of established and emerging scholars who examine women in law and in lawmaking issues in the nineteenth and twentieth centuries in a framework that seeks to challenge disciplinary categories.

Despite working from different areas, the authors share the ambition of using some of the richest methodologies from the humanities and social sciences. Their chapters involve heuristics, data collection and interviews within such frameworks as sociology of law and gender theory. The authors also include narrative accounts and many case studies, which brings the actors in their stories to life and allows greater access to the experiences of those who have lived

---

3 Rosemary Auchmuty, 'Whatever Happened to Miss Bebb? *Bebb v The Law Society* and Women's Legal History', *Legal Studies*, 31/2 (2011): p. 200.

through this period.[4] In bringing some of the most valuable aspects of their specialities to their research – the extensive archival research, the interpretation of empirical data, participant observation – the authors stimulate women's studies by showing what historians can learn from jurists, legal sociologists from anthropologists and so on, as well as what specialists in subfields such as private law, public policy, intellectual studies, labour history and gender studies can contribute to the field of contemporary European history.

Some methodological and theoretical choices that are made in several of the chapters require a brief explanation. First, one of the authors (Maria Rita Bartolomei) turned to participant observation and oral accounts as one means of gathering material. An advantage of studying contemporary Europe is precisely in having access to men and women who can recount their experiences.[5] However, the author has not relied solely on interviews: she has used them as a complement to quantitative data, which provides a valuable interpretative element to her study. Second, the political sociology and sociology of law-inspired approach of actors and of social movements and the emphasis on the role of social networks are evident in several chapters (Sara L. Kimble, Marion Röwekamp, Mary Jane Mossman). With their combined focus on the broader women's movement in its historical context and the particularities of individual actors' emancipation within different nation states, they explain the political and professional participation and activism of women who may or may not have had access to the legal field and to suffrage, and who remained largely at the margins of traditional institutions. The authors here try to understand the ways in which state institutions, professional behaviour, social discourses and national culture affect women's opportunities, especially their access to citizenship and to the judiciary.

Next, the contribution of gender theory is evident in all chapters, and in particular in those by Aurore François and Christine Machiels, Sara L. Kimble, Marion Röwekamp and Mathieu Brûlé, who dwell upon the impact of the essentialist discourse versus the equality concept on women's labour participation in the nineteenth and first half of twentieth centuries (Röwekamp refers to relational versus individualist feminism). Finally, the chapters of Dave De ruysscher, Evdoxios Doxiadis and Nadezda Belyakova and Taisya Belyakova join in with the more conventional legal scholarship, based on legal sources. With their emphasis on critical historical and political moments, they pursue the work undertaken by legal historians and social scientists and add a compelling longitudinal dimension to the study of women in law. Next to the

4 On this element of storytelling that helps to enliven historical research, see also: Wendy Pojmann, 'Introduction', in Wendy Pojmann (ed.), *Migration and Activism in Europe since 1945* (New York, 2008), p. 3.

5 Ibid.

obvious focus in this volume on private law, and to a lesser degree on public law, the authors of the last two above-mentioned chapters have also taken Canon law and religious belonging into their accounts of women's rights and participation in the legal field.

This book is divided into three parts, including in each part chapters that handle similar themes in different contexts. Part I considers women's access to legal professions in Belgium, France and Germany during the first half of the twentieth century. Part II offers a long-term look at the impact of gender constructions on jurisprudence in – once again – Belgium and France, and in two Catholic Orthodox countries at the southern and eastern borders of Europe, Greece and Russia, with a special emphasis on periods of changing cultural and legal norms during the nineteenth century. Part III examines the issue of gendered legal cultures in a global perspective, yet with a focus on contemporary Italy in the first contribution and Western Europe, the United States and some British colonies in the late nineteenth and early twentieth centuries in the second contribution. A more detailed description of each of the three parts follows.

Part I: History of Women in the Legal Profession

The chapters in Part I focus on the historical development of women's access to the legal profession, revealing the roots of present-day and well-known barriers to gender equality in legal careers. They show that there is an historical explanation of both the problematic representation of women within the top judiciary[6] and the often encountered limitation of jurist women's competences in specific fields such as youth delinquency and protection of the family.

Aurore François and Christine Machiels explain how child protection became one of the first domains in which women got involved socially, politically and professionally. From the end of the nineteenth century onwards, there was a growing debate in Belgium and on the international level about the role women could play in the juvenile justice system and in the specialised courts dealing with delinquent children that at that time emerged all around Europe. A 1912 law created the first juvenile courts in Belgium. From probation officers to juvenile judges later, from women doctors to female police officers, women got involved in child protection in multiple ways. Yet each of these positions or duties was the

[6] Although the judiciary has gained a much more equal representation in recent years, this does not apply to the upper echelons of the judicial system, where it remains a male bastion. Recent European studies show that the proportion of female judges in higher courts still tends to decrease the higher the level in the hierarchy. Fewer women than men are court presidents and the majority of women are gathered in courts of first instance and in lower judicial positions. See: European Commission for the Efficiency of Justice (CEPEJ), *European Judicial Systems: Efficiency and Quality of Justice. An Overview* (Strasbourg, 2012).

subject of fierce discussion and negotiation concerning the specificity – and even legitimacy – of women's formal participation in the labour market in this field of social action. Based on parliamentary debates records, contemporary sources on child protection, juvenile courts' archives, accounts and writings of Belgian feminists engaged at the national or the international level (League of Nations, International Council of Women), François and Machiels analyse the arguments and ideas brought forward by different actors dealing with juvenile delinquency.

It was in the area of child welfare policy, closely linked to the traditional family and private sphere, that women first claimed new roles for themselves and transformed their emphasis on motherhood into public policy. When in Belgium eventually the first juvenile courts were created, the professional opportunities for women in the field were however immediately restricted. The opening of the position of juvenile judge to them was not even discussed by the predominantly male and Catholic members of the Belgian Parliament. The spirit of the age remained connected to the Christian charity model inherited from the nineteenth century that favoured the selfless interventions of philanthropists engaged in youth protection rather than the creation of jobs related to the field. Financial compensation, one of the most obvious characteristics of professionalisation, would allegedly alter the pureness of the actions and the quality of the interventions within families. Only in the middle of the 1930s, when the professionalisation of the sector became a pressing issue and when the role of the police and the judiciary came up for discussion, did the volunteers make way for trained social workers and civil servants.

Yet it is worth mentioning that what eventually managed to convince male decision makers about women's access to the professions in relation to child protection were not egalitarian speeches that promoted gender equality on the basis of the universality of human nature. It was rather a set of arguments putting forward the intrinsic qualities of women, which men were allegedly lacking, and that resulted in a model based on the different but complementary nature of men and women, adapted to the respective skills of both sexes. This essentialist discourse, claiming the specificity of women, was not perceived as antagonistic to the concept of equality by Belgian feminists themselves, who did not perceive the egalitarian views as strategically successful. These women activists did not seem to be aware that the emphasis on 'natural skills' could limit the involvement of women in the public sphere. Even if it allowed women to actively participate in fields connected to their 'innate expertise', like social work with families, it did not help them obtain positions that were considered unrelated to the traditional roles of women in the domestic sphere, at least in the short term.

Aurore François and Christine Machiels argue that the Belgian actors involved in the debates dealing with juvenile delinquency in the twentieth century are in many ways emblematic of the complementary-based model this trend in feminism produced in practice. Women's involvement at the local level followed this discourse of 'natural qualifications' where women's roles were distributed according to a pattern in which men took care of older teenagers and women were in charge of younger children and girls. Files and tasks were thus distributed by gender standards. If from the 1930–40s onwards it resulted in women's access to public spheres that previously were closed to them, the essentialist argument only had a limited impact. It could even be turned against those upholding it. Transposed to other issues, the notion of typically female competencies did not always result in emancipating women. On the contrary, the argument was often used to invite women to opt for the place where their natural competencies were best exercised: the hearth. François and Machiels' findings concur with the notion of 'professional territories', as described by political scientist Juliette Rennes: as since the end of the nineteenth century women were entering professions previously reserved to men, their contribution, and in particular in the professions known as 'prestigious', was intended for a restricted clientele (women and children); and they also remained confined to a undervalued terrain, not positioning themselves as competitors to their male colleagues.[7]

State institutions were slow to adapt to the claims of women. As Ulrike Schultz and Gisela Shaw have put it, the judiciary is a field that has, historically, tended to disregard women as a resource, and even today is curbing full equality of opportunities.[8] Resistance against women in the judiciary is the result of its predominantly masculine image that has lasted until recent times. (Male) judges were (and are) representatives and servants of the state, exerting authority, incorporating the ideal of objectivity, covering their individuality with a black robe. Femininity, on the contrary – classically associated with qualities such as empathy, mercifulness, indulgence and tolerance – threatens the familiar and established image of the judiciary.[9] This explains women's relatively late access to the profession. It is only after World War II that both in Belgium and in France women were granted full access to the judiciary (although they could already sit in labour courts, commercial courts and in industrial tribunals). The political circumstances in the post-war years and the general tendency towards renewed democracy offered opportunities for the women's movement that saw some of their principal demands being agreed to.[10] In the bar, though, the first breaches of the male monopoly had already been made at the turn of the century. The opening of the profession of lawyer to French women in 1900 provided several women lawyers with the opportunity to demonstrate their skills as *advocates*,

---

7 Juliette Rennes, *Le mérite et la nature. Une controverse républicaine: l'accès des femmes aux professions de prestige (1880–1940)* (Paris, 2007), pp. 414–19.

8 Schultz and Shaw, 'Introduction', p. 5.

9 Ibid., pp. 24–5.

10 Eva Schandevyl, 'Portia ten tonele: de feminisering van de Belgische magistratuur', in Dirk Heirbaut, Xavier Rousseaux and Alain Wijffels (eds), *Histoire du droit et de la justice: une nouvelle génération de recherches* (Louvain-la-Neuve, 2009), pp. 565–77.

critical thinkers and orators. Following the admission of women to the bar, new debates unfurled on the role of gender in legal work.

The contribution of Sara L. Kimble to this volume shows how a group of French jurist women in the first half of the twentieth century participated in social protest against legal discrimination in different manners: by taking their cases to the courtroom to gain access to the legal profession; by their involvement in national and international women's rights organisations to provide and exchange legal expertise on Civil code reform; by winning over male colleagues and mostly left-wing politicians to their cause; by lecturing or publishing on legislation, justice and social morality in the press and journals to influence public opinion; by letter-writing campaigns to achieve more state intervention on women's behalf; and by participating in extra-parliamentary legal commissions that acted as pressure groups on the authorities and government officials. In each of these examples, these women shaped political situations and did not simply react to existing circumstances and legislation.

Kimble describes how in France a feminist lawyers' movement was since the turn of the century engaged in varied forms of activism for legal reform related to mothers' and married women's rights, women's rights to work and their political rights. The model legislation that was drafted by those female lawyers active in the movement was, however, restrained by their lack of formal rights since they were excluded from political power. The Civil code was a central source of women's subordination in the family, as was the Constitution, both confirming women's incapacity and legal inferiority. Moreover, the breakthrough in European civil law that constituted French women's admission to the bar simultaneously reinforced their legal inferiority, as the law granting them this access also explicitly endorsed the tradition that they could not serve as judges, prosecutors, court clerks or notaries. No provisions were granted to admit them to a variety of posts for which, except for gender, they would have been qualified. Opposing forces argued that women's ineligibility for the judiciary rested with their biological, social and political inequality. As for their claims for individual rights, this ultimately became the central legacy of this feminist lawyers' movement and its political activism in twentieth-century France.

From Kimble's chapter it appears that women's demand for entry into legal office was tightly interwoven with other contentious areas, a proposition that she also advances in her other writings.[11] Kimble states that protest against gender discrimination in the legal field intrinsically encompassed the demand for equal citizenship and voting rights. One of the arguments opposing women's access to the judiciary had indeed been that admission to such a 'ministerial office' required candidates to have full political and civil rights. However, when

---

[11] Sara L. Kimble, 'No Right to Judge: Feminism and the Judiciary in Third Republic France', *French Historical Studies*, 31/4 (2008): pp. 609–41.

French and Belgian women in 1946–48 at last gained the right to judge, this did not so much happen as the recognition of their 'exceptional qualities' or as the result of a global striving for 'equality'. It was principally presented as a token of esteem for the role they had played during the war and the suffering they had experienced during those years.

France had been the first civil law country in Europe to grant access to the bar through a legislative act. Germany was one of the last countries in Europe to admit women, in 1922, but it was also one of the very few countries to permit women to act as judges before World War II. Marion Röwekamp explains how in Germany two facts were responsible for the even higher institutionalised obstacles to women gaining access to the legal profession. Firstly, there was the tradition of legal education in Germany, which was a highly regulated state institution; and secondly, there was the fact that the resources of male power were strongly institutionalised within professional corporations, which in case of the advocacy were semi-tied to bureaucracy. Lawyers who protected the access to their profession largely occupied civil service structures. Through a system of study time at university combined with apprenticeship and state exams, legal education in Germany formed a very homogenous professional group of lawyers with the ability to work in all legal professions, and who occupied the most influential spheres of society, including the judiciary, state administration, civil service and legislative bodies. Women's non-admission to those state exams thus presented an extra barrier to the bar.

For German women the possibility of a legal process to force access to the bar was not an option, and neither was there a constitutional court legally competent to hear their cases. Yet, armed with their new constitutional and political rights under the regime of the Weimar Republic, the women's movement changed its strategy from pressuring ministries to adjust their interpretations of the law, to bringing all requests in the parliaments of all the states. They were able to lodge their requests via the new female MPs on an all-party level. Here again, full citizenship rights were at stake and not only the question of whether women would be able to judge over men, but also the prospect of women gaining access to real power positions, as within the German state the lawyer was the most influential of all professions. It eventually needed a social democratic Reichsministry of Justice to impose on the governments of the single states the reform project that granted women access to the entire legal profession, including the judiciary – that is, until the Nazi takeover in 1933 when women were excluded again.

Many of the newly appointed female judges wanted to reveal the human side of law. In their effort to change conventional gender roles they moved cautiously. Instead of breaking the rules, they believed in bending them. Their activism can be defined as a new way of exercising the profession of lawyer at the junction of law and politics. There is a similarity with the picture that Kimble draws of those French female lawyers who used special political and rhetorical strategies to defend their clients and to criticise inequalities of power in society. Often, they took on test cases and made moral arguments during trials. Their reform-orientated strategies addressed specific topical concerns such as the organisation of justice, family law, civil and criminal law, and women's and children's social and political rights. Kimble draws a parallel with legal theorists describing contemporary behaviour in this model as altruistic lawyering or 'cause lawyering'.

This legal practice seems to confirm the essentialist argument related to the complementary-based model. It also supports the dominant moderate tendency in social feminism that was acting through a gradual strategy of bending the law rather than radically opposing it and of women jurists looking for support from male colleagues rather than confronting them. As different as the cases are, these countries as drawn above also show many similarities between them when it comes to women in law. Firstly, there is the fact that the controversy about the possibility of female judges was primarily a political one. The fact that women were already eligible to serve in labour courts and in commercial courts starting from the beginning of the twentieth century shows that the issue was not only ability but also women's civil and political status. Secondly, female lawyers, social welfare workers and professionals in the judicial field defended a more humanitarian vision of law. Often, they acted as moral activists whose reform campaigns were designed to introduce an ethical language in their countries' sites of power, or they tried to educate and empower people through educational activities and publications. Besides, several female legal activists were involved in transnational women's rights organisations. In these capacities, feminist lawyers provided legal expertise that facilitated efforts to communicate with political leaders. This was especially important when lawyers could make their voices heard on matters of constitutional or Civil code reform. Thirdly, women have frequently operated according to multiple forms of identity, combining their gendered and professional identities. In Kimble's account the two often went hand in hand; in Mary Jane Mossman's chapter further in this book, however, both were in conflict with each other. Mossman gives the example of British, Canadian and American women lawyers around the turn of the century, who illustrate a stance frequently seen in relation to women in leadership positions: they take care to adapt as closely as possible to male standards, thus providing a masculinised performance in the attempt to avoid any criticism linked to their femininity.

In sum, it seems that women jurists have experienced several possible gendered and judicial identities: assimilation to masculine judicial norms; the ideal of the disembodied neutral judicial officer who is neither male nor female; a gender-aware female judge or lawyer or a feminist judge or lawyer.[12] Yet it

---

12 Schultz and Shaw, 'Introduction', p. 43.

stands without doubt that those last ones have, through their critique of existing legal regimes, delineated the way to change, and that feminism has constituted a factor for transformation of the administration of justice and the theory of law.

Part II: Gender Constructions and their Impact on Jurisprudence

The chapters in Part II examine the impact of gender constructions on jurisprudence. At the intersection of law, labour history and politics, a first chapter offers new insights on nineteenth-century labour arbitration. The following three chapters in this section address family law-related topics such as marriage property law, divorce and parental custody in different national contexts. The chapters in this section go beyond just an examination of existing law in relation to women's rights. They also offer new insights into the response of women to the legal regimes in their countries. While women's poor status in nineteenth-century Europe has attracted the interest of many scholars in recent years, the authors of these chapters question to what degree women's emancipation has been possible inside legal systems and political regimes that have a strong history of female subordination and male dominance.

Mathieu Brûlé's chapter joins the wider field of legal history that emphasises the interaction of working-class people with the legal system. Through an extensive study of more than 4,000 cases, Brûlé examines the ways in which female workers in the northern French textile city of Tourcoing viewed and used the labour arbitration boards known as *conseils des prud'hommes* as an avenue for achieving justice for workplace grievances. These boards were created in the beginning of the nineteenth century under the direction of Napoleon, with the means of resolving workers' and employers' differences through conciliation rather than through collective action. Both male and female workers were allowed access to the boards as plaintiffs and defendants. Brûlé examines how the presence of male workers on the boards – only men could since 1848 run as candidates for the boards – affected the *conseils des prud'hommes*' rulings in cases involving female workers.

The increasing presence of working-class women using the boards' services in the second half of the nineteenth century seems to indicate that the presence of their male counterparts on the boards improved their view of the boards as a site of redress against perceived injustices at work. Brûlé points out though that the female working class under study was far from being an homogeneous category. This is illustrated through an analysis of the ways in which a plaintiff's gender intersected with class, occupational skill-level, education and age to impact their performance at the *conseils des prud'hommes*: the higher the skill-level the higher the rate of success and, on the whole, the levels of success of working-class female plaintiffs were higher than those of men. The growing number of working-class women using their services indicates that the presence of a working-class voice, regardless of its gender, increased women's confidence in the ability of the *conseils des prud'hommes* to deliver justice. However, the presence of a working-class voice also contributed to the emergence of political and class-based tensions. The increased tension at the boards in the last decade of the nineteenth century, as influential unions and the socialist party increasingly saw the boards as a tool in the class struggle, provoked a decline in female working-class use of the boards' services.

Increased tensions at the boards affected women's confidence in the institution, especially as the tensions largely concerned issues that were out of reach of women, such as the election of and power struggles between board members. As a result of the absence of female voting rights, the socialist party did not actively seek support from female workers and this contributed to the marginalisation of women's issues. Therefore, whatever progress had been made in increasing female working-class confidence in the boards was by the end of the nineteenth century largely undone by the impact of class relations between worker and employer representatives serving on the *conseils des prud'hommes*.

Only in 1907–1908 could women run for the elected positions on the *conseils de prud'hommes* and, at least by 1930, they were serving as judges on an equal basis with men. This fact, in combination with women's eligibility in commercial courts from 1900 onwards, demonstrates that the discussion about the possibility of women becoming judges, as treated in Part I of this book, was not only a matter of competence but also of women's incapacity imposed by the Civil code and the Constitution. A main issue in feminist judicial reform was indeed married women's civil rights and, more specifically, the fact that they were subject to spousal approval under the Civil code – including their right to work, to appear in court and to contract.

As in many other European regions, the French Civil code, which was imposed on the southern Netherlands (today's Belgium) by the French occupants, remained in force in Belgium throughout the nineteenth century. The Civil code was compiled in 1804 under Napoleon, and combined elements from Roman and French law into a coherent set of standards that govern relations between individuals. The influence of the Civil code spread across Europe both directly during Napoleonic conquests and indirectly when it was used as a model during legal reform elsewhere. As Sara L. Kimble reminds us in her chapter, the articles of the Civil code concerning marriage stipulated that husbands owed protection to their wives, and wives owed obedience to their husbands. Patriarchal authority within the family depended upon the subordination of women. Napoleon likened women to possessions who were 'destined to make children'. Under the Civil code, a husband had marital authority over his wife, her body, her children and her property. He had nearly unchecked powers over the running of the household; a right to supervise his wife's personal conduct and movements; the right to forbid her actions; and the imposition of his nationality upon marriage. In practical terms, married women could not move or travel where they wished; they could not open an individual bank account; and they could not make contracts or work without marital authorisation. The Civil code essentially stripped married women of their basic rights and rendered them 'eternal minors' in legal terms.

This general position of married women and their incapacity in relation to the Napoleonic Civil code has been a recurrent theme in publications on legal history, but the interpretation of this rigid Civil code in Belgian legal practice of the nineteenth century is still largely a black box. De ruysscher's contribution in this book fills in this blind spot. In addition, he comes to remarkable conclusions regarding women's rights to contract under Belgium's nineteenth-century legal regime.

In his chapter he argues that already in the nineteenth century, Belgian legal practice did acknowledge some contractual rights of married women. Based on a thorough analysis of judgements and legal literature from the first half of the nineteenth century, De ruysscher shows how judges and legal scholars made use of the few escape routes that were found within the Civil code, in order to recognise the part a wife could have in running the family estate and in managing her property. Legal authorities, however, did not want a fundamental revision of the legal articles regarding the position of married women: even if in legal practice some of the harsh provisions of the law were mitigated, gender equality as such was not a goal, and legal discrimination of married women did not decrease substantially during the nineteenth and a large part of the twentieth century. The incapacity of wives that had been laid down in the Civil code was, and particularly when being compared with the rules of the Old Regime, extreme. In the seventeenth and eighteenth centuries, many areas in France and the Southern Netherlands had allowed married women to acquire and alienate assets and had known rules based on cooperation between spouses. The provisions of the Civil code were much stricter than legislation of the previous periods, as they took the omnipotence of the husband and the obedience of his wife rather than the conjugal partnership as starting points.

The Civil code contained nevertheless provisions allowing some autonomous actions of married women, in particular the exception of the relative – and thus not absolute – nullity rule for profitable contracts. This relative nullity rule allowed a wife to convince her husband after she had signed a contract, even when the other contracting party had not been aware of the women's marital status and wanted to attack the contract on the basis of that argument. Authorisation could be given after concluding the contract, or the husband could let the parties to the contract know that he would not seek annulment. It was a rule of the Old Regime that a beneficial and reciprocal contract could not be attacked, even if it had been signed by a married woman without her husband's cooperation. The relative nullity rule within the Civil code made it also possible that the wife, with a general authorisation of her husband, led the household and managed the assets of the community property. A married woman could in principle only sign contracts, sell belongings or engage in mortgage following the express and detailed authorisation of her husband; but if the latter made it clear to the contracting parties that he generally agreed with his wife's actions, it was impossible to have such actions annulled. These legal exceptions were, however, limited. Moreover, the rule of relative nullity brought about that women were met with distrust when acting in public; those who engaged in contracts with them had to be absolutely sure that their husbands consented in what they were doing. Benevolent judges and jurists could thus bend some of the rules to the advantage of married women, even though such interpretations mostly served the interests of creditors. Their approach aimed more at the safeguarding of the rights of those parties who had contracted with a woman than with a full recognition of married women's rights. Judges of tribunals in the central Belgian province of Brabant and its main legal centre, Brussels, circumvented the gender-biased rules of law mostly to protect the economic interests of the third parties involved.

Up until the middle of the twentieth century only some minor legal improvements were made for married women in Belgium and in France. It was only 10 years after general suffrage had been accorded to women in 1948 that the Belgian legislator formally abandoned the marital authority regime of the Civil code. World War II was a catalysing event in these changes as, in its wake, voting rights were extended to women. Even so, the reform of the legal position of women was slow, and in private law even slower than in public law. This slowness of legislative reform was a clear indication of the reluctance of a predominantly male parliament towards the necessary legal changes.

Taken together then, Mathieu Brûlé and Dave De ruysscher offer a complex look at the history of legal practice in the French and the France-orientated Belgian contexts as modelled by the Napoleonic code. The chapters by Evdoxios Doxiadis and Nadezda Belyakova and Taisya Belyakova on Southern and Eastern Europe add a compelling transnational component to discussions over the complexity of mixed legal regimes. The cohabitation of different rules of law – family law based on Byzantine norms, custom law and Canon law – in the cases of nineteenth-century Greece and Russia seems to have resulted in very complex and eventually inefficient and dissatisfying legal regimes. Only slowly did the principles of the Civil code as a model for legal reform seep through in both countries, under the influence of a Western trained native legal elite. This happened, however, without a clean-cut rupture with past regimes. But from the contributions of Dave De ruysscher, Evdoxios Doxiadis and Nadezda Belyakova and Taisya Belyakova we gather that women's rights under these old regimes were in several aspects more progressive than under nineteenth-century codification. These chapters confirm that the modern state has not been especially kind to women, particularly in matters of law – where women in the transition from the Early Modern to the Late Modern period and with the adoption of the Civil code suffered considerable erosion of their rights, especially property rights.

Evdoxios Doxiadis begins his chapter by examining the relationship of women, law and property rights when Greece was still a province of the Ottoman Empire, and then looks at the effects of the modern state of Greece. He draws his analysis from Greek state government archives and from notarial documents and communal records from urban as well as agricultural and maritime areas for the period from the mid eighteenth century to the mid nineteenth century. Doxiadis explains how the Greek Ottoman legal tradition finds its roots in Byzantine law, which stated that a woman's dowry was inalienable and was to be returned to her upon the dissolution of marriage. Although the husband managed his wife's property, there was no question of common conjugal property in marriage. Evidence shows that women were quite active in Byzantine courts, seeking control over their wealth. Besides, they also sought justice in the ecclesiastical courts of the Orthodox Church, where the caseload concerned issues of marriage, dowries and inheritance. The influence of Canon law in these matters was dominant, even under Ottoman rule and after the emergence of the Hellenic Kingdom. Yet in commercial cases, judicial authority often resided in local councils that functioned as communal courts with easy access for any member of the community. With their absence of standardised codes by which to judge (local customs were applied instead) these councils resembled the Islamic courts that every inhabitant of the Ottoman Empire, despite his or her religion, could also choose to appeal to. Despite legal fragmentation and the multiplicity of authorities, legal options and legal practices available, women everywhere were very active as litigants, and their presence reveals a remarkable knowledge of their rights.

With the overthrowing of the Ottoman authorities and the establishment of the modern state of Greece, new forms of administration and justice were sought. Attempts to create uniform legal codes, however, were predictably countered by proponents of customary law. Despite the governmental efforts to install a modern and hierarchical judicial system, there was a lack of procedural clarity within an administrative and judicial labyrinth that was in almost perpetual flux. In the end, the physical structure of a modern justice system was set up, before the state had a comprehensive system of laws. It would turn out that the emergence of a completely new judicial structure determined women's legal status in Greece much more than the law itself, most significantly by physically excluding them from courts that were situated too far away for them to travel to. That resulted in making women dependent upon men and professional lawyers as their representatives and reduced their incentive to know and keep up with the changes regarding the laws impacting property rights. Knowledge of law became increasingly a male prerogative and source of influence and power.

Moreover, in accordance with evolutions and Romantic ideals elsewhere in Europe, the concept of common marital property under supervision and authority of the husband was slowly emerging and the former clear divisions between properties of husband and wife were breaking down. Legal discrimination was present throughout the newly enacted laws, which on the one hand saw the need to protect women and on the other valued them considerably less than men. Doxiadis concludes that the relative deterioration of women's rights with the establishment of the modern state of Greece was, however, not necessarily due to erosion of the rights they had, but to increasing male rights such as suffrage and education. It is also worth mentioning that Doxiadis sees a difference between legal practice in urban and in agricultural areas, with the former maintaining a more strict/restrictive attitude, whereas the latter seems more flexible. The legalistic attitudes of newly created courts stuck to the letter and forms of jurisprudence as opposed to old communal courts, which used to be more interested in substance than in formality. This difference between urban areas – where state law and codification proponents won ground more easily – and rural areas – where custom law remained dominant – is also present in Nadezda Belyakova and Taisya Belyakova's chapter.

Just as Evdoxios Doxiadis does, Nadezda Belyakova and Taisya Belyakova follow a long-term perspective, which allows assessing the role of the Byzantine legal tradition and its influence on Christian legislation from the Middle Ages onward. Their contribution focuses on women's rights in late imperial Russia in relation to the change in legislation concerning the divorce procedure and property rights. Based on legal literature of the nineteenth century, they focus on the contradicting patriarchal norms in the family sphere on the one hand and the independent property principles for women in the financial sphere on the other. In contrast to European nineteenth-century legislation and practice, the Russian legal system preserved and further developed the principle of separate property of spouses, a tradition that was connected with the norms of medieval Byzantine family law. The dowry or any other property of the wife was considered her private possession and was inviolable. This relative high and independent property status of women in the Russian Empire stood in contradiction with the low legal status of Russian women in society at large, and their rightless status in the family sphere.

Nadezda Belyakova and Taisya Belyakova describe the lack of unified and developed family law in imperial Russia, where no civil marriage or divorce procedure existed. This was hampered by the concept of sacramental marriage. Throughout the nineteenth century, the conclusion and dissolution of marriage remained in the competence of confessional structures, the state reserving for itself the regulation of the forms of the procedures only – despite several reform projects and attempts at civil marriage registration. Next to the Russian Orthodox Church norms, family law remained also regulated by custom law, most so in the traditional agricultural regions where, for example, peasants' courts functioned in the related areas. In late imperial Russia we thus find a combination of primitive family law shaped by Byzantine tradition and conservative religious concepts imposed by the clerical state and Church ideologues, which had legal force.

Russian social life in the nineteenth century was affected by the same processes as elsewhere in Europe: the influence of the patriarchal family norm in contradiction with the shift in women's role in society and their aspiration for emancipation and for legal and financial independence. The rejection of the civil marriage procedure was in contradiction with the realities and social necessities of the nineteenth century. The authors argue that the keeping of divorce in the competence of the Church, with its prohibitive approach, resulted in the crisis of the family as an institution. It also contributed to the growth of dissatisfaction towards Church authorities, which in turn contributed to anticlericalism and to the revolutionary developments at the beginning of the twentieth century. One of the first acts of the new Soviet government would be a decree about divorces that withdrew all marriage procedures from the Church's competence.

Nadezda Belyakova and Taisya Belyakova thus offer a concrete example of how an inadequate legal system can influence social and political developments in society. Underpinning the chapters by Mathieu Brûlé, Dave De ruysscher and Evdoxios Doxiadis, it seems that political upheavals, wars and revolutions generate transformations of judicial institutions and practices with new elements – import products from other countries or judicial systems as in Belgium, or innovative doctrines and ideologies that differ from formerly prevailing ideas and values as in France – that are embedded in or annihilate the former system. Brûlé expressively and the other authors in Part II of this book implicitly inscribe themselves in the trend to see legal institutions as a process of interaction, protest and collaboration between the state, political authorities and its subjects. In doing so, they follow other scholars who adhere to the tendency of recognising the agency of men and women in their interactions with the law.

Part III: Gendered Legal Cultures in Global Perspective

To better assess present debates, Maria Rita Bartolomei deals with recent developments. Even when focusing on contemporary legal culture, she is aware though of the changes that have occurred during the twentieth century. The contribution of Mary Jane Mossman examines the relationships between gender and professionalism in the lives of women in law at the beginning of that century. Both authors touch upon subjects that remain of topical interest today, such as the pressure to conform to prevailing professional identities that often disregard gender; and resistance against this by women jurists, and their roles in transforming legal practice.

The contributions to Part III of this volume examine gendered legal cultures in a global perspective. Next to considering women jurists' organising to challenge dominant practices, they also consider these women's work, often 'outside the boundaries' of the legal profession, to reshape the meaning of legality and to engage with women's rights activities. At the same time these two contributions reflect on how women's discrimination embedded in legal discourse and in the legal profession has shaped these women's choices in their private and public lives. The individual historical settings and experiences of women in Western Europe, the United States and some British colonies are therefore relevant in understanding women's relationships with law in its different aspects. Both chapters consider the difficult balance between gender and professional identities.

Mary Jane Mossman argues that notwithstanding the close connection that existed between early claims for access to the legal profession and the broader issue of the feminist movement, by the turn of the twentieth century different women lawyers in a variety of different jurisdictions began to focus their attention more pointedly on their professional activities rather than providing ongoing support to women's rights struggles. For these women lawyers, the priority was to succeed in being accepted within the (male) professional culture and to be recognised as lawyers rather than as women lawyers. In turn, none of the women who did successfully succeed in combining their professional and gendered identities in the women's rights struggles acquired formal admission to their respective legal professions.

With regard to women's presence in the legal profession, it was particularly in the countries where voting rights were achieved after World War I (including common law countries as the United States and Britain) where women lawyers increasingly embraced a professional identity, for many of them considered that the goals of the women's movement had been achieved. Their downplaying of a gendered identity seems also to have been the result of the necessity of earning a living. Lastly and most importantly there was the pressure – also self-imposed – to conform to the culture of dispassionate professionalism in law, which was supposedly characterised by its neutral, objective and meritocratic ideology. Mary Jane Mossman here once again connects with present debates on differences between male and female practice of law. Arguments in that debate are extensively discussed in Ulrike Schultz and Gisela Shaw's recent work and come down to the question: does gender make a difference to the way judicial professionals work, and is gender-blindness a built-in prerequisite of judicial objectivity? Shultz and Shaw summarise as follows: the vast majority of scholars believe that women's voices differ from those of men and that their ethic is one of care as opposed to a male ethic of justice. At the same time, Schultz and Shaw point to the fact that tracking down and providing evidence for effects of difference due to the gender of the lawyer or the judge is difficult because of the fact that male and female gender always intersects with other aspects of difference such as age, family background, class/social stratum and religion, as well as with an individual's social and legal qualities.[13] The contributors' findings in this present book however point out that women in law and lawmaking do indeed offer a specific contribution. Apart from their greater sensitivity to, and advocacy of, human rights, minority group claims and needs, youth protection and domestic violence – as witnessed by the contributions of François and Machiels, Kimble, Röwekamp and Bartolomei below – women seem inclined to promote substantive justice. Schultz and Shaw's above-cited work confirms that women do choose a more interdisciplinary approach, avoiding the rigid application of universal rules and narrow doctrinal issues.[14] In the light of diverging results and ambiguous answers to the question of whether women lawyers and judges act differently from men, Schultz and Shaw quote Rosemary Hunter's suggestion that speculation as to the contribution women might make to the judicial field should cease, and rather the impact of the presence of feminist lawyers and judges should be examined. This stands for a 'chosen' difference in attitude and mind related to a political opinion, which implies that the women's question has always to be kept in mind and asked.[15]

In her chapter on recent developments in Italy, Maria Rita Bartolomei uses specific cases to illustrate how women lawyers transform themselves, their working sphere and the lives of ordinary women, especially with regard to a better global understanding of domestic violence. In contrast with the other chapters of this book that examine the historical position of women in law, Bartolomei's chapter covers the contemporary position of women in law, and stands therefore somewhat as an exception in this book. The author focuses on the Italian situation, but several of her conclusions are present in almost all European countries today: the relatively recent feminisation of the judicial world coupled with a horizontal professional segregation by speciality – women most strongly represented within family law, juvenile law and migration law – that women themselves, however, do not necessarily perceive as problematic. Simultaneously, there does remain a vertical segregation by which women are generally excluded from important and remunerative interesting financial and political cases; nor do they in general have access to the highest policy-related positions where decisions are made concerning recruitment and promotion

---

13 Schultz and Shaw, 'Introduction', pp. 29–30.

14 Ibid, p. 33.

15 Rosemary Hunter, 'Can Feminist Judges Make a Difference?', *International Journal of the Legal Profession*, 15/1–2 (2008): pp. 7–36.

issues. For this existing imbalance Bartolomei enumerates once more the well-known causes: women's late access to the legal field historically; the lack of family-friendly policies in the legal profession; institutional impediments and glass ceiling mechanisms. Based on interviews with Italian women lawyers and with victims of domestic violence in order to assemble a life history collection, Bartolomei explores both groups' ideas and narratives about law and also frames these within the concept of 'legal consciousness'. Bartolomei explains how the women lawyers under study deploy legal meanings in new settings and make innovative use of existing legal paradigms. She gives the example of Italian women lawyers' contribution to the legal qualification of domestic violence against women as a violation of human rights, where previously this was rarely regarded as a crime. At the same time, these women witness that legal knowledge provides them with social norms they use not only at work but also to understand their everyday experience. Their struggles for a prospective gender-orientated professional agenda thus refer to discrimination inside as well as outside the courtroom: these women's legal strategies reveal the aim and effort to challenge the prevailing gender bias in jurisprudence and in legal practice as well as in their personal lives (such as existing impediments to upward professional mobility, the difficult balancing of the demands of work and family). They make use of legal arguments and specific strategies to overcome the many barriers they meet in their careers. In doing so, they fully join in with the twentieth-century feminist tradition.

The chapters in this book show that whereas the professionalisation of law from the end of the eighteenth century onwards involved the gradual exclusion of women, we later see an inverse movement. In the twentieth century the further development and specialisation of legal theory and legal practice was accompanied by the (re)introduction of women. Indeed, twentieth-century feminist demands for granting new (or previously lost) rights to women – such as access to the legal profession, property rights, rights within the family sphere and voting rights – were not seldom accompanied by claims to more professionalism wherein ideas regarding gender and plans for legal reforms crossed each other (as in the case of juvenile law).

The twentieth century was a time of optimism with regard to liberal changes in society and new opportunities for women, including access to education, training and participation in the labour market. The notion of masculine rationality – and the courts and the judiciary were traditionally being identified with the unmistakable masculinity of public offices – was slowly being exposed as a mere cliché that justifies dominant behaviour (and that as a relational model in contrast with femininity necessitates that all women are stamped as irrational). As this book indicates, this critical stance towards gendered power relations in the legal field remains of topical interest even today, at the beginning of the twenty-first century.

The contributors and I hope that this book will facilitate the understanding of women's issues in law and lawmaking in nineteenth- and twentieth-century Europe. Of course this volume is not exhaustive, and some subjects remain absent or underexposed. Although attention does go to areas where customary law was prevalent, the main focus lies with civil law countries and, to a much lesser degree, with common law countries. For that, we limit ourselves by referring to Schultz and Shaw's above-mentioned work, where they comprehensively go into the striking difference between common law and civil law countries regarding not only women's entry to and career progression within the judiciary, but also the respective reception of this process (large media and political attention in the common law countries and relative absence of public interest in civil law countries) which has everything to do with the fact that as a rule in civil law countries success in examinations determines access to the judiciary. In common law countries, in contrast, judges are chosen from among experienced legal practitioners; and in this professional visibility, evaluations of professional achievement and access to networks are of crucial weight. Yet it seems that whatever procedure is applied, there is one feature which remains in place, namely that men control access and resources, and that stereotypical perceptions of masculinity and femininity play an important part.[16]

The authors wish that this book will stimulate research and inspiring discussion on women in law and lawmaking in the modern and contemporary era. We look forward to further collaborate with historians and social scientists in dealing with the many issues raised here and welcome you to share our piece of work.

Bibliography

Auchmuty, Rosemary, 'Whatever Happened to Miss Bebb? *Bebb v The Law Society* and Women's Legal History', *Legal Studies*, 31/2 (2011): 199–230.

European Commission for the Efficiency of Justice (CEPEJ), *European Judicial Systems: Efficiency and Quality of Justice. An Overview* (Strasbourg: Council of Europe, 2012), http://www.coe.int/T/dghl/cooperation/cepej/evaluation/2012/Synthese_Version_fi nale_en.pdf.

Hunter, Rosemary, 'Can Feminist Judges Make a Difference?', *International Journal of the Legal Profession*, 15/1–2 (2008): 7–36.

Kimble, Sara L., 'No Right to Judge: Feminism and the Judiciary in Third Republic France', *French Historical Studies*, 31/4 (2008): 609–41.

Pojmann, Wendy, 'Introduction', in Wendy Pojmann (ed.), *Migration and Activism in Europe since 1945* (New York: Palgrave Macmillan, 2008).

16 Schultz and Shaw, 'Introduction', pp. 5–6, 15–16, 20.

Rennes, Juliette, *Le mérite et la nature: une controverse républicaine: l'accès des femmes aux professions de prestige (1880–1940)* (Paris: Fayard, 2007).
Schandevyl, Eva, 'Portia ten tonele: de feminisering van de Belgische magistratuur', in Dirk Heirbaut, Xavier Rousseaux and Alain Wijffels (ed.), *Histoire du droit et de la justice: une nouvelle génération de recherches* (Louvain-la-Neuve: Presses universitaires, 2009).
Schultz, Ulrike, and Gisela Shaw (ed.), *Gender and Judging* (Oxford: Hart, 2013).

PART I
History of Women in the Legal Profession

Chapter 1

From Philanthropists to Juvenile Judges: Women Dealing with Juvenile Delinquency. International Debates and Local Practices in Belgium (1890–1960)

Aurore François and Christine Machiels

On 15 May 1912, after several years of harsh debate, members of the Belgian Parliament enacted the country's first law on child protection.[1] This law notably established juvenile courts, which concretized a wish inherited from the previous century: to withdraw delinquent minors from the penal law. From that point on, children were no longer to be judged as adults but by one single specialized judge. Despite its humanitarian tone, the actual intentions of this legislation entailed further ramifications. The law of 1912 was the first great form of the realization of the so-called *défense sociale* doctrine.[2] It was focused on children who were victims, delinquents or just 'difficult', in the sense of generating a social risk. The law provided for interventions that would affect families directly, some preventive and some curative, involving placement of 'children at risk' in institutions.

This shift from the penal field to the social (but still judicial) field went together with the emergence of new parties concerned: the juvenile judge and the *délégué(e) à la protection de l'enfance*, a function which was claimed to be

---

[1] 'Loi du 15 mai 1912 sur la protection de l'enfance', in *Moniteur Belge*, 27–29 May 1912, pp. 3457–67. On the law's development process and its orientation, see: Jenneke Christiaens, *De geboorte van de jeugddelinquent (België 1830–1930)* (Brussels, 1999); Françoise Tulkens and Thierry Moreau., *Droit de la jeunesse. Aide, assistance, protection* (Brussels, 2000); Marie-Sylvie Dupont-Bouchat, *De la prison à l'école. Les pénitenciers pour enfants en Belgique au XIXe siècle (1840–1914)* (Kortrijk-Heule, 1996); Marie-Sylvie Dupont-Bouchat and Éric Pierre (ed.), *Enfance et justice au XIXe siècle. Essais d'histoire comparée de la protection de l'enfance 1820–1914. France, Belgique, Pays-Bas, Canada* (Paris, 2001).

[2] Jean Trépanier and Françoise Tulkens, *Délinquance & protection de la jeunesse. Aux sources des lois belge et canadienne sur l'enfance* (Montreal-Ottawa-Brussels, 1995); Françoise Tulkens, *Généalogie de la défense sociale en Belgique 1880–1914* (Brussels, 1988).

inspired by probation officers in the United States.[3] These probation officers led enquiries into the families in preparing the judge's decision and supervising children who were to stay with their family following a judge's decision.

Their mission was twofold: proceed to a social investigation into the minor and his family in order to supply the judge with information on the possible fate to be reserved for the child appearing before him; supervise the child should he or she be placed under the mode of *release on probation*, by submitting a report to the judge on the child's schooling, work, frequentations, behaviour and so on.

Throughout the debates in parliament, extending over two decades, the emphasis was placed on the success of the methods used in the US, and particularly the positive repercussions of the officers' work, in terms of relapse for example.[4] Some of these foreign institutions (Chicago, New York and Canadian municipal courts), the names of which regularly came up in the debates, often employed women as probation officers or even magistrates. Indeed, at the international level, child protection was one of the first fields where women were socially, politically and professionally involved. At the end of the nineteenth century, a reflection emerged about the part they could play in specialized courts dealing with children, which were created all around Europe. As Seth Koven and Sonya Michel mentioned, the rise of women's social action movements is connected to the emergence of state welfare policies, and women succeeded in 'shaping one particular area of state policy: child welfare. It was in this area, closely linked to the traditional female sphere, that women first claimed new roles for themselves and transformed their emphasis on motherhood into public policy'.[5]

The foreign (mainly American) innovative institutions, regularly quoted in Belgian debates for their exemplary ways of working, influenced Belgian lawmakers. The institutions employed female officers with real professional training in juvenile delinquency management, under various statuses and conditions. They were either full-fledged civil servants or employees paid thanks

---

3 Aurore François, 'Une phalange de collaborateurs pour "une tâche de cœur": les délégués à la protection de l'enfance (Belgique, 1912–1949)', *Histoire et Sociétés. Revue européenne d'Histoire sociale*, 25–6 (2008): pp. 212–25.

4 According to *La section centrale*, the committee in charge of studying the project, release on probation would have produced in the United States 'the happy result of reducing recidivism, which ranged from 30 to 40 per cent, to around 10 to 20 per cent'. Rapport fait au nom de la Section centrale par R. Colaert. Chambre des Représentants, documents, séance du 31 janvier 1912 (Session de 1911–12), p. 504.

5 Seth Koven and Sonya Michel, 'Womanly Duties: Maternalist Politics and the Origins of Welfare States in France, Germany, Great Britain, and the United States (1880–1920)', *American Historical Review*, 95/4 (1990): pp. 1076–7.

to private fundraising.[6] Their salaries were often quite low, but nonetheless regarded as a stable career employment.

In conceiving the 1912 law, Belgian members of parliament were aware of foreign experiences linking women to child protection. Therefore, it seemed justified to women to benefit from the opportunity that the creation of a new judicial territory related to child protection in Belgium might represent for them. It should be immediately specified that the choices made by members of parliament, led by the Catholic minister Carton de Wiart, quickly restricted professionalization opportunities in the field as well as the opening of these positions to women. The opening of the juvenile judge position to women was not even discussed, since it was decided to recruit these new judges among magistrates in office, who at that time were all men (women did not have access to the magistracy until 1948).

Probation officers, juvenile judges, women doctors, female police officers ... Although women's commitment in child protection was large and varied, every function or duty involving women had to be negotiated, and the specificity – or even the legitimacy – of women's official participation in the field of child protection was debated with sometimes considerable vigour. How did women appear as privileged auxiliaries of justice or the police with regard to juvenile delinquency treatment? How did their commitment, often presented as 'natural' in some discourses, materialize in practical experiences? Was their integration really that evident? And, finally, how was their work received, evaluated or criticized?

This chapter aims to explore these issues, from the early parliamentary debates in 1890 when the first law project on child protection was elaborated, up to achievement after World War II, when women succeeded in their efforts to be integrated into child protection programmes and institutions as real professionals. Sources for exploring these questions are numerous and rich. We used parliamentary debates records (*annales parlementaires*); specialized literature in the field of child protection – journals or practitioners' reports; and writings of Belgian feminists engaged at the national or international level (League of Nations). The analysis of these ideological debates was complemented

---

6 Deputy Denis thus appears to have been quite well informed on the evolution of the status of delegates in Chicago. Chambre des Représentants, annales parlementaires, séance du 19 avril 1912, p. 1751. On probation officers, their status and means of financing their function, see: Steven L. Schlossman, *Love and the American Delinquent: The Theory and Practice in Progressive America* (Chicago, 1977), pp. 61–2; Joan Sangster, *Girl Trouble: Female Delinquency in English Canada* (Toronto, 2002); Anne Meis Knupfer, *Reform and Resistance: Gender, Delinquency, and America's First Juvenile Court* (New York, 2001), pp. 48–9; David Niget, *La naissance du tribunal pour enfants. Une comparaison France-Québec, 1912–1945* (Rennes, 2009), p. 61.

by a study of the juvenile courts' archives, which inform us on the practices of child protection services and workers.

The *Délégué(e) à la Protection de l'Enfance* (1912–1935): A Charitable Model

Let us now discuss the role of the *délégué(e) à la protection de l'enfance* for which Belgian parliament members opted, yet with a quite different approach than that of the American success stories they at first claimed to have been inspired by. It is true that Carton de Wiart directly advocated the 'recruitment' of women as probation officers (we will deal with this issue later). However, he ruled out all the arguments that favoured a professionalization of the position, turning down the amendment proposed by the socialists presented by the deputy, Hector Denis, according to which probation officers were to be appointed by the government instead of the judges. The Catholic minister replied that his objective was 'to foster dedication rather than to create job opportunities'.[7] He opposed any form of professionalization of the probation officers, and wished the position to be given to volunteers rather than to civil servants.[8] Thus, the *délégué(e)*'s mission fitted into the purest paternalistic tradition inherited from the nineteenth century, with a recruitment of its lifeblood from philanthropic organizations and local social actors: 'visitors to the poor, teachers, members of the Saint Vincent de Paul Society and the Sisters of Mercy.'[9]

According to this model based on charity, financial compensation, one of the most obvious characteristics of professionalization, would allegedly alter the pureness of the actions and the quality of the interventions within families. The charity model favoured the selfless interventions of philanthropists rather than the intrusion of beggars (*quémandeurs*, as Carton de Wiart termed them) looking for a small salary at the state's expense.

The Catholics used as their main argument that it was advisable for women to intervene in the noble cause of child protection so as to rule out the idea of financial compensation. Indeed, paying the *délégué(e)s à la protection de l'enfance* would result in philanthropic women and women from the upper middle-class involved in charity disengaging themselves, their social rank being incompatible with the notion of salary. 'We should avoid ruling out any contribution due

---

7 Chambre des Représentants, annales parlementaires, séance du 19 avril 1912, p. 1750.

8 Ibid.

9 Ibid. But, as Marie-Sylvie Dupont-Bouchat notes, 'even thought the discourse remains characterized by paternalism, something new is happening, when an official appeal is made to women to be justice auxiliaries. It may be seen as a public sign of recognition, in addition to their traditional motherhood role.' Marie-Sylvie Dupont-Bouchat, 'Femmes philanthropes. Les femmes dans la protection de l'enfance en Belgique (1890–1914)', *Sextant. Femmes de culture et de pouvoir*, 13–14 (2000): p. 109.

to conditions that might scare people with very delicate sensibilities away', as Carton de Wiart put it.[10]

The *délégué(e)s* à *la protection de l'enfance* had to be filled with devotion, and as such, the task had to be performed by volunteers. Volunteering was seen as favouring the participation of women already involved in the field. Their presence was strongly encouraged through maternalist arguments, praising the typical qualities of the intervention of women in dealing with delinquent children and their families. Carton de Wiart explained:

> Women's cleverness, when used to do good, contains an infinite diversity and energy. As they are more in touch with the small details of everyday life, and are more intimate confidants of hidden woes, women will often be better able to soothe the former and discreetly show interest in the latter.[11]

This opening of the delegate position to women illustrates this will to build a truly protective model around delinquent children. Protecting rather than punishing, 'depenalizing' without 'dejudicializing' are all leitmotivs justifying the setting up of systems around children reminiscent of a harmonious family structure, with a sensitive and understanding mother-like probation officer on the one hand, and a paternalistic and protective judge on the other hand.

Indeed, debates in the Belgian Parliament heavily insisted on this notion of the paternalistic figure of the judge, therefore notably ruling out collegiality – preferring a single judge instead of a collegial exercise of jurisdiction – and stressing the necessity of recruiting experimented and stable magistrates for these positions. Some deputies went further, as did the socialist politician Georges Hubin, who pleaded for restricting access to this function to family men:

> I do not consider a bachelor as able to properly judge children. (...) In order to be able to judge a child (...) one has to have children of his own, to have felt the sufferings that are incurred in bringing them up. One needs the experience of their education and of their souls.[12]

We should add that this kind of argument was only used for men. The experience of motherhood as an ultimate skill was never required for women. This illustrates once more how these qualities were perceived as innate and natural, rather than personal: there was no necessity, for women, to experience

10 Chambre des Représentants, annales parlementaires, séance du 19 avril 1912, p. 1750 (our translation).

11 Ibid.

12 Chambre des Représentants, annales parlementaires, séance du 3 avril 1912, p. 1517 (our translation).

motherhood in order to be recognized as experts in the field. Maternalist discourses, aiming at promoting women's involvement in the field of child welfare, exalted women's capacities as mothers, and extended to society as a whole their values of care, nurturance and morality.[13]

In the end, parliament members agreed on hiring volunteers. There was only one exception: some paid permanent probation officers were hired in major urban centres in order to assist the judges. But no formal training was required of them at the outset.[14]

Ten years later, in a guide (published in 1923) for offering advice to the *délégué(e)s*, the arguments of Carton de Wiart favouring the intervention of women, was used again by the Brussels juvenile judge Paul Wets, who put forward their intrinsic qualities:

> Women (...) often have, by instinct, a thorough knowledge of child psychology. They have that patient softness that lowers the barriers and leads hardened and hostile hearts to open (...). Their interventions in families are often better welcomed; the seeming weakness of their sex helps their personal and individual energies to come to the fore, without running in the face of that defensive state, passive or active, which so often sets awry our best intentions. They are better at obtaining certain confidences and bandaging certain wounds than men.[15]

The Failure of the Philanthropic Approach (1935–1947)

How was this new system set up? Judicial files reveal very distinct situations according to the districts, the judges in office and their personal involvement in philanthropic networks. While a particularly involved judge such as Wets in Brussels was able to gather hundreds of volunteers, files from other districts

---

[13] Seth Koven and Sonya Michel, *Mothers of a New World: Maternalist Politics and the Origins of Welfare States* (New York, 1993), p. 4.

[14] Their number grew as time went on: Brussels counted five in 1929; Charleroi three; Antwerp, Liège and Mons two; and Ghent one. Aimée Racine, *Les enfants traduits en justice. Étude d'après trois cents dossiers du tribunal pour enfants de l'arrondissement de Bruxelles* (Liège, 1935), p. 14.

[15] Paul Wets, *Le guide du délégué à la protection de l'enfance* (Liège, 1923), p. 83 (our translation). More generally, Henri Velge offered in 1919 an overview of women's contribution to the vast domain of child welfare in Belgium. See: Henri Velge, 'L'activité féminine dans les Œuvres de Protection de l'Enfance', *La femme belge* (May 1919): pp. 29–34. Concerning the specific role of women in the child welfare movement in Belgium, consult Dupont-Bouchat, 'Femmes philanthropes', pp. 97–105.

show recourse to alternatives such as sending police officers to provide reports on family situations.[16]

At the level of the juvenile courts' files, what do we learn about the recruitment of women as probation officers? First of all, that there was a smaller proportion of women than men occupying this function (about one-third versus two-thirds). Secondly, that women dealt with more files than their male counterparts, for whom the task could only represent a small part of their daily activities due to their professional occupations. The impression left by the files is that the female delegates spent more time in the field than their male counterparts, leading to the conclusion that the first ones were very active in the field. The *délégué(e) à la protection de l'enfance* was typically represented by a female figure. In recruitment posters or circulars, the word *déléguée* was almost always written in the feminine form.

As for permanent probation officers, the function was often (but not always) occupied by women, some of whom had graduated from the first, pioneering *écoles sociales* (graduate schools of social work). The increasing proportion of women in the field was not always met with favourably. Juvenile judge Wets for instance, while advocating the professionalization of the position, deplored in 1934 that there were only a few male social workers. Of course, job insecurity was an issue too. The salary for the job was very low, while it demanded a constant presence and a certain level of qualification (writing skills).

Judicial files provide us with some explanation for Wets' reluctance towards a complete feminization of the *délégué(e)s à la protection de l'enfance*. Indeed, a Brussels judge got into the habit of distributing his files by gender standards: girls and the youngest boys were entrusted to female delegates, while teenagers were entrusted to the men. Those teenagers accounted for the bulk of cases presented before the juvenile courts, and were also those who most often had to go through probationary periods.

These files also shed light on the true supervision mission of delegates, which strongly contrasts with the soothing portrait of women's intervention as presented in the speeches. Indeed, we are dealing with what might be described as a *police des familles*[17] in many ways, even if the supervision aspect did not

[16] The following doctoral theses illustrate the very different practices in Antwerp, Brussels and Namur: Margo De Koster, *Weerbaar, weerspannig of crimineel? Meisjes en jonge vrouwen tussen emancipatie en delinquentie tijdens de eerste helft van de twintigste eeuw*, PhD diss. (Brussels, 2003) (unpublished); Els Dumortier, *De jeugdrechter in twijfel. Een onderzoek naar het ontstaan en de praktijk van de kinderrechter*, PhD diss. (Brussels, 2006) (unpublished); Aurore François, *Guerres et délinquance juvénile (1912–1950): Un demi-siècle de pratiques judiciaires et institutionnelles envers des mineurs en difficulté* (Bruges, 2011).

[17] Jacques Donzelot, *La police des familles* (Paris, 1977). On the subject of British female police forces' practices, Louise Jackson described similar dynamics of 'control' and 'protection', as well as a quite nuanced reception of their actions by the population, sometimes

always rule out a very positive intervention towards endangered minors (some *délégué(e)s* denounced correctional institutions with scandalous practices). But most of the time, the *délégué(e)s'* actions were related to a project of acculturation to the elite's social standards: for example a nearly obsessive care for order and hygiene; the morality of parents, and especially that of mothers. The intervention of *délégué(e)s* in families was often a bad experience for families, who considered them as representatives of the threatening figure of the judge.

A few years of practice in the field were enough to put an end to the charitable model. Besides, the opening of the first social schools during the interwar years played a role in the arrival of trained staff in juvenile courts, as permanent delegates or trainees. Judges were delighted with the quality of the work performed by this new staff, some of whom had devoted extensive time to training. As time went on, the gap between these social workers and volunteers grew wider and wider. The jurist and sociologist Aimée Racine had already uttered criticism, for example. In her study on the juvenile court of Brussels, published in 1935, she aligns with the criticism from some judges she surveyed, about the difficult recruitment and lack of assiduity of some *délégué(e)s*.[18] Changes in judges' perceptions of social work gave rise to criticism regarding volunteers' lack of technique and method. Put differently, they lacked professionalism. So, only two decades were enough to push some of the conceptions inherited from the nineteenth century into the background.[19] If, before the interwar period, science and charity had been perceived as 'neither antagonistic nor mutually exclusive categories',[20] during the interwar years the two began to be considered as separate discourses.

---

welcomed, sometimes resisted. See on this subject: Louise Jackson, *Women Police: Gender, Welfare and Surveillance in the Twentieth Century* (Manchester, 2006); Louise Jackson, 'Care or Control? The Metropolitan Women Police and Child Welfare, 1919–1969', *Historical Journal*, 46/3 (2003): pp. 623–48.

18 Racine, *Les enfants traduits en justice*, pp. 380–81. Aimée Racine was a Belgian lawyer and sociologist known for her work on juvenile delinquency. She was involved in feminism and took part in the work of the National Council of Belgian Women (CNFB).

19 For the same period, concerning work with children, Claudine Marissal notes that 'voluntary engagements are often criticized or even considered to be ineffective'. She sees this as a sign of an evolution in 'the way in which social action is conceived from the interwar period on, owing to the effect of specialization and professionalization'. Claudine Marissal, 'Travail ou non travail? Le bénévolat féminin dans les œuvres de l'enfance', *Cahiers de la Fonderie*, 39 (2008): p. 23.

20 Mariana Valverde, *The Age of Light, Soap, and Water: Moral Reform in English Canada, 1885–1925* (Toronto, 2008), p. 160. Mariana Valverde situates the separation of moral and scientific discourses overseas at around 1910. This confirms the difference in elapsed time between the two continents.

The 'empirical and sentimental charity', denounced by specialists like Aimée Racine, gave way to social intervention regarded as 'scientific'.[21] Yet that did not prevent moral considerations from remaining very present in the practice and even in the criminological theories in vogue, confirming, if needed, 'the significant lines of filiations between the emergent social sciences and moral regulation activism'.[22] In a first phase at least, this movement of professionalization of probation officers did not modify the criteria of evaluation of families, which hardly varied between volunteers and social workers. The social schools, too, contributed to anchoring the maternalist argument, which underlay the investment of women in the social field from the professional point of view.[23] Yet over time, modernization became an affair of methods, techniques and socio-professional status.

Probation Officers, Police Functions, the Judiciary, and the Complementary Model (1912–1947)

The issue of *délégué(e)s à la protection de l'enfance* may then be seen as but one aspect of the wider debate on professional women in the field of juvenile delinquency prevention and management that also includes the police and the magistracy. There was a particularly harsh debate on an international scale from the 1920s on, notably at international congresses dedicated to child protection and the struggle against white slavery, and within transnational institutions like the League of Nations.

These discussions were animated by a wide range of social actors (politicians, professionals in child welfare, militant women and feminist organizations) who all recommended remedies for these particular social questions. International women's organizations, perceived by them as 'moral experts' in the field of protecting women, childhood and the family, benefited from these new international spaces for exchanges and negotiations to put forward their arguments in favour of a professionalization of the role of women in the three areas of probation, magistracy and police.[24] Women's associations, seldom heard

---

21 Racine, *Les enfants traduits en justice*, p. 379.

22 Alan Hunt, *Governing Morals: A Social History of Moral Regulation* (Cambridge, 1999), p. 101.

23 See on this subject: Guy Zélis, 'Maternalisme dans le travail social féminin 1920–1940', *Travailler le social & Chronique féministe*, 41 (2008): pp. 135–47.

24 The benevolent women's organizations, represented at the League of Nations, were not all 'feminist', but were more located at the crossroads of the moral reform movement and the feminist movement, closely dovetailed. See: Carol Miller, *Lobbying the League: Women's International Organizations and the League of Nations*, PhD diss. (Oxford, 1992) (unpublished), p. 7.

from on national levels, particularly placed enormous confidence in the League of Nations, supposed to encourage positive reforms in its members.[25]

In Belgium, the feminization of legal professions came up on the political agenda from time to time, notably with the committee set up by the socialist Minister of Justice Eugène Soudan in 1935 on the participation of women in the struggle against juvenile delinquency, as *déléguées*, magistrates or police officers. This committee was composed of representatives of two social schools, Marie Mulle (headmistress of the lay school for Social Service) and Maria Baers (president of the committee for Flemish social Catholic schools); three feminists, among whom two lawyers (Paule Lamy and Marcelle Renson) and Jeanne Vandervelde (a doctor and anthropologist for prisons); and Aimée Racine, jurist and sociologist who specialized in juvenile delinquency. The committee was presided over by the Brussels juvenile judge Paul Wets and M. Bekaert, who was a director in the Ministry of Justice. Attorney Grandjean-Kowalski ensured the secretariat.

Some elements put forward in the debates on women's employment within the police or as magistrates deserve to be dwelled on, in view of what has been said regarding the *délégué(e)s*. The rhetorical strategy of the sustainers of women's access to these functions was mostly based on complementary rather than on egalitarian notions, either in terms of skills or target audiences. Clearly the notion of 'professional territories', as described by French political scientist Juliette Rennes, was at work here.[26] Women were certainly entering professions hitherto reserved to men. But they were intended for a restricted clientele (women and children) and remained confined to an undervalued terrain, not positioning themselves as competitors. This argument goes beyond the context of child welfare explored here. It draws its roots from debates ongoing since the last century, particularly as to the access of women to professions known as 'prestigious' (medicine, the bar, the judiciary, politics etc.).

Women are more 'qualified' than men (who are clumsy and tactless) to take on missions involving children, declared Avril de Sainte-Croix, a French feminist who was deeply involved in the League of Nations debates:

> Indeed, let us imagine the role that women can play with regard to children on public byways, on squares, parks and gardens. Who would dream of denying that women are more qualified than men to fulfil this role? A woman will always gain the confidence of children much more quickly, will be able to protect them and

[25] Brussels, CARHIF, Fonds du Conseil international des femmes (Social Welfare Work of SDN). *Commission consultative des questions sociales. Organisations bénévoles. 1ère session. Rapport annuel pour 1936. Organisations féminines internationales* (Geneva, 19 April 1937).

[26] Juliette Rennes, *Le mérite et la nature. Une controverse républicaine. L'accès des femmes aux professions de prestige (1880–1940)* (Paris, 2007), pp. 414–19.

intervene efficiently where a man, as well disposed as he might be, will remain clumsy or embarrassed.[27]

In the Belgian debate too, this argument prevailed and was prolonged by the question of morals: 'It has always seemed highly shocking to us, in reading the files of vice cases, that little girls or teenagers should be questioned in so much detail on such issues by male police officers', explained Belgian specialist Aimée Racine in 1947.[28]

This 'complementary system' and strain of thought had as a consequence that many suggested models proposed a task distribution between men and women, usually based on the age and sex of the children. The proposed strategies were gradual and progressive. In the international debate on female police, for example, Avril de Sainte-Croix suggested restricting interventions to pre-emptive actions (safeguarding of female youth, protecting children 'in moral danger') to begin with, then extending it to the repression of minors and prostitution, or even to delinquent youth as a whole (a first interrogation, a court appearance, inquiries relative to these cases, surveillance of parks, placement offices, dance halls, and so on).[29]

The strategic position of de Sainte-Croix, recommending a method of 'small steps', referred to two models of 'female police forces', corresponding to various foreign experiments: some of these were based on the concept of equality (in Poland for instance), others on the complementary model (as in the Netherlands).[30] The two options were known and discussed among judicial authorities, as well as in the associative sector. The National Committee of Belgian Women opted for the second model. It estimated that it was better to support a proposal circumscribed to a female police force confined to preventive action than to ask for equal rights for all juvenile delinquency professionals (in particular women judges for children) but to obtain nothing at all.[31] The choice

---

[27] Geneva, United Nations Library, Advisory Committee on Traffic in Women and Children. Employment of Women Police (box 677), doc. 58965, *Rapport présenté par Guénia Avril de Sainte-Croix (6e session de la Commission de la traite)* (April 1927). Our translation.

[28] Mons, Mundaneum, Fonds CNFB, 10, Moralité-guerre.

[29] Geneva, United Nations Library, Advisory Committee on Traffic in Women and Children: Employment of Women Police (677), doc. 58965, *Rapport présenté par Mme Avril de Sainte-Croix (6e session de la Commission de la traite, avril 1927).*

[30] The two experiments in the field were notably presented to various associations on the occasion of an international congress of social morals (Budapest, 1934). On the female police force in Rotterdam, see: Nelleke Manneke, *Vrouwen van kaliber. Politievrouwen in de twintigste eeuw* (Apeldoorn, 1998).

[31] Geneva, United Nations Library (Archives and Historical Collections), Première période (1919–27), Section 12 (section sociale), 676, Employment of Women Police, *Lettre du comité belge contre la traite (Isidore Maus) au ministre de l'Intérieur* (19 March 1925).

was tactical: in a gradual logic some, like de Sainte-Croix, imagined that in the long run a shift might be made from the complementary model (first stage) to that of equality (second stage).

This way of seeing things was shared by the Soudan committee members. The committee leaned towards the model of a female police force incorporated in the judicial police but with a female chief dependent on the Prosecutor General, and 'specialized' according to her 'particular aptitudes'. One could find the same type of arguments in the debate on women's access to the judiciary. In relation to this issue, the Soudan committee advocated a transitional period, during which cases would be distributed between a male judge and a female judge according to the sex and/or the age of the minors.

It should be noted that despite the dynamism of feminist lobbies and the audience they gradually gathered in the field of child protection, the path was full of obstacles. The nature of the issues to be faced was due to the difficult socio-political climate of the 1930s and the mentality issue, which was particularly acute in some sectors, like the judiciary.

As regarding the police, Belgian towns' tradition of autonomy slowed down the application of a general reform for female police forces. Lawmakers refused to directly intervene at the level of local administration, which had total liberty of action in organizing their police forces.[32] Except for Antwerp, which had tried to incorporate female agents into its vice squad in 1925, communal authorities remained quite indifferent to the issue.

Reform claims in relation to the judiciary transcended the narrow perimeter of juvenile courts. The 1912 law stipulated that juvenile judges should be recruited among members of the courts of first instance (*tribunal de première instance*) and that women's access to the judiciary had to be granted consequently. However, if actors in child welfare demanded the opening of courts to women, it also caused virulent opposition among many magistrates. A testimony to this is the standpoint taken by the acting Prosecutor General of the Liège Court of Appeals, Léo Delwaide, who at the time of his opening session speech in September 1946 delivered a real diatribe against opening the profession to women, basing his argument on the following aspects:

1. *physiological* ('It is foundationally a question of glands'; 'at around forty-five years of age, their sexual life withdraws, leaving them with a deep sentiment of a diminution in their being. At that moment, the woman

[32] Geneva, United Nations Library (Archives and Historical Collections), Première période (1919–27), Section 12 (section sociale), 676, Employment of Women Police, doc. 28694, Dossier concerning Belgium, réponse du ministre de l'Intérieur à la sollicitation d'Isidore Maus extraite de *Lettre du ministère des Affaires étrangères (Émile Vandervelde) à Éric Drummond* (Brussels, 12 August 1926). Our translation.

puts on weight and becomes a matron. Wouldn't one consequently have to advance the retirement age for women magistrates with fifteen years?');

2. *psychological* ('Psychologists generally recognize that a woman is more emotive and subjective; that she allows herself to be led by sympathy; that she contents herself with intuition while a man analyses and reflects; that she lacks independence and critical spirit; that she has a very weak capacity for abstraction');
3. *pragmatic* ('The law forbids putting women to work in the four weeks following childbirth. A provision of this sort would undoubtedly have to be inserted into the law of judicial organization if there were women magistrates. We will also have to install a nursery in the courthouse, complete with nurses and suspend sessions at the hours of breastfeeding');
4. *linked to the bourgeois family schema and the distribution of roles at its centre* ('It is quite certain that because of the necessities of service, one cannot think of appointing a married woman to the magistracy. (...) A woman who would leave meals unprepared, her house in disorder, his/her children in rags or feverish, how do you expect her to lock herself up in her office with her files?').[33]

First Achievements in the Post-World War II Years

During the interwar period, and despite the lobbying of women associations, all requests or initiatives concerning juvenile delinquency professionals, delegates for child protection, female police forces or women judges for children were weighted down by a difficult socio-political and economic climate. The crisis of the 1930s slowed the possible resolution of social demands, as well as that of the professionalization of women in general. Among other initiatives, and under the cover of natalist and economic arguments (e.g. the struggle against unemployment), the Catholic senator Georges Rutten submitted in May 1934 a proposition of law aimed at limiting the work of married women in factories, workshops, on building sites and in offices.[34]

World War II pushed back debates on the question of the role of women in child welfare. However, the occupation gave rise to new experiments, in particular the institution in April 1943 of a female police force of German inspiration, made up of two services (morals and youth).[35] Twenty-six inspectors

---

33 'Discours de rentrée de L. Delwaide', *Journal des tribunaux*, 13 October 1946, pp. 465–70. Our translation.

34 Sénat, annales parlementaires, 13 February 1934, p. 433.

35 Such an initiative is typical of the occupation practices deployed by the Germans in Belgium during World War II, namely the occupant instigating the development of structures whose implementation was nevertheless entrusted to local authorities. On this subject,

were recruited in Brussels, one of whom was a female student of the *École ouvrière supérieure*, Marcelle Bouchy, who drew from her experience a report amounting to an unprecedented testimony on the period. It illustrates the fact that a good number of women active in the field, educated in the so-called social schools, naturally endorsed the 'maternalist' (and bourgeois) conceptions that underlay women's investment in the field of the child welfare. Thus, this student was said, in connection with her practice, to have done 'educational work' among 'deficient' mothers of the popular class, by inculcating in them 'elementary concepts of hygiene and cleanliness'.[36] She was convinced that 'the female police force should have a social character and only rarely act in a repressive way'.[37]

The first initiatives of women's professionalization in the field of child welfare were only to be successful in the years immediately following World War II. Successive 'legislative victories' were part of a favourable trend following the war years, when the struggle for women's suffrage was also finally won. Women's associations benefited from the support of female members of parliament in the public sphere, who were open to new ideas. Female members of parliament who combined their efforts and transcended political cleavages to defend a common cause carried legal propositions on female police forces and women's access to the judiciary to victory.[38] Moreover, the bill that was introduced in parliament by the liberal Senator Georgette Ciselet, and that would eventually become the law of 21 February 1948 that regulated women's access to all offices in the Belgian judiciary (civil and military courts, as judges and as public prosecutors), had been co-supported by male supporters of women's emancipation. To the argumentation that a modernized and (thus) woman-friendly administration of justice was necessary for the future of democracy in Belgium, the Minister of Justice added a reference to the past. He defended the bill as homage to the part that Belgian women had played in the war, during which they had been examples of civil virtuousness.[39]

---

see: Benoît Majerus, *Occupations et logiques policières. La police bruxelloise en 1914–1918 et 1940–1945* (Brussels, 2007).

36 Brussels, Institut Émile Vandervelde, mémoires de l'École ouvrière supérieure, Marcelle Bouchy, *La police des mœurs et la création d'une police féminine à Bruxelles* (1944), p. 40 (our translation).

37 Ibid., pp. 60–61 (our translation). That police force, considered as suspect for being known as on the side of the German occupier, was disbanded with the Liberation.

38 Catherine Jacques, *Le féminisme en Belgique de la fin du 19e siècle à 1970* (Brussels, 2009), pp. 42ff.

39 Eva Schandevyl, 'Vrouwelijke rechters: de eerste pioniers, 60 jaar geleden', in Eva Schandevyl, Sophie Bollen and Machteld De Metsenaere (ed.), *In haar recht? Vrouwe Justitia feministisch bekeken* (Brussels, 2009), pp. 35–47; Eva Schandevyl, 'Portia ten tonele: de feminisering van de Belgische magistratuur', in Dirk Heirbaut, Xavier Rousseaux and Alain

After several false starts (different legal propositions in the 1930s), female police officers were mentioned in the 21 August 1948 law on the suppression of *maisons de tolérance* (brothels). A women's police service was created in 1953, after which female officers were then incorporated into the police, on the municipal level as well as in the new judicial police linked to the country's prosecution offices. Yet despite the abundance of candidates (nearly 350), the *parquet* (prosecution office) of Brussels only appointed three women in 1953. It took a number of years for new experiences and initiatives to appear.[40] A statutory text foresaw a mixed but differentiated distribution of policing tasks. For some, like the Royal Prosecutor of the Court of first instance of Brussels, Raymond Charles, diversity constituted a logical and inescapable consequence of justice at the end of World War II:

> Justice having become more human and more understanding – its solicitude for the individual makes it an organ of social protection. The woman finds her place there quite naturally. The public has the right to expect something different from the police force than punitive measures. It has become a vast organ of social protection, a social service whose role is the prevention of offences.[41]

When law courts were opened to women, the juvenile judge's position was quoted as an example in the parliamentary debates.[42] However, the full integration of women into the judiciary was a difficult process that happened very slowly, especially in the higher courts; there, the discrepancy between the numbers of men and women remains blatant, even today. The first woman children's judge, Rosette Dubuisson, was named to the Charleroi court of first instance in 1949.

And only in 1949 the law professionalized the function of *délégué(e) à la protection de l'enfance*, after another two years of parliamentary debates regarding the required diplomas.

Conclusion

In 1947, Aimée Racine presented women's access to the judiciary as a totally legitimate claim, whereas she had remained quite discreet on the matter for

Wijffels (ed.), *Histoire du droit et de la justice. Une nouvelle génération de recherches* (Louvain-la-Neuve, 2009), pp. 565–77.

40 Catherine Jacques, 'Quand la police se décline au féminin', *Cahiers de la Fonderie*, 39 (2008): pp. 41–5.

41 Mundaneum, CNFB 11. Séance du Conseil National des Femmes Belges, 7 March 1956.

42 Catherine Jacques, 'À l'assaut d'un bastion masculin. L'accès des femmes à la magistrature', *Cahiers de la Fonderie*, 39 (2008): pp. 51–5.

years, except within feminist circles. It is indeed noteworthy that what managed to persuade decision makers was not the recourse to egalitarian speeches, promoting gender equality on the basis of the universality of human nature. The feminist themselves did not perceive those views as strategically successful. In contrast, convincing was a set of arguments putting forward the intrinsic qualities of women, which men were allegedly lacking, that resulted in the complementary model of men and women, adapted to the respective skills of both sexes.

This essentialist discourse, claiming the specificity of women, was not perceived as antagonistic to the concept of equality. Belgian feminists did not seem to be aware that this insistence on natural skills could limit the involvement of women in the public sphere. Even though it allowed women to actively participate in fields connected to their 'natural expertise', like social work with families, it did not help them to obtain positions that were considered unrelated to the traditional roles of women in the domestic sphere, at least in the short term.

The three Belgian actors of child protection (magistrates, policewomen and delegates) that were involved in the debates and practices dealing with juvenile delinquency since the early twentieth century are in many ways emblematic of the 'relational feminism' described by Karen Offen,[43] and the complementary model this trend in feminism produced in practice.

First, the *délégué(e)s à la protection de l'enfance*, whose role was distributed according to a model in which men took care of older teenagers and women were in charge of younger children and girls. Second, the female police officers, whose mission was to morally help endangered young girls. Third, the association of female and male magistrates in the distribution of files involving boys and girls, as suggested in the first juvenile court projects.

If it resulted in women's access to public spheres that previously were closed to them, the essentialist argument only had a limited impact. It could even be turned against those upholding it. Transposed to other questions, the assertion of typically female competencies did not always result in emancipating women.

[43] 'Viewed historically, arguments in the relational feminist tradition proposed a gender-based but egalitarian vision of social organization. They featured the primacy of a companionate, non-hierarchical, male-female couple as the basic unit of society (...) Relational feminism emphasized women's rights *as women* (defined principally by their childbearing and/or nurturing capacities) in relation to men. It insisted on *women's* distinctive contributions in these roles to the broader society and made claims on the commonwealth on the basis of these contributions.' Karen Offen, 'Defining Feminism: A Comparative Historical Approach', *Signs*, 14:1 (1988): pp. 135–6.

On the contrary, the argument was often mobilized to invite women to opt for the place where their natural competencies were best exercised: the hearth.[44]

The confinement of female police officers to vice cases particularly raises questions regarding child protection if we consider that girls only accounted for 30 per cent of minors reported to prosecution offices and that vice cases accounted for less than half of those 30 per cent, at the most.[45] Similarly, speeches describing the tasks of social workers remained, even after the reform of 1947–49, filled with the same arguments as those of the nineteenth century. They considered this occupation as a very womanly one, 'one of the most beautiful professions, filled with nuances and love'.[46]

Belgian delegates, policewomen and magistrates illustrate to what extent the official involvement of women in the child protection field created its own paradoxes and challenges. Indeed, the step-by-step method was successful in some way, but also faced drawbacks and created its own barriers. Although it enabled progress regarding women's access to child protection activities, even when women did not have a professional status, it also confined them to a very restricted role for a long period of time.

Bibliography

Bribosia, Paul, *Enfants de juges et juges d'enfants* (Namur: Editions du Soleil Levant, 1964).

Christiaens, Jenneke, *De geboorte van de jeugddelinquent (België 1830–1930)* (Brussels: VUB Press, 1999).

De Koster, Margo, *Weerbaar, weerspannig of crimineel? Meisjes en jonge vrouwen tussen emancipatie en delinquentie tijdens de eerste helft van de twintigste eeuw*, PhD diss., Vrije Universiteit Brussel, 2003 (unpublished).

Donzelot, Jacques, *La police des familles* (Paris: Minuit, 1977).

Dumortier, Els, *De jeugdrechter in twijfel. Een onderzoek naar het ontstaan en de praktijk van de kinderrechter*, PhD diss., Vrije Universiteit Brussel, 2006 (unpublished).

Dupont-Bouchat, Marie-Sylvie, *De la prison à l'école. Les pénitenciers pour enfants en Belgique au XIXe siècle (1840–1914)* (Kortrijk-Heule: UGA, 1996).

---

[44] Aimée Racine herself paid a price for her convictions. Describing, in an etiologic analysis on juvenile delinquency, how the absence of mothers at the hearth was liable to affect the wellbeing and morality of children, Racine's study was picked up on by Senator Rutten in his argumentation against married women at work, held up as a factor in juvenile delinquency. Aimée Racine, 'Les conditions économiques de la famille comme facteur de la délinquance juvénile', *Revue de l'institut de sociologie*, 3 (1932): pp. 540–63.

[45] François, *Guerres et délinquance*, pp. 42–3.

[46] Paul Bribosia, *Enfants de juges et juges d'enfants* (Namur, 1964), p. 36.

Dupont-Bouchat, Marie-Sylvie, 'Femmes philanthropes. Les femmes dans la protection de l'enfance en Belgique (1890–1914)', *Sextant. Femmes de culture et de pouvoir*, 13–14 (2000): 81–117.

Dupont-Bouchat, Marie-Sylvie, and Éric Pierre (ed.), *Enfance et justice au XIXe siècle, Essais d'histoire comparée de la protection de l'enfance 1820–1914. France, Belgique, Pays-Bas, Canada* (Paris: PUF, 2001).

François, Aurore, 'Une phalange de collaborateurs pour "une tâche de cœur": les délégués à la protection de l'enfance (Belgique, 1912–1949)', *Histoire et Sociétés. Revue européenne d'Histoire sociale*, 25–6 (2008): 212–25.

François, Aurore, *Guerres et délinquance juvénile (1912–1950). Un demi-siècle de pratiques judiciaires et institutionnelles envers des mineurs en difficulté* (Bruges: Die Keure, 2011).

Hunt, Alan, *Governing Morals: A Social History of Moral Regulation* (Cambridge: Cambridge University Press, 1999).

Jackson, Louise, 'Care or Control? The Metropolitan Women Police and Child Welfare, 1919–1969', *Historical Journal*, 46:3 (2003): 623–48.

Jackson, Louise, *Women Police: Gender, Welfare and Surveillance in the Twentieth Century* (Manchester: University of Manchester Press, 2006).

Jacques, Catherine, 'Quand la police se décline au féminin', *Cahiers de la Fonderie*, 39 (2008): 41–5.

Jacques, Catherine, 'À l'assaut d'un bastion masculin. L'accès des femmes à la magistrature', *Cahiers de la Fonderie*, 39 (2008): 51–5.

Jacques, Catherine, Le féminisme en Belgique de la fin du 19e siècle à 1970 (Brussels: Centre de recherche et d'information socio-politiques (CRISP), 2009).

Koven, Seth, and Sonya Michel, 'Womanly Duties: Maternalist Politics and the Origins of Welfare States in France, Germany, Great Britain, and the United States (1880–1920)', *American Historical Review*, 95/4 (1990): 1076–108.

Majerus, Benoît, *Occupations et logiques policières. La police bruxelloise en 1914–1918 et 1940–1945* (Brussels: Académie royale de Belgique, 2007).

Manneke, Nelleke, *Vrouwen van kaliber. Politievrouwen in de twintigste eeuw* (Apeldoorn: Verloren, 1998).

Marissal, Claudine, 'Travail ou non travail? Le bénévolat féminin dans les œuvres de l'enfance', *Cahiers de la Fonderie*, 39 (2008): 20–23.

Meis Knupfer, Anne, *Reform and Resistance: Gender, Delinquency, and America's First Juvenile Court* (New York: Routledge, 2001).

Miller, Carol, *Lobbying the League: Women's International Organizations and the League of Nations*, PhD diss., University of Oxford, 1992 (unpublished).

Niget, David, *La naissance du tribunal pour enfants. Une comparaison France-Québec, 1912–1945* (Rennes: PUR, 2009).

Offen, Karen, 'Defining Feminism: A Comparative Historical Approach', *Signs*, 14:1 (1988): 119–57.

Pièces parlementaires (annales et documents) (Brussels: Belgian Senate and Chamber of Representatives, since 1831).

Racine, Aimée, 'Les conditions économiques de la famille comme facteur de la délinquance juvénile', *Revue de l'institut de sociologie*, 3 (1932): 540–63.

Racine, Aimée, *Les enfants traduits en justice. Étude d'après trois cents dossiers du tribunal pour enfants de l'arrondissement de Bruxelles* (Liège: Thone, 1935).

Rennes, Juliette, *Le mérite et la nature. Une controverse républicaine. L'accès des femmes aux professions de prestige (1880–1940)* (Paris: Fayard, 2007).

Sangster, Joan, *Girl Trouble: Female Delinquency in English Canada* (Toronto: Between the Lines, 2002).

Schandevyl, Eva, 'Vrouwelijke rechters: de eerste pioniers, 60 jaar geleden', in Eva Schandevyl, Sophie Bollen, and Machteld De Metsenaere (ed.), *In haar recht? Vrouwe Justitia feministisch bekeken, Brussel* (Brussels: VUB Press, 2009).

Schandevyl, Eva, 'Portia ten tonele: de feminisering van de Belgische magistratuur' in Dirk Heirbaut, Xavier Rousseaux and Alain Wijffels (ed.), *Histoire du droit et de la justice. Une nouvelle génération de recherches* (Louvain-la-Neuve: Presses univeritaires de Louvain, 2009).

Schlossman, Steven L., *Love and the American Delinquent: The Theory and Practice in Progressive America* (Chicago: University of Chicago Press, 1977).

Trépanier, Jean, and Françoise Tulkens, *Délinquance & protection de la jeunesse. Aux sources des lois belge et canadienne sur l'enfance* (Montreal–Ottawa–Brussels: Presses de l'Université de Montréal, Presses de l'Université d'Ottawa, De Boeck Université, 1995).

Tulkens, Françoise, *Généalogie de la défense sociale en Belgique 1880–1914* (Brussels: Storia Scientia, 1988).

Tulkens, Françoise, and Thierry Moreau, *Droit de la jeunesse. Aide, assistance, protection* (Brussels: Larcier, 2000).

Valverde, Mariana, *The Age of Light, Soap, and Water: Moral Reform in English Canada, 1885–1925* (Toronto: University of Toronto Press, 2008).

Velge, Henri, 'L'activité féminine dans les Œuvres de Protection de l'Enfance', *La femme belge* (May 1919): 29–34.

Wets, Paul, *Le guide du délégué à la protection de l'enfance* (Liège: Thone, 1923).

Zélis, Guy, 'Maternalisme dans le travail social féminin 1920–1940', *Travailler le social & Chronique féministe*, 41 (2008): 135–47.

Chapter 2
Feminist Lawyers and Legal Reform in Modern France, 1900–1946

Sara L. Kimble

Introduction: Pioneering Lawyers as Activists

In the early twentieth century, France was home to the largest concentration of female lawyers anywhere in the world. Women were officially admitted to the bar first in France (1900), Romania (1901), the Netherlands (1903), Norway (1904) and Denmark (1906). Frenchwomen rapidly moved into the profession and advocated for their clients in a variety of courts, from criminal to military. By 1921, women constituted perhaps 8 per cent of the French legal profession, while in the US, by comparison, women accounted for only 1.4 per cent.[1] By contrast, women in Britain and Germany could not practise law at all until 1922.

This research considers how French female lawyers participated in legal reform during the period from 1900 to 1940. Frenchwomen were admitted to the legal profession in 1900 by an act of parliament and this reform brought political implications in its wake. My research on the first cadres of female lawyers illustrates that they were unusually politically active. As unequal members of the profession and unequal citizens in society many of these new professionals engaged in a vigorous defence of equality and justice.[2]

Reform-oriented French women were disadvantaged by the fact that they could not vote until 1944. Socialist politician René Viviani once said that

---

[1] Christine Bard, *Les Filles de Marianne. Histoire des féminismes 1914–1940* (Paris, 1995), p. 178.

[2] The sources for this research arise primarily from printed and manuscript material found in French archives and library collections. The history of women's presence in the Paris Faculté de droit can be derived in part from the archival materials at the Archives nationales. I have drawn on legal testimony from civil and criminal cases (from the Archives de Paris) and newspaper articles in order to illustrate how feminist lawyers used the courts and the mass media to disseminate legal knowledge, defend women's existing rights, and advocate for new laws. A few lawyers wrote memoirs, letters, articles, and pamphlets about their personal experiences at work. These materials, some housed at the Bibliothèque Marguerite Durand (BMD), the Centre des Archives du Féminisme (in Angers) and the Bibliothèque Historique de la Ville de Paris (BHVP), are essential for restoring their voices to the historical record.

'legislators make the laws for those who make the legislators', meaning that those who do not vote, do not count in French society.[3] Feminists' efforts to reform women's rights, especially to revise the antiquated Civil code that was a central source of women's subordination in the family, seemed impossible without the enfranchisement of women. Nevertheless, in the face of their formal exclusion from political power, *avocates* (female lawyers) used varied means to articulate their demand for women's emancipation and foster support for substantive legal reform. These activities constitute serious political engagement such that many of the leading lawyers should be seen as *avocates engagées* (politically engaged lawyers). The evidence of the collective activities of these historical actors reveals the presence of a collective feminist lawyers' movement.

French female lawyers also used special political and rhetorical strategies to defend their clients and to critique inequalities of power in society. *Avocates* were moral activists who worked on behalf of others in the following ways: first, their reform campaigns were designed to introduce a humanitarian vision and ethical language into national and international sites of political power. Second, they took on test cases and made moral arguments during legal trials. Third, they educated and empowered the public through educational activities and publications. These reform-oriented strategies addressed specific topical concerns such as the organization of justice, family law, civil and criminal law, and women's and children's social and political rights. Legal theorists describe contemporary behaviour in this model as altruistic lawyering or 'cause lawyering'.[4] This chapter draws on such insights and applies them to the historical record.

The movement of politically engaged female lawyers was an urban phenomenon centred in the French capital where the highest concentration of lawyers also worked. Nevertheless, this urban movement was not exclusively Parisian. Feminist lawyers in Algiers, Avignon, Bordeaux, Toulon, Toulouse and Marseilles networked with their peers across the nation.[5] Across the nation and in the French colonies, feminist lawyers were also involved in a host of related organizations such as groups of university women, professional and non-political groups of lawyers and judges, social welfare groups concerned with juvenile justice and some religious organizations. The interplay between the

---

3 Steven Hause and Anne Kenney, *Women's Suffrage and Social Politics in the French Third Republic* (Princeton, 1984), quoted p. 32.

4 See Austin Sarat and Stuart A. Scheingold (ed.), *Cause Lawyering: Political Commitments and Professional Responsibilities* (New York, 1998); Austin Sarat and Stuart A. Scheingold (ed.), *Cause Lawyers and Social Movements* (Stanford, 2006).

5 See Sara L. Kimble, 'Justice Redressed: Women, Citizenship, and the Social Uses of the Law in Modern France, 1890–1939', PhD diss. (University of Iowa, 2002), and her forthcoming book, *Women, Feminism, and the Law in Modern France: Justice Redressed* (New York, 2015).

women's rights movement and the feminist lawyers' movement was mutually supportive and generally fruitful.

Moreover, international lawyers and feminists made connections through correspondence and travel from the end of the nineteenth century. For example, the intrepid Jeanne Chauvin, who was responsible for opening the bar to women in France, was connected to American reformers from the 1890s when she was invited to participate in the Chicago conference of the International Council of Women (ICW) of 1893.[6] This is but one example of *avocates*' transatlantic and pan-continental alliances that grew strong between the 1890s and 1940s.[7] French female lawyers were also involved in national and international women's rights organizations. In these capacities, feminist lawyers provided legal expertise that facilitated organizational efforts to communicate with political leaders nationally and internationally. This was especially important when lawyers could make their voices heard on matters of constitutional, international or national code reform. The close intersection between the feminist movement and women's participation in the legal profession had its origins in the history of the profession itself.

The Role of Gender in Access to the Legal Profession in France

France was the first civil law country in Europe to grant women access to the bar through a legislative act. The question of women's right to practise law in France emerged after the issue had arisen in neighbouring countries such as Italy and Belgium during the 1880s.[8] The French effort was spearheaded by Jeanne Chauvin, the daughter of a provincial notary, who requested the right to join the Paris bar after completing her doctorate in law. Chauvin's controversial doctoral dissertation, *A Historical Study on the Professions Accessible to Women* (1892), argued that the appearance of women's inequality was the result of their inferior educational opportunities, the constraints of law and legislation, and other

[6] Jeanne Chauvin, 'La Condition juridique de la femme française', *Société pour l'amélioration du sort de la femme et la revendication de ses droits. Rapports adressés au Congres des femmes représentantes tendu à Chicago, 1893* (Paris, 1893).

[7] On the Franco-American relationship see, Sara L. Kimble, 'Portia's Sisters: Transatlantic Networks for Women in the Legal Professions', paper presented at the American Historical Association Annual Meeting, Chicago, 8 January 2012.

[8] On Italy see Vittorio Olgiati, 'The Case of the First (Failed) Woman Lawyer in Modern Italy', in Ulrike Schultz and Gisela Shaw (ed.), *Women in the World's Legal Professions* (Oxford; Portland, 2003), pp. 419–35. See also Mary Jane Mossman, *The First Women Lawyers* (Oxford; Portland, 2006).

social oppressions.[9] She believed that women were as capable as men to practise law because the modern liberal professions required gender-neutral standards of merit that women could meet by fulfilling the same procedures established for men, namely: academic study and apprenticeship. Moreover, she argued that the French republican tradition obligated the government to grant equal rights and duties to women. Although the faculty at the Sorbonne praised Chauvin's intellectual achievements, male students disrupted her defence and protested her ideas.[10]

The fact that Chauvin was already known as a supporter of women's rights likely exacerbated the negative reaction to her ideas among students. A republican feminist, Chauvin advocated women's equal rights in the family, education, the workplace and under the law. Her most important fin-de-siècle political commitment was to Jeanne-Elisabeth Schmahl's civil rights-oriented group *L'Avant Courrière* (The Front Runner), where she drafted and promoted model legislation on the issues of married women's right to serve as witnesses and autonomous control over their earned income.[11] Legislative progress was made on both fronts in 1897 and 1907 respectively. Chauvin would also publish a well-received introductory legal textbook promoting legal education for girls and based on her own experience as a girls' schoolteacher.[12]

In pursuit of women's right to work in the legal profession, Chauvin approached the Paris bar association with a request to become a practising lawyer, a demand supported by the feminist movement and the burgeoning feminist press. Her request was refused and her case rejected by the *cour d'appel* (appeals court) in 1897. The French court was influenced by the preceding Italian and Belgian decisions that had cited women's biological inequality and the French Civil code of 1804 as sources that justified the exclusion of women from the bar. Nevertheless, she found sympathetic politicians in the Chamber of Deputies and the Senate who were willing to champion her cause.[13]

Independent socialist and Deputy René Viviani sponsored a bill that would allow women to become lawyers for the purpose of putting into action 'the grand principles of liberty and equality in education and in work for all women as it

---

9 Jeanne Chauvin, *Des professions accessibles aux femmes en droit romain et en droit français évolution historique de la position économique de la femme dans la société* (Paris, 1892).

10 Henri Dabot, *Calendriers d'un bourgeois du quartier latin du 1 janvier 1888 au 31 décembre 1900* (Paris, 1905), pp. 103–4.

11 Jeanne Chauvin, 'La Capacité légale des femmes', *La Fraternité*, 3 May 1893.

12 Jeanne Chauvin, *Cours de droit professé dans les lycées de jeunes filles de Paris* (Paris, 1895). See also Archives nationales de France, AJ/16/1012, dossier, *Jeanne Chauvin*.

13 See Kimble, 'Justice Redressed'; Christine Alice Corcos, 'Lawyers for Marianne: The Nature of Discourse on the Entry of French Women into the Legal Profession, 1894–1926', *Georgia State University Law Review*, 12/2 (1996): pp. 435–75.

is for all men'.[14] His legislation received support from solidarist deputies who believed that everyone needed 'equal opportunity [gained] through education, guaranteed employment, comprehensive welfare and social security services'.[15] Jeanne's brother, Émile Chauvin, was a deputy in the Chamber at the time but he remained silent on the official public record concerning the bill brought on his sister's behalf. The wide-ranging parliamentary debate evoked strong language about the threats posed by feminism and socialism to the family on the one hand, and the enlightenment promised by emancipation on the other. Anxiety about the transformation of gender roles aside, the Chamber of Deputies voted 312 in favour and 160 against on 30 June 1899 to admit women to the bar as lawyers. When the Senate finally took their vote on 13 November 1900, the bill passed by 172 in favour and 34 against, a wider margin.[16] The resulting law of 1 December 1900 was hailed by optimists as a revolutionary feminist triumph and acknowledged by pragmatists as a modest step forward.

The most significant limitation of the legislation passed on Chauvin's behalf was the fact that it created two unequal paths within the legal profession. Women in France who joined the bar before 1946 were not authorized to become judges, magistrates, prosecutors, notaries or other officials of the court. The structural inequality within this otherwise landmark legislation was a result of instructions issued by the Ministry of Justice and the failure of the legislative champions to insist on the equal treatment of women.[17] Despite the law's limitations, historians see its passage as an extraordinary breakthrough in European civil law.[18]

The law of 1900 did nothing to address the anomaly that women had the right to argue cases in various courts – from military to criminal – but they could not serve as judges or prosecutors. Although men were eligible for the bar before the age of majority, the women's civil inferiority made them 'eternal minors' under the law.[19] In other words, the jurisprudence of the era translated thusly: women did not have the right to judge because they did not have the right to vote.

The inequality of the law of 1900 had several consequences beyond the fact that it simultaneously opened up a professional opportunity and also reinforced women's legal inferiority. The limitations of the law politicized the women who entered the profession under unequal conditions who saw the need to fight for equal treatment. By extension, these lawyers remained cognizant of the role that

---

14 *Chambre des Députés de l'Assemblée Nationale. Annales et documents parlementaires, 1871–1942*, no. 3145 (22 March 1898), vol. 54 (Paris, 1898), p. 924.

15 J.E.S. Hayward, 'The Official Social Philosophy of the French Third Republic: Léon Bourgeois and Solidarism', *International Review of Social History*, 6/1 (1961), p. 30.

16 André Daniel, *L'Année politique 1900* (Paris, 1901), p. 324.

17 Archives nationales de France, AN C//5595 Dossier 1892.

18 Bard, *Les Filles de Marianne*, pp. 178–9.

19 See Kimble, *Women, Feminism, and the Law*.

the Constitution and the Civil code played in defining all women's inequality in the family and society. The revolutionary nature of the law, however, inspired much discussion throughout Europe on the evolution in gender roles. The opening of this profession provided women with the opportunity to demonstrate their skills as advocates, critical thinkers and orators. The occasion engendered discussions about the nature of gender-appropriate legal work. The traditionally male legal profession had monopolized the field of juvenile justice and the admission of women into the legal field raised questions about women's potential roles with delinquent youth and the newly emerging juvenile courts (established in 1912).[20] Broadly speaking, the central issues for the following decades were the interplay between women's experiences in the legal profession and women's struggle for equality under the law.

Cause Lawyering and Moral Arguments

In French history, politically engaged lawyers used the courts as sounding boards for *idées-forces*, ideas that were capable of influencing the mentality of others and the structures of their society. Commitment to political ideas was not always the best way to win a case, but it could be an effective strategy to influence public opinion. Political engagement by lawyers could be signalled in court by the use of a rhetorical technique called *la plaidoirie de rupture* wherein the lawyer espoused the political opinions of his or her client, attacked the establishment and spoke in defence of individual liberties.[21] French legal sociologist Lucien Karpik found that lawyers have also used their defence arguments as 'political pedagogy', generating explanations that liberal forces outside the judicial system could use to 'consolidate and extend true civil and political citizenship'.[22] The work of the pioneering French feminist lawyers engaged in such strategies to benefit the women's rights movement and other republican-based political movements.

Maria Vérone was among the exemplars of politically engaged lawyers who used legal knowledge to advocate for judicial and legal change inside and outside the courtroom. A true *doyenne* (leader) of the Paris bar, Vérone's female colleagues saw her as a mentor and admired how her professional work

---

20 Sara L. Kimble, 'No Right to Judge: Feminism and the Judiciary in Third Republic France', *French Historical Studies*, 31/4 (2008), pp. 609–41.

21 Bernard Sur, *Histoire des avocats en France, des origines à nos jours* (Paris, 1997), pp. 196–9.

22 Lucien Karpik, 'Builders of Liberal Society: French Lawyers and Politics', Nora Scott trans., in Terence C. Halliday and Lucien Karpik (ed.), *Lawyers and the Rise of Western Political Liberalism: Europe and North America from the Eighteenth to Twentieth Centuries* (New York, 1997), p. 109.

reflected her ideological commitments.[23] Moreover, she advocated individual rights by means of *la plaidoirie de rupture* and was one of the few pioneers to receive wide approbation during her lifetime.[24] Vérone was born into a family of modest means in Paris where her father worked as an accounting clerk, and her mother worked in shops as a *fleuriste-plumassière* decorating women's hats and clothes with feathers and fabric flowers.[25] Her father, Gustave Vérone, was among a small cohort of men and women who established the National Federation of the Free Thinkers, an organization Maria joined while still a teenager. In this group, Maria likely met a handful of influential professional women, including education inspector Pauline Kergomard, Maria Pognon, and Marie Bonnevial, the president and secretary-general of the French Women's Rights League.[26] After Vérone was fired from her first teaching job for a speech on secular education, she was fortunate to land at Marguerite Durand's *La Fronde* as a reporter. In the late 1890s, starting at the age of 23, she wrote about legal topics under the pseudonym 'Themis', Greek goddess of good counsel and social order. As historian Steven Hause noted, Vérone and her colleagues 'forced exclusively masculine institutions such as the stock exchange to accredit women as journalists for the first time'.[27] At that time, Vérone was one of the few women who also secured admission to professional journalism associations and briefly became a pioneering legal reporter.[28] Vérone entered law school while simultaneously working for *La Fronde* (1897–1905) and serving as general secretary of the French Women's Rights League. She would complete her law degree in 1907 and become the fifth woman to join the Paris bar.

Vérone believed that women's political participation and legislative reform were the keys to improving the condition of the disadvantaged. She was involved in many social justice and women's rights organizations, the most important of which were the French Women's Rights League and the National Council of French Women (an ICW affiliate). From 1912 on, she also served on the influential extra-parliamentary Committee to Defend Children in the Justice System and revised the law to improve the treatment of delinquent youth.

---

23 Vérone's involvement in the feminist movement has been described most comprehensively by Hause and Kenney, *Women's Suffrage*, and Bard, *Filles de Marianne*.

24 See Raymond Hesse and Lionel Vastorg (ed.), *Leur Manière* (Paris, 1925).

25 Hause and Kenney, *Women's Suffrage*, p. 53.

26 Jacqueline Lalouette, *La Libre pensée en France: 1848–1940* (Paris, 1997), pp. 94–5. On these women see Linda L. Clark, *Women and Achievement in Nineteenth-Century Europe* (Cambridge, 2008).

27 Hause and Kenney, *Women's Suffrage*, p. 35.

28 Sara L. Kimble, 'Popular Legal Journalism in the Writings of Maria Vérone and *Le Droit des femmes*', paper presented at the Western Society for French History conference, Portland, 12 November 2011.

She is credited with catalysing votes on at least three laws related to juvenile welfare alone.[29]

By 1909, Vérone had developed a grand vision of republican universalism that she would promote throughout her lifetime that held:

> Woman, a human being like man, endowed liked him with reason, giver of life and first teacher to the child, bound to the same duties in the family and society as he, vulnerable to the same pains as he, must possess the same rights as man and participate in the creation of laws with him.[30]

She argued that the declaration of the *Rights of Man and Citizen* from 1789 was 'one of the best steps in the path of human progress' and that a proclamation of human rights needed to be issued to affirm the equality of the sexes.[31]

During the first full year of her career, Vérone cemented her reputation as an *avocate engagée*. In 1908, Vérone argued on behalf of Henriette Roussel, a young florist who had been arrested in July 1907 along with 41 others for posting antimilitarist flyers at a train station in Paris. This incident was part of a series of explosive antimilitarist demonstrations that emerged as an outgrowth of the early twentieth-century French labour movement.[32] When she was arrested, Roussel had copies of an antimilitarist pamphlet in her possession, the *Young Recruits' Manifesto*, a document that incited soldiers to desert the military. In her defence argument, Vérone did not try to persuade the jury that her client was innocent; rather, she characterized Roussel as a pacifist and argued that it was women's duty to protest against war. Vérone was 'armed with evidence, spoke with a clear voice, and made graceful gestures' to justify Roussel's participation in anti-government demonstrations.[33] Vérone claimed that pacifists strengthened the nation in their effort to preserve the lives of their children, brothers and husbands. Moreover, she claimed that women's campaigns for peace were not a threat to society (unlike the anarchists), and rather that women had a special stake in the prevention of war and disease.[34] Drawing on contemporary ideas about women's moral superiority, Vérone argued that women should be allowed to take a greater role in society, to civilize it in the interests of peace even

---

29 Maurice Hamburger, *Nos grands avocats* (Paris, 1930), pp. 170–76.

30 Maria Vérone, *Appel à la justice adressé par le Conseil national des femmes françaises à la Chambre des députes et au Sénat. Rapport de la section du suffrage du Conseil national présente par Mme Maria Vérone* (Paris, 1909), p. 20.

31 Ibid.

32 Gordon Wright, *France in Modern Times* (New York, 1987), p. 263.

33 'Antimilitarisme en Cour d'assises', in *Revue des grands procès contemporaine*, in Emile de Saint-Auban (ed.), vol. 26 (Paris, 1908), p. 302.

34 Ibid., p. 307.

when such participation violated the law. Vérone's arguments won Roussel her freedom; she was acquitted of all charges.[35]

Later that same year, Vérone sought to test the 1885 court decree that prohibited women from exercising political rights. In this extra-judicial affair, Vérone served as the legal counsellor to Jeanne Laloë, a candidate for the Municipal Council of Paris. Laloë ran on a feminist platform calling for free nurseries and greater government subsidies for housing. The newspaper *Le Matin* supported Laloë's candidacy as a kind of publicity stunt. Vérone, however, used the occasion to promote women's electoral rights. Vérone's persistence and willingness to challenge authority enabled Laloë to hold an electoral meeting on public property, despite the obstructionism of the local mayor.[36]

In the final tally of ballots cast by men in the Paris municipal elections of 1908, Laloë received approximately 22 per cent of the votes. Election officials ruled her candidacy invalid and annulled these ballots because women did not have the right to run for or be elected to office. Vérone protested the official decision to dismiss the ballots, arguing that the administration was attempting to substitute its own will for popular sovereignty as expressed in the contested ballots. She asserted that public opinion and jurisprudence were on the side of feminism and that equality and justice would prevail.[37] In the end, Vérone succeeded by facilitating the first electoral campaign, though not the election, of a female candidate in twentieth-century France. At the July 1908 Congress on women's civil rights and suffrage, she argued that the time was ripe to push for political rights on the municipal level. The following year, the National Council of French Women, the largest women's rights organization in France, decided to lobby for voting rights at this level.

Many of the women who followed Vérone into the legal profession were equally motivated to address feminist issues as matters of law and social policy. The stars of this generation included Agathe Dyvrande, Suzanne Grinberg, Marcelle Kraemer-Bach, Andrée Lehmann, Yvonne Netter and Odette Simon-Bidaux. These women followed Vérone's example in their dedication to the legal profession, their engagement with legal issues through journalism and public speaking, and their leadership in social justice and women's rights organizations. The most important campaigns included securing women's right to work on an equal basis, reforming women's rights in the Constitution and under the Civil code, and building alliances with other female lawyers across national borders.

---

35 'La première défenderesse en cour d'assises', *La Française*, 12 January 1908.

36 Steven C. Hause and Anne Kenney, 'Women's Suffrage and the Paris Elections of 1908', *Laurels*, 1/41 (1980): pp. 21–32.

37 Maria Vérone, 'Actualité. Victoire Féministe', *La Française*, 10 May 1908.

Equality for Women in the French Legal Profession and 'the Right to Judge'

Throughout the early twentieth century, female lawyers objected to the fact that their career opportunities were truncated because they were women. The law of 1 December 1900 was written so narrowly as to admit women only as *avocates*. No provisions were granted to admit them to a variety of posts for which, except for gender, they would have been qualified. This meant that women could not work as court clerks or notaries, and they were ineligible for appointments to the judiciary or public prosecution. Attorney Agathe Dyvrande faulted the narrowness of the 1900 law for 'establishing an inequality, prejudicial to women, between lawyers of the two sexes; it closes the door by which women have already entered into the sanctuary of justice itself'.[38] Dyvrande, the daughter of a prosecutor, had an active legal career from 1907 and vigorously supported the women's rights movement.[39] In 1911, while working for the successful lawyer Eugène Balliman, she requested that women be admitted to plead cases in the higher courts. Specialized lawyers, such as Balliman, enjoyed a near monopoly over all cases heard before the high court, with the exception of electoral ones. The governing council of the bar rejected her argument on the grounds that such access constituted admission to a 'ministerial office' and thus required candidates to have full political and civil rights.[40] This was a convenient argument that put voting rights as an explicit prerequisite for the judiciary.

Feminist lawyers did not relent in their search for ways to convince the members of their profession and the legislature that women merited the opportunity for 'the right to judge'. One of the important battles in this campaign occurred during the debates about the creation of the French juvenile courts. Juvenile court reformers and feminists both hoped to see women employed as juvenile court judges. Since 1907, when a precursor of the juvenile court system opened to serve the Paris region, the new cohort of female lawyers was disproportionately assigned to represent juvenile defendants. The *avocates* could speak from experience about the limitations of the current system. Maria Vérone observed that the juvenile trials were chaotic and fruitless. She criticized the judges for their lack of specialized knowledge, their superficial treatment of individuals and for meting out punitive rather than rehabilitative sentences. She faulted the system for creating unworkably heavy caseloads and providing scanty pre-hearing evidence.[41] Drawing on maternalist rhetoric, Vérone argued

38 Mme [Ghénia] Avril de Sainte-Croix (ed.), *Dixième congrès international des femmes. Oeuvres et institutions féminines, droits des femmes. 2 Juin 1913, Paris* (Paris, 1914), pp. 577, 407, 397.

39 'Une Nouvelle 'avocate', *Le Temps*, 6 November 1907.

40 'A Travers Paris', *Le Figaro*, 1 April 1911.

41 André Moufflet, 'Le meeting du 27 Juin 1911', *Le Droit des femmes*, January 1912, pp. 12–15. See Kimble, 'No Right to Judge'.

for the employment of women as judges in the future juvenile courts because women 'know how to love and to forgive, and also to correct and punish'.[42] The influential jurist Emile Garçon, who opined in 1911 that 'no eloquent, persuasive speeches' were required to justify women's 'obvious and logical role' in the juvenile courts, supported her position.[43] Despite the appeal of such argument, the issue of women's right to serve as judges in the juvenile courts was not so easily resolved. Appointments to the juvenile court bench were made through the same procedures as other jurisdictions, and no special dispensation was then granted to women.

The controversy about the possibility of female judges was primarily a political one. The fact that women were eligible to serve in the commercial courts demonstrated that the issue was not ability but women's civil and political status. In the commercial courts, women could vote and be elected as judges in the lower labour arbitration courts by 1900 and the superior courts by 1903.[44] In the case of the *conseils de prud'hommes* (labour courts) that oversaw disputes between employers and employees, women had been eligible to run for the elected positions since the laws of 1907 and 1908, and, at least by 1930, women were serving as lay judges on an equal basis with men.[45]

The fact that women's unequal citizenship made them ineligible for judicial appointments rankled experienced female lawyers. In the aftermath of World War I, when too few male lawyers were available to fill judicial positions, the National Association of Lawyers debated the issue. Vérone argued passionately for the admission of women to the judiciary, remarking that more than 200 women then worked at the Paris bar alone, and following such a reform, the proportion of female law students would certainly increase from its current 12 per cent.[46] Anticipating that veteran female lawyers would seek places on the bench, Vérone counselled that it would be 'much better to plead in front of a capable competent, experienced woman' than to have one's case judged by a young, inexperienced and less competent man.[47] Her argument was rejected

[42] Jean Lefranc, 'Les enfants coupables et leur protectrice', *Le Temps*, 14 May 1911.

[43] Emile Garçon, 'Quelques observations sur le projet de loi relatif aux tribunaux pour enfants', *Revue politique et parlementaire*, 70 (1911), p. 72.

[44] Georges Scelle, 'La Représentation politique', *Revue du droit public*, 28 (1911), p. 547.

[45] Articles 5–6 of the law of 27 March 1907 extended voting and electability to women. See René Bloch and Henry Chaumel, *Traité théorique et pratique des conseils de prud'hommes* (Paris, 1925), p. 10. Vérone, *Appel à la justice*, p. 9.

[46] Based on total enrolment of 9,971 law students, academic year 1929–30. *Annuaire statistique de la ville de Paris, 1929, 1930 et 1931* (Paris, 1933), p. 533.

[47] Maria Vérone, 'Le Congrès de Marseille', *Le Droit des femmes* (December 1930), 298–300; *Le Congrès d'Alger de l'Association nationale des avocats (22–24*

in favour of lowering the age qualification for men to 23 with the law of 16 July 1930.

As I argue elsewhere at greater length, female lawyers were vigorous and persistent campaigners to open the judiciary to women.[48] They believed their cause would simultaneously advance women's rights, the welfare of defendants and the needs of the nation. The opposition forces argued that women's ineligibility for the judiciary rested with their biological, social and political inequality.[49] Judicial reformers also struggled against the fact that married women's civil rights – including their right to work, to appear in court and to contract – were subject to spousal approval under the Civil code. While these constraints were viewed increasingly as anachronistic, they constituted a bulwark to change nonetheless. The reform movement was disadvantaged not only by law but also by culture. Cultural prejudices painted women as lacking the essential characteristics that judges typified, that is intellect, sangfroid, objectivity and impartiality. Consequently, the battle to remove the gender requirement from the judiciary was a challenge to male hegemony in society.

Although feminists fought for decades to secure those rights, among others, women did not gain the right to become judges until 1946, two years after they were enfranchised. The right to judge would be secured by special legislation initiated by new female representatives in the Constituent Assembly.[50] Dyvrande's demand from 1911 that women be admitted to the ranks of the lawyers arguing in the highest courts was a long time coming. In 1976, Martine Luc-Thaler became the first woman admitted to this exclusive group.[51]

Female Lawyers and Civil Code Reform

Feminist jurisprudence on French Civil code was the special purview of female lawyers. The Civil code was compiled in 1804, under Napoleon, and combined elements from Roman and French law into a coherent national set of standards. The French Civil code proved to be more enduring than any of France's constitutions. Over the past two centuries, the French have lived under 10

avril 1930). Bulletin de l'Association nationale des avocats inscrits aux barreaux de France, des colonies et pays de protectorat (Paris, 1930), pp. 111–12.

48 See Kimble, 'No Right to Judge', pp. 609–41.

49 On *capacité politique* in the 1930s, see Anne Boigeol, 'Les femmes et les Cours. La difficile mise en œuvre de l'égalité des sexes dans l'accès à la magistrature', *Genèses*, 22 (March 1996), p. 111.

50 Kimble, 'No Right to Judge', pp. 635–6.

51 'Luc-Thaler (Martine)' in *Who's Who in France. Dictionnaire biographique de personnalités françaises vivant en France et à l'étranger, et de personnalités étrangères résidant en France* (Paris, 2009).

constitutions but only one Civil code. Civil law is the 'heart' of French law, and governs relations between individuals – in the family, property, contracts, marriage and succession.[52] Moreover, the influence of the Code spread across Europe both directly during Napoleonic conquests, and indirectly when it was used as a model during legal reform elsewhere.

The Civil code inscribed women's inequality for the purpose of securing public virtue through control of private virtue. The articles of the Code concerning marriage (Articles 212–26) stipulated that husbands owed protection to their wives, in exchange for which wives owed obedience to their husbands. Patriarchal authority within the family depended upon the subordination of women. Napoleon likened women to possessions – notably fruit-bearing trees – who were 'destined to make children'.[53] Under the Code, a husband had *puissance maritale* (marital authority) over his wife, her body, her children and her property which included, a right to supervise his wife's personal conduct and movement, the right to forbid her actions, and, by extension, the imposition of his nationality upon marriage. In practical terms, married women could not move or travel where they wished; they could not open individual bank accounts; and they could not make contracts or work without marital authorization. The Code essentially stripped married women of their basic rights and rendered them 'eternal minors' in legal terms.

Dismantling the inequality inherent in the Civil code was a priority for feminist lawyers. By 1896, Jeanne Chauvin optimistically declared that 'today, more young women and women of the world dare to call themselves feminists, and are convinced of the injustice of the Code'.[54] Chauvin predicted that women who identified with feminism would increasingly hesitate before getting married because of their knowledge of the Civil code, and would also feel empowered to communicate their desire for legal reform to lawmakers.[55] By the centenary of the promulgation of the Civil code in 1904, the collective feminist position was clear: 'It crushes women!'[56] Shortly after the feminist protests, the French government organized its first extra-parliamentary commission to review the possibility of revising the Civil code. The commission contained 60 men and no women. The Fraternal Union of Women lodged a protest that eligible women, notably lawyers Marguerite Dilhan and Chauvin, had been excluded from the

52 René David, *French Law: Its Structure, Sources, and Methodology*, trans. Michael Kindred (Baton Rouge, 1972), pp. 108–12.

53 Albert Damez, *Le Libre salaire de la femme mariée et le mouvement féministe* (Paris, 1905), quote p. 22.

54 Jeanne Chauvin, 'La Question féministe devant les chambres françaises', *La Ligue. Organe Belge du droit des femmes* (1896): 57–65; quote p. 64.

55 Ibid., pp. 57–65.

56 Felicia Gordon, *The Integral Feminist: Madeleine Pelletier, 1874–1939* (Oxford, 1990), p. 86.

new commission.[57] An independent citizens' commission of men and women was formed to provide an alternative proposal. Their plan to make 'civil equality of the two sexes' the 'fundamental principle of modern law' translated into a proposal to change 83 articles of the Code.[58] This idealistic plan signalled a vision for reform where eventual enactment in 1938 would require cooperation from male legislators and government officials.[59]

Although feminists would have preferred to see women's legal inferiority swept away in one effective overhaul, the actual process was gradual. Married women were granted small rights through legislative action in a piecemeal fashion through the cooperation of feminists and their political supporters. For example, married women gained limited financial autonomy to open savings accounts (1881, 1895); control over their salaries (1907); to serve as guardians in the family (1917); to join a union without marital permission (1920); and to choose their own nationality (1927). All women gained the right to serve as witnesses in civil acts (1897), file paternity suits (1912), and a right to equal pay (1919). The government responded to the post-war demographic crisis and the financial fragility of families by establishing penalties for family abandonment (1921), extending paid maternity leaves (1928), and providing other assistance to families with children. Feminists had a hand in all these changes.[60]

Feminist lawyers were particularly active in the effort to legalize paternity suits. Paternity suits were essentially outlawed by the Civil code in Article 340 to protect the 'legitimate family', with little regard to the quality of life for out-of-wedlock children.[61] Jeanne Chauvin argued in a public speech that Article 340 of the Civil code should be rewritten to permit paternity suits and require fathers to pay for the food, living expenses and education of their children. She also wanted mothers to be able to file suits claiming damages and interest against fathers. In 1900, at the Second International Conference of Feminine Organizations, Chauvin and radical republican lawyer and *homme politique* Marc Réville proposed legal strategies to pursue absent fathers to provide for

---

[57] 'Le Mouvement féministe', *Le Devoir*, 29 (1905), p. 105.

[58] Henri Coulon quoted in Iwan Bloch, *The Sexual Life of Our Time: In Its Relations to Modern Civilization* (London, 1908), pp. 219–20; quote p. 220. See also Henri Coulon and René de Chavagnes, *Le Mariage et le divorce de demain* (Paris, 1908).

[59] The reforms enacted in 1938 did little to alter the legal powers of the husband. See Paul Smith, *Feminism and the Third Republic: Women's Political and Civil Rights in France* (Oxford, 1996), pp. 163–211.

[60] See Bard, *Filles de Marianne*; Laurence Klejman and Florence Rochefort, *L'Égalité en marche. Le féminisme sous la Troisième République* (Paris, 1989); and Karen M. Offen, *European Feminisms 1700–1950: A Political History* (Stanford, 2000).

[61] See Rachel G. Fuchs, *Contested Paternity: Constructing Families in Modern France* (Baltimore, 2008).

their children through the court system.[62] Chauvin's vision of social justice for women depended on reforming legislation, consciousness-raising and court enforcement of laws. To combat women's own ignorance of the law, Chauvin offered free law classes at the city hall on family law topics including paternal authority and mother's rights.[63]

The right to file paternity suits was finally enacted in 1912, yet feminist lawyers criticized the law for its shortcomings and strict evidentiary requirements. The new 1912 law gave single mothers the right to sue fathers for child support until the child reached the age of majority. Single mothers had to prove that they had been raped or kidnapped at the time of conception, or had cohabited, or could provide proof of a promise of marriage or other concrete evidence of the father's recognition of paternity of the child. Lawyers Vérone and Kraemer-Bach formulated the position for the National Council of French Women that these restrictive requirements came at the expense of the needs of children.[64] *Avocate* Hélène Miropolsky used a court case to criticize the 1912 law for failing to provide adequate protection for seduced mothers and their children. She argued that under the Code a 'woman is almost fatally condemned to become a complete victim. In cases of seduction, for a woman to obtain recourse, it is necessary to prove the man's clear intention to cause her harm', and such proof was difficult to acquire.[65] Moreover, rigid application of the evidentiary requirements undermined the usefulness of the law. At the time, news of this modest legislative advancement reached few of the women who might have benefited from the law. Few women fully understood what kind of evidence they needed to collect that could help them in court, or that they needed to act quickly to improve their chances of success. To educate the public, female lawyers publicized legal changes through their free law clinics, speech tours, newspaper columns and other publications.

Mothers' rights were just one aspect of the broad campaign by feminist lawyers for equality. Vérone put legal equality at the top of the platform in her role as President of the French Women's Rights League (1919–38). In 1920, Vérone published her most important and comprehensive guide to women's legal status: *La Femme et la loi*.[66] Composed in direct and unpretentious language, this work addressed issues of civil law, labour legislation, institutions of social assistance and penal law. In the area of civil law, she was most concerned with reforming married woman's nationality to free it from its state

---

62 Léon Parsons, 'Les Congrès de l'exposition. Oeuvres et Institutions féminines', *Revue Bleue*, 4/14 (7 July 1900): pp. 56–9.

63 Maria Martin, 'Le féminisme marche', *Journal des femmes*, December 1900.

64 Ann Taylor Allen, *Feminism and Motherhood in Western Europe 1890–1970: The Maternal Dilemma* (New York, 2005), p. 147.

65 Suzanne Dudit, 'Quand un seul paie pour deux', *Minerva*, 2 April 1933.

66 Maria Vérone, *La Femme et la loi* (Paris, 1920).

of dependency. Her publication argued that legal inequalities impinged upon women's freedom and their ability to act for the wellbeing of their family.

By 1925, a delegation of Radical Party women went to the minister of justice to request the abrogation of the Civil code articles that dictated women's inequality within marriage. This resulted in a new extra-parliamentary commission to prepare legislation to improve married legal women's status. The participating female jurists included Grinberg, Kraemer-Bach, Netter, and Simon-Bidaux. As Grinberg remembered it, the central purpose of the commission was not a moral and legal revolution but rather an adaptation of the law to present needs.[67] Kraemer-Bach had believed at the beginning that it would be 'facile' to pass a series of 'short and distinct' laws that would partially modify the Code. She soon learned that this was 'impossible' because one reform to the Code pulls on another, threatening to unravel the entire structure. She supported total revision and defended such an approach as the effective way to 'protect women and children'.[68]

Simultaneously, the national feminist movement lent its weight to push for reform. The 1926 Paris meeting of the International Alliance of Women for Suffrage and Equal Citizenship provided feminist lawyers the opportunity to offer their 'witty' and 'destructive' criticism of the Civil code.[69] Grinberg argued that advanced industrial societies recognized men and women as human beings of equal worth. To bring such an ideal to fruition, laws and institutions must be reformed to end the alienation and subordination of women. She believed that the growing consensus that women were equal was a consequence, in part, of women's participation in traditionally masculine professions. Moreover, women's participation in paid work, which had always been high in France, also required new rights to facilitate their movement in the public world. Optimistically, Grinberg noted that 'little by little, ideas are overturning and reversing established traditions'.[70] Ending discrimination in the Civil code was thus essential to true progress.

In 1929, Vérone called for the total suppression of the incapacity of married women under the law at the Etats-Généraux du Féminisme congress. Vérone served then as the president of the legislative section for the National Council

67 'D'un romantisme à l'autre et le fameux Code Napoléon. Conference dialoguée de Mme Suzanne Grinberg et de M. Jacques Ditte', *Confeéencia*, 20 February 1930, p. 232 in Bibliothèque Marguerite Durand, dossier Code Napoléon.

68 Marcelle Kraemer-Bach in Albert Blas (ed.), 'Séance Commune de l'Institut de droit comparé et de la Société de législation comparée, 31 mai 1933', *Bulletin de la Société de législation comparée*, 62/7 (July–September 1933): pp. 355–9.

69 International Alliance of Women for Suffrage and Equal Citizenship, *Report of Tenth Congress. Paris, France May 30th to June 6th, 1926* (London, 1926), pp. 38–9.

70 Suzanne Grinberg, 'Le Congrès de l'Alliance internationale pour le suffrage des femmes', *La Renaissance politique, littéraire, artistique* (1926): pp. 1–2.

of French Women. From this powerful position she urged other delegates to see that the Code was at the heart of women's position as civil minors, leaving them 'along with the insane and with children' with few rights. The law must be modernized 'since everything in the law relative to the family is based on the principle of the husband's authority and the obedience of the wife'.[71] She easily persuaded the conference to support a resolution calling for the radical alteration of the Civil code. By 1933, Vérone was impatient to see the Civil code reform (then in the form of the 'Renoult' bill) brought to fruition. She lamented that 'in the country of the Rights of Man, we are still waiting for the proclamation of the Rights of Woman'.[72]

When a Civil code reform was finally approved, it altered 71 articles of the Code, abrogated another 24 and added new articles on community property.[73] Judge and legal theoretician Marc Ancel claimed that the improvements were a 'result of the feminist movement'.[74] However, the law did not provide for the comprehensive overhaul that feminist had envisioned. With the resulting creation of the law of 18 February 1938, married women theoretically gained the right to exercise a profession, to control their private correspondence, and to apply for passports and identity cards.[75] Husbands retained the right to control where the family lived, and many of their traditional paternal powers. A husband also retained the right to oppose a wife's separate profession (Article 216) if he argued that such work interfered with the interests of the family or housekeeping. Vérone criticised the results :

> [That the law constituted] only weak progress towards addressing the current situation. The law claims to give the wife her full civil capacity but it leaves to the husband the right to choose the domicile and the right to oppose his wife's profession; it suppresses obedience due ... but it acknowledges the husband as the *chef de famille* [head of the family].[76]

---

71 *La Française*, 29 February 1929, quoted in Smith, *Feminism*, p. 178.

72 Maria Vérone, 'Droits civils ou droits politiques', *L'Oeuvre*, 1 July 1933.

73 Marc Ancel, 'Le Projet français sur la capacité de la femme et les enseignements du droit comparé de l'Université de Paris I', *Annales de l'Institut de droit comparé de l'Université de Paris* I (1934): pp. 145–68.

74 Ibid., p. 149.

75 The right to passports and identity cards was previously granted by the circular of 14 June 1937.

76 Maria Vérone, 'La Femme devant la loi à travers le monde', *Bulletin de l'Association juridique internationale* (December 1937), p. 22.

Kraemer-Bach argued that the need to create equality between parents remained 'urgent'.[77] Consequently, feminist lawyers carried on their campaign for full emancipation. After World War II, Andrée Lehmann, feminist lawyer and President of the French Women's Rights League, demanded that the Civil code be 'revised so that the husband and wife are considered to be two associates in law and that any action involving family life should be agreed upon by the two spouses'.[78] Further revisions were approved piecemeal throughout the 1950s, 1960s and 1970s.

The strength of the feminist lawyers' activity in France was facilitated by the vivacity of womens's suffrage groups and the rising effectiveness of professional organizations to facilitate networking. Every women's association had its lawyers who wrote for feminist periodicals, spoke at conferences, and drafted or lobbied for specific legal reform.[79] These lawyers were spread out across the left and centre of the political spectrum, representing socialists (Germaine Picard-Moch and Simone Weiler), Catholics (Marie-Thérèse Moreau), the republican Radical Party (Marcelle Kraemer-Bach), and the Parti Démocrate Populaire (Germaine Poinso-Chapuis). These women and their colleagues belonged to numerous other political and professional organizations, and they pushed each one to campaign for women's rights.

Simultaneously, feminist lawyers were involved in associations to build solidarity with other women across national lines. The Franco-American alliance between lawyers cultivated during the belle époque spawned new associations, but they could not expand into other European countries until those locations began to graduate women from law schools and admit them to the profession. A wave of progress in this regard occurred after World War I when new nations, eager to reconstruct their fragile democracies along egalitarian lines, granted women a variety of equal rights. Nevertheless, Paris remained the headquarters for many of the important women's associations, such as the enduring International Federation of Women in Legal Careers (FIFCJ).[80]

During the interwar years, lawyers played key roles in the new organizations formed to protect and defend the interests of educated and working women, such

---

77 Marcelle Kraemer-Bach, 'La Capacité de la femme mariée en droit français (loi du 18 février 1938) et en droit comparé', *La Revue pratique de droit international*, 26 (1937), p. 23.

78 *Le Droit des femmes*, March–April 1946 quoted in Sylvie Chaperon, '"Feminism is dead. Long live feminism!" The Women's Movement in France at the Liberation, 1944–1946', in Claire Duchen and Irene Bandhauer-Schöffmann (ed.), *When the War Was Over: Women, War and Peace in Europe 1940–1956* (London, 2000), pp. 146–60; quote p. 155.

79 Smith, *Feminism*, p. 170.

80 On the FIFCJ, see Sara L. Kimble, 'Women, Law and Friendship: Activities of the International Federation of Women in Legal Careers between the Two World Wars', paper presented at the Social Science Historical Association Conference, Minneapolis, 5 November 2006.

as the International Federation of University Women (IFUW); the International Federation of Business and Professional Women (IFBPW); the Open Door International (ODI); and the FIFCJ. The FIFCJ played an important role in the early twentieth century to forge bonds between 'modern Portias', especially those female lawyers newly emerging in Europe.[81] Feminist jurists understood well that they had to fight on multiple fronts – at international legal forums, within women's organizations, and through national legislation – to advance the cause of women's equality. They worked together to support reform efforts in the Second Spanish Republic, France and Estonia. They also opposed legal clauses that discriminated against Jews in Hungary, Romania, Poland and Germany. The hallmarks of their approach included persistence and flexibility at evoking sympathy for their priorities, even from somewhat reluctant partners. These lawyers recognized that 'the growing interconnectedness of the modern world meant that questions of labour legislation, nationality, and the traffic in women could only be addressed on the international plane'.[82] Consequently, these groups worked together to pressure international organizations such as the League of Nations and the International Labour Office to enact measures to advance women's equality.

The Pen and the Black Robe: Journalism and Lawyering

Lawyers engaged not only in legal practice and political activity; they were also passionately engaged in writing for the average reader. Numerous lawyer-journalists contributed to greater knowledge about women's status under the law by publishing in the 'women's press', the legal papers and the mainstream news. Writing for the women's press began to flourish after the censorship rules were profoundly relaxed by the Press Law of 1881. This period saw the rise of feminist press, including Hubertine Auclert's paper *La Citoyenne* (1881–91) wherein she advocated the end of women's subordinate legal status under the Civil code and called for women's equality under the law. Most famous was Marguerite Durand's daily newspaper *La Fronde*, published by a nearly all-female staff, which stayed in print from 1897 to 1905.[83] The weekly *La Française*, created in 1906 by journalist Jane Misme, was a paper about 'feminine progress'.

[81] Marcelle Kraemer-Bach, *Les Inégalités légales entre l'homme et la femme* (Paris, 1927), p. 2.

[82] Leila Rupp, *Worlds of Women: The Making of an International Women's Movement* (Princeton, 1997), p. 155.

[83] See Sara Kimble, 'Popular Legal Journalism in the Writings of Maria Vérone', *Proceedings of the Western Society for French History*, vol. 39 (2011), pp. 224–235. On *La Fronde* see Mary Louise Roberts, 'Copie subversive. Le journalisme féministe en France à la fin du siècle dernier', *Clio*, 6 (1997): pp. 230–47; and Sandrine Lévêque, 'Femmes,

Le Droit des femmes was founded in 1869 by Léon Richer and Maria Deraismes as an outlet for the French League for Women's Rights, and its publication run extended from 1869 to 1971 with only brief interruptions during the World Wars. *Le Droit des femmes* was an important site for discussion about gender discrimination, feminist protest, and functioned as a watchdog of women's equal rights. Chauvin and Vérone were among a large group of female lawyers who eagerly published on legal topics.

By the interwar period there were a sufficient number of female lawyers moonlighting as journalists writing in a style that can plausibly be labelled 'feminist legal journalism'. This form of journalism attempted to use the power of the popular press to change laws, soften hearts and promote gender equality in modern French society. Such writing put gender at the centre of legal analysis and the articles were written in such a way as to democratize legal knowledge. Unlike courtroom pleadings, journalism was more conducive to expressing political opinions. This was particularly true for interwar era France, when newspapers were often sponsored by, or aligned with, political organizations.[84]

During her 40-year journalistic career, Vérone wrote for at least 16 journals, published four books and pamphlets, and contributed chapters to three other books. Her articles and columns appeared in centrist or left-wing publications – including *L'Oeuvre*, *Le Matin*, *La Paix*, *La Bataille Syndicaliste*, *La France Libre* – and in the women's press with feminist leanings: *La Française*, *Le Journal des femmes*, *Minerva* and *L'Action féministe*. Her huge corpus of articles – numbering easily 1,500 – provides scholars with important sources of her ideas and activism. Vérone published approximately 500 articles in *L'Oeuvre* alone in a regular column that ran from 1926 to 1936 on Wednesdays. In her columns Vérone typically offered legal advice and provided socio-political commentary, promoted feminism and called for legal reforms to improve the treatment of women and children in society. The primary purpose of Vérone's articles in *Le Droit des femmes* and *L'Oeuvre* was to bring women's concerns to the forefront while exploring the conflict between existing laws and the reality of women's lives. Most frequently, she addressed the themes of women's inequality under the law; offered critiques of the judiciary; and illustrated the role of feminism in addressing legal questions.[85]

Yvonne Netter was also devoted to addressing the injustice of women's legal situation. Netter had joined the bar in 1920 following an unhappy marriage and divorce. While raising her son, she was active in feminist and Zionist

féministes et journalistes. Les rédactrices de *La Fronde à* l'épreuve de la professionnalisation journalistique', *Le Temps des médias*, 1/12 (2009): pp. 41–53.

[84] For French press history, see Claude Bellanger (ed.), *Histoire générale de la presse française. Tome 3: De 1871 à 1940*; Christophe Charle, *Le Siècle de la presse: 1830–1939* (Paris, 2004); and René de Livois, *Histoire de la presse française*, vol. 2 (Paris, 1965).

[85] Kimble, 'Popular Legal Journalism'.

organizations while maintaining a successful legal practice and writing for the French press. She wrote hundreds of articles on legal topics for *La Femme de France* and contributed articles on family and civil law for a dozen other newspapers. Netter's column in *La Femme de France* ran from 1928 to 1937. Her topics were invariably practical ones, including the staples of family law: prenuptial agreements, divorce, paternal power, paternity suits, married women's right to earned income (law of 1907) and illegitimate children. She also wrote on political topics such as the suffrage campaign, the efforts to secure an independent nationality for married women and other feminist activities. She regularly incorporated news of current lawsuits, especially those involving murders or family law matters. Her articles and books were a direct response to the kinds of questions she was repeatedly asked in her professional capacity as a volunteer counsellor at the town hall and her decades in private practice. She published legal manuals for lay readers, including *La Code de la femme et enfant* (1926), *Code pratique de la femme et de l'enfant* (1930), and *Plaidoyer pour la femme française* (1936).

Similarly, Marcelle Kraemer-Bach, a Parisian lawyer of immigrant origins, started and edited her own monthly newspaper devoted precisely to providing legal information for women. Kraemer-Bach's *L'Information féminine* (1927) was intended to dispel common confusions about civil and family law. She called her journal the 'First French Revue of Law and Women's Interests'. This periodical spoke in particular about the reform of the Civil code to permit women to become autonomous actors in the public sphere, regardless of their marital status. The purpose of the periodical was to address common confusions about civil and family law from correspondents. The letters from readers testified to married women's difficulty in obtaining passports, opening bank accounts or obtaining joint custody of their children after divorce. The letters also highlighted a lack of awareness about the ways in which the Civil code constrained women's civil rights, particularly those granting the husband authority over his wife, or the legislative gains that improved women's control over their own property.[86] Despite the obvious uniqueness of the monthly magazine it only survived for a few months in 1927. After the paper folded, Kraemer-Bach continued to write legal articles for the popular press and academic journals, as she had done in prior years.

The discussions of legislation, justice and social morality that peppered feminist lawyers' articles constitute central topics in French legal journalism. Such legal discussions had a place in ordinary periodicals because one of the central conceptions of law in French society holds that law is essential for creating justice. As legal historian René David explained, French law is based

[86] The most complete copy of the *revue* exists at the BMD (396 INF Bul; Per B F° Bob. 28).

on 'universality and ... the perfection of a just society'.[87] David argued that the very purpose of law in France is to make (and remake) the social order through the articulation of its principles. Thus, law also instructs citizens on proper behaviour in accordance with communal ideas of morality and justice. Feminist lawyers, with their allies in the women's emancipation movement, sought to change the Civil code and the Constitution precisely because law functions as an expression of social morality and an organizing principle for society.[88]

The rich materials that constitute feminist legal journalism from the interwar period, introduced briefly here, lead to four central observations. First, lawyers' legal columns often included free advice to readers on how – if they faced divorce, wanted to file a paternity suit or file a property claim – they might secure the best outcome for themselves. Consequently, lawyers both shared their reflections on the common workings of the justice system and offered counsel to potential clients. Second, these articles encouraged readers to become more knowledgeable about the impact of the law on their lives. These legal columns were almost invariability about women's legal condition, so plausibly the anticipated readership was female. Third, as lawyers promoted their vision of legal reform they often invoked the good work done by feminist organizations to make the broader movement relevant to readers. Finally, these journalistic activities benefited the authors by solidifying their reputations as public intellectuals. Moreover, journalism generated supplemental income that would have been especially helpful for lawyers such as these who were well known for taking on many pro bono cases.

In this historic context, feminist legal journalism was informed by a view of the world that privileged the clients' experience and anticipated legal ramifications of cases going to court. These legal articles were filled with life lessons that urged ordinary folk to try not to fall into existing traps. If feminist legal journalism succeeded in demonstrating the utility of lawyers to society – primarily as legal counsellors and political critics – then the reputation of the profession might well have received a corresponding boost. These journalistic efforts suggest that the lawyers were invested in pushing the profession away from its connotations as self-serving and apolitical towards an image of lawyers who operated with a moral conscience on behalf of the disadvantaged.

Conclusion

Recent scholarship by sociologist Anne Boigeol and lawyer Ludovic de Boisbrunet on the post-war French legal profession found that improvements

[87] David, *French Law*, p. 75.

[88] See Kimble, *Women, Feminism, and the Law*.

in the representation of women in the profession only began in the 1970s. Discrimination, harassment and hostility towards women have declined gradually. Ironically, the impressive numbers of women entering the profession since the 1990s has prompted governmental inquiries into this 'feminization' of the profession for its threat to status and earnings.[89]

The history of women's participation in the French legal profession indicates that the republican tradition of political engagement was a defining characteristic for many of the pioneering *avocates*. French female lawyers of the early twentieth century were often engaged in altruistic service or 'cause lawyering', using their professional work and expertise to build a better society. In the face of discrimination and in the climate of burgeoning social change, the early *avocates* articulated feminist ideals and joined the politically influential republican and left-wing organizations of the era. By modelling a politics of care and professional excellence, these *avocates* put a positive face on the profession, and made the idea of lawyering both more political and more humane. Given this history, perhaps it should come as no surprise that the profession now attracts historic numbers of women. As of 2010, women constitute 51.2 per cent of the profession.[90]

During the first half of the twentieth century, the feminist lawyers' movement engaged in varied forms of activism, from test cases to outright political activism for legal reform. Feminist legal criticism was expressed vehemently and widely, whether at conferences, in the press and publications or in the courtroom. While not all female lawyers were feminists, the leadership of the bar was unabashedly committed to campaigning for equality under the law. An important segment of the women who joined the French legal profession in the early decades of the twentieth century were also committed to feminist socio-legal change. Their activism for women's rights and legal reform led to changes in positive law and impacted gender roles. These lawyers demonstrated through their professional work and political activism that women could act as citizens even when they did not have the right to vote or stand for election. Yet, their arguments and actions clearly aligned them with the values of their French republican society: meritocracy, justice and social solidarity. Not only did they value their republic but they also firmly believed in women's capacity to contribute to the greater perfection of society. Their political engagement was signalled by their

---

89 Boigeol, 'Les Femmes et les Cours'; and Ludovic de Boisbrunet, *La Justice des femmes. Essai sur la féminisation de la magistrature française* (Paris, 2003). On the feminization of the legal profession, see Marie-Claude Calot, 'Les Femmes et la magistrature', *Revue de la recherche juridique. Droit Prospectif*, 2 (1997): pp. 733–41; Martial Kaminske (ed.), *Les Femmes dans les professions liberales* (Paris, 1995); Carrie Menkel-Meadow, 'Feminization of the Legal Profession: The Comparative Sociology of Women Lawyers', in Richard Abel and Philips Lewis (ed.), *Lawyers in Society: An Overview* (Berkeley, 1995), pp. 221–80.

90 Observatoire du Conseil National des Barreaux, 'Avocats: évolutions et tendances de la profession' (Paris, 2011), p. 24.

willingness to serve on extra-parliamentary commissions, engage in letter-writing campaigns to government officials and make public arguments about rights. Although *avocates* drafted model legislation and articulated feminist jurisprudence, there is no doubt that their ability to influence the rewriting of the French Constitution and the Civil code was restrained by the lack of formal rights.

These lawyers were also deeply concerned with the administration of justice. They worked frequently, though not exclusively, for poor clients and underage defendants. Consequently, they expressed misgivings about the current system by criticizing the weaknesses of existing formal protections and mechanisms for the delivery of justice. *Avocates*' argument that experienced professional women ought to be incorporated into the judiciary, especially at a time of great need following the devastation of World War I, was a result of their desire to see women serve the nation through the courts. At this point, among others, they were unwavering defenders of women's right to work and the high moral and intellectual quality of such work.

French feminist lawyers were a numerical minority but they made a disproportionate impact on their society. They challenged gender roles by demonstrating women's capacity to succeed in this traditionally masculine legal profession. As political activists, they claimed fundamental individual rights enshrined in such documents as the *Declaration of the Rights of Man and Citizen* (1789) as the birth right of women too. The defence of individual rights was ultimately the central legacy of the feminist lawyers' movement of twentieth-century France.

Bibliography

Manuscript Sources

Archives nationales de France, Paris, C/5595; C/5659; AJ/16/1012.

Bibliothèque Marguerite Durand, Paris: individual dossiers, including Dyvrande, Grinberg, Kraemer-Bach, Lehmann, Vérone; dossier Code Napoleon.

Bibliothèque Historique de la Ville de Paris, Fonds Bouglé.

Centre des Archives du Féminisme, Angers, Fonds Brunschvicg; Fonds CNFF; 2 AF 111.

Printed Sources

'A Travers Paris', *Le Figaro*, 1 April 1911.

'La première défenderesse en cour d'assises', *La Française*, 12 January 1908.

'Le Mouvement féministe', *Le Devoir*, 29 (1905): 105.

'Une Nouvelle 'avocate'', *Le Temps*, 6 November 1907.

Allen, Ann Taylor, *Feminism and Motherhood in Western Europe 1890–1970: The Maternal Dilemma* (New York: Palgrave Macmillan, 2005).

Ancel, Marc, 'Le Projet français sur la capacité de la femme et les enseignements du droit comparé de l'Université de Paris I', *Annales de l'Institut de droit comparé de l'Université de Paris* I (1934): 145–68.

Annuaire statistique de la ville de Paris, 1929, 1930 et 1931 (Paris: Imprimerie Municipale, 1933).

Avril de Sainte-Croix, Mme [Ghénia] (ed.), *Dixième congrès international des femmes. Oeuvres et institutions féminines, droits des femmes. 2 Juin 1913, Paris* (Paris: Giard et Brière, 1914).

Bard, Christine, *Les Filles de Marianne. Histoire des féminismes 1914–1940* (Paris: Fayard, 1995).

Bellanger, Claude (ed.), *Histoire générale de la presse française. Tome 3: De 1871 à 1940* (Paris: PUF, 1972).

Blas, Albert (ed.), 'Séance Commune de l'Institut de droit comparé et de la Société de législation comparée, 31 mai 1933', *Bulletin de la Société de législation comparée*, 62/7 (July–Septempber 1933): 331–72.

Bloch, Iwan, *The Sexual Life of Our Time: In Its Relations to Modern Civilization* (London: Heinemann, 1908).

Bloch, René, and Henry Chaumel, *Traité théorique et pratique des conseils de prud'hommes* (Paris: Dalloz, 1925).

Boigeol, Anne, 'Les Femmes et les Cours. La difficile mise en œuvre de l'égalité des sexes dans l'accès à la magistrature', *Genèses*, 22 (March 1996): 107–29.

Boisbrunet, Ludovic de, *La Justice des femmes. Essai sur la féminisation de la magistrature française* (Paris: Copytop, 2003).

Calot, Marie-Claude, 'Les Femmes et la magistrature', *Revue de la recherche juridique. Droit Prospectif*, 2 (1997): 733–41.

Chambre des Députés de l'Assemblée Nationale. Annales et documents parlementaires, 1871–1942, vol. 54 (Paris: Imprimerie du journal officiel, 1898).

Chambre des Députés de l'Assemblée Nationale. Annales et documents parlementaires, 1871–1942, vol. 140 (Paris: Imprimerie du journal officiel, 1930).

Chaperon, Sylvie, '"Feminism is dead. Long live feminism!" The Women's Movement in France at the Liberation, 1944–1946', in Claire Duchen and Irene Bandhauer-Schöffmann (ed.), *When the War Was Over: Women, War and Peace in Europe 1940–1956* (London: Leicester University Press, 2000).

Charle, Christophe, *Le Siècle de la presse: 1830–1939* (Paris: Seuil, 2004).

Chauvin, Jeanne, *Des Professions accessibles aux femmes en droit romain et en droit français évolution historique de la position économique de la femme dans la société* (Paris: Giard et Brière, 1892).

Chauvin, Jeanne, 'La Capacité légale des femmes', *La Fraternité*, 3 May 1893.

Chauvin, Jeanne, 'La Condition juridique de la femme française', *Société pour l'amélioration du sort de la femme et la revendication de ses droits. Rapports adressés au Congres des femmes représentantes tendu à Chicago, 1893* (Paris: Meyer, 1893).

Chauvin, Jeanne, *Cours de droit professé dans les lycées de jeunes filles de Paris* (Paris, Giard et Brière, 1895).

Chauvin, Jeanne, 'La Question féministe devant les chambres françaises', *La Ligue. Organe Belge du droit des femmes* (1896): 57–65.

Clark, Linda L., *Women and Achievement in Nineteenth-Century Europe* (Cambridge: Cambridge University Press, 2008).

Corcos, Christine Alice, 'Lawyers for Marianne: The Nature of Discourse on the Entry of French Women into the Legal Profession, 1894–1926', *Georgia State University Law Review*, 12/2 (1996): 435–75.

Coulon, Henri, and René de Chavagnes, *Le Mariage et le divorce de demain* (Paris: Flammarion, 1908).

Dabot, Henri, *Calendriers d'un bourgeois du quartier latin du 1 janvier 1888 au 31 décembre 1900* (Paris: Doal, 1905).

Damez, Albert, *Le Libre salaire de la femme mariée et le mouvement féministe* (Paris: Rousseau, 1905).

Daniel, André (ed.), *L'Année politique 1900* (Paris: Carpentier, 1901).

David, René, *French Law: Its Structure, Sources, and Methodology*, trans. Michael Kindred (Baton Rouge: Louisiana State University Press, 1972).

Dudit, Suzanne, 'Quand un seul paie pour deux', *Minerva*, 2 April 1933.

Fuchs, Rachel G., *Contested Paternity: Constructing Families in Modern France* (Baltimore: Johns Hopkins University Press, 2008).

Garçon, Emile, 'Quelques observations sur le projet de loi relatif aux tribunaux pour enfants', *Revue politique et parlementaire*, 70 (1911): 63–88.

Gordon, Felicia, *The Integral Feminist: Madeleine Pelletier, 1874–1939* (Oxford: Polity Press, 1990).

Grinberg, Suzanne, 'Le Congrès de l'Alliance internationale pour le suffrage des femmes', *La Renaissance politique, littéraire, artistique* (1926): 1–2.

Hamburger, Maurice, *Nos grands avocats* (Paris: Redier, 1930).

Hause, Steven C., and Anne Kenney, 'Women's Suffrage and the Paris Elections of 1908', *Laurels*, 1/41 (1980): 21–32.

Hause Steven, and Anne Kenney, *Women's Suffrage and Social Politics in the French Third Republic* (Princeton, NJ: Princeton University Press, 1984).

Hayward, J.E.S., 'The Official Social Philosophy of the French Third Republic: Léon Bourgeois and Solidarism', *International Review of Social History*, 6/1 (1961): 19–48.

Hesse, Raymond, and Lionel Vastorg (ed.), *Leur Manière* (Paris: Grasset, 1925).

International Alliance of Women for Suffrage and Equal Citizenship, *Report of Tenth Congress: Paris, France May 30th to June 6th, 1926* (London: London Caledonian Press, 1926).

Kaminske, Martial (ed.), *Les Femmes dans les professions libérales* (Paris: Délégation interministérielle aux professions libérales, 1995).

Karpik, Lucien, 'Builders of Liberal Society: French Lawyers and Politics', Nora Scott trans., in Terence C. Halliday and Lucien Karpik (ed.), *Lawyers and the Rise of Western Political Liberalism: Europe and North America from the Eighteenth to Twentieth Centuries* (New York: Oxford University Press, 1997).

Kimble, Sara L., 'Justice Redressed: Women, Citizenship, and the Social Uses of the Law in Modern France, 1890–1939' (PhD diss., University of Iowa, 2002).

Kimble, Sara L., 'Women, Law and Friendship: Activities of the International Federation of Women in Legal Careers between the Two World Wars', paper presented at the Social Science Historical Association, Minneapolis, 5 November 2006.

Kimble, Sara L., 'No Right to Judge: Feminism and the Judiciary in Third Republic France', *French Historical Studies*, 31/4 (2008): 609–41.

Kimble, Sara L., 'Popular Legal Journalism in the Writings of Maria Vérone', *Proceedings of the Western Society for French History*, 39 (2011): 224–35.

Kimble, Sara L., 'Portia's Sisters: Transatlantic Networks for Women in the Legal Professions', paper presented at the American Historical Association Annual Meeting, Chicago, 8 January 2012.

Kimble, Sara L., *Women, Feminism, and the Law in Modern France: Justice Redressed* (New York: Routledge, forthcoming).

Klejman, Laurence, and Florence Rochefort, *L'Égalité en marche. Le féminisme sous la Troisième République* (Paris: Fondation nationale des sciences politiques, 1989).

Kraemer-Bach, Marcelle, *Les Inégalités légales entre l'homme et la femme* (Paris: PUF, 1927).

Kraemer-Bach, Marcelle, 'La Capacité de la femme mariée en droit français (loi du 18 février 1938) et en droit comparé', *La Revue pratique de droit international*, 26 (1937): 3–30.

Lalouette, Jacqueline, *La Libre pensée en France: 1848–1940* (Paris: Michel, 1997).

Le Congrès d'Alger de l'Association nationale des avocats (22–24 avril 1930). Bulletin de l'Association nationale des avocats inscrits aux barreaux de France, des colonies et pays de protectorat (Paris: Bulletin de l'ANA, 1930).

Lefranc, Jean, 'Les enfants coupables et leur protectrice', *Le Temps*, 14 May 1911.

Lévêque, Sandrine, 'Femmes, féministes et journalistes. Les rédactrices de *La Fronde* à l'épreuve de la professionnalisation journalistique', *Le Temps des médias*, 1/12 (2009): 41–53.

Livois, René de, *Histoire de la presse française*, vol. 2 (Paris: Société française du livre, 1965).

Martin, Maria, 'Le féminisme marche', *Journal des femmes* (December 1900): 105.

Menkel-Meadow, Carrie, 'Feminization of the Legal Profession: The Comparative Sociology of Women Lawyers', in Richard Abel and Philips Lewis (ed.), *Lawyers in Society: An Overview* (Berkeley: University of California Press, 1995).

Mossman, Mary Jane, *The First Women Lawyers* (Oxford; Portland: Hart, 2006).

Moufflet, André, 'Le meeting du 27 Juin 1911', *Le Droit des femmes* (January 1912): 12–15.

Observatoire du Conseil National des Barreaux, 'Avocats: évolutions et tendances de la profession' (Paris: Conseil National des Barreaux, 2011).

Offen, Karen M., *European Feminisms 1700–1950: A Political History* (Stanford: Stanford University Press, 2000).

Olgiati, Vittorio, 'The Case of the First (Failed) Woman Lawyer in Modern Italy', in Ulrike Schultz and Gisela Shaw (ed.), *Women in the World's Legal Professions* (Oxford; Portland: Hart, 2003).

Parsons, Léon, 'Les Congrès de l'exposition. Oeuvres et Institutions féminines', *Revue Bleue*, 4/14 (7 July 1900): 56–9.

Roberts, Mary Louise, 'Copie subversive. Le journalisme féministe en France à la fin du siècle dernier', *Clio*, 6 (1997): 230–47.

Rupp, Leila, *Worlds of Women: The Making of an International Women's Movement* (Princeton, NJ: Princeton University Press, 1997).

Saint-Auban, Emile de (ed.), *Revue des grands procès contemporaine*, vol. 26 (Paris: Calmann-Levy, 1908).

Sarat, Austin, and Stuart A. Scheingold (ed.), *Cause Lawyering: Political Commitments and Professional Responsibilities* (New York: Oxford University Press, 1998).

Sarat, Austin, and Stuart A. Scheingold (ed.), *Cause Lawyers and Social Movements* (Stanford: Stanford University Press, 2006).

Scelle, Georges, 'La Représentation politique', *Revue du droit public*, 28 (1911): 525–57.

Smith, Paul, *Feminism and the Third Republic: Women's Political and Civil Rights in France* (Oxford: Clarendon Press, 1996).

Sur, Bernard, *Histoire des avocats en France, des origines à nos jours* (Paris: Dalloz, 1997).

Vérone, Maria, 'Actualité. Victoire Féministe', *La Française*, 10 May 1908.

Vérone, Maria, *Appel à la justice adressé par le Conseil national des femmes françaises à la Chambre des députes et au Sénat. Rapport de la section du suffrage du Conseil national présente par Mme Maria Vérone* (Paris: s.l., 1909).
Vérone, Maria, *La Femme et la loi* (Paris: Larousse, 1920).
Vérone, Maria, 'Le Congrès de Marseille', *Le Droit des femmes* (December 1930): 298–300.
Vérone, Maria, 'Droits civils ou droits politiques', *L'Oeuvre*, 1 July 1933.
Vérone, Maria, 'La femme devant la loi à travers le monde', *Bulletin de l'Association juridique internationale* (December 1937): 20–24.
Who's Who in France. Dictionnaire biographique de personnalités françaises vivant en France et à l'étranger, et de personnalités étrangères résidant en France (Paris: Lafitte, 2009).
Wright, Gordon, *France in Modern Times* (New York: Norton, 1987).

Chapter 3

Women's Admission to the Legal Profession in Germany between 1900 and 1933

Marion Röwekamp

In most European countries women gained access to the practice of medicine and other academic professions before they could practise law, in some cases decades earlier. In a handful of nations women obtained entrance to legal professions around the turn of the century; in the majority of countries they won admission only after World War I. This was also the case in Germany. Though the only so far existing survey on the entrance of European women into legal professions has found many similarities between the different national cases,[1] the entry of women in German legal professions reveals a unique pattern. While it was one of the last countries in Europe to admit women, in 1922, it was also one of the very few countries to permit women to act as judges before World War II. From 1922, German women were allowed to sit the two necessary state exams which were required to enter legal professions.

Resistance to women's access to legal professions was particularly harsh in Germany. In 1921 the feminist Marie Stritt (1855–1928), founder of the Legal Aid Institution for Women and former president of the *Bund Deutscher Frauenvereine* (BDF, National Council of Women), Germany's umbrella organization for most of the bourgeois women's associations, claimed: 'Not even against woman suffrage ..., especially from the professional circles, has [resistance] ever been so hard and stubborn as on this one.'[2]

Paradoxically, Germany was at the same time one of the few countries were female judges were quickly rising in numbers, working alongside female attorneys – until the rise of nationalism curtailed their right to work. By choosing the example of Germany, I will show that in the historical research on the (late) access of women to legal professions, important questions have not yet been considered and answered. This is, for example, the case for the role of

---

1 James Albisetti, 'Portia ante Portas. Women and the Legal Profession in Europe, ca. 1870–1925', *Journal of Social History*, 33/4 (2000): pp. 825–57.

2 Marie Stritt, 'Germany', *The International Woman Suffrage News*, April 1921, p. 107.

the women's movement, or for the arguments that women used to gain access to legal professions. Besides these questions, I will consider the difference of the legal admission of women to the bar and to the judiciary, and the political implications resulting from this difference.

In order to make women lawyers' voices of the past come alive, this chapter will draw on a variety of sources, basically printed and manuscript material found in various archives and library collections, such as the Bundesarchiv (German federal archive); different German state archives; the Marie Munk Collection at the Landesarchiv Berlin; the Sophia Smith Collection of Smith College in Northampton, Massachusetts, and the Leo Baeck Institute in New York. Methodologically, this chapter combines research questions drawn from different disciplines: social history, gender studies, empirical data research, legal history, and intellectual history.

Studying Law in Imperial Germany (1900–1918)

Access to legal professions was not a priority for the German women's movement when it asked for the opening of universities to women. It was mainly the opening of medical and philosophical faculties that German women were interested in. It was easier to see the daughters of the bourgeoisie working as medical doctors and teachers than as lawyers. Both of these first-mentioned professions had the advantage that their inclusion of women meant a 'natural extension' of already existing traditional roles and professions for them: in the case of medicine to heal and care for in precedent professions like midwifery or nursing; and in the case of teaching to raise children, as in precedent professions like kindergarten employee or schoolteacher.[3] No such previous profession existed in the law that could just naturally extend women's role into legal professions.

Furthermore, legal professions were perceived as downright male professions. The law required objectivity, rationality, and authority: all of them characteristics that were not thought of as part of female nature. In fact, they were the absolute opposite of the abilities women were generally attributed. In Germany cultural stereotypes that shaped gender roles were particularly strong. As occurred in the debates on women's admission to the bar in most Western countries, German women and their allies in the battle for professional equality appealed to the idea of fairness and to what female attorneys and judges could do for other women

[3] Barbara Harris, *Beyond Her Sphere: Women and the Professions in American History* (Westport, CT, 1978), p. 110; Leslie Howsam, '"Sound-Minded Women": Eliza Orme and the Study and Practice of Law in Late Victorian England', *Atlantis*, 15/1 (1989): p. 47.

and for society as a whole. Their opponents, in contrast, emphasized women's alleged innate characteristics.

Masculinity stood not only central in all characteristics deemed necessary to exercise legal professions, but the law itself was also influenced by the social relations between the sexes by legitimizing prejudicial cultural attitudes and justifying inequitable practices. Although the law usually claims neutrality, it is not gender-neutral and sexual discrimination is embedded in it. This is very apparent in family law as well as in all the laws that were referred to in order to exclude women from entering legal professions. In Germany, gender difference had been codified in the German Civil code of 1900 (*Bürgerliches Gesetzbuch*, BGB) to define married women outside the category of 'legal persons'. This means that, under the so-called 'gender tutelage', as a rule women could not undertake legal action without a male guardian. Especially the legal identity of a married woman was merged into that of her husband's, drastically restricting her civil and political as well as her property rights, leaving her basically no legal existence apart from her husband. Although allegedly it was only married women who lacked legal personhood under German civil law, single women too were affected by the legal system that was underpinned by longstanding ideas about gender differences, such as not being able to vote or to exercise any chosen profession. Judicial reformers in the late nineteenth and the beginning of the twentieth century fought against the fact that married women's civil rights – including their right to work, to appear in court, and to contract – were subject to spousal approval under the Civil code.[4] While these constraints were since the second half of the nineteenth century increasingly viewed as anachronistic by judicial reformers and by the women's movement, they constituted a bulwark against the claims for women's judicial eligibility as lay judges and as professionals. The women's rights reform movement was disadvantaged not only by tradition and culture, but also by law because masculinity belonged to the principles and the essence of the law.

As opposed to the small radical wing of the German women's movement that campaigned for female suffrage as a priority, the bourgeois women's wing of the late nineteenth and early twentieth centuries was more prompted to 'relational' or 'maternalist' feminism.[5] It believed that the question of

[4] Ute Gerhard, *Gleichheit ohne Angleichung. Frauen im Recht* (Munich, 1990); Stephan Meder et al. (ed.), *Frauenrecht und Rechtsgeschichte. Die Rechtskämpfe der deutschen Frauenbewegung* (Cologne/Weimar/Vienna, 2006); Dieter Schwab, 'Gleichberechtigung und Familienrecht im 20. Jahrhundert', in Ute Gerhard (ed.), *Frauen in der Geschichte des Rechts. Von der Frühen Neuzeit bis zur Gegenwart* (Munich, 1997), pp. 790–827.

[5] Ute Gerhard, *Feminismus und Demokratie. Die europäischen Frauenbewegungen der 1920er Jahre* (Kronberg/Ts., 2001); Sylvia Paletschek and Bianca Pietrow-Ennker (ed.), *Womens's Emancipation Movements in the 19th Century: A European Perspective* (Stanford, 2004).

women's rights was based on education, and it promoted the notion of special women's talents and the need for them in fields like medicine and teaching. The reasoning went that women preferred women as doctors, especially as gynaecologists, and that women were also needed to teach female students who started to get into higher schooling. According to this reasoning, there was, at least until 1888, when the German Civil code came up for revision, no obvious reason why the women's movement should need female lawyers. This changed drastically after the women's movement failed to change the gender-discriminating clauses in the German Civil code that was finally codified in 1900. Replacing the former Prussian Civil code from 1794, the more liberal *Preußisches Allgemeines Landrecht* in the first drafts revealed unfavourable changes for women, especially in the field of family law. Only when the first big reform movement against these dispositions failed[6] did the women's movement start to understand how decisive schooled female lawyers could be in the battle for equal rights. Anita Augspurg (1857–1943) – a radical feminist, journalist and women's rights activist who had, as one of the first women, studied law in Switzerland – formulated around 1894 the slogan of the next century: that is that the question of women's rights was based on education and law.[7] Yet the call for women lawyers was for Imperial Germany's society still too far-fetched to make a strong case: even for the women's movement the idea of women in the law was perceived to be contrary to the nature of women. In 1900 the pioneering feminist, teacher, and women's rights activist Auguste Schmidt (1833–1902) conceded: 'We were convinced that the profession of … the lawyer could be exercised by women in a sufficient way, but we knew that this opinion wouldn't be considered compatible with common sense. Thus we kept quiet.'[8]

If it is true that in every country it seemed to be 'more difficult to become a lawyer than a doctor … because the legal profession was institutionalized and had, in general, been granted licensing powers earlier than the medical profession', as legal scholar Robert Stevens[9] has argued for the United States, in Germany two facts were responsible for the even higher institutionalized obstacles to women gaining access to legal professions: the tradition of legal education in Germany, which was a highly regulated state institution; and the fact that the resources

---

6 Christiane Berneike, *Die Frauenfrage ist Rechtsfrage. Die Juristinnen der deutschen Frauenbewegung um das Bürgerliche Gesetzbuch* (Baden-Baden, 1995); Tanja-Carina Riedel, *Gleiches Recht für Frau und Mann. Die bürgerliche Frauenbewegung und die Entstehung des BGB* (Cologne/Weimar/Vienna, 2008).

7 Anita Augspurg, 'Gebt acht, solange noch Zeit ist!', *Die Frauenbewegung,* 1 (1895): 4–5; Berneike, *Frauenfrage ist Rechtsfrage*, pp. 44–66.

8 Auguste Schmidt, 'Juristinnen', *Neue Bahnen*, 25/3 (1900): p. 32.

9 Robert Stevens, *Law School: Legal Education in America from the 1850s to the 1890s* (Chapel Hill, NC, 1983), p. 82.

of male power were strongly institutionalized within professional corporations, which in case of advocacy were semi-tied to bureaucracy. Lawyers, protecting access to their profession, largely occupied civil service structures.

Legal education in Germany formed so-called *Einheitsjurists*, lawyers with the ability to work in all legal professions. Law students did not only 'go to law school'; they also had to complete a three-year apprenticeship that prepared them for the legal professions. Study time at university was concluded not with an intern exam, but by a first state exam in which all students had to participate.[10] The so-called second state exam ended the apprenticeship time of the *Einheitsjurists* and thus produced a highly uniform and homogenous professional group that soon occupied the most influential spheres of society: obviously the judiciary, but also the legislative bodies. Another particularity of the German system was the fact that its administration was basically also staffed by lawyers. In fact, a position in the administration was considered to be the most prestigious among the ones in the legal professions, followed by that of the judge and the attorney.[11] All of these professions were considered elite jobs among the other academic professions. The possibility that women would become judges or civil servants partly explains the resistance against women's access to legal education. In Germany there was much more at stake than in the other European nations, as this admission implied full citizenship for women.[12] Since the judiciary was defined as a public office, women needed the vote first.

The admission of women to legal faculties, such as those in Baden in 1900 and Bavaria in 1903, did not prove to be the big obstacle in the German case, as women were simply excluded from participation in the state exams; yet they could finish their studies with a doctorate in law.[13] Controversy only arose when Prussia, the largest and most influential state in Germany, considered opening its universities to women. As government officials were concerned about whether it would be possible to exclude them in the long term from the state exams, the plan was delayed for some years. When in 1908–09 women finally got admitted

10 Peter Krause, 'Geschichte der Justiz- und Verwaltungsausbildung in Preußen und Deutschland', in Christian Baldus et al. (ed.), *Juristenausbildung in Europa zwischen Tradition und Reform* (Tübingen, 2008), pp. 95–125.

11 Kenneth F. Ledford, *From General Estate to Special Interest: German Lawyers 1878–1933* (Cambridge/New York, 1996).

12 Albisetti, 'Portia ante Portas', pp. 825–57; Sara L. Kimble, 'No Right to Judge: Feminism and the Judiciary in Third Republic France', *French Historical Studies*, 31/4 (2008): pp. 609–41.

13 Marion Röwekamp, *Die ersten deutschen Juristinnen. Eine Geschichte ihrer Professionalisierung und Emanzipation (1900–1945)* (Cologne/Weimar/Vienna, 2011), pp. 41–60.

to university, an explicit proviso barred them from participating in the state exams and the apprenticeship in law.[14]

Hence, once Alix Westerkamp (1876–1944)[15] earned her doctorate at the University of Marburg in 1906 as the first woman in Germany, nobody was scandalized or nervous since she could not sit the legal state exams and thus not work in the legal professions. Westerkamp started to work in a legal aid clinic for women, an institution created by Marie Stritt in 1894 in Dresden that was supposed to give free legal advice to women, mainly those of the lower classes. The women who worked there on a charity basis were confronted with the injustice of misogyny laws and were thus aware of the existing need for female lawyers, not only for their institutions but also for the women's movement and for women's rights in general.[16] Women lawyers working in these institutions usually liked their jobs for two reasons: they felt they could 'do good' – the motivation that had inspired them to study law to begin with; and they could work in a field that was closely related to the traditional legal professions.[17] Besides these legal aid clinics women lawyers also taught in women's schools for social work, and had minor positions in law offices or in welfare agencies and in juvenile care.[18] Most of them did not earn enough money to make ends meet and had to be supported by their families or held two or three jobs at the same time. That is why women lawyers complained that the effort to make a decent living needed disproportional amounts of effort in courage and energy that usually were already spent before they started to get onto the real job market.[19] What they really wanted was to work in the legal professions they had studied for.

This unsatisfying situation led to a first attempt of the women's movement to request access of women to legal professions. In May 1908 the progressive women's association *Frauenbildung-Frauenstudium* (Women's Education-

14 James Albisetti, *Schooling German Girls and Women: Secondary and Higher Education in the Nineteenth Century* (Princeton, 1988), p. 247ff.

15 Marion Röwekamp, *Juristinnen. Lexikon zu Leben und Werk* (Baden-Baden, 2005), pp. 430–32.

16 Beatrix Geisel, *Klasse, Geschlecht und Recht. Vergleichende sozialhistorische Untersuchung der Rechtsberatungspraxis von Frauen- und Arbeiterbewegung (1894–1933)* (Baden-Baden, 1997).

17 Beatrix Geisel, '"Alle Juristinnen haben ihre Stellung der Frauenbewegung zu verdanken!" Dem langen Kampf um die Robe folgte der noch immer nicht beendete Streit um die Gleichberechtigung', *Ariadne*, 30 (1996): pp. 52–9.

18 Erna von Langsdorff, 'Die Berufsaussichten der Juristin in Deutschland', *Die Frau*, 20 (1912/13): pp. 603–9; Margarete Bernhard, 'Vorbildungs- und Berufsverhältnisse der deutschen Nationalökonominnen und Juristinnen', *Volkswirtschaftliche Blätter*, 12/5–6 (1913): pp. 54–9.

19 Margarete Berent, 'Die Zulassung von Frauen zu den juristischen Berufen', *Die Frau*, 27 (1919–20): p. 332.

Women's Studies) put in a request to the Ministry of Justice of the state of Baden to admit women to the state exams as well as to the bar.[20] Feeling self-confident that the admission of women, even if only to the bar, was beyond any possibility, the ministry asked the board of the bar in Karlsruhe for an assessment.[21] Attorney Max Hachenburg – one of the very few male supporters of women's admission to legal professions – backed up the request, and after an agitated debate the board endorsed the admission of women to the bar by six votes to three.[22] It stated that arguments of justice made them favour their positive stand in this question.[23] The minority rejecting the request adopted in contrast the prevailing opinion championed within the legal professions and the Ministry of Justice. The latter opinion was based on the interpretation of norms from the German Judicature Act (GVG), the Order on Lawyers, the Code of Civil Procedure, and the Code of Criminal Procedure. This interpretation concerned especially §2 and §4 GVG from 1877 and its new version from 1910 that regulated the conditions of admission to legal professions. According to §2 GVG, admission was dependent on passing the two state exams or, according to §4 GVG, dependent on holding a full tenure position at a law faculty of a German university. None of the paragraphs explicitly made admission subject to being of the male sex; but the common legal opinion and the legislature took it for granted that women would not make use of this right. The positive opinion of the Karlsruhe bar was received with silence in the Ministry of Justice, which was a strict believer in the prevailing opinion in this question and thus rejected the request of Baden's women's association. But since the women's movement of the small state of Baden was acting in this case without national support, the request had no further consequences and remained almost unknown.

At the national level, the German women's movement needed some more time to agree on women's admission to legal professions and legal administrative offices. In reality, this issue was only a small part of its claims, as priority went to the question of women's right to act on juries, especially in the new established institution of juvenile courts. Within the context of the reform debates on the revision of the German Code of criminal procedure in 1909 and the German Judicature Act in 1910, as well as the German Juvenile Court Act from 1912, the women's movement saw reasons for strong agitation:[24] the demand for women acting as jurors in juvenile courts was requested not only at the general assemblies of the *Bund Deutscher Frauenvereine* but also at the popular and well-

---

20 Generallandesarchiv Karlsruhe (G.L.A. KA), 234 No. 4186.

21 Ministry of Justice, 5 December 1908, G.L.A. KA 234 No. 4186; Max Hachenburg, *Lebenserinnerungen eines Rechtsanwalts* (Düsseldorf, 1927), p. 247.

22 Hachenburg, *Lebenserinnerungen*, p. 247.

23 Board of the Bar, 10 August 1908, to Ministry of Justice, G.L.A. KA 234 No. 4186; Hachenburg, *Lebenserinnerungen*, p. 247f.

24 Vera Lowitsch, *Die Frau als Richter* (Berlin 1933), p. 55.

visited rally for the 'Day of the Female Juror' in March 1911. Many of the female Juris Doctors were actively participating in these campaigns, either as referees or sitting on panels.[25] These campaigns stirred the public and especially the so-called *Jugendgerichtstag* (congress of all the professions that participated in juvenile trials and dealt scientifically with juvenile criminality). The *Jugendgerichtstag* during its second congress in Munich in 1910 backed up the participation of women as jurors in juvenile trials[26] and launched a petition that was supported by 500,000 women.[27]

The German women's congress of 1912 in Berlin offered another occasion to broach the issue of the admission of women to legal professions and the opening of the legal state exams to them.[28] To facilitate women's participation in all the legal professions, the BDF in its tenth general assembly of October 1912 agreed within the context of the draft for new laws concerning criminal trials against juveniles on a plan based on two main pillars: to petition the Reichstag on a regular basis; and to start a major offensive following the example of the protest against the codification of the German Civil code before 1900, the so-called *Frauenlandsturm*.[29] The BDF planned to organize mass rallies in most major German cities.[30] Alongside the BDF, the German women's movement too started in 1913 a big offensive by organizing mass rallies in 14 major cities: a hall seating 2,000 was not large enough in Berlin for the attending audience, and in Hamburg the event attracted 1,000 participants.[31] But, unfortunately, the outbreak of World War I would cause the women's movement to prioritize national patriotism over political goals. The bourgeois women's movement stopped their fight for equal rights to support the war effort from 1914 to 1918, expecting to be granted full equal rights for their help after the war. This *Burgfrieden* (class truce) policy of the German women's movement towards their national government in these years prevented success for almost all campaigns for equal rights.

---

25 Landesarchiv Berlin (LA Berlin), B Rep. 235–12 (BDF), Frau als Laien und Berufsrichter, Fiche 2786.

26 'Zweiter Deutscher Jugendgerichtstag, 29. September–1. Oktober 1910 in München', *Die Frauenbewegung*, 16/21 (1910): p. 169.

27 Herbert Ruscheweyh, *Die Entwicklung des deutschen Jugendgerichts. Schriften des Ausschusses für Jugendgerichte und Jugendgerichtshilfen* (Weimar, 1918), p. 67.

28 Bund deutscher Frauenvereine (ed.), *Deutscher Frauenkongreß, Berlin, 27. Februar–2. März 1912. Sämtliche Vorträge* (Leipzig/Berlin, 1912).

29 The *Frauenlandsturm* was a campaign in 1900 of the German women's movement against the codification of the new Civil code and its misogynistic family laws.

30 BDF, Jan. 1913, LA Berlin, B Rep. 235–12, Fiche 2787.

31 'Kundgebung für die Zulassung der Frauen als Schöffen', *Die Frau*, 20 (1912–13): p. 376; Gertrud Bäumer, 'Zwei Kundgebungen zur Einheitlichkeit der deutschen Frauenbewegung', *Die Frauenfrage*, 15/1–2 (1913–14): p. 2.

Being left to themselves, the German women lawyers founded in 1914 in Berlin their own professional organization, the *Deutscher Juristinnenverein* (DJV, German Women Lawyers' Association). The founders were Dr. Margarete Berent (1887–1965), Dr. Margarete Muehsam-Edelheim (née Meseritz, 1891–1975), and Dr. Marie Munk (1885–1978), all of them from a Jewish background and among the first women to study law in Germany.[32] The idea was 'to promote the interests, especially the professional and scientific further legal training of women lawyers.'[33] The DJV was independent, functioned above party lines, and was non-denominational. Compared to other female professional groups, it had an early start. The Union of German Women Doctors, for example, was founded only 10 years later – female doctors had better professional chances than women lawyers, and thus the creation of a professional group had been less urgent – though in numbers it would become much larger. As a result of the small number of German women studying law, the DJV remained a tiny organization. In its founding year it had 28, in 1916–17, 35, and in 1919, 85 members. It was a very active organization that played an important role in German women's endeavour for equal rights.[34]

Fighting for Access in the Early Weimar Republic, 1918–1922

In the aftermath of the revolution of 1918, German women got suffrage. The new constitution of Weimar was passed in 1919, and in its Art. 109 and Art. 128 it promised equality for women in principal terms. It thus also promoted the cause of women lawyers. Equipped with these new rights, feminists finally had arguments in their hands to push for legal change, yet the constitution's immediate impact on the legal status of women remained limited. It needed some more political pressure still until the Reichstag in 1922 finally passed a law that permitted women lawyers to work in legal professions. The Weimar constitution had marked a new ideal of full equal rights for men and women. By formulating this principle, these rights were suddenly near at hand and women lawyers, as well as the women's movement, were ready to use their new advantages.

Contrary to the examples of Lidia Poët and Teresa Labriola in Italy, Marie Popelin in Belgium, Adolphine Kok in the Netherlands, Jeanne Chauvin in France, Eliza Orme in England, and others who could apply directly to the bar, German women first had to tackle the opening of the state exams and official institutions.[35] When European women were being denied access to the bar,

---

32 Röwekamp, *Juristinnenlexikon*, pp. 36–40; 271–4; 275–8.
33 Marie Munk, Autobiography, LA Berlin, B Rep. 235–12, IX, 4.
34 Röwekamp, *Die ersten deutschen Juristinnen*, pp. 546–52.
35 Albisetti, 'Portia ante Portas', pp. 828–38.

they could turn to courts to appeal these decisions. These courts in some cases relented; in others they did not, but all decisions were precedents, each with the possibility of being granted by one judge sympathetic to the case. In some countries legislation was needed beyond recourse to the courts.[36] For German women, on the contrary, the possibility of a legal process was not open; there was neither a legal basis for their claims, nor was there a constitutional court legally competent to hear their cases. German female lawyers could only take the way of convincing the justice administrations to let them sit the exams, or they had to convince the legislature to change the law.

Armed with the new constitutional equality rights, they were determined to do so. Having now voting rights, they were no longer dependent on the formula of petitions to parliaments, but were now able to lodge their requests immediately via the new female members of parliament. The options to bring their demands forward into parliamentary sessions increased drastically. Together, the DJV, the female members of the parliaments, the party faction of the German Democratic Party (DDP) and the Social Democrats (SPD) achieved success.[37]

The DJV started its relentless struggle with a petition to the Prussian Ministry of Justice in March 1919.[38] It was characteristic of the campaigns of the DJV that

---

[36] Ibid., pp. 844–7.

[37] Reglindis Böhm, 'Der Kampf um die Zulassung der Frauen als Rechtsanwältinnen und zum Richteramt', in Ministry of Justice of Hesse (ed.), *Frauen in juristischen Berufen.Ein Brevier für Referendare und Referendarinnen* (Wiesbaden, 1987), pp. 11–19; Stefan Bajohr and Katrin Rödiger-Bajohr, 'Die Diskriminierung der Juristin in Deutschland bis 1945', *Kritische Justiz*, 13 (1980): pp. 39–50; Oda Cordes, 'Die Frau als Organ der Rechtspflege? Über die historisch wichtigsten Stationen der Zulassung von Frauen in der deutschen Rechtspflege', in Stephan Meder et al. (ed.), *Frauenrecht und Rechtsgeschichte. Die Rechtskämpfe der deutschen Frauenbewegung* (Cologne/Weimar/Vienna, 2006), pp. 279–301; Deutscher Juristinnenbund, *Juristinnen in Deutschland. Die Zeit von 1900 bis 1998* (Baden-Baden, 2003); Barbara Dölemeyer, 'Die Zulassung von Frauen zur Rechtsanwaltschaft und ihr Ausschluß in der NS- Zeit', in Mario Ascheri et al. (ed.), *'Ins Wasser geworfen und Ozeane durchquert'. Festschrift für Knut Wolfgang Nörr* (Cologne/Weimar/Vienna, 2003), pp: 151–64; Sibylla Flügge, 'Der lange Weg in die Gerichte. Von der Männlichkeit des Staates und vom Ende holder Weiblichkeit', *Streit*, 4 (1984): pp. 149–53; Hiltrud Häntzschel, 'Justitia – eine Frau? Bayerische Positionen einer Geschlechterdebatte', in Hiltrud Häntzschel and Hadumod Bußmann (ed.), *Bedrohlich gescheit. Ein Jahrhundert Frauen und Wissenschaft in Bayern* (Munich, 1997), pp. 194–213; Claudia Huerkamp, *Bildungsbürgerinnen. Frauen im Studium und in akademischen Berufen 1900–1945* (Göttingen, 1996); Heino Schöbel, 'Frauen in der bayerischen Justiz. Der Weg zum Richteramt', *Bayerische Verwaltungsblätter*, 44/129, 1–12 (1998): pp. 65–73, 106–10; Ulrike Schultz, 'The Status of Women Lawyers in Germany', in Ulrike Schultz and Gisela Shaw (ed.), *Women in the World's Legal Professions* (Oxford/Portland, 2003), pp. 271–93.

[38] Geheimes Staatsarchiv (GStA) Rep. 84 a Nr. 579, Fiche 12981, 120f.

it not only used the formal way, but also strove towards personal contacts and lobbying policy-makers. It contacted the social democrat Minister of Justice, Wolfgang Heine, in order to raise his sympathy for the cause.[39] Simultaneously, the Committee on Petitions of Saxony's parliament and the government of Saxony were confronted with a novelty: a petition by female law students of the University of Leipzig, asking for admission to the legal exams.[40] Clueless about how to handle this, the Minister of Justice contacted his colleagues in the other federal-state administrations of justice departments to look for advice. While the parliamentary debates on the petition took place in June 1919, the other administrations of justice departments rejected the plea.[41] The female law students got the same negative answer as the DJV had had before: admission to the law exams 'had to be considered consistently for the entire empire by the Imperial ministry of justice.'[42]

Defenders of women's rights stressed the social benefits of women's work: women in legal offices were there to protect other women, children and minorities. Their presence would also improve the legal system that was suffering a crisis of confidence as it was said to be missing humanity and impartiality. Many more petitions of single women lawyers, of the DJV and of the women's movement finally made the administration of the Justice departments understand that their stance was no longer sustainable. The Reichsministry of Justice that so far had taken the role of observer rather than main player felt this political pressure. It therefore asked the governments of all German states in April 1919 how they wanted to treat the admission of women to legal offices and professions in the future. The states were more or less united in their opinion that women should be able to function as members of the jury, but that they should not be allowed to exercise legal professions, especially not those of judges.[43]

Yet before all the reports of the states were returned to the Reichsministry of Justice, the Prussian Minister of Justice, Hugo am Zehnhoff, in May 1919, passed a decree that allowed women to sit the first state exam, although without the right to participate in legal apprenticeships.[44] The reasoning went

39 Margarete Edelheim (DJV) to Ministry of Justice, 3/12/1919, GStA Rep. 84 a Nr. 579, Fiche 12981, 122.

40 Ministry of Saxony, March 1919, Bayerisches Hauptstaatsarchiv (BayHStA) MJu 9829.

41 GStA Rep 84 a Nr. 579 Fiche 12982, 135.

42 'Die Zulassung der Frauen zu den juristischen Prüfungen und zum Vorbereitungsdienst', *Die Frau*, 27 (1919–20): p. 349.

43 Reichsministry of Justice, 4/14/1919, to all State Ministries of Justice, BA Berlin R 3001 4180, 91 ff.; BayHStA MJu 9829; GSTA Rep 84 a Nr. 579, Fiche 12982, 125.

44 Justizministerialblätter 1919, 288; GStA Rep. 84 a Nr. 579, Fiche 12981, 118; Berent, 'Zulassung', pp. 332–4.

that by admitting women to the first state exam, this could distract them from exercising their constitutional rights to enter every chosen profession. There were no principle considerations against admitting women to the state exams, but due to current overcrowding of all legal professions it was argued to be inconsiderate to expose male members of the professions to new competition.[45] Considering the small number of women lawyers ready to sit the exams, this argument seemed rather curious. Obviously aware of this, Prussia in the end admitted women – though only informally – to legal apprenticeships without, however, granting them the right to participate in the second state exam.[46]

The question of the standardized admission of women to legal professions was debated in November 1919 in the presence of all states in the Reichsministry of Justice. This department for the first time declared there were no legal obstacles to admitting women to the exams and to apprenticeships; it suggested at least opening the first of the two required state exams. This meant a considerable change of the legal situation. So far the Reich and states had both denied their jurisdiction in this question.[47] The change of policy happened under the liberal Minister of Justice Eugen Schiffer, who took over the ministry from the conservative politician Rudolf Heinze in October 1919. Schiffer was not only a DDP colleague of the DJV executive board, but also a close friend of DJV board member Marie Munk. Most states now opened the first state exams to women. Baden and Saxony, the more liberal ones, even officially permitted women into the apprenticeship service. Prussia and Bavaria, on the other hand, came together in strong opposition: Prussia because it was in the unfortunate position that, due to its laws, everybody who had passed the second state exam had to be appointed to a position in the justice administration,[48] while other states still had the option of not appointing women as judges. Bavaria represented the Catholic, backward position towards everything that was deemed to be modern.

Caught in this complex jurisdiction conflict, the women's movement and the DJV came to the conclusion that changes in the legal situation could not be achieved by convincing ministries to adjust their interpretations of the new equal rights for women as provided by the new constitution. A formal change of existing laws was required, and thus a change in strategy. Priority was now given to bringing in all requests in the parliaments of all the states. Yet progress was slow, as DJV-board member Margarete Muehsam-Edelheim reported after a debate in the Prussian parliament:

---

45 Ministerialdirektor Nüßlein to the Bavarian Ministry of Justice, 5 September 1919, BayStA MJu 9829.

46 Röwekamp, *Juristinnen*, pp. 247–57.

47 Ibid., pp. 257–66.

48 Curt Zimmer and Friedrich Klee, *Die juristische Ausbildung in Preußen. Zusammenstellung der Gesetzes- und Verwaltungsvorschriften* über *Rechtsstudium, juristische Prüfungen und Vorbereitungsdienst nebst erläuternden Bemerkungen* (Berlin, 1930), p. 19.

> The reasons he [the Prussian Minister of Justice] gave for the rejection, could not pass objective survey so it cannot be helped to feel that the gentlemen in the ministry, all of them old style, simply *don't want it*, and for this not wanting it they had to find a false pretence.[49]

Only a new attempt by Saxony's Minister of Justice, the social democrat Dr. Rudolf Harnisch (b. 1864), who continued negotiations with the Reichsministry of Justice, got things moving again.[50] This attempt made all the other administration of justice departments nervous; hectically they assured each other that they would stick to their negative attitude. But the Reich reckoned that 'Saxony's wish in the current situation was justified', and invited new negotiations. During the entire year of 1920, a number of motions of the DDP and SPD factions were debated in the Reichstag and the state parliaments. Unparalleled was the cooperation of all 32 female members of the Reichstag on an all-party level, who together requested the admission of women to the legal state exams.[51] Unusually active and eloquent for the cause of women lawyers was the DDP member of the Reichstag, Marie-Elisabeth Lüders (1878–1966). She not only constantly reported and used her parliamentarian rights to interrogate, but also channelled all requests to the DDP faction and other female Reichstag members. As a member of the BDF board of executives, she also acted as the contact person of the DJV when the association wanted to introduce a new motion via different party factions.

Based on a positive resolution of its state parliament, the Prussian Ministry of Justice yielded to the DJV pressure and passed a second decree in January 1921 that nullified the decree from May 1919. It permitted women to participate in legal apprenticeship in the same way as male legal candidates. Still excluded though was the right to sit the second state exam. Pressured by Prussia's solo attempt, the Reichsminister of Justice could not avoid addressing all the states again to find a uniform regulation for the entire Reich.[52] This attempt did not find many friends, especially in Bavaria and in Hesse, but the smaller states relented in the new directive. While the Reichstag, the women's movement and women lawyers worked together towards a legal draft, and the Reichsministry of Justice and the State Ministries of Justice passed the buck to each other, the

49 Margarete Meseritz, 'Die Prüfung der Juristinnen', *Vossische Zeitung*, 23 February 1920.

50 Saxony's Ministry of Justice to Reichsministry of Justice, 30 April 1920, GStA Rep. 84 a Nr. 579, Fiche 12983, 250; BA Berlin R 3001 4181, 244ff., BayHStA MJu 9829; Hess. StA DA G 21 A 67/3.

51 Petition Mrs. Agnes and companions, 12 February 1920, No. 1035, Hearings of the Reichstag vol. 365, printed matter 1035, Reichstag I. election period 1920, 705.

52 Reichsministry of Justice, 23 February 1921, to all State Ministries of Justice, BA Berlin R 3001/4181, 25.

German Judge Association expressed its understanding of the question as the first legal professional group. At its fourth congress in March 1921, and after a long and agitated debate, it voiced with 245 against five votes that it deemed women to be unfit to practise law, at least as judges. The association went to great lengths explaining that, based on their nature, women were unfit to exercise the profession, either physically or psychologically; women working as judges would also endanger the authority of the entire state apparatus.[53]

It was not so much the competition of women that was feared, as the number of women entering legal professions was too small to pose a real threat. At stake were the full citizenships rights and the question of whether women would be able to judge over men (an unthinkable image) and women gaining access to real power positions. Let us remind ourselves that law in itself did not only represent a system of moral values of which lawyers saw themselves as the keepers; within the German state it was also the most influential of all professions. While medicine and education were more or less clearly defined within specific areas of competence and influence, the law was omnipresent in all niches of society: lawyers did not only hold influential positions in governments and parliaments, but also in the economy, in banks and in the stock exchange. Furthermore, the law is by definition the only area that has a power structure that can enforce its decisions – all reasons enough to keep women out of its power ranks. That was why Marie Stritt wrote in 1921, visibly irritated:

> It is an old claim of the National council of women, of the former Suffrage Societies, and other large organisations that woman law-students shall be admitted to the last qualifying examinations and the preparatory service which is obligatory for lawyers as well as for the judiciary and administrative careers. But on no other point – not even against woman suffrage – the resistance, especially of the professional circles, has ever been so hard and stubborn as on this one. It seems, indeed, as if the idea of women with judicial powers and functions was quite unbearable to men in all lands.[54]

During the entire year of 1921 the issue of admission of women as jurors and as professional lawyers was debated in the Reichstag. In January 1922 the German Bar Association in its annual congress also disputed the question.[55] On the side of the attorneys, votes were more divided than was the case for the judges (43:32), yet still they opinionated that 'the woman is not suited to work as an

[53] 'Verhandlungen des 4. Richtertages', *Deutsche Richterzeitung*, 13 (1921): pp. 196–206.

[54] Stritt, 'Germany', p. 107.

[55] Reichsministry of Justice to the board of the German Attorneys Association, 5 October 1921, BA Berlin R 3001 4181, 167.

attorney or a judge. Her admission would lead to a damage of the judicature and therefore is rejected.'[56]

As common (?) in the unstable Weimar Republic the government had changed once again: the social democrat Prof. Dr. Gustav Radbruch took over the Reichsministry of Justice. Radbruch, as opposed to most other ministers, was a supporter of the admission of women to legal professions and immediately set out to draft a law permitting women to work in legal careers.[57] Before introducing his project into the Reichstag, he had contacted the governments of the single states.[58] 'Nobody who is interested in a steady, stable legal development will be able to take the responsibility for this step', Bavaria warned a last time.[59] Other states found the reform draft 'radical' and 'an enormous risk.' Yet without any problems the project came through the Reichstag and finally also passed the vote of the Reichsrat (Imperial State Council). It was to become the law of 11 July 1922.[60]

From 1922 to Nazi Takeover in 1933: Women Lawyers at Work

But what was the actual working situation of female jurists after their successful entry? We will dwell upon this issue in the following pages.

Female Attorneys

Immediately after 1922, women lawyers in Germany set out to conquer the legal professions. The majority of them became attorneys. The first female advocate in Germany, Maria Otto, was admitted that year to the bar in Munich. Elfriede Meißen followed her in 1924 at the bar of Dresden; Marie Munk, Edith Sußmann and Edith Hegemann-Springer at the bar in Berlin; and Margarethe Esch at the bar in Cologne. Every year the number of female attorneys increased considerably. In 1933, when the national socialists took power and slowly started to limit women's access to legal professions, Prussia counted 60 female attorneys, Saxony 10 and Munich eight female attorneys. Altogether, the number of female

56 'Verhandlungen des Anwaltstages', *Juristische Wochenschrift*, 51 (1922): pp. 1247, 1255.

57 Handwritten note by Radbruch, 2 March 1922, BA Berlin R 3001/4181, 198.

58 Proceedings of the Reichsgovernment 2 January 1922, BA Berlin R 3001 4181, 200f.

59 Bavaria's Ministry of Justice to Foreign Office, 17 February 1922, BayHStA MJu 9829.

60 *Reich Law Gazette*, 1/51 (1922): pp. 573–4.

attorneys in Germany should at that time have been around 120.[61] They were for the major part active in the larger cities.[62]

The first years for these women lawyers were often characterized by economic hardship. Their first clients were poor women, who preferred to use the service of women whom they trusted easier than men.[63] Clients were relieved to unburden their worries with a woman since they could establish an easier contact, characterized by confidence, intimacy and mutual understanding.[64] Male clients, too, slowly found their way to female attorneys. While in the beginning female attorneys were mainly sought for family law-related cases,[65] soon they had law offices like their male colleagues.[66] Yet it appears that female attorneys often had to work more than their male colleagues to achieve a safe and equivalent economic position.[67] Very few male colleagues were willing to accept women as partners in their offices; the elder attorneys, especially, were often worried that their clients would meet female colleagues with some disapproval.[68] Since young attorneys usually joined an office in order to have a steady salary and learn under the expertise of more experienced colleagues, for women it was far harder to enter the profession, being either unaffiliated or only in an office-sharing situation (meaning sharing costs but not expertise).[69]

Most female attorneys shared a different working ethos than male attorneys. They understood that to help their clients a more human approach was as important as the legal advice itself.[70] The relationship between Bremer advocate Emmalene Bulling (1900–59) and her clients were described thus: 'She took

---

61 Röwekamp, *Juristinnen*, pp. 468–70.

62 Ibid., p. 470.

63 'Sind weibliche Schöffen und Geschworene, Richter und Anwälte notwendig und wünschenswert?', *Stadt-Anzeiger*, 13 May 1926.

64 Marie Munk, 'Legal Training in Germany', *The Double Tau, National League Sorority*, 9/1 (1938): pp. 11–13, 30, 43–4.

65 Marie Munk, Pioneer Women Judge, Sophia Smith Collection, Smith College/Northampton, SSC, IV, 4; Dorothee Breucker and Gesa Ingendahl, 'Emmy Rebstein-Metzger: Rechtsanwältin und Frauenrechtlerin', in Dorothee Breucker and Gesa Ingendahl, *Leben und Arbeit von Frauen in Ravensburg* (Tübingen/Stuttgart, 1993), pp. 58–62.

66 Margarethe von Erffa and Ingeborg Richarz-Simons, 'Der weibliche Rechtsanwalt', in Julius Magnus, *Die Rechtsanwaltschaft* (Leipzig, 1929), p. 476; Käthe Gaebel, 'Die Berufslage der Akademikerinnen', *Die Frau*, 34 (1926–27), p. 223.

67 Marie Munk, *Die Juristin. Merkblätter für Berufsberatung* (Berlin, 1928), p. 7.

68 Erffa and Richarz-Simons, 'Weibliche Rechtsanwalt', p. 476; Erna Haßlacher-Friedenthal, 'Die Juristin', in Erich Janke, *Das moderne Buch der weiblichen Berufe* (Minden, 1928), p. 218.

69 Gaebel, 'Berufslage', p. 223.

70 Margarete Berent, 'Die Frau in den juristischen Berufen', *Die Frau der Gegenwart*, 11 (1917): p. 157.

care of them.'[71] They also felt that the profession of attorney corresponded to 'the need of a woman, to advise and help', as attorney Erna Haßlacher-Friedenthal wrote.[72] They conceived their profession in the tradition of so-called 'organized motherhood.'[73] Their other duty was to change the gendered interpretation of existing laws, as attorney Margarete Berent stressed.[74]

Female Judges

Obviously, female attorneys and judges shared a common struggle but compared with attorneys, judges to be met with much stronger resistance. To judge, in the eyes of many, was not a function that could be performed by women. Since the appointment of judges was the responsibility of the states, some like Bavaria or the small state of Oldenburg simply decided not to appoint women. Female judges in fair numbers were only to be found in Prussia and Saxony. Judges were first always employed in temporary positions; to later gain a lifetime appointment took, depending on the state, between six and 10 years. Thus the first female judges with lifetime positions were to be found by the end of the 1920s. The first female judge in Germany was Maria Hagemeyer, who had passed her second state exam in October 1924 in Prussia. She was first employed by the Prussian Ministry of Justice, and in May 1927 was appointed *Amts- und Landrichterin* (local and regional) judge in Bonn. In June 1928 she was promoted to a lifetime position and received the first established post as a female judge in Bonn.[75] She was followed in 1929 by Dr. Gertrud Cichorius, who was placed in a full post in Chemnitz,[76] by Dr. Gertrud May in Leipzig[77]

---

[71] Christine Bartlitz, 'Justitia ist weiblich. Emmalene Bulling. Bremens erste Rechtsanwältin', in Eva Schöck-Quinteros (ed.), *Buten un Binnen, Wagen un Winnen. Erste Bremerinnen auf dem Weg ins akademische Leben* (Berlin, 1998), p. 110.

[72] Haßlacher-Friedenthal, 'Juristin', p. 217.

[73] Henriette Schrader-Breymann coined the term 'organized motherhood' or 'extended motherhood' in 1870. It expressed the view that motherhood in no way presupposed physical maternity. The German women's movement referred to it in relation to demands for employment and participation by childless women, arguing that ('spiritual') maternity was in principle a quality of all women, as it did not express having a family. For some of the leading feminists, spiritual motherhood in fact counted more than physical motherhood. Irene Stoehr, '"Organisierte Mütterlichkeit": Zur Politik der deutschen Frauenbewegung um 1900', in Karin Hausen (ed.), *Frauen suchen ihre Geschichte. Historische Studien zum 19. und 20. Jahrhunder* (Munich, 1983), pp. 221–49.

[74] Berent, 'Frau', p. 157.

[75] Röwekamp, *Juristinnenlexikon*, p. 123.

[76] Cichorius, Gertrud, BA Berlin R 3001 053503.

[77] May, Gertrud, Staatsarchiv Leipzig, LG 8008.

and by Elisabeth Krumme in Essen.[78] In 1930 Marie Hurtzig was appointed in Chemnitz,[79] Marie Munk (who is often wrongly cited as the first female judge) in Berlin, and Hedwig Brann-Frank in Frankfurt.[80] By 1933 Germany counted an estimated 13 lifetime female judges and over 100 female judges in judicial training.[81] The difference between judges appointed for life and those assigned to fixed-term positions became all too apparent for non-Jewish female judges in 1934. Despite continued prejudice against female jurists (Hitler's antipathy towards them was notorious), the few of them with a lifetime position were not sacked by the Nazis but simply shifted to less publicly visible positions. This was obviously not the case for female judges of Jewish descent; they all lost their jobs, following the Law for the Restoration of the German Career Civil Service in 1933.

The opposition towards women in legal professions, especially women in the judiciary, carried on after 1922. The same arguments that previously were used to prevent women entering the profession now served to steer them into certain areas of the law which allegedly they were better suited for, like divorce, guardianship and juvenile law.[82] But female judges themselves also felt they had a special duty as women in their new field: 'I always make a point of not disregarding the human side of the trial alongside the legal assessment, and I try to avoid at any cost the arrogant tone common to officials,' said Judge Viktoria Eschke.[83] After all, female jurists had been demanding access to legal professions with the argument that their participation would humanize justice. When describing their way of sentencing, female judges usually argued that first and foremost they used an objective and logical approach, but also a stronger sense of intuition.[84] While strictly adhering to the norms, standards and traditions of their profession, they also wanted to reveal the 'human' side of the law. The

78 Röwekamp, *Juristinnenlexikon*, p. 214.

79 Hurtzig, Marie, BA Berlin R 3001 061499.

80 Röwekamp, *Juristinnenlexikon*, p. 275.

81 Röwekamp, *Juristinnen*, p. 451.

82 Sibylle Böge, *Weibliche Juristen? Eine historisch-soziologische Analyse des Zugangs von Frauen zu juristischen Professionen* (Master diss., University of Kassel, 1992); Sibylle Böge, 'Geschlecht und "horizontale" Segmentierungen in der juristischen Profession', in Angelika Wetterer (ed.), *Die soziale Konstruktion von Geschlecht in Professionalisierungsprozessen. Vom kollektiven Frauenausschluss zur Integration mit beschränkten Möglichkeiten* (Frankfurt/Main, 1995), p. 139; Ilse Costas, 'Gesellschaftliche Umbrüche und das Verhältnis von Profession und Geschlecht. Die juristische Profession im deutsch-französischen Vergleich', in Wetterer, ibid, p. 121; Hildegard Koll, 'Die Frau im Richterberuf', in *Städtisches Gymnasium und Realgymnasium in der Kreuzgasse zu Köln, 1828–1928. Festschrift zur Jahrhundertfeier der Anstalt 13. bis 15. Okt. 1928* (Cologne, 1928), p. 103.

83 Sims, 'Erste Kammergerichts-Richterin', *Der Montag (Lokal-Anzeiger)*, 22.4.1929, w.p.

84 Koll, 'Frau im Richterberuf', p. 100.

way the law was applied they considered as too cold, with the feminine element missing. In sum, the law was their tool to guarantee justice, and that is how they interpreted it.

The Social Side of the Law and New Career Strategies

But there was yet another part that was new to the professional attitude of many female lawyers. They developed career strategies that involved social change through political and legal processes. Concern about the protection of the socially disadvantaged was at the core of their professional behaviour and did not limit itself to court cases, but also to legal reforms. Indeed, courtroom experience seems to have increased their compassion and conviction to tackle social problems in society. Concern for the protection of children was a priority for many women lawyers, who made attempts to end the stigmatization of illegitimate children. Women lawyers also stood up for better welfare laws for women and children and equal salaries for equal work. They pushed for reforms in family law, including equal spousal responsibilities; easier divorce procedures not based on the guilt principle; common custody law; equal goods acquired during marriage in case of divorce; and equal citizenship rights for women. The attorney Marie Munk for example outlined the BDF's claims concerning the legal position of illegitimate children in 1918.[85] Together with attorney Margarete Berent she wrote in 1920 suggestions for the draft of a new Judicature Act, including women as laymen.[86] The latter in 1932 also sketched a BDF petition to the Reichstag for a change in citizenship law for women.[87] Berent and Munk drafted together a number of suggestions for family law reform that were accepted in 1921 by the BDF plenum.[88] Later, Munk was asked by the BDF to draft a more comprehensive memo for family law reform that should contain all claims of the women's movement for a change of the Civil code. It was published in 1923 and widely discussed among the lawyers in the Weimar Republic.[89] Marie Munk and attorney Emmy Rebstein-Metzger gave important lectures at

---

85 LA Berlin B Rep. 235–01 Fiche 2765.

86 LA Berlin B Rep. 235–12 Fiche 2787.

87 LA Berlin B Rep. 235–01 Fiche 2782, 2783.

88 LA Berlin B Rep. 235–12 Fiche 3016.

89 Marie Munk, *Vorschläge zur Umgestaltung des Rechts der Ehescheidung und der elterlichen Gewalt nebst Gesetzesentwurf. Denkschrift des Bundes Deutscher Frauenvereine* (Berlin, 1923); LA Berlin B Rep. 235–12, Fiche 2762; Marie Munk, Autobiographie, IX, 6, LA Berlin B Rep. 235–12, Fiche 3507.

the prestigious biannual meeting of all German lawyers.[90] In fact, a number of women lawyers published their claims for legal changes in prominent journals.[91]

While pushing for equal rights for women, their activities were mostly headed under the banner of 'relational' feminism rather than 'individualist' feminism.[92] In their effort to change conventional gender roles, they moved cautiously. Instead of breaking the rules, they believed in bending them. As a group, women lawyers catalyzed legal, political and cultural changes to end discrimination in the law, especially in the Civil code, in legal professions and in society in general. Their activism can be defined as a new way of exercising the profession of lawyer at the junction of the law and politics.[93]

Conclusion

Striving for justice characterized German female lawyers' activism during the first decade of the twentieth century. Their struggle for access to legal professions was one against discrimination, and after 1918 also for the fulfilment of the promise of the Weimar Republic that all citizens were equal before the law. Women's access to legal professions was more controversial than that of other academic professions because the law was closely associated with political rights. The question of women's right to work in law unfolded in a historical period when women's place in society was changing. Women started to work in growing numbers, but social changes were blocked by the new Civil code of 1900 that tried to convey an image of the traditional family. Much more than before 1900,

---

[90] Marion Röwekamp, 'Der Deutsche Juristentag und seine Juristinnen', *Zeitschrift des Deutschen Juristinnenbundes* (*djbZ*), 4 (2010): pp. 181–3; Röwekamp, *Juristinnen*, pp. 583–8; 598–606.

[91] Röwekamp, *Juristinnen*, pp. 604–6.

[92] Karen Offen – who described the first as more typical of Anglo-American arguments, and the latter as dominating European feminism – has drawn the distinction between 'individualist' and 'relational' feminism. These terms have also been described as feminism based on 'equality' and 'difference'. Arguments relational feminists used referred to equal rights for women as a result of their different but distinctive and equally important contribution to society in their roles as mothers and women, whereas individualist feminists demanded equality based irrespective of sex or gender as human beings. They stressed concepts of human rights and personal independence in all aspects of life and society while diminishing all socially constructed roles as insignificant. See Karen Offen, 'Toward an Historical Definition of Feminism: The Case of France', in *Center for Research on Women*, Working Paper no. 22 (Stanford: Center for Research on Women, 1984); Lorraine Code (ed.), *Encyclopedia of Feminist Theories* (New York, 2000); Ute Gerhard, *Frauenbewegung und Feminismus. Eine Geschichte seit 1789* (Munich, 2009).

[93] Röwekamp, *Juristinnen*, pp. 629–35.

the new Civil code prevented women from acting as legal persons and allowed discrimination in the family in a way that was unknown before. Politically engaged women felt the need to confront these discriminations. Even though their efforts met strong resistance, women lawyers had by 1933 succeeded in not only opening all legal professions to women, but also in gradually establishing their position as attorneys, judges and civil servants, law experts and scientists. The fact that they succeeded was also due to a strong women's movement that supported the battle of women lawyers.

Female judges enforced the law themselves and managed to change certain aspects of legal interpretations, and attorneys demanded legal compliance to ensure that the promise of law was fulfilled. But they also facilitated reform pressure in misogyny laws, especially in family and citizenship law, because they felt their duty was to use the law to make changes for the better for women and children. More than their male colleagues, they worked in the overlapping areas of politics and law, and social work and law. The history of women's participation in legal professions in Germany, until they were excluded again when Hitler took power in 1933, reveals magic moments of German feminism. By exercising their professions they promoted an image of 'new women' capable of full participation in public life and exercising full citizenship rights.

Bibliography

Printed Primary Sources

Augspurg, Anita, 'Gebt acht, solange noch Zeit ist!', *Die Frauenbewegung,* 1 (1895): 4–5

Bäumer, Gertrud, 'Zwei Kundgebungen zur Einheitlichkeit der deutschen Frauenbewegung', *Die Frauenfrage*, 15/1–2 (1913–14): 2ff.

Berent, Margarete, 'Die Frau in den juristischen Berufen', *Die Frau der Gegenwart*, 11 (1917): 153–7.

Berent, Margarete, 'Die Zulassung von Frauen zu den juristischen Berufen', *Die Frau*, 27 (1919–20): 332–4.

Bernhard, Margarete, 'Vorbildungs- und Berufsverhältnisse der deutschen Nationalökonominnen und Juristinnen,' *Volkswirtschaftliche Blätter*, 12/5–6 (1913): 54–9.

Bund deutscher Frauenvereine (ed.), *Deutscher Frauenkongreß, Berlin, 27. Februar–2. März 1912. Sämtliche Vorträge* (Leipzig/Berlin: Teubner, 1912).

'Die Zulassung der Frauen zu den juristischen Prüfungen und zum Vorbereitungsdienst', *Die Frau*, 27 (1919–20): 349.

Erffa, Margarete von, and Ingeborg Richarz-Simons, 'Der weibliche Rechtsanwalt', in Julius Magnus, *Die Rechtsanwaltschaft* (Leipzig: Moese, 1929), 471–85.

Gaebel, Käthe, 'Die Berufslage der Akademikerinnen', *Die Frau*, 34 (1926–27): 218–24; 278–82.

Hachenburg, Max, *Lebenserinnerungen eines Rechtsanwalts* (Düsseldorf: Neue Brücke Verlag, 1927).

Haßlacher-Friedenthal, Erna, 'Die Juristin', in Erich Janke, *Das moderne Buch der weiblichen Berufe* (Minden: Köhler, 1928), 211–20.

Koll, Hildegard, 'Die Frau im Richterberuf', in *Städtisches Gymnasium und Realgymnasium in der Kreuzgasse zu Köln, 1828–1928. Festschrift zur Jahrhundertfeier der Anstalt 13. bis 15. Okt. 1928* (Cologne: Kölner Görres Haus, 1928), 99–104.

'Kundgebung für die Zulassung der Frauen als Schöffen', *Die Frau*, 20 (1912–13): 376.

Langsdorff, Erna von, 'Die Berufsaussichten der Juristin in Deutschland', *Die Frau*, 20 (1912–13): 603–9.

Lowitsch, Vera, *Die Frau als Richter* (Berlin: Heymann, 1933).

Meseritz, Margarete, 'Die Prüfung der Juristinnen', *Vossische Zeitung*, 23 February 1920.

Munk, Marie, *Vorschläge zur Umgestaltung des Rechts der Ehescheidung und der elterlichen Gewalt nebst Gesetzesentwurf. Denkschrift des Bundes Deutscher Frauenverein* (Berlin, 1923).

Munk, Marie, *Die Juristin. Merkblätter für Berufsberatung* (Berlin: Trowitzsch, 1928).

Munk, Marie, 'Legal Training in Germany', *The Double Tau, National League Sorority*, 9/1 (1938): 11–13, 30, 43–4.

Ruscheweyh, Herbert, *Die Entwicklung des deutschen Jugendgerichts. Schriften des Ausschusses für Jugendgerichte und Jugendgerichtshilfen* (Weimar: Dietsch & Brückner, 1918).

Schmidt, Auguste, 'Juristinnen', *Neue Bahnen*, 25/3 (1900): 32.

Sims, 'Erste Kammergerichts-Richterin', *Der Montag (Lokal-Anzeiger)*, 22.4.1929, w.p.

'Sind weibliche Schöffen und Geschworene, Richter und Anwälte notwendig und wünschenswert?', *Stadt-Anzeiger*, 13 May 1926.

Stritt, Marie, 'Germany', *The International Woman Suffrage News*, April 1921: 107.

'Verhandlungen des Anwaltstages', *Juristische Wochenschrift*, 51 (1922): 1241–68.

'Verhandlungen des 4. Richtertages', *Deutsche Richterzeitung*, 13 (1921): 196–206.

Zimmer, Curt, and Friedrich Klee, *Die juristische Ausbildung in Preußen. Zusammenstellung der Gesetzes- und Verwaltungsvorschriften* über *Rechtsstudium, juristische Prüfungen und Vorbereitungsdienst nebst erläuternden Bemerkungen* (Berlin: Preuß. Dr.- u. Verl.-AG, 1930).

'Zur Frauenbewegung. Die Zulassung von Juristinnen zur Staatsprüfung', *Die Frau*, 26/10 (1918–19): 318.

'Zweiter Deutscher Jugendgerichtstag, 29. September–1. Oktober 1910 in München', *Die Frauenbewegung*, 16/21 (1910): 169ff.

Secondary Sources

Albisetti, James, *Schooling German Girls and Women: Secondary and Higher Education in the Nineteenth Century* (Princeton, NJ: Princeton University Press, 1988).

Albisetti, James, 'Portia ante Portas. Women and the Legal Profession in Europe, ca. 1870–1925', *Journal of Social History*, 33/4 (2000): 825–57.

Bajohr, Stefan, and Katrin Rödiger-Bajohr, 'Die Diskriminierung der Juristin in Deutschland bis 1945', *Kritische Justiz*, 13 (1980): 39–50.

Bartlitz, Christine, 'Justitia ist weiblich. Emmalene Bulling – Bremens erste Rechtsanwältin', in Eva Schöck-Quinteros (ed.), *Buten un Binnen, Wagen un Winnen. Erste Bremerinnen auf dem Weg ins akademische Leben* (Berlin: Schriftenreihe des Hedwig Hintze Instituts Bremen, 1997), 97–123.

Berneike, Christiane, *Die Frauenfrage ist Rechtsfrage. Die Juristinnen der deutschen Frauenbewegung um das Bürgerliche Gesetzbuch* (Baden-Baden: Nomos, 1995).

Böge, Sybille, *Weibliche Juristen? Eine historisch-soziologische Analyse des Zugangs von Frauen zu juristischen Professionen* (Master diss., University of Kassel, 1992).

Böge, Sybille, 'Geschlecht und "horizontale" Segmentierungen in der juristischen Profession', in Angelika Wetterer (ed.), *Die soziale Konstruktion von Geschlecht in Professionalisierungsprozessen. Vom kollektiven Frauenausschluss zur Integration mit beschränkten Möglichkeiten* (Frankfurt/Main: Jenior & Pressler 1995), 139–54.

Böhm, Reglindis, 'Der Kampf um die Zulassung der Frauen als Rechtsanwältinnen und zum Richteramt', in Ministry of Justice of Hesse, *Frauen in juristischen Berufen. Ein Brevier für Referendare und Referendarinnen* (Wiesbaden 1987), 11–19.

Breucker, Dorothee, and Gesa Ingendahl, 'Emmy Rebstein-Metzger: Rechtsanwältin und Frauenrechtlerin', in Dorothee Breucker and Gesa Ingendahl (ed.), *Leben und Arbeit von Frauen in Ravensburg* (Tübingen/Stuttgart: Silberburg 1993), 58–62.

Code, Lorraine (ed.), *Encyclopedia of Feminist Theories* (New York: Routledge, 2000).

Cordes, Oda, 'Die Frau als Organ der Rechtspflege? Über die historisch wichtigsten Stationen der Zulassung von Frauen in der deutschen Rechtspflege', in Stephan Meder et al. (ed.), *Frauenrecht und Rechtsgeschichte. Die Rechtskämpfe der deutschen Frauenbewegung* (Cologne/Weimar/Vienna: Böhlau, 1996), 279–301.

Costas, Ilse, 'Gesellschaftliche Umbrüche und das Verhältnis von Profession und Geschlecht. Die juristische Profession im deutsch-französischen

Vergleich', in Angelika Wetterer (ed.), *Die soziale Konstruktion von Geschlecht in Professionalisierungsprozessen: vom kollektiven Frauenausschluss zur Integration mit beschränkten Möglichkeiten* (Frankfurt/Main: Jenior & Pressler, 1995), 121–38.

Deutscher Juristinnenbund, *Juristinnen in Deutschland. Die Zeit von 1900 bis 1998* (Baden-Baden: Nomos, 2003).

Dölemeyer, Barbara, 'Die Zulassung von Frauen zur Rechtsanwaltschaft und ihr Ausschluß in der NS- Zeit', in Mario Ascheri et al. (ed.), *'Ins Wasser geworfen und Ozeane durchquert'. Festschrift für Knut Wolfgang Nörr* (Cologne/Weimar/Vienna: Böhlau, 2003), 151–64.

Flügge, Sibylla, 'Der lange Weg in die Gerichte. Von der Männlichkeit des Staates und vom Ende holder Weiblichkeit', *Streit*, 4 (1984): 149–53.

Geisel, Beatrix, '"Alle Juristinnen haben ihre Stellung der Frauenbewegung zu verdanken!" Dem langen Kampf um die Robe folgte der noch immer nicht beendete Streit um die Gleichberechtigung', *Ariadne*, 30 (1996): 52–9.

Geisel, Beatrix, *Klasse, Geschlecht und Recht. Vergleichende sozialhistorische Untersuchung der Rechtsberatungspraxis von Frauen- und Arbeiterbewegung (1894–1933)* (Baden-Baden: Nomos 1997).

Gerhard, Ute, *Gleichheit ohne Angleichung. Frauen im Recht* (Munich: Beck, 1997).

Gerhard, Ute, *Feminismus und Demokratie. Die europäischen Frauenbewegungen der 1920er Jahre* (Kronberg/Ts.: Ulrike Helmer, 2001).

Gerhard, Ute, *Frauenbewegung und Feminismus. Eine Geschichte seit 1789* (Munich: Beck, 2009).

Häntzschel, Hiltrud, 'Justitia – eine Frau? Bayerische Positionen einer Geschlechterdebatte', in Hiltrud Häntzschel and Hadumod Bußmann (ed.), *Bedrohlich gescheit. Ein Jahrhundert Frauen und Wissenschaft in Bayern* (Munich: Beck, 1997), 194–213.

Harris, Barbara, *Beyond Her Sphere: Women and the Professions in American History* (Westport, Conn: Greenwood Press, 1978).

Howsam, Leslie, '"Sound-Minded Women": Eliza Orme and the Study and Practice of Law in Late Victorian England', *Atlantis* 15/1 (1989): 44–55.

Huerkamp, Claudia, *Bildungsbürgerinnen. Frauen im Studium und in akademischen Berufen 1900–1945* (Göttingen: Vandenhoeck & Ruprecht, 1996).

Kimble, Sara L., 'No Right to Judge: Feminism and the Judiciary in Third Republic France', *French Historical Studies*, 31/4 (2008): 609–41.

Krause, Peter, 'Geschichte der Justiz- und Verwaltungsausbildung in Preußen und Deutschland', in Christian Baldus et al. (ed.), *Juristenausbildung in Europa zwischen Tradition und Reform* (Tübingen: Mohr Siebeck, 2008), 95–125.

Ledford, Kenneth. F., *From General Estate to Special Interest: German Lawyers 1878–1933* (Cambridge/New York: Cambridge University Press 1996).

Meder, Stephan et al. (ed.), *Frauenrecht und Rechtsgeschichte. Die Rechtskämpfe der deutschen Frauenbewegung* (Cologne/Weimar/Vienna: Böhlau 2006).

Offen, Karen, 'Toward an Historical Definition of Feminism: The Case of France', in *Center for Research on Women*, Working Paper no. 22 (Stanford: Center for Research on Women 1984).

Paletschek, Sylvia, and Bianca Pietrow-Ennker (ed.), *Womens's Emancipation Movements in the 19th Century: A European Perspective* (Stanford: Stanford University Press, 2004).

Riedel, Tanja-Carina, *Gleiches Recht für Frau und Mann. Die bürgerliche Frauenbewegung und die Entstehung des BGB* (Cologne/Weimar/Vienna: Böhlau, 2008).

Röwekamp, Marion, *Juristinnen. Lexikon zu Leben und Werk* (Baden-Baden: Nomos, 2005).

Röwekamp, Marion, 'Der Deutsche Juristentag und seine Juristinnen', *Zeitschrift des Deutschen Juristinnenbundes* (*djbZ*), 4 (2010): 181–3.

Röwekamp, Marion, *Die ersten deutschen Juristinnen. Eine Geschichte ihrer Professionalisierung und Emanzipation (1900–1945)* (Cologne/Weimar/Vienna: Böhlau, 2011).

Schöbel, Heino, 'Frauen in der bayerischen Justiz. Der Weg zum Richteramt', *Bayerische Verwaltungsblätter*, 44/129, No. 1–12 (1998): 65–73, 106–10.

Schubert, Werner, *Die Projekte der Weimarer Republik zur Reform des Nichtehelichen-, des Adoptions- und Ehescheidungsrecht* (Munich/Zürich: Schöningh, 1986).

Schultz, Ulrike, 'The Status of Women Lawyers in Germany', in Ulrike Schultz and Gisela Shaw (ed.), *Women in the World's Legal Professions* (Oxford/Portland: Hart, 2003), 271–93.

Schwab, Dieter, 'Gleichberechtigung und Familienrecht im 20. Jahrhundert', in Ute Gerhard (ed.), *Frauen in der Geschichte des Rechts. Von der Frühen Neuzeit bis zur Gegenwart* (Munich: Beck 1997), 790–827.

Stevens, Robert, *Law School: Legal Education in America from the 1850s to the 1890s* (Chapel Hill: University of North Carolina Press, 1983).

Stoehr, Irene, '"Organisierte Mütterlichkeit": Zur Politik der deutschen Frauenbewegung um 1900', in Karin Hausen (ed.), *Frauen suchen ihre Geschichte: Historische Studien zum 19. und 20. Jahrhunder* (Munich: Beck, 1983), 221–49.

Witz, Anne, *Professions and Patriarchy* (London/New York: Routledge, 1992).

PART II
Gender Constructions and their Impact on Jurisprudence

Chapter 4

Arbitrating Class and Gender: Working-class Women and Labour Arbitration in Tourcoing, 1848–1894[1]

Mathieu Brûlé

Created in 1806 under the direction of Napoleon, the French labour arbitration boards known as the *conseils des prud'hommes* were established to provide France's workers and employers with the means of resolving some of their more minor differences through conciliation rather than through collective action. Although male and female workers were allowed access to the boards as plaintiffs and defendants, the right to run as and vote for candidates for the *prud'hommes* before 1848 was reserved solely to male employers. With the creation of the Second Republic in 1848 and the subsequent extension of universal male suffrage, male workers were given the right to elect their own representatives to the *prud'hommes*, where their representation became numerically equal to that of employers. While this represented a step forward in the democratization of this legal institution, it was nevertheless a limited step as the same rights were not extended to women.

This chapter addresses the question of how this reform affected the ways in which female workers viewed and used the *prud'hommes* as an avenue for achieving justice for workplace grievances. It also examines how the presence of male workers on the boards affected the *prud'hommes*' rulings in cases involving female workers. Did male worker representatives elected to the board adopt a gendered bias, or did their presence make the *prud'hommes* a less hostile place for all workers? This study also considers the impact of other legal reforms over the second half of the nineteenth century: the legalization of strikes in 1864, as well as the legalization of unions in 1884. Did the prospect of settling workplace disputes through collective means, such as strikes and unions, prove to be more

[1] This chapter benefitted greatly from numerous conversations with Béatrice Craig, Patricia Kmiec and the Toronto Labour History Reading Group. I owe them a debt of gratitude for their assistance. I am also grateful to the editor of this volume for her valuable feedback. Finally, I would like to acknowledge the financial support provided by the Department of History at the University of Ottawa.

attractive to female workers than settling them individually at the *prud'hommes*? How did experiences at the *prud'hommes* differ among women, whose results were shaped by much more than their gender? It also considers changes brought to the structure of the *prud'hommes* in this period and their potential impact on their use and rulings.

As an important centre in one of France's greatest textile regions, Tourcoing serves as an excellent site for a case study of this nature. Situated on the Franco-Belgian border, Tourcoing had served as an important textile centre since the Middle Ages. Its importance grew with the mechanization of the textile industry in the early nineteenth century, a change that saw work previously performed in the home moved into larger mills and factories, as well as a shift in the gendered nature of specific textile jobs.[2] The mix-gendered nature of its workforce also presents us with an interesting case. In addition to playing an important role in the region's textile industry, the sentiment towards female workforce participation was generally positive among both workers and employers. A study of the region's workforce by Béatrice Craig points to an 1873 survey of the region's employers in which they were asked to comment on the availability of work for women, as well as on any efforts that may have been made to keep them out of the workplace. As Craig points out, none of the answers provided indicated any problem with female waged labour, stating instead that there was plenty of work available for women wishing to earn a wage. Unlike other industrial centres, the male breadwinner ideology did not take hold in this region as it did elsewhere.[3]

In addition to the importance of its industry and the nature of its workforce, the availability of sources relating to its *conseil des prud'hommes* also adds to Tourcoing's appeal for this project. These sources are extensive and provide researchers with an excellent picture of the types of cases being heard. While the voices of individual men and women who appeared before the *prud'hommes* are largely absent from the records, these documents nevertheless provide details on the gender, profession and city of residence for both plaintiffs and defendants of each case, as well as the nature of the conflict and its outcome. This provides researchers with a wealth of material to conduct a thorough quantitative study of the city's *prud'hommes*. This study consists of an examination of 4,400 cases over 21 years between 1848 and 1894.[4] Years included in the sample

[2] For more on the changes brought about by the mechanization of the textile industry in northern France, see: Béatrice Craig, 'La structure de l'emploi féminine dans une ville en voie d'industrialisation: Tourcoing au XIXe siècle', *Canadian Journal of History/Annales canadiennes d'histoire*, 28 (August 1992): pp. 299–332; and Béatrice Craig, 'Salaire, niveaux de vie et travail féminin, dans l'arrondissement de Lille au XIXè siècle', *Canadian Journal of History/Annales canadiennes d'histoire*, 33 (August 1998): pp. 215–47.

[3] Craig, 'Salaire, niveaux de vie et travail féminin', 242.

[4] These years include four different periods: a short period following the 1848 reforms

were chosen to obtain a picture of the conditions at the *prud'hommes* before and after the reforms of 1848, the legalization of strikes in 1864 and of unions in 1884, as well as the general strike in the textile industry that gripped the city and the surrounding region in 1880. The study concludes in the early 1890s as the political make-up in the region was shifting to the left with the election of socialist candidates to a number of political offices in the region.

This analysis of these cases reveals that the inclusion of male working-class representatives on the *conseils des prud'hommes* in 1848 proved to be beneficial to both female and male workers. Compared to the pre-1848 period, workers' performance as both plaintiffs and defendants at the boards improved as the number of cases lost by working-class women and men fell and those settled through compromise rose. This improved performance in turn led to an increased use of the *prud'hommes* by working-class women, suggesting that, although they were not represented on the boards as women, the presence of their male counterparts encouraged them to continue to view the *prud'hommes* as a means of obtaining redress for perceived infractions by their employers. Conversely, employers saw their rate of success drop dramatically and replaced with cases settled through compromise, indicating that the post-1848 *prud'hommes* were no longer the employer-friendly environment they had once been. This resulted in an almost total abandonment of the *prud'hommes* by the city's employers, who all but disappeared as plaintiffs by the end of the century.

Interpretations of the *conseils des prud'hommes* by legal and social historians have differed and evolved in varying ways. The initial impulse of early scholarship on the *prud'hommes* by legal historians such as Marcel David, William H. McPherson and Frederic Meyers was to point to the original composition and structure of the boards as evidence of their use as repressive instruments of French employers against workers. They argued that the structure of the boards was intentionally designed to place as much power in the hands of employers as possible.[5] Although the structure of the boards provided workers with little formal power in the first half of the nineteenth century, the view of the *prud'hommes* as essentially coercive tools was challenged by social and gender historians who made the boards the subjects of their research.

Rather than focus on the structure of the *prud'hommes*, other historians have instead examined the uses of these institutions. Authors such as Paul Delsalle and Béatrice Craig challenged the notion that employers used the boards against workers. This was done through an examination of the cases and

---

(1848, 1852 and 1855); the eight years following the legalization of strikes (1866–74); the eve of the legalization of unions (1880–83); and the early 1890s (1890–94).

[5] William H. McPherson and Frederic Meyers, *The French Labor Courts: Judgment by Peers* (Urbana, 1966); Marcel David, 'L'évolution historique des conseils de prud'hommes en France', *Droit Social*, 2 (February 1974): pp. 3–21.

rulings issued by the boards, demonstrating that, despite their lack of control over the *prud'hommes* before 1848, workers made great use of the boards' services to challenge their employers, often successfully. Delsalle's study of the *prud'hommes* in Tourcoing's neighbouring city of Roubaix demonstrated that workers in that city were not deterred by the lack of a working-class voice on the boards before 1848 and made great use of their services to defend their working conditions.[6] However, despite the popularity of the *prud'hommes* among the region's working-class, certain groups of workers were less likely than others to view them as a source of justice for workplace grievances.

Béatrice Craig's study of the rulings issued by Tourcoing's *conseil des prud'hommes* before 1848 revealed that the city's working-class women were underrepresented among plaintiffs at the *prud'hommes*. Craig explains this by pointing to the masculine culture of the *prud'hommes* and the economic barriers that would have made giving up a day's wage to attend a hearing a more difficult task for female workers than for men. These factors, Craig argues, made the *prud'hommes* a less attractive option to working-class women.[7]

The study of the working-class use of the *prud'hommes* allows scholars to shed light on how workers in general, and women in particular, interacted with and responded to conciliatory forms of justice. This shift in the view of the *prud'hommes* speaks to similar trends in the wider field of legal history that emphasizes the interaction of working-class people with the legal system and its subsequent implications. The importance of this trend is emphasized in a number of works on both legal and gender history. Wim Mellaerts' study on the working-class uses of legal aid services in late nineteenth-century Caen argues that the extent of popular uses of more accessible forms of justice, such as the *prud'hommes*, emphasizes the need to revisit what he refers to as the 'common assumption of hostility among workers towards the justice system'.[8] Mellaerts argues instead that the construction of these institutions was a process of 'interaction, contest and collaboration' between the state and working-class people.[9] Other scholars have also noted the trend of recognizing the agency of

---

6 Paul Delsalle, 'Tisserands et fabricants chez les prud'hommes dans la région de Lille-Roubaix-Tourcoing (1840–1848)', *Le Mouvement social*, 141 (October–November 1987): pp. 61–80.

7 Béatrice Craig, 'Justice bourgeoise? Justice masculine? Les conseils de prud'hommes au début du XIXe siècle: l'exemple de Tourcoing', *Histoire sociale*, 25/50 (November 1992): pp. 277–8.

8 Wim Mellaerts, 'In the Shadow of Justice: Popular Uses of the Law in Urban Normandy, c. 1880–1905', *French History*, 14/2 (2000), p. 198.

9 Ibid., p. 199.

men and women in their interactions with the law, noting its importance in shaping the fields of legal and gender history.[10]

More recently, scholars have analysed the relationship between the *prud'hommes* and unions. Sociologist Jérôme Pélisse's research on the influence of the law on unions has demonstrated the important role that institutions such as the *prud'hommes* played in shaping unions in France. He argues that, because unions recognized the importance of legal bodies like the *prud'hommes*, they formed strategies to control and reform these institutions in their favour.[11] Similarly, historian Claire Lemercier has examined the relationship between unions and the *prud'hommes* and argued that the labour movement was especially active in strategizing around the boards during their elections, as a victory at the *prud'hommes* was useful in providing unions with legitimacy.[12] This chapter on how working-class men and women made use of Tourcoing's *conseil des prud'hommes* addresses the trend of considering interactions of working-class men and women in two ways: by examining the impact of the inclusion of male worker representatives on the board after 1848, namely how this shaped the institution's response to working-class plaintiffs; and by outlining the ways in which this shaped female working-class attitudes towards Tourcoing's *prud'hommes*. It examines the role the gender of plaintiffs played in shaping the board's response to their cases. It also recognizes that one's lived experiences are never defined by one sole aspect of one's identity, and that Tourcoing's female working class was far from being a homogeneous category. This is addressed through an analysis of the ways in which a plaintiff's gender intersected with class and age to impact their performance at the *prud'hommes*.

Legal Reform and the Structure of the *Conseil des Prud'hommes*

Structurally, the *conseil des prud'hommes* in Tourcoing was divided into four categories, each representing a different sector of the textile industry. Although candidates were required to run in the category representing their own professional sector, a frequent shortage of candidates often forced the board to allow board members to represent sectors other than their own. Tourcoing's board was typically composed of 16 members, two for each sector per class

[10] Suzanne Desban and Jeffrey Merrick (ed.), *Family, Gender, and Law in Early Modern France* (University Park, 2009); Jean-Claude Farcy, *L'histoire de la justice française de la révolution* à *nos jours* (Paris, 2001).

[11] Jérôme Pélisse, 'Les usages syndicaux du droit et de la justice', in Jacques Commaille and Martine Kaluszynsk (ed.), *La fonction publique de la justice* (Paris, 2007), pp. 165–89.

[12] Claire Lemercier, 'Discipliner le commerce sans corporations. La loi, le juge, l'arbitre et le commerçant à Paris au XIXe siècle', *Le Mouvement social*, 224 (July–September 2008): pp. 61–74.

represented, with elections usually held every three years. Although the services of the *prud'hommes* were available to mostly any worker or employer, those wishing to sit on the board were forced to meet specific residential, professional and literacy requirements. As a result, working-class representatives tended to be from among the city's more skilled and educated professions. The opposite was true of employer representatives, who tended to be owners of mid to small-scale operations, reducing the socio-economic gap between worker and employer representatives.

The *prud'hommes* typically heard and attempted to settle smaller-scale disputes between workers and employers. In Tourcoing, the most common cases were those revolving around accusations of breach of contract and wage-related disputes. While most cases reached conciliation at the first instance of the *prud'hommes*, known as the *bureau particulier*, those failing to do so would be judged by the entire board at the *bureau générale*. Only rulings involving penalties over 100 francs could be appealed to the city's commercial courts.[13]

In the event of a tied vote, the president of the board would serve as a tiebreaker. This obvious power invested in the president's position therefore made it an easy target for political conflict. As a result, every legal reform of the *prud'hommes* initiated in the second half of the nineteenth century involved the manner in which the president was chosen. After 1848, the positions of president and vice-president were elected by board members from within their ranks and had to alternate, with an employer occupying one and a worker occupying the other. This changed in 1852 with the fall of the Second Republic, as a new reform of the *prud'hommes* put an end to the election of the president, leaving the power to appoint this position to the government. This continued until 1880, when a new law passed by the Third Republic reinstated the election of the president and vice-president, as well as the alternating nature of the positions.[14]

This continuous shifting of the position of president led to some conflict between worker and employer board members in *prud'hommes* across France, including in Tourcoing. While these tensions between worker and employer representatives on Tourcoing's *prud'hommes* were largely internal, they may have also played a role in shaping the ways in which working-class women and men viewed the board. This will be discussed in greater detail later in this chapter.

---

13 For more details on the election of Tourcoing's *conseil des prud'hommes* as well as the cases heard by its representatives, see: Mathieu Brûlé, *Reforming Arbitration: Class, Gender and the Conseil des Prud'hommes in Tourcoing, 1848–1894* (Master diss., University of Ottawa, 2009).

14 For more on the structure and legal reforms of the *conseils des prud'hommes*, see: McPherson and Meyers, *The French Labor Courts*; David, 'L'évolution historique des Conseils de prud'hommes en France'; Monique Kieffer, 'La législation prud'homale de 1806 à 1907', *Le Mouvement social*, 141 (October–December 1987): pp. 9–23.

Tourcoing's Female Working Class and the *Prud'hommes*

The number of working-class women approaching Tourcoing's *conseil des prud'hommes* in the second half of the nineteenth century increased; but who were these women? Details contained in the records of the *prud'hommes* are very scarce and provide very little information on the details of their cases, but studies conducted on the working lives of women in Tourcoing do shed some light on the identity of those who engaged in paid labour in Tourcoing, and were therefore likely to look to the *prud'hommes* as a means of settling workplace disputes.

Most of the women bringing their workplace disputes to the *prud'hommes* were young, unmarried and without children. According to the findings of a study of working women in Tourcoing throughout the nineteenth century, young unmarried women had a much higher rate of workforce participation than married women and widows. The 1886 census indicates that 78 per cent of unmarried women in Tourcoing held an occupation.[15] This stands in contrast to the married women, of whom only 20 per cent were listed as holding a paid occupation, and widows, a majority of which were either listed as not holding an occupation or were self-employed.[16] Therefore, it is likely that women making use of the *prud'hommes* tended to be young and unmarried.

Of those women who were engaged in the workforce and brought their cases to the *prud'hommes*, an overwhelming majority were from unskilled occupations (Table 4.1).

Table 4.1. Gender of working-class plaintiffs from skilled and unskilled occupations, 1848–1894

	Male plaintiffs		**Female plaintiffs**	
Period	*Skilled (%)*	*Unskilled (%)*	*Skilled (%)*	*Unskilled (%)*
1848, 1852, 1855	85.0	11.5	42.8	48.2
1866–74	71.7	24.5	11.8	78.2
1880–83	75.4	21.4	10.2	89.1
1890–94	71.9	20.1	14.4	79.7

Source: Archives départementales du Nord (ADN), 5U1–18, 5U1–20, 5U1–21, 5U1–22, Régistre des conciliations.

15 Craig, 'La structure de l'emploi féminine', pp. 325–6.

16 Ibid., pp. 311, 321.

The increase in the presence of female plaintiffs from unskilled occupations speaks to the impact of mechanization of the textile industry on Tourcoing's workforce. According to Craig, mechanization of the textile industry led to the elimination of a number of skilled occupations dominated by female workers, including that of spinning (*fileuses*).[17] Therefore, not only were female working-class plaintiffs predominately from unskilled occupations, but they were also a workforce in the midst of a transformation.

Use of the *Prud'hommes*, 1848–1884

One measure of the impact of the inclusion of male workers on the *conseil des prud'hommes* in Tourcoing is the rate at which its services were used. A comparison of the number of cases brought to the board before and after 1848 reveals that their numbers increased, from an average of 72 cases per year between 1821 and 1836, to an average of 242 in the decades following the reform. This alone would suggest that the presence of male worker representatives increased the institution's attractiveness among Tourcoing's workers and employers. However, despite this 240 per cent increase, the number of cases brought to the *prud'hommes* did not keep up with the city's demographic growth, which increased by 267 per cent in the same period.[18] Therefore, although more cases were brought to the attention of the *prud'hommes*, proportionally, fewer people sought this method of dispute resolution.

This proportional decrease in the use of the boards is in part the result of fewer employers choosing to bring their cases to the *prud'hommes* after 1848. While employers accounted for almost two-fifths of plaintiffs before 1848, their numbers dropped to just under one-fifth despite the fact that their numbers within the population remained relatively stable throughout this period. This trend continued until the 1880s, with the exception in the 1866–1874 period (Table 4.2).

A look at the gender distribution of those initiating cases at the *prud'hommes* indicates that working-class women made up an increasingly larger portion of working-class plaintiffs in this period. The same cannot be said for female employers, whose numbers among plaintiffs were comparable to those of working-class women before 1848, but fell to slightly over 1 per cent by the early 1880s (Table 4.3).

Although an increasingly large number of people brought their cases to Tourcoing's *prud'hommes* after 1848, the decrease in the number of employers

17 Ibid., pp. 316.

18 Ibid., pp. 299–332.

Table 4.2 Class of plaintiffs, 1821–1894

		Employer plaintiffs		**Worker plaintiffs**	
Period	*Total cases*	*Total*	*Per cent*	*Total*	*Per cent*
1821–36	1,087	416	38.3	672	61.8
1848, 1852, 1855	726	142	19.6	574	79.1
1866–74	2,087	588	28.2	1,494	71.6
1880–83	875	153	17.5	722	82.5
1890–94	712	20	2.8	691	97.1

Source: Archives Municipales de Tourcoing (AMTg), Conseil des prud'hommes de Tourcoing, Plumitif no. 1, 1821–37; ADN, 5U1–18, 5U1–20, 5U1–21, 5U1–22, Régistre des conciliations.

Table 4.3 Class and gender of plaintiffs, 1821–1894

	Employer plaintiffs			**Worker plaintiffs**		
Period	*Total cases*	*Male (%)*	*Female (%)*	*Total cases*	*Male (%)*	*Female (%)*
1821–36	416	87.7	12.2	672	84.2	15.6
1848, 1852, 1855	142	95.7	2.8	574	83.4	16
1866–74	588	98.6	1	1,494	82.2	17.5
1880–83	153	94.7	1.3	722	79.5	20.3
1890–94	20	100	0	691	89.7	9.9

Source: AMTg, Conseil des prud'hommes de Tourcoing, Plumitif no. 1, 1821–37; ADN, 5U1–18, 5U1–20, 5U1 21 5U1–22, Registre des conciliations.

interested in doing so contributed to the failure of the board to keep its rate of use in proportion to the city's demographic growth. Consideration of the paternalistic attitude of employers in Tourcoing and northern France as a whole can shed light on their decreased presence among plaintiffs. As a number of scholars have noted, northern France's textile employers were notoriously paternalistic. In her study of the socialist politics of the region, Patricia Hilden notes that many of the region's employers tended to look down on their employees with a degree of pity and scorn motivated by the belief that workers' poor conditions were the result of their inability to adopt good morals. To employers, the working class were like children in need of supervision.[19] Employers were therefore unlikely to have welcomed the changes to the *prud'hommes*' structure in 1848 that not only allowed workers to judge their employers, but which also provided them with increased power through equal numerical representation, as well as access to the power inherent in the position of board president. The fact that the presence of employers among plaintiffs increased in the 1860s and 1870s, when the board president was appointed by the government rather than elected, suggests that the appeal of the *prud'hommes* to Tourcoing's employers was at least partially proportional to the amount of power over the institution the law placed in the hands of workers.

While the attitude of employers towards the *prud'hommes* was clearly shifting, so was that of working-class women, whose proportion among working-class plaintiffs increased steadily between 1848 and 1883. If the masculine culture of the *prud'hommes* discouraged working-class women from using their services before 1848, as Craig suggested, then their increased presence after that date suggests that the presence of working-class male representatives increased the familiarity of the boards among Tourcoing's female workforce. Although the reforms of 1848 continued to exclude women, the fact that they opened up the *prud'hommes* to male workers would have provided female workers with the opportunity to be judged by those with life experiences that more closely resembled their own than did those of male employers. Regardless, the presence of working-class male representatives clearly did not deter working-class women from using the services of the *prud'hommes*. Despite the impact that the presence of male workers may have had on the levels of familiarity of the *prud'hommes*, it is unlikely that this was the sole contributing factor to the increased presence of women among working-class plaintiffs. Other factors, such as their performance at the board, must also be taken into consideration.

Gender and Class in the Rulings of the *Prud'hommes* after 1848

Although the new structure of the *prud'hommes* proved unappealing to employers, it is unlikely that this fact alone would have driven them away from the board at the rates seen in the years after 1848. It is equally unlikely that the presence of working-class men on the board was the sole reason behind the

[19] Patricia Hilden, *Working Women and Socialist Politics in France, 1880–1914: A Regional Study* (Oxford, 1986), p. 76. For more on the paternalism among northern French employers, see: Claude Willard, 'Les attaques contre notre-dame de l'usine', *Le Mouvement social*, 57 (October–December 1966): pp. 203–9; Thibault Tellier, 'Les nouvelles clôtures urbaines à l'âge industrielle. L'encadrement religieux des jeunes ouvrières du textile dans l'agglomération lilloise à la fin du XIXe siècle', *Histoire,* économie *et société*, 24/2 (2005): pp. 421–31.

increase in the number of working-class women using its services as a means of settling workplace disputes. An examination of the rulings of the *prud'hommes* could shed light on this.

Cases brought to Tourcoing's *conseil des prud'hommes* could have had a number of outcomes. For the purpose of this chapter, these outcomes of cases heard by the board have been categorized into five distinct categories: wins, losses, compromises and non-conciliation, with a final category comprising those cases whose outcomes were not clear. A case was considered won when the plaintiff's reason for initiating the complaint was met. For example, on 24 September 1868, Élise Hortemaine, a *soigneuse* (a female textile worker in charge of the bobbins) from Tourcoing, appeared before the *prud'hommes* complaining that her employer, Fidèle Strat, had failed to pay her wages. Her case was deemed successful, as the members of the board ruled in her favour, stating that her employer was to pay her wages in full.[20] A loss would occur when the plaintiff's case was either thrown out or if the end result favoured the defendant. Explanations justifying a decision to throw out a case were rarely provided, but board members sometimes found that a plaintiff's complaint was unfounded. This was the case on 18 April 1867 when Adéline Legley, a *rattacheuse* (spinner's assistant) from Tourcoing, asked that her employer, Darras Lemaire, allow her to complete 15 final days of work before being dismissed from her work, a practice common among textile employers, known as *la quinzaine*. After hearing arguments, which are unfortunately not indicated in the records, the *prud'hommes* ruled that Legley's claim was unfounded and subsequently threw it out.[21]

In addition to losing or winning cases, disputes could also be settled through compromise. These occurred when neither party obtained exactly what they sought from the board. Board members often achieved conciliation through compromise by awarding plaintiffs sums less than the amount requested.[22] Such a case occurred in November of 1880 when Julie Deswazière, a *rattacheuse* from Tourcoing, complained that her employer, Deherripen Classe, had terminated her employment by refusing to provide her with work. Deswazière requested two francs per day of unemployment. As a solution the *prud'hommes* proposed that, rather than award the plaintiff the requested sum of money, the defendant would instead provide her with two weeks' worth of work before officially terminating her employment.[23]

---

20 ADN, 5U1 21, Régistre des conciliations.

21 ADN, 5U1–22a, Régistre des conciliations.

22 While it is possible that plaintiffs requested sums exceeding what they believed they were owed in hopes of obtaining an amount closer to the desired amount, limits imposed by the sources would make determining this a difficult task, one that would also fall outside the scope of this study.

23 ADN, 5U1–22, Régistre des conciliations.

When neither party agreed to the solution proposed by the members of the *prud'hommes*, it was considered a case of non-conciliation. For example, on 21 January 1864 Amélie Poret, a *tisserande* (weaver) from Bonduel, was brought to the *prud'hommes* by her employers, Courmont frères. Her employers were demanding that she complete the work that they had given her the previous October. They asked that she be given 15 days to complete this work, after which she would be fined one franc for every day it continued to be late. Although the records unfortunately do not provide information on the ruling of the *prud'hommes* in this case, or the responses from either party, conciliation proved to be impossible.[24] When non-conciliation occurred, disputes were sent to the entire board at the *bureau générale* where a ruling was considered final.

As Béatrice Craig's study reveals, Tourcoing's *prud'hommes* before 1848 was a friendly environment for the city's employers. This is demonstrated by the fact that employers who brought their cases to the *prud'hommes* were successful in 77 per cent of their cases and lost less than 10 per cent of their disputes. Their rate of success was higher and rate of loss much lower than those of working-class plaintiffs, who won almost a third of their cases, while losing a quarter. Employers were also forced to compromise with working-class defendants much less often than workers. Settlement of cases was more likely in worker-initiated cases than in cases with employer defendants, as fewer of their cases ended in non-conciliation.[25]

Given the tendency of the all-employer *prud'hommes* to rule in their favour, employers had no reason not to view the board as an effective means of pursuing their workers for perceived injustices. Their good fortunes, however, would not last forever as the reforms of 1848 ushered in a new era in Tourcoing's *conseil des prud'hommes*. Among the biggest changes in the performance of employer plaintiffs was the decrease in their rate of success.

Worker plaintiffs experienced a similar shift as their rates of success fell by approximately two-thirds and losses dropped to less than one-fifth. Equally notable is the increase in the number of cases settled through compromise, as these rose from slightly over 40 per cent for worker-initiated cases before 1848, to over 47 per cent after the reforms. This increase in the number of cases settled through compromise pales in comparison to the increase experienced by employer plaintiffs, who saw their rate of compromise increase from less than 10 per cent to one half of their cases in the decade following the introduction of male working-class representatives. Perhaps as an indication of growing tension at the *prud'hommes*, the number of cases ending in non-conciliation more than doubled for both workers and employers (Table 4.4).

---

24 ADN, Régistre des conciliations, 5U1–20.

25 Non-conciliation occurred when one or both parties rejected a settlement proposed by members of the *conseil des prud'hommes*.

Table 4.4 Outcome of employer- and worker-initiated cases, 1821–1883

Employer-initiated cases					
Period	*Win (%)*	*Loss (%)*	*Compromise (%)*	*Non-conciliated (%)*	*Other/ unspecified (%)*
1821–36	77.2	7.9	8.9	6	0
1848, 1852, 1855	21.7	4.8	50	12.9	3.2
1866–74	6.4	2.8	74	8.4	8
1880–83	5.3	1.1	81.1	2.1	10.5
Worker-initiated cases					
Period	*Win (%)*	*Loss (%)*	*Compromise (%)*	*Non-conciliated (%)*	*Other/ unspecified (%)*
1821–36	29.4	25.9	41.1	3.6	0
1848, 1852, 1855	11	17.7	47.4	7	16.7
1866–74	8.1	21.3	47.4	12.3	10.6
1880–83	7.8	24.9	47.1	9.6	10.6

Note: The number of employer-initiated cases in 1890–94 is too small to generate any meaningful data through a comparison with those of worker-initiated cases.
Source: AMTg, Conseil des prud'hommes de Tourcoing, Plumitif no. 1, 1821–37; ADN, 5U1–18, 5U1–20, 5U1–21, Régistre des conciliations.

These numbers indicate that the introduction of male workers on the board did not work to the advantage of Tourcoing's employers who sought to settle their workplace disputes in this way. Although workers and employers experienced similar changes, these were much more abrupt for employers and therefore less likely to have been as acceptable as they were for workers. While both groups experienced decreases in the number of victories, the difference between pre- and post-1848 levels was much greater for employers than for workers. Employers, who had previously almost never had to compromise to settle their disputes, found themselves having to do so in half of their cases. This transformed the *prud'hommes* into an institution much less sympathetic to employers than it had been previously, which contributed to their reluctance to use it as a means of settling workplace disputes.

Equal representation in terms of class helped shift the balance of power on Tourcoing's *conseil des prud'hommes* more equitably; but what effect did it have on the performance of working-class plaintiffs in terms of gender? How did the performance of female workers compare to that of their male counterparts? Did the presence of male worker representatives make Tourcoing's board a friendlier place for working-class women, or did the all-male *prud'hommes* favour other male plaintiffs? The increase in the number of working-class women who made use of the *prud'hommes* between 1848 and 1883 would suggest that the reforms of 1848 were in some ways beneficial (Table 4.4).

An analysis of the results of cases brought to Tourcoing's *prud'hommes* by working-class plaintiffs before 1848 indicates that female workers who initiated cases fared better than their male counterparts. Working-class women won more and lost less than working-class men. As a result of their success, they settled for compromise less often.

The changes in performance experienced by male and female worker plaintiffs in the decade following 1848 were similar to those experienced by employers and workers in general: levels of success and loss both fell, while the number of cases settled through compromise increased, particularly for women, as did the overall rates of non-conciliation. As with workers and employers, the overall impact of the introduction of working-class male representatives on Tourcoing's *conseil des prud'hommes* on its rulings in the decade after 1848 was to make them more equitable by emphasizing compromise as a means of settling disputes (Table 4.5).

One change that stands out after 1848 is the significant decrease in the number of cases initiated by working-class women that resulted in victories. Their numbers decreased to a degree comparable to that of employer-initiated cases. Why then, if their rates of success fell so dramatically, did women's presence among working-class plaintiffs increase, whereas the same effect drove employers away? Aside from the fact that the transition into the new, post-1848 *prud'hommes* was an easier task for working-class women than it was for employers, their increased presence among plaintiffs may also lie in the limited number of legal options available to workers. Employers would typically have had much less to lose in settling a dispute with a worker by dismissing them rather than by bringing the case to the *prud'hommes*, especially if the worker worked in an unskilled trade, which many women did, as this made them much easier to replace. The same cannot be so easily said about workers, whose low wages made it much more difficult to risk living extended periods without an income. Therefore, the fact that the *prud'hommes* remained one of the only legal means of settling workplace disputes available to workers contributed to the continued presence of female workers among those using the board's services.

Table 4.5 Outcome of male and female worker-initiated cases, 1821–1894

	Male worker-initiated cases				
	Win (%)	*Loss (%)*	*Compromise (%)*	*Non-conciliated (%)*	*Other/ unspecified (%)*
1821–36	27.5	26.5	42.1	3.9	0
1848, 1852, 1855	11.2	18.6	49.6	7	13.3
1866–74	8	22.5	44.9	13.1	11.2
1880–83	6.7	24.5	47.1	10.7	10.7
1890–94	13.7	3.3	42.5	16.6	23.6
	Female worker-initiated cases				
	Win (%)	*Loss (%)*	*Compromise (%)*	*Non-conciliated (%)*	*Other/ unspecified (%)*
1821–36	40	23.8	34.3	1.9	0
1848, 1852, 1855	9.3	16	46.6	8	22.2
1866–74	8.7	15.4	61.7	7.3	6.7
1880–83	10.2	22.4	22.4	1.3	43.5
1890–94	25.7	0	40	14.2	22.8

Source: AMTg, Conseil des prud'hommes de Tourcoing, Plumitif no. 1, 1821–37; ADN, 5U1–18, 5U1–20, 5U1–21, 5U1–22, Régistre des conciliations.

The Legalization of Strikes and the *Conseil des Prud'hommes*, 1864–1883

The *conseil des prud'hommes* was one of the only legal means for workers to address workplace issues and settle disputes with their employers until the legalization of strikes in 1864. Although the *prud'hommes* did not involve themselves in strikes, an examination of the use of its services following the legalization of strikes could shed light on whether the availability of legal collective action attracted workers away from settling disputes individually.

Strikes were never a popular means of solving workplace issues in Tourcoing. The city's police recorded only five strikes between 1848 and 1864, all of which were short-lived and rarely involved more than a dozen workers. While female workers played a significant role in the city's textile industry, sectors affected by strikes were those with a predominantly male workforce. While it is possible that women did play some role in these actions, it is unlikely that they made up a large percentage of strikers.[26]

Tourcoing's workers were reluctant to adopt confrontational methods to settle workplace disputes, and the legalization of strikes in 1864 did little to change this. Tourcoing's police records recorded very few strikes between 1864 and the end of the century. One exception to this was the large textile strike of 1880, which affected the region's textile industry. According to police records, the strike, which began in neighbouring Roubaix and spread throughout the region, affected 42 workplaces in Tourcoing. Correspondence between local authorities would suggest that this number may have been as high as 57 workplaces, with as many as 5,820 workers out on strike.[27] Regardless of their numbers, for two weeks a variety of workers from a number of sectors of the textile industry took to the streets demanding higher wages and shorter workdays. Although police records and correspondence rarely took the gender of strikers into account, some evidence exists to suggest that a number of women participated in the strike. For example, a number of *soigneuses* were noted to have been among the strikers. In addition to the fact that the word *soigneuses* is a female noun, the 1886 census records of Tourcoing indicate that this occupation was overwhelmingly, if not entirely, female.[28] Police records indicate that at least 1,186 of the strikers were *soigneuses*, which suggests that women may have made up to 20 per cent of the city's strikers. Although some workers began to return to work before the end of the strike on 13 May, a number of sectors with the resources to remain on strike were able to secure wage increases, including a 10 cent increase for the region's *soigneuses*.[29]

Although the strike of 1880 demonstrates that Tourcoing's working class were willing and capable of withholding their labour in order to obtain concessions from their employers, this strike was clearly an exceptional event. The rarity of strikes before and after 1864, as well as the relative stability of the number of workers among plaintiffs in 1864–83, indicates that the legalization of strikes was not enough to convince Tourcoing's workers to settle their workplace grievances collectively rather than individually. The *prud'hommes* served a purpose in the lives of Tourcoing's working class, one that could not be replaced by collective action.

The minimal effect of the legalization of strikes can also be seen in the rulings of the *conseil des prud'hommes* in the decade after the reform, as well as the three

---

26 Archives départementales du Nord (ADN), Grèves 1846–52, M 620 1–15; ADN, Grèves 1860–69, M17 1–9.

27 ADN, Grèves 1880, Tourcoing, M 619 3. Cens, to *L'Écho du Nord*, 8 May 1880; Jacques Marseille and Martine Sassier, *'Si ne veulent point nous rinquérir in va bientôt tout démolir!' Le Nord en grève, avril/mai 1880* (Paris, 1982), 11.

28 Archives Municipales de Tourcoing (AMTg), Recensement de Tourcoing, 1886.

29 Marseille and Sassier, *Le Nord en grève*, p. 120.

years following the general strike of 1880. In the case of worker and employers plaintiffs, the changes in performances noted after 1848 continued virtually uninterrupted (Table 4.3). Even after the legalization of strikes and almost 40 years after the introduction of male workers on the *prud'hommes*, the changes the reform of 1848 brought on the rulings of the board continued unabated: very few of the cases brought to the *prud'hommes* were won; and employers, by the 1880s, found themselves having to settle through compromise in four-fifths of the cases they initiated. Although workers continued to lose cases at a much higher rate than employers, they were now for the first time winning more than their employers.

Post-1848 trends noted among working-class male and female plaintiffs also continued into the decade following the legalization of strikes, as rates of success remained low and compromise high. However, this period saw the situation of male and female worker plaintiffs begin to differ. While both were winning at similar rates, female workers were much less likely to lose their cases and much more likely to settle through compromise. They were also half as likely to not reach a settlement as their male counterparts.

As for the early 1880s, they proved to be a relatively kinder period for female working-class plaintiffs at the *prud'hommes* than for male workers. Both groups were more likely to lose their case, but women were twice as likely to win as men. Although the number of compromises fell to a level equal to that of men, their rate of non-conciliation was almost half of what it was for male workers, indicating that they continued to be more likely to walk away from their cases with a settlement. The only downfall for the performance of working-class women was the near doubling of their rate of loss.

Overall, in comparison to the performance of working-class male plaintiffs, the introduction of male workers on the *prud'hommes* helped improve the situation of working-class women who went on the offensive. Although their levels of success dropped, they remained above those of men and levels of non-conciliation were significantly lower than those of male workers by the 1880s. Therefore, the continued levels of success and conciliation met by female workers gave them little reason to turn their backs on the board.

Problematizing Gender: Skill and Age at the *Prud'hommes*

While the inclusion of male worker representatives on Tourcoing's *conseil des prud'hommes* was generally an improvement for working-class women who used the board's services, this was not the case for all women. This situation changes when the categories of gender are broken down even further and divided by age and occupational skill level.

A comparison of the performance of female worker plaintiffs overall and those from unskilled occupations makes it clear that the skill level of one's occupation played a direct role in shaping their experience at the *prud'hommes*. Female worker plaintiffs from unskilled occupations won less, lost more and settled fewer cases through compromise than female worker plaintiffs overall. While male worker plaintiffs from unskilled occupations also had lower rates of success and compromise than male worker plaintiffs as a whole, they also experienced a lower rate of loss. This proves that male and female gender always intersects with other aspects of difference such as class and social background.

The socio-economic standing of these workers may also have been responsible for their lower rate of non-conciliation. Although records do not indicate which party refused the conciliation proposed by the *prud'hommes*, the tendency of workers from unskilled occupations to receive lower wages may have affected their ability to reject a proposed solution. Because attending a hearing at the *prud'hommes* required missing work, the decision to miss a day would therefore not have been taken as lightly by unskilled workers as it would have been for men and those from a skilled occupation The fact that rejecting conciliation would have meant missing a second day of work, not to mention the possibility of an unfavourable ruling, would have made rejection a more difficult proposition for unskilled workers, particularly women, whose wages were already typically lower than that of men. Overall, the fact is that working-class plaintiffs from unskilled occupations, regardless of their gender, received less favourable treatment at the *prud'hommes* than workers as a whole, and that the skill level of one's occupation may have played an important role, perhaps as important as gender, in shaping the outcome of one's case in the post-1848 period (Table 4.6).

The comparative performance between male and female plaintiffs also changes when the distinction is made between minor and adult working-class plaintiffs. The records of Tourcoing's *prud'hommes* were not always consistent in their recording of the age of plaintiffs. The only sample period in which the records indicated whether the plaintiffs were minors or not was the 1880–83 period.[30]

If this sample is representative of the trend in other periods, it would suggest that the performances of male and female working-class minors at the *prud'hommes* differed from those of male and female working-class plaintiffs in general. This suggests that age, like skill, could affect the outcome of one's case.

---

30 The age of the plaintiffs was never provided, but the French Law of 20 September 1792 defines the *âge de la majorité civile* as 21 years for both men and women.

Table 4.6 Outcome of male and female unskilled worker-initiated cases, 1821–1894

Male unskilled worker-initiated cases					
Period	*Win (%)*	*Loss (%)*	*Compromise (%)*	*Non-conciliated (%)*	*Other/ unspecified (%)*
1821–36	35	30	19	3	0
1848, 1852, 1855	7.1	19.6	42.8	1.7	12.5
1866–74	8.6	11.9	26.4	4.9	5.5
1880–83	2.4	21.9	21.1	7.3	2.4
1890–94	10.4	1.6	32	5.6	16.8
Female unskilled worker-initiated cases					
Period	*Win (%)*	*Loss (%)*	*Compromise (%)*	*Non-conciliated (%)*	*Other/ unspecified (%)*
1821–36	40	23.8	34.2	1.9	0
1848, 1852, 1855	8.3	14.5	29.1	10.4	16.5
1866–74	4.3	9.2	35.6	2.9	3.9
1880–83	6.8	12.2	20.6	2.2	3.8
1890–94	9	0	23.6	5.4	10.8

Source: AMTg, Conseil des prud'hommes de Tourcoing, Plumitif no. 1, 1821–37; ADN, 5U1–18, 5U1–20, 5U1–21, 5U1–22, Régistre des conciliations.

Table 4.7 Outcome of male and female minor working-class plaintiffs, 1880–1883

	Male		**Female**	
	All (%)	*Minors (%)*	*All (%)*	*Minors (%)*
Win	6.7	5.5	10.2	3.3
Loss	24.5	22.2	22.4	26.6
Compromise	47.1	26.3	22.4	53.3
Non-conciliated	10.7	2.7	1.3	6.6
Other/ unspecified	10.7	43	43.5	10

Source: ADN, 5U1–21, Régistre des conciliations.

Unions, Socialists and Tourcoing's *Conseil des Prud'hommes*

Between the introduction of working-class male representatives in 1848 and the legalization of unions in 1884, Tourcoing's employers turned their backs on the city's *conseil des prud'hommes*. The board was no longer the employer-friendly institution that it had once been. The rulings of the board were now more equitable, with many more cases settled through compromise rather than clear victories or losses. Unlike the legalization of strikes, the legalization of unions and the growing influence of socialism in the city and surrounding region had a more noticeable impact on the *prud'hommes*.

Police files on unions recorded only 12 active unions headquartered in Tourcoing during the second half of the nineteenth century, but this did not mean that workers did not belong to other organizations.[31] Several unions in northern France were regional in nature and encompassed multiple cities within their jurisdiction. Five of the 12 recorded unions in Tourcoing included workers from outside the city and carried names such as the *Syndicat des ouvriers de l'industrie textile de Tourcoing et environs* (Union of Textile Industry Workers of Tourcoing and Surrounding Region). A number of these unions were later absorbed into larger regional unions. For example, Tourcoing's *Chambre syndicale ouvrière de l'industrie textile 'l'union fraternelle des travailleurs' de Tourcoing et ses environs* (Union of Textile Industry Workers 'the fraternal union of workers' of Tourcoing and Surrounding Region) was absorbed into the *Chambre syndicale ouvrière textile de Roubaix et environs* (Union of Textile Workers of Roubaix and Surrounding Region) in May of 1896.[32]

Although unions were illegal before 1884, workers in Tourcoing and neighbouring cities had a history of organizing to protect their common interests. Police records on union activity indicate that at least five unions were headquartered in the city before 1884, with some organizing openly as early as 1881. This would suggest that, although illegal, local authorities nevertheless tolerated unions. Unfortunately, information on union membership is very limited. Those records that do provide information on members only seem to have done so after 1894, leaving little information on their size before this date. At this date, however, union membership was not particularly high, ranging from the 10 registered members of the *Chambre syndicale des ouvriers en bâtiments* (Union of Construction Workers) to the 150 members in the *Chambre syndicale des ouvriers tapissiers en grosse moquette* (Union of Workers in Large Carpeting).[33]

The political activities of Tourcoing's unions also attracted the attention of the police, as the authorities feared that they would provide a breeding ground

31 ADN, Syndicats ouvriers à Tourcoing, M 596 61–9.

32 Ibid.

33 Ibid.

for socialist agitation, a fear that was not altogether unfounded. As Patricia Hilden points out, the activities of the socialist *Parti ouvrier Français* (French Workers' Party, hereafter POF) were so closely linked to the activities of many textile unions that union meetings often doubled as party meetings.[34] One of Tourcoing's unions, the *Chambre syndicale ouvrière textile de Tourcoing et des environs*, was described by police as being 'composed entirely of workers who, following their beliefs, belong to the socialist party and occupy themselves more with questions of politics than work.'[35] It was also noted that another union, the *Chambre syndicale ouvrière de l'industrie textile 'L'union fraternelle des travailleurs' de Tourcoing et ses environs*, served as more of a 'centre of propaganda rather than a union as it concerned itself with political questions rather than working conditions.'[36]

Some of this 'propaganda' and political work involved the *conseil des prud'hommes*. As previously mentioned, scholars such as Pélisse and Lemercier have argued that the *prud'hommes* played an important role in shaping the strategies of the union movement. Unions were particularly interested in the role of the *prud'hommes* in settling workplace disputes. Because it provided a forum to confront employers and win gains for workers, many unions adopted policies and procedures to regulate their relationship with the board. A number of unions made references to the *prud'hommes* in their bylaws and constitutions, with many viewing it as a positive institution that could be incorporated into their tactics and strategies. In fact, most unions offered support for members who initiated cases at the *prud'hommes*. This support was usually financial or came in the form of providing experts who could serve as witnesses or could evaluate a worker's performance, depending on the nature of the conflict.[37]

Like unions, the POF also encouraged members to make use of the *prud'hommes* to challenge their employers. For the socialists in the POF, the *prud'hommes* were another battleground in the class struggle against employers, and for this reason they argued that workers had 'the duty to bring their case to the attention of the *conseil des prud'hommes*' and fight for whatever they felt there were entitled to.[38] In other words, conciliation was not their preferred method of settlement. In addition to encouraging workers to use the board, the POF also regularly ran their own candidates in board elections, sometimes successfully, claiming that it was the only way to ensure that working-class representatives were free from the influence of employers.[39]

---

34 Hilden, *Working Women and Socialist Politics in France*, 123.

35 Ibid.

36 Ibid.

37 ADN, Syndicats ouvriers à Roubaix, M 596 59. Chambre syndicale des ouvriers lainiers: projet de statuts.

38 *Le Cri du Travailleur*, 4–11 February 1888.

39 Ibid., 26 October–8 November 1888.

The use of the *prud'hommes* declined significantly in the years following the legalization of unions, from an average of 218 cases per year in 1880–83, to 142 in the first half of the 1890s. This decrease is in large part due to the fact that, by the 1890s, the disinterest of employers in using the *prud'hommes* had caused them to all but abandon the board altogether. In a decade, the number of cases initiated by employers fell from 17.5 per cent to less than 3 per cent, leaving only 20 employer-initiated cases in the first half of the 1890s.

Perhaps more surprising than the decline of employer plaintiffs is the sudden decrease in the use of the *prud'hommes* by female workers, whose numbers among plaintiffs was cut in half in the early 1890s. What is most curious about this is that their numbers fell at a time when their results at the board were as good as they had ever been. In the early 1890s, female workers who initiated cases were winning more frequently and losing less frequently than they had in the past.

The rate of success for female working-class plaintiffs was at its highest since before 1848, yet female workers were using the *prud'hommes* in fewer numbers. The only noticeable significant decline in the performance of female worker plaintiffs was a slight decrease in the compromises and an increase in the number of cases resulting in non-conciliation. Factors other than performance are therefore likely to have contributed to their reluctance to use the *prud'hommes*. One such factor was the growing political tension at the *prud'hommes* between worker and employer representatives.

Correspondence from Tourcoing's *prud'hommes* indicates that union and socialist interests in the *prud'hommes* in the 1880s were viewed by some board members as a disruptive influence on the city's workers. For example, in the 1883 annual report on the board's activities, board president and employer representative Louis-Bernard Cuvillier elaborated on the *prud'hommes*' relations with the city's working-class. He stated that these relations would be perfect had some workers not been so 'completely dominated by the labour unions that seem to oppose our mission, which is conciliation. It is impossible to reach conciliation in these circumstances.'[40] Cuvillier repeated these sentiments in the following year's report. Once again commenting on board members' relationships with workers, Cuvillier stated that these would be without problems if it were not for the unions demanding that the board issue rulings at the *bureau générale* instead of offering conciliation at the *bureau particulier*.[41] While some employer representatives might have pointed to the number of cases failing to settle through conciliation as the result of union and socialist interference in *prud'hommes* business, some worker representatives laid the blame for this squarely at the feet

---

40 ADN, Correspondance, 1884–1904, M-5U1–38, État des travaux du Prud'hommes en 1883.

41 ADN, Correspondance, 1884–1904, M-5U1–38, État des travaux du Prud'hommes en 1884.

of employer representatives. One such accusation was made in 1886 by worker representative Victor Liétard, who accused the board's secretary of actively discouraging workers from pursuing their employers at the *prud'hommes*. This accusation was later substantiated by the board's president, Cuvillier, who, in a statement exemplifying the paternalism of the region's employers, admitted that the secretary had only done so to prevent workers from losing their cases.[42] Similar accusations were made in 1892, when Liétard, as well as Joseph Volt-Catteau, a POF candidate and worker representative on the board, accused employers on the board of systematically ruling against workers.[43]

Tension between worker and employer representatives in this period was not unique to Tourcoing, as the reforms of 1880 launched a series of contests for control of the *prud'hommes* across France. One of the reasons for this competition was the redefining of the positions of president and vice-president as elected positions. According to Marcel David, employers saw this as an attack on their supremacy in the *prud'hommes* as the president could cast the deciding vote in the case of a tie at the *bureau générale*.[44] This fear of worker-controlled boards was made more serious in the 1880s, when working-class organizations such as unions and the POF not only encouraged workers to reject conciliation with their employers, but also called on worker representatives to adopt their *mandat impératif*, a pledge to always vote to support the claims of working-class plaintiffs.[45] Although it is unclear whether Tourcoing's worker representatives ever adopted the *mandat impératif*, the increase in victories and the decrease in losses experienced by working-class plaintiffs in the early 1890s would suggest that it might have been adopted by some of the city's board members. This would in turn suggest that the POF's message to workers and working-class representatives to put the cause of workers before the cause of conciliation found a receptive audience among at least part of Tourcoing's working class.

By the end of the nineteenth century, all of these came together to create an environment of increased tension and competition at Tourcoing's *conseil des prud'hommes*. In addition to contributing to the spike in the number of cases that failed to reach a settlement through conciliation, the increased tension at the *prud'hommes* may have also been a contributing factor in the decline in female working-class use of the board's services. As Craig has argued, the low female use of the board before 1848 was likely attributable to its status as a site of male

[42] ADN, 5U1–38, Correspondance 1884–1902, Louis Bernard Cuvillier, Président du Conseil des Prud'hommes de Tourcoing, to Maire de Tourcoing, 30 December 1886.

[43] ADN, 5U1–38, Correspondance 1884–1902, Lemaire-Caulliez, Président du Conseil des Prud'hommes de Tourcoing, to Maire de Tourcoing, undated.

[44] David, 'L'évolution historique des conseils de prud'hommes en France', p. 15.

[45] The *mandat impératif* was encouraged as a strategy from 1880 until 1905, when a new law replaced the power to break a tie by the president of the board and it was granted to a justice of the peace instead. Pélisse, 'Les usages syndicaux du droit et de la justice', p. 167.

sociability, therefore decreasing the attractiveness of the institution as a site for justice for women. If, as the numbers suggest, working-class women after 1848 grew more comfortable with and confident in the ability of the *prud'hommes* to provide them with justice, it is possible that increased tension at the board affected their confidence in the institution. This may especially be the case given that the tension was largely over issues that were out of the reach of women, that is the election of and power struggles between board members. As for the role of unions and the POF in this tension, as Hilden points out, although women were not formally excluded from their ranks, the attention given to women's issues was negligible at this point, as the POF's success at the polls had encouraged them to focus on electoral politics rather than grassroots mobilization. The absence of female suffrage therefore provided the party with little incentive to pursue support from female workers and contributed to the marginalization of women's issues, and to some extent women themselves, within the POF.[46] The POF's appeal for workers to refuse compromise at the *prud'hommes* may therefore have been better heeded by working-class men than by their female counterparts, once again transforming the board into an increasingly masculine space and undoing some of the progress achieved with the introduction of working-class representatives half a century earlier.

Conclusion

Tourcoing's *conseil des prud'hommes* before 1848 was a friendly environment for the city's employers. Not only was control of the institution completely in their hands, but also the rulings issued tended to lean heavily in their favour. This changed following the limited, and gendered, democratization of the *prud'hommes* that saw the introduction of working-class male representatives in 1848. After this date, the *prud'hommes* ceased to be the employer-friendly place it had once been as cases were settled through compromise rather than by assigning clear victories or defeats. The paternalistic worldview of employers made the idea of sharing power with and being judged by workers difficult to accept. This was made even more so when the rulings at the *prud'hommes* ceased to grant them the number of victories it once had, forcing them settle through compromise instead. This did not bode well for employers, whose use of the *prud'hommes* consequently began to decline. By the end of the nineteenth century, employers had ceased to use the board almost altogether.

Despite the negative impact of this reform on the views of employers towards the *prud'hommes*, the increased presence of working-class women using the board's services suggests that the presence of their male counterparts on

46 Hilden, *Working Women and Socialist Politics in France*.

the board improved their view of the *prud'hommes* as a site of redress against perceived injustices at work. Although the prevalence of compromise after 1848 also came at the cost of the number of cases won by workers, the more equitable rulings did not lead to an exodus of workers from the *prud'hommes* as it had for employers.

These trends continued largely unabated between 1848 and the mid 1880s, but the political atmosphere in Tourcoing and at the *prud'hommes* changed by the last decade of the century. Unions and the socialist *Parti ouvrier Français* took a particular interest in the board, seeing it as a tool in the class struggle. The tension caused by their attention to the *prud'hommes*, especially at a time of heightened tension between worker and employer representatives over control of the board, contributed to a growing climate of tension and confrontation at the board that resulted in more cases failing to settle through conciliation. Unsurprisingly, the increased tension and inability of board members to settle cases drove employers further away from the *prud'hommes*. However, the increasingly hostile climate seemed to have had an unexpected side effect of deterring female workers from using the *prud'hommes*' services, as their proportion among plaintiffs fell to their lowest levels ever.

Overall, the act of opening up the *prud'hommes* to male workers in 1848 had a mixed impact on the use of their services in Tourcoing. While the more equitable distribution of power between worker and employer representatives caused employers to turn their backs on the board, the growing number of working-class women using its services indicates that the presence of a working-class voice, regardless of its gender, increased their confidence in the ability of the *prud'hommes* to deliver justice. However, the presence of a working-class voice also contributed to the emergence of political and class-based tensions. By the end of the century, these tensions, combined with the added influence of unions and of the POF, had culminated to create a situation in which the conciliation and compromise that had been in part made possible by the reforms of 1848 were increasingly difficult to achieve. Therefore, while the reforms of 1848 and the inclusion of male worker representatives were positive in terms of increasing female working-class confidence in the *prud'hommes*, whatever progress was achieved through these reforms was in large part undone by their impact on the state of class relations between worker and employer representatives serving on Tourcoing's *conseil des prud'hommes*. This evolution seems to confirm early feminist theory based on difference, stating that women more than men are inclined towards acting in terms of autonomy and consensus, withdrawing themselves whenever political antagonism starts prevailing over conciliation and individual approaches. It also painfully illustrates the marginalization of women's issues by early socialist party and union politics.

Bibliography

Manuscript Sources

Archives départementales du Nord (ADN), 5U1–18, 5U1–20, 5U1–21, 5U1–22, Régistre des conciliations.

Archives Municipales de Tourcoing (AMTg), Conseil des prud'hommes de Tourcoing, Plumitif no. 1, 1821–37; ADN, 5U1–18, 5U1–20, 5U1–21, 5U1–22, Régistre des conciliations.

Printed Sources

Brûlé, Mathieu, *Reforming Arbitration: Class, Gender and the Conseil des Prud'hommes in Tourcoing, 1848–1894* (Master diss., University of Ottawa, 2009).

Craig, Béatrice, 'La structure de l'emploi féminine dans une ville en voie d'industrialisation: Tourcoing au XIXe siècle', *Canadian Journal of History/ Annales canadiennes d'histoire*, 28 (August 1992): 299–332.

Craig, Béatrice, 'Justice bourgeoise? Justice masculine? Les conseils des prud'hommes au début du XIXe siècle: l'exemple de Tourcoing', *Histoire sociale*, 25/50 (November 1992): 257–82.

Craig, Béatrice, 'Salaire, niveaux de vie et travail féminin, dans l'arrondissement de Lille', *Canadian Journal of History/Annales canadiennes d'histoire*, 33 (August 1998): 215–47.

David, Marcel, 'L'évolution historique des conseils de prud'hommes en France', *Droit Social*, 2 (February 1974): 3–21.

Delsalle, Paul, 'Tisserands et fabricants chez les prud'hommes dans la région de Lille-Roubaix-Tourcoing (1840–1848),' *Le Mouvement social*, 141 (October–November 1987): 61–80.

Desban, Suzanne, and Jeffrey Merrick (ed.), *Family, Gender and Law in Early Modern France* (University Park: Pennsylvania State University Press, 2009).

Farcy, Jean-Claude, *L'histoire de le justice française de la révolution à nos jours* (Paris: Presses Universitaires de France, 2001).

Hilden, Patricia, *Working Women and Socialist Politics in France, 1880–1914: A Regional Study* (Oxford: Clarendon Press, 1986).

Kieffer, Monique, 'La législation prud'homale de 1806 à 1907', *Le Mouvement social*, 141 (October–December 1987): 9–23.

Lemercier, Claire, 'Discipliner le commerce sans corporations. La loi, le juge, l'arbitre et le commerçant à Paris au XIXe siècle', *Le Mouvement social*, 224 (July–September 2008): 61–74.

Marseille, Jacques, and Martine Sassier, *'Si ne veulent point nous rinquérir in va bientôt tout démolir!' Le Nord en grève, avril/mai 1880* (Paris: Jacques Marseille-Martine Sassier, 1982).
McPherson, William H., and Frederic Meyers, *The French Labor Courts: Judgment by Peers* (Urbana: University of Illinois, 1966).
Mellaerts, Wim, 'In the Shadow of Justice: Popular Uses of the Law in Urban Normandy, c. 1880–1905', *French History*, 14/2 (2000): 174–200.
Pélisse, Jérôme, 'Les usages syndicaux du droit et de la justice', in Jacques Commaille and Martine Kaluszynski (ed.), *La fonction publique de la justice* (Paris: La Découverte Recherches/Territoires du politique, 2007).
Tellier, Thibault, 'Les nouvelles clôtures urbaines à l'âge industrielle: l'encadrement religieux des jeunes ouvrières du textile dans l'agglomération lilloise à la fin du XIXe siècle', *Histoire, économie et société*, 24/2 (2005): 421–31.
Willard, Claude, 'Les attaques contre Notre-Dame de l'usine', *Le Mouvement social*, 57 (October–December 1966): 203–9.

Chapter 5

Bending the *Code Civil*: Married Women, their Capacity to Engage in Contracts and the Partnership between Spouses (Belgium, 1804–*c.* 1865)

Dave De ruysscher

Introduction

It is a surprising fact that the contractual incapacity and the general position of married women in private law in nineteenth-century Belgium and France has not often been studied, even though it is a recurrent theme in generalizing publications of legal history.[1] The respective contents of the 1804 French (Napoleonic) Civil code, which was imposed on the Southern Netherlands (that is today's Belgium) by French occupants and which remained in force in Belgium throughout the 1800s, are often presented without much consideration for their detail and full legal implications. Moreover, the interpretation of the rigid 1804 Civil code in Belgian legal practice of the nineteenth century is still largely a black box.[2] The legal context is nonetheless important for assessments of the role of women in nineteenth-century society, and for the history of the

---

[1] Traditional and generalizing views on these matters can be found in the secondary literature cited in footnote 10, and in most course handbooks of continental legal history. An exception in this regard is David Deroussin, *Histoire du droit privé (XVIe–XXIe siècle)* (Paris, 2010), pp. 196–204. The history of the sections of the 1804 Civil code regarding married women has been detailed by Jean Gay. See: Jean Gay, 'Capacité de la femme mariée et puissance maritale dans l'élaboration du Code civil', *Revue de l'Institut Napoléon*, 161 (1993/2): pp. 33–65, 162 (1994/1): pp. 51–64, and 163 (1994/2): pp. 19–43. A summarized version of this chapter has been published in *Mémoires de la Société pour l'histoire du droit et des institutions des anciens pays bourguignons, comtois et romands* (1993), pp. 129–45.

[2] This is so for many themes of nineteenth-century Belgian private law. See: Dirk Heirbaut, 'Les juges belges face au Code civil aux 19ième et 20ième siècles: l'exemple des troubles de voisinage', in Barbara Dölemeyer, Heinz Mohnhaupt and Alessandro Somma (ed.), *Richterliche Anwendung des Code civil in seinen europäischen Geltungsbereichen außerhalb Frankreichs* (Frankfurt am Main, 2006), pp. 257–8.

family of this period. Historians and sociologists have recently underscored that in the course of the nineteenth century, in Belgium and elsewhere, there was a progressive trend towards reappraisal of the mother, which came along with a modest, egalitarian approach within marriage.[3] Legal history may help further nuancing such views.

In this chapter, it is argued that already in the early nineteenth century Belgian legal practice went some way in acknowledging contractual rights of married women. Both in the French and in the France-orientated Belgian legal scenes, for this issue legal scholars and judges made use of the few escape routes that were found within the 1804 Civil code in order to juristically acknowledge the part a wife could have in running the family estate and in managing her property. However, in spite of some softening approaches, in Belgium over the whole period of the nineteenth century legal discrimination of married women did not decrease substantially. In legal practice some of the harsh provisions of the law were mitigated, but gender equality as such was not a goal. Belgian judges, together with French legal authors, reacted against some of the Civil code's inconsistencies, but they did not want a fundamental revision of the legal articles regarding the position of married women.

The 1804 Civil code was clearly discriminatory, and it is remarkable that many of its biased sections continued to be applied even in the twentieth century. It was only in the first decades of the 1900s that political will, albeit slowly, made a thorough change of the law possible. The philosophy behind the articles of the original 1804 Civil code required a woman's submission to her husband following marriage. Exceptions to this underlying principle mostly resulted from situations in which the husband was unable to administer the household, or from his cooperation. The agreement between spouses as to the community of property, which is foremost found in the marriage contract, was for a large part irrelevant for the legal position of the wife, and even contractual separation of assets did not always revive the wife's rights. It has been pointed out that these strict rules, as well as other provisions of law that were issued under the French Consulate and Empire of Napoleon, purported to prevent illegitimate births and to stimulate family unity and parental responsibility.[4] Such articles of law did not correspond with the rules that had applied in the Belgian regions before the French occupation in 1795, and the tempering responses of Belgian jurists after 1804 were also inspired by these older legal solutions.

---

[3] Koen Matthijs, 'Changing Patterns of Familial Sociability: Family Members as Witnesses to (Re)Marriage in Nineteenth-Century Flanders', *Journal of Family History*, 31 (2006): pp. 115–43; Bart Van de Putte et al., 'The Rise of Age Homogamy in 19th Century Western Europe', *Journal of Marriage and Family*, 71 (2009): pp. 1234–53.

[4] June K. Burton, *Napoleon and the Women Question: Discourses of the Other Sex in French Education, Medicine and Medical Law, 1799–1815* (Austin, 2007), pp. 201–2; Suzanne Desan, *The Family on Trial in Revolutionary France* (Berkeley, 2004), pp. 283–310.

In this contribution, judgements and legal literature for the period between 1804 and until around 1865 are analysed.[5] The geographical focus is on the kingdom of Belgium, and mostly on the province of Brabant and its main legal centre, Brussels. Yet, since the intertwinement between French and Belgian legal science remained very strong even after the end of Napoleon's power over the Belgian provinces in 1814,[6] the interactions between French legal literature and Belgian legal practice are also considered. As in France, Belgian jurists remained generally conservative throughout the nineteenth century, even though in both countries some exceptions to the general sexist legal principles were gradually broadened. The end date of 1865 marks the first feminist protests against the Civil code in France.[7] The *Principes de droit civil* (1870) and the proposed reforms of the (Belgian) Civil code (1879–82), which were drafted by the Belgian jurist and law professor François Laurent and which incorporated the mentioned interpretations of legal practice too, conclude this period. In order to illustrate the stickiness of the 1804 legal regime regarding married women, however, the final paragraph goes into the legislative initiatives

[5] The studied judgements were all published in legal journals such as *Pasicrisie belge* (hereinafter *Pasicrisie*, sometimes specified with *(Arrêts des Cours d'Appel)* when two volumes were published in a same year, one for judgements of the Cassation Courts and one containing judgements of Courts of Appeal) and *La Belgique Judiciaire*. The first journal printed the complete text of remarkable judgements of Belgian and French Courts of Appeal and of the Cassation Courts of both countries since 1832. The second one was started in 1842, and contains (Belgian and French) verdicts that were pronounced by Courts of Appeal and the Cassation Courts, but also some that were issued by other tribunals. Both journals published the arguments of the claimant and defendant as summarized in the judgement. For a general overview of nineteenth-century Belgian law journals, see: Dirk Heirbaut, 'Law Reviews in Belgium (1763–2004): Instruments of Legal Practice and Linguistic Conflicts', in Michael Stolleis and Thomas Simon (ed.), *Juristische Zeitschriften in Europa* (Frankfurt am Main, 2006), pp. 343–67. In principle, no exhaustive conclusions can be drawn from such published judgements, since for diverse reasons many nineteenth-century judicial decisions remained unpublished. See, in this respect: Régine Beauthier, 'Le juge et le lit conjugal au XIXe siècle', in Marie-Thérèse Coenen (ed.), *Corps de femmes: sexualité et contrôle social* (Brussels, 2002), pp. 40–41. This notwithstanding, the consistency between legal doctrine and the judgements analysed hereafter allows for an assessment of crucial developments.

[6] Dirk Heirbaut, 'The Belgian Legal Tradition: Does it Exist?', in Hubert Bocken and Walter De Bondt (ed.), *Introduction to Belgian Law* (Brussels, 2000), pp. 10–13.

[7] In the 1860s, Léon Richer and Maria Deraismes started lobbying for a change of legal status of married women in France. In 1868, Richer founded the journal *Droit des femmes*. In Belgium, the feminist movement was launched only in the later 1880s. See: Eliane Gubin, 'Du politique au politique: parcours du féminisme belge (1830–1914)', in Hans Moors (ed.), *Fabrics of Feminism: Comparative Analysis of Nineteenth-Century Gender Discourse in Belgium and the Netherlands* [*Revue belge de philologie et d'histoire*, 77 (1999)] (Brussels, 1999), pp. 370–82.

of the later nineteenth century and of the twentieth century on this subject and into their protracted results.

The 1804 Civil Code, the Double Standard and the Conjugal Bond

The French Civil code of 1804 contained several detailed rules regarding the rights of married women in contractual and private law affairs, and with regard to their place within the household. In many respects, this codification enshrined the double standard. A striking example concerns the authorization of parents as to a marriage of their children. According to the Civil code, both the mother and father had to consent. However, it was also provided that, if the parents disagreed between themselves, the father had the deciding opinion.[8] Another example relates to the unequal freedom of choice of domicile. A married woman was held to follow her husband and live together with him. Only the husband had the right to decide where the household would be established, and not the wife.[9]

With regard to the position of married women in contractual affairs, the compilers of the Civil code designed a strict regime. According to the Civil code, marriage reduced the wife to incapacity, which could only be remedied by the cooperation of her husband. A married woman was considered to be on the same level as minors and as persons being incapable because of 'idiocy, insanity, or madness' (sections 489 and 1124). Most compilers of the Civil code, and jurists commenting on its articles, stressed that the – then commonly accepted – *faiblesse de sexe* of women was not the prime motive for these rules, but rather the fact that marriage entailed a partnership between husband and wife (*société conjugale*, conjugal partnership). The husband was deemed to be the only *chef et organe* of this association.[10] The fact that he was considered to

---

[8] Section 148 Civil code.

[9] Sections 213–14 Civil code. Section 213 explicitly provided that the wife owed obedience to her husband.

[10] *Discours préliminaire*, in Pierre-Antoine Fenet, *Recueil complet des travaux préparatoires du Code civil* (15 vols, Paris, 1827–28), vol. 1, p. 486. Doctrinal views along these lines can be found in: André Jean Simon Nougarède de Fayet, *Lois du mariage et du divorce, depuis leur origine dans le droit romain* (Paris, 1816), pp. 353–4; Carl Salomé Zachariae, *Le droit civil français (avec des annotations de G. Massé et CH. Vergé)* (5 vols, Paris, 1854–60), vol. 1, p. 231. See also: Michèle Bordeaux, 'Le maître et l'infidèle. Des relations personnelles entre mari et femme de l'ancien droit au Code civil', in Irène Théry and Christian Biet (ed.), *La famille, la loi, l'état de la Révolution au Code civil* (Paris, 1989), pp. 432–5; Philippe Godding, 'La femme sous puissance maritale (1804–1958)', in Luc Courtois, Jean Pirotte and Françoise Rosart (ed.), *Femmes et pouvoirs. Flux et reflux de l'émancipation féminine depuis un siècle* (Louvain-la-Neuve, 1992), pp. 19–20; Gabriel Lepointe, 'La femme au XIXe siècle

be the director of the partnership existing between the spouses is clear in the paragraphs of the Civil code imposing authorization for most property-related and contractual acts of the wife. Section 217, for example, stipulated that a married woman could not give, alienate, pledge or acquire by free or chargeable title without the concurrence of her husband in the act or without his consent in writing. As *organe* of the matrimonial partnership, the husband was supposed to organize and oversee the household. He represented the matrimonial community of property, and as a result, he always had to be summoned to court for debts involving this community. Only exceptionally – when the husband was incapable, absent or detained – could his wife act independently.[11]

The incapacity of wives that had been laid down in the Civil code was, and particularly when being compared with the rules that had applied in the Old Regime, extreme. In the seventeenth and eighteenth centuries, many localities in France and the Southern Netherlands had allowed married women to acquire assets and to incur obligations when the contracts signed were beneficial for the matrimonial community or for the husband. These rules were often combined with a right to retreat. If a married woman had signed a contract that proved detrimental afterwards, she could have the contract annulled. In many places this was not accepted if the contract had been reciprocal (ie if the benefits of the agreement compensated the contractual duties), or if some other profit for the community property could be demonstrated. As a result, a profitable contract signed by a married woman, even without the prescribed assistance or authorization of her husband, was nonetheless valid.[12] A second difference

en France et dans le monde de l'Europe occidentale', in *La Femme* [Recueils de la Société Jean Bodin pour l'histoire comparative des institutions, 12] (Brussels, 1962), p. 504. Even though these authors refer to the eighteenth-century views of Pothier, who had underscored a natural weakness of women, and to comparable remarks made by compiler Portalis, other authors of the Civil code and most commentators did not support such considerations. Most of them remarked on the inconsistency with the legal position of unmarried women. Because the latter were capable of signing contracts, incapacity for married women could not be based on the argument of 'natural' characteristics pertaining to sex. See: Régine Beauthier, 'Construction du divorce et des relations entre époux dans les travaux préparatoires du Code Napoléon', in Anne Devillé and Olivier Paye (ed.), *Les femmes et le droit. Constructions idéologiques et pratiques sociales* (Brussels, 1999), pp. 80–83.

11 Section 222 Civil code.

12 See: Dave De ruysscher, 'The Capacity of Married Women to Engage in Contracts: Emancipation Through *Ius Commune* in the Southern Netherlands (12th–18th Centuries)', in Grethe Jacobsen and Heide Wunder (ed.), *East Meets West: A Gendered View of Legal Tradition* (forthcoming). For France, see: Pierre Petot and André Vandenbossche, 'La femme dans les pays coutumiers français', in *La Femme* [Recueils de la Société Jean Bodin pour l'histoire comparative des institutions, 12] (Brussels, 1962), pp. 246–7 and p. 249, footnote 7. When academic doctrine (*ius commune*) became more accepted in France in the fifteenth and sixteenth centuries, the concept of nullity was projected onto older rules.

with the older legislation concerned the property regime during marriage. In the Civil code, the type of marriage contract that had been chosen by the spouses had virtually no impact on the legal position of the wife. Even when a matrimonial community had been excluded and the spouses were completely separate in property, the wife could not alienate her privately owned immovable assets without her husband's consent (sections 217 and 1449). This had not been the case in many legal systems of the Old Regime.[13]

Limited Legal Possibilities for Household Management by Married Women

These provisions within the Civil code have led many authors to present the incapacity of married women in nineteenth-century France and Belgium, with regard to private law (contracts, matrimonial property, land law), as absolute.[14] However, within the Civil code some exceptions to the mentioned articles of law were acknowledged as well. The rule that was most far-reaching in this respect provided that only the husband, the wife and their heirs could raise the nullity of a contract that had been signed by the wife without her husband's consent (section 225). This nullity was relative, and not absolute. This meant that such a contract could be declared invalid, but only if the mentioned parties objected to the contract. The agreement was not null and void by law, but voidable. If the contracting woman and her husband acknowledged its contents, or refrained from a complaint, the contract was and remained lawful. The number of persons who could apply for annulment was limited. The parties who had signed a contract with a married woman could not challenge the validity of such a contract for the reason of absence of marital consent. This was so even when the woman with whom they had negotiated had been married but had not mentioned the fact, or when she had pretended to act with the consent of her husband.[15] Creditors could neither prevent nor reverse a nullity that was sought

---

The *Coutumes* of Paris of 1580 (section 223), for example, imposed nullity of the act that had been performed by a married woman without her husband's authorization. However, this was a relative nullity, which could only be invoked by the husband, the wife and their heirs. This section served as an example for section 225 of the Civil code. See: Petot and Vandenbossche, 'La femme', p. 247, footnote 3.

13 Ibid., p. 249.

14 Gustaaf Baeteman and Jean-Pierre Lauwers, 'Le statut de la femme dans le droit belge depuis le Code civil', in *La Femme* [Recueils de la Société Jean Bodin pour l'histoire comparative des institutions, 12] (Brussels, 1962), p. 581; Godding, 'La femme sous puissance maritale (1804–1958)', pp. 26–7; Lepointe, 'La femme', p. 504.

15 Charles-Bonaventure-Marie Toullier, *Le droit civil français, suivant l'ordre du Code civil ...* (13 vols, Paris, 1824–28), vol. 2, 17 (nos 622–3); Jean Viaud, *De la puissance maritale considérée sous les rapports historique, philosophique et juridique ...* (Paris, 1855), p. 377.

by the husband.[16] In short, the relative nullity rule allowed a wife to convince her husband after she had signed a contract, even when the other contracting parties had not been aware of the woman's marital status. An informal endorsement by the husband was sufficient, even though the husband could let the parties to the contract know that he would not seek annulment.[17]

The rule of relative nullity had important disadvantages for those who had signed a contract with a married woman that was afterwards rejected by her husband. Sections of the Civil code provided that creditors of contested contracts could not expropriate assets of the common fund of marriage or those properties belonging privately to the husband. Debts within such contracts were considered to be the wife's, and only her property served as collateral for them (section 1426). This was often disadvantageous because the personal property of the wife was usually less valuable than the communal assets or those owned by the husband. Moreover, when expropriation of the wife's property was sought, even when it concerned her personal debts, the husband had to be summoned to court together with his wife. If he refused to grant authorization to his wife to appear in court for this purpose, a separate proceeding had to be started in order to obtain judicial authorization (section 2208). Furthermore, because expropriation against the personal assets of a married woman was thought to be potentially dangerous for the household, the judge weighed the interests of the family and the household against those of the creditors. If the wife's private property was used for the family, the claimants could be required to postpone expropriation against such assets until dissolution of the marriage (by death of a spouse or following divorce). They could not obtain separation of communal property between the spouses before the end of marriage (section 1446). Because of all this, those who intended to enter an agreement with a woman needed to have an idea of her marital status or her financial situation. If the negotiating parties knew that she was married, they surely asked her to submit proof of her husband's consent if the woman had not done so herself. It seems that, in early nineteenth-century France, delivery upon a sale agreed with a married woman was often postponed until evidence of her husband's authorization was presented.[18]

However, regardless of the legal disadvantages for creditors, the mentioned relative nullity rule made it possible that a wife, with the consent of her husband, led the household and managed the assets of the community property. A married woman could in principle only sign contracts, sell belongings or

However, in those circumstances, the contracting party could still attack the contract on the basis of fraud (*dol*) if he had contracted because of the stratagems of the woman (section 1116 Civil code).

[16] Zachariae, *Le droit civil français*, vol. 1, p. 244.

[17] Toullier, *Le droit civil français*, vol. 2, p. 27.

[18] Viaud, *De la puissance maritale*, pp. 373–4.

engage in hypothecs, with communal property, following the express and detailed authorization of her man; but if the latter generally agreed with his wife's actions, it was impossible to have such actions annulled. The Civil code prescribed a specific (silent or express) authority for such actions (section 223), but if the husband had decided to not question the contracts of his wife, this rule had no consequences.

Also in some other respects the Civil code allowed wives to act autonomously. In the Civil code and in French legal doctrine it was acknowledged that they could perform *actes d'administration* (administrative acts) with respect to their private assets (movable and immovable) if separation of property or a general authorization of administration had been provided in the marriage contract (sections 223, 1449 and 1536). Such acts comprised the sale of movables, maintenance of buildings, and the enjoyment of rewards and revenues. Sums that were periodically due, for example those stemming from rent contracts or loans, could lawfully be cashed.[19] However, the *actes d'administration* did not encompass alienations of immovable property, as was expressly provided in the Civil code (section 1449 *in fine*). For such actions, cooperation of the husband was required as a principle.

Another type of operation that was – according to French legal writers commenting on the Civil code – lawful for a wife, even without her husband's agreement, was *actes conservatoires* (conservatory acts). *Actes conservatoires* were deemed necessary because of an immediate threat against the wife's property, and swift action was required in order to prevent (further) damage. Because of the urgency, the wife could perform acts of importance such as *inter alia* seizure of assets, engagement in hypothecs and sending of protests.[20] Furthermore, with regard to some decisions concerning children (even communal children), the wife could act alone. She could, for example, accept a donation that was made to them.[21]

A further and well-known exception to the legal principle of incapacity of married women related to the so-called *mandat domestique*. This entailed a silent and presumed mandate of the husband to the wife allowing her to buy and sell to the extent that such operations concerned necessary supplies and provisions for the household. If the wife transgressed this mandate, by making excessive costs or by selling goods under value, the contracts that she had signed could not embarrass the husband or the matrimonial community.[22] In French doctrine

[19] Charles Demolombe, *Cours de code civil* (15 vols, Brussels, 1847–82), vol. 2, pp. 275–6 (no. 154).

[20] Ibid., pp. 270–71 (nos 131–3); Zachariae, *Le droit civil français*, vol. 1, p. 236, footnote 34.

[21] Toullier, *Le droit civil français*, vol. 2, p. 19 (no. 630); Zachariae, *Le droit civil français*, vol. 1, p. 236.

[22] Zachariae, *Le droit civil français*, vol. 1, p. 241, footnote 51.

that was written in comment on the Civil code, the difference between *mandat* and *autorisation* was underscored. The wife was presumed to have a *mandat domestique*, whereas she was not presumed to have authorization. Therefore, she was held to present or mention the authority of her husband to the parties with whom she negotiated a contract, but she did not have to evidence her mandate for those contracts that concerned foodstuffs and clothing. The contracting parties were supposed to be aware of the silent 'domestic mandate', and they were certain as to their recourse against the matrimonial community.[23] After a while, the theoretical difference between mandate and authorization allowed reducing the negative effects of the black-letter law of other provisions in the Civil code (see hereafter).[24]

The husband had many powers regarding his consent or authorization. He could easily refuse. The wife could thereupon contest this decision before a tribunal and the judge had to consider the interests of both spouses when deciding on the grounds of the refusal.[25] If the judge regarded the lack of cooperation from the husband as unfounded, he could decide that the wife was allowed to perform the act under question. The verdict then served as authorization. However, such an appeal to the judiciary was often a mere theoretical remedy because, even when the judgement granted authority to the wife, the married woman could in principle only engage her own assets and not the matrimonial community (section 1426).[26] As mentioned before, in that case the claims of her creditors could be reduced in the interest of the family, and they could not ask for separation of communal property (section 1446).

The mentioned legal exceptions as to the Civil code's principle of authorization by the husband were, all in all, limited. Married women could not preside over the sale of their immovable property, not even when it was strictly personal. Their legally acknowledged powers concerned the preservation and maintenance of private assets rather than a full capacity to acquire and transfer. The husband directed the matrimonial community, and the role of the wife was in this respect even more restricted than with regard to her private estate. The

23 Désiré Dalloz, *Répertoire méthodique et alphabétique de législation, doctrine et jurisprudence* (Paris, 1852), p. 220 (no. 1007) and p. 384 (no. 1857).

24 Another difference between *mandat* and *autorisation* was procedural. As to the *mandat domestique*, the husband could simply point to the excessiveness of the costs incurred by his wife when refusing payment or delivery. The other contracting party then had to take the initiative of bringing suit on the matter. Under the regime of authorization, a complaint of the husband was required in order to annul a contract that been signed without his consent.

25 Zachariae, *Le droit civil français*, vol. 1, p. 239, footnote 44.

26 Section 1427 of the Civil code provided some very minimal exceptions to section 1426. These exceptions comprised judicially confirmed agreements that had been made in order to liberate a woman's husband from prison, or for the 'establishment' of the children.

rule of relative nullity meant that women were met with distrust when acting in public and that they negotiated on their own behalf when their husband did not support their actions. Those who engaged in contracts with a woman had to be absolutely sure that she was either single or – if she was married – that her husband consented to what she was doing. However, benevolent judges and jurists could bend some of these rules, and especially the one regarding relative nullity, to the advantage of married women, even though such interpretations mostly served the interests of creditors. They were not so much equality driven.

French Doctrine and Belgian Judgements Circumventing the Civil Code (1804–*c.* 1865)

In some respects, French doctrine of the early 1800s had walked away from the strict provisions of the Civil code, and Belgian tribunals followed its lead. An example of this is clear in the views of the Court of Appeal of Brussels regarding the relation between *autorisation* and *mandat/procuration*, which it developed in close relation with the relative nullity rule of the Civil code. In this latter respect, the judges in Brussels attempted to revive some of the Brabant law that had applied before the French occupation. They were original with regard to other legal problems as well.

Contemporary French commentators emphasized that the more lenient mandate could replace the strict requirements of authorization. The picky rules applying to the latter did not hinder the former. A mandate could be broad and general, whereas an authorization had to be precise and had to be linked to one operation only (section 223). A husband could empower his wife to 'do all things necessary' to 'administer a business'. Such descriptions were deemed sufficient to have the legal effect of a mandate, also for precise operations and even for those acts for which according to the Civil code a specific and detailed authorization was required. A general mandate could be conferred on the wife, allowing her to buy and sell for the benefit of the matrimonial community or in the interest of the husband.[27]

---

[27] Demolombe, *Cours de code civil*, vol. 2, p. 284 (no. 170); Alexandre Duranton, *Cours de droit civil suivant le code français …* (12 vols, Brussels, 1841), vol. 1, pp. 350–51 (no. 1035); Demolombe, *Cours de code civil*, vol. 2, p. 284 (no. 170); Toullier, *Le droit civil français*, vol. 2, p. 25 (no. 644). This same insight was also mentioned in the first edition of Duranton's commentary, dating from 1825. See: Alexandre Duranton, *Cours de droit français suivant le code civil …* (21 vols, Paris, 1825–37), vol. 2, p. 417 (no. 448). Demolombe's treatise dates from 1847. Toullier's was published in 1824 and it most certainly was a source for Duranton's remarks. After Toullier's death, Duranton completed and edited the unfinished fifth edition of Toullier's *Le droit civil français*.

In February 1818, the Brussels Court of Appeal heard an appeal that had been brought against a judgement of the Commercial Court of Brussels. The latter had condemned a certain Mr Coché, a merchant living in Brussels, to pay out four letters obligatory that had been drawn on him and his wife for a sale of movables, and which had been signed for acceptance by his wife alone, with the added note of hers that she had acted '*par procuration de son mari*' (on the basis of a mandate of her husband). The strategy of Mr Coché during the proceedings before the Commercial Court suggests that his wife regularly undertook commercial activities, together with him or with his consent. Mr Coché's advocates indeed did not bring up the incapacity of Madam Coché as a married woman, but merely referred to the fact that she had not been given a specific mandate (*procuration*) for the acceptance of the bills obligatory under question. On 19 June 1817, the Brussels Commercial Court had produced a provisional judgement inviting the claimant to produce evidence of a mandate by Mr Coché, or as to the legal status of Madam Coché. If the latter had been conducting business as an independent tradeswoman at the time of the acceptance of the bills, and if the bills were related to this separate trade, according to the court the acceptance of the bills should be considered valid. In that case, the claimant could prosecute his claim against the assets of the community property, as was provided in the Civil code. Wives with separate businesses, authorized by their husband, could bind the matrimonial community property (section 1426). The point of the separate trade by Madam Coché was proven, and thereupon Mr Coché was convicted. In response, the latter lodged an appeal against this judgement. The Brussels Court of Appeal untangled the many legal questions that had been raised. It rightly stated that either Madam Coché had had a separate trade, or that her husband was liable because of a given or presumed mandate for the acceptance of the bills. Because it was believed that the bills obligatory had not been drawn for the purpose of a separate trade of Madam Coché (she had accepted them on behalf of her husband), the Brussels Court of Appeal did not follow the reasoning of the first instance Commercial Court, which had accepted the relation between the bills and Madam Coché's separate business.

Instead, and rather surprisingly, the Brussels Court of Appeal judged that even when no express mandate by the husband could be demonstrated, the creditors of the bills could bring suit against Mr Coché on the basis of an action *de in rem verso*, if the deliveries following the sale had been made to him. In that case, he had profited from the contract, and therefore he should respond to the debts stemming from that contract. This action *de in rem verso* was, according to the late medieval and early modern legal doctrine in which it had been developed, related to the profits that had been made. It was a remedy against unjustified enrichment.[28] The Brussels Court of Appeal nonetheless suggested that the claim could be brought for the totality of merchandise that had been delivered, and not only for the gains that had been made out of it.[29] In this regard, the judgement was important. It clearly derogated from contemporary French legal doctrine, which allowed this action *de in rem verso* only for the surplus acquired by the defendant, that is the actual profit.[30] If – in the cited example – Mr Coché had received and sold the deliveries, the classical action *de in rem verso* could only regard the difference between the selling and buying price. The creditors of the bills obligatory, who had delivered the goods bought, could accordingly recover their debts to the maximum of this difference, which was always smaller than the total billing cost. However, in the interpretation of the Brussels Court of Appeal, the full debt for the deliveries could be claimed from Mr Coché.

In the Coché case, the Brussels Court of Appeal used the French doctrinal distinction between *mandat* and *autorisation* by explicitly not requiring that the rules of *autorisation* apply in case of *mandat/procuration*. Moreover, the Brussels Court of Appeal linked these opinions to the Brabant law of the Old Regime, and blended the latter with the *actio de in rem verso*. This *actio* was broadened for the hypothesis of reciprocity in the contractual relation between the wife and her contracting parties, and in this respect the Brussels Court of Appeal went considerably further than French doctrine. Before 1789, it had been a common rule in Brabant that when the matrimonial community or the husband benefitted from a profitable but unauthorized agreement, the latter should be fulfilled. The importance of this innovative legal interpretation was that it permitted bringing a substantial claim against the husband for contracts against payment that had been made by his wife. Also, from another legal viewpoint, this solution was no less than revolutionary. According to the letter of the Civil code, a person falsely presenting himself as an agent of another person should be considered liable for damages and compensation out of the contracts which he signed with such pretentions, and no claim could be raised against the falsely represented (section 1998). Thus, according to the black-letter provisions of the Civil code, when these rules had been applied, and because the mandate remained unproven, Madam Coché had to be held responsible for the bills. That would have meant

28 Daniël Visser, 'Das Recht der ungerechtfertigten Bereicherung', in Robert Feenstra and Reinhard Zimmermann (ed.), *Das römisch–holländische Recht. Fortschritte des Zivilrechts im 17. und 18. Jahrhundert* (Berlin, 1992), pp. 369–428.

29 Court of Appeal Brussels 10 February 1818, *Pasicrisie*, 1818 [published in 1843], pp. 29–31.

30 Duranton, *Cours de droit civil*, vol. 1, p. 365 (no. 1095); Philippe Antoine Merlin, *Répertoire universel et raisonné de jurisprudence* (17 vols, Paris, 1812), vol. 1, p. 519 (no. 8); Claude-Etienne Delvincourt, *Cours de code civil* (3 vols, Paris, 1819), vol. 3, p. 36; Zachariae, *Le droit civil français*, vol. 1, p. 342, footnotes 10 and 42.

that the creditors could not seek payment for their debt against the assets of the community property (section 1426). The legal understanding proposed by the Brussels Court of Appeal must therefore foremost be evaluated as a measure tackling such inadequacies, which under the circumstances of the case went against the good faith of the creditor of the bills obligatory. It is clear that the Brussels Court of Appeal circumvented the gender-biased rules of law, mostly to protect the economic interests of the third parties involved.

Other judgements of the Brussels Court of Appeal explored the legal elements that had been set out in the former case. An interesting example, dating from 1860, related the mentioned new views to the rule of relative nullity. Madam Laureys and her son had signed *billets à ordre* (promissory notes), which they had not paid afterwards. The beneficiary of those notes was Madam Verbeemen. The latter summoned Madam Laureys and her son in payment before the Commercial Court of Mechelen. Madam Laureys was married at the time of the signing of the *billets*, and in court she mentioned that she had acted without the *autorisation* of her husband, who was not present in the courtroom. Only later, before the Brussels Court of Appeal, it appeared that her husband had left her some 20 years before. Madam Laureys insisted in appeal that the promissory notes were null and void because she had signed them without permission of her husband. The advocate-general emphasized the principle that a contract signed by a wife without her husband's authority should be honoured if it contributed to the matrimonial community. He stressed that the right to revoke such a contract was subject to the condition that the contract had not been reciprocal. Also, the advocate-general's conclusion was that, in principle, the action *de in rem verso* should be limited to the profits that had been made. However, he suggested that because the husband of Madam Laureys had left, he had to be considered legally absent. Therefore, Madam Laureys had to be qualified as the director of the household at the time of the signing of the notes, and the full amount of the debt had to be compensated. Also, the advocate-general interpreted the *mandat domestique* very broadly, in the sense of a mandate for the benefit of the matrimonial community and not only for buying groceries and clothes. The Brussels Court of Appeal followed the advocate-general's advice, which thus set forth an exception to the relative nullity rule for profitable contracts.[31] In this

---

31 Court of Appeal Brussels 9 May 1860, *Pasicrisie (Arrêts des Cours d'Appel)*, 1860, pp. 158–62. The latter interpretation of *mandat domestique* refined decisions of the same Court of Appeal. See, for example, Court of Appeal Brussels 8 January 1851, *Pasicrisie (Arrêts des Cours d'Appel)*, 1851, p. 327–8, at p. 327 (the *mandat domestique* '*concern[e] les objets nécessaires* à *l'alimentation et* à *l'entretien de la famille*' ['relates to objects that are necessary for the feeding and maintenance of the family']). See, for a decision comparable with the verdict of 9 May 1860, Court of Appeal Brussels 7 November 1840, *Pasicrisie (Arrêts des Cours d'Appel)*, 1841, pp. 13–14.

latter respect, the Brussels Court of Appeal further endorsed the older legal rules with regard to the contractual capacity of married women.

The Brussels Court of Appeal was, also with regard to other legal questions, innovative. In the 1850s, it decided for example that a silent authorization from the husband could be deduced from the insertion into an official deed of the expression *dûment autorisée par son mari* (duly authorized by her husband).[32] At around that same time, it again stated – with reference being made to the mentioned Coché verdict – that the fact that an unauthorized contract was profitable for the husband brought about his liability.[33] The position of the Brussels Court of Appeal was, when being compared with other Courts of Appeal, quite progressive. Many of the mentioned judgements concerned commerce, which was important not only in the city of Brussels but also in Mechelen and Antwerp. The latter cities resorted under the jurisdiction of the Brussels Court of Appeal and before 1795 they had known rules based on cooperation between spouses.[34] In other Belgian Courts of Appeal, for example in Ghent and Liège, decisions were stricter and they remained closer to the provisions of the Civil code, most probably because they did not so much concern trade. Differences in decisions between the Court of Appeal of Brussels and other Courts of Appeal, for example, concerned the specific or general authorization for commerce,[35] and whether a silent authorization of the husband could be deduced from circumstances or customs.[36] In verdicts of the

---

32 Court of Appeal Brussels 15 May 1855, *Pasicrisie (Arrêts des Cours d'Appel)*, 1855, pp. 394–9.

33 Court of Appeal Brussels 1 June 1857, *Pasicrisie (Arrêts des Cours d'Appel)*, 1857, pp. 272–4.

34 For Antwerp, see: De ruysscher, 'The Capacity of Married Women'. For Mechelen, see: Guillaume De Longé (ed.), *Coutumes de la seigneurie de Malines. Coutumes de la ville de Malines* (Brussels, 1879), p. 64 (ch. 9, section 9).

35 See, for an overview of judgements between 1870 and 1900 regarding the requirement of a specific authorization for trade, François Laurent, *Supplément aux principes de droit civil* (8 vols, Paris, 1898–1903), vol. 1, p. 378 (no. 575). In Ghent and Liège, specific authorizations were imposed, whereas in Brussels a more lenient interpretation prevailed.

36 Compare Court of Appeal Ghent 6 August 1862, *Pasicrisie (Arrêts des Cours d'Appel)*, 1863, pp. 54–9 (an authorization cannot be silent and must be express) with Court of Appeal Brussels 25 February 1852, *Pasicrisie (Arrêts des Cours d'Appel)*, 1852, pp. 340–42, at p. 340 ('*le consentement tacite du mari constitue une autorisation suffisante*' ['the silent consent of the husband is sufficient as an authorization']). See also: Court of Appeal Brussels, *Pasicrisie (Arrêts des Cours d'Appel),* 1860, pp. 240–41, at p. 240 ('*l'autorisation peut résulter des circonstances*' ['the authorization can result from circumstances']). A similarity in judgements, which was beneficial to women, concerned the interpretation of the 1851 law regarding hypothecs. This law was explained in the sense that women could still register the silent hypothec for their dowry after a judgement had declared their husband to be bankrupt.

Brussels Court on such themes, the link with economic benefits and the rights of creditors was evident.

Minimal and Unachieved Projects for Reform (*c.* 1870–*c.* 1960)

The mentioned developments in Belgian legal practice and French doctrine had some impact on Belgian legislation. In December 1872, for example, a legislative change was made to the Belgian *Code de commerce* (Commercial code), in the sense that a woman with a trade separate from her husband's was henceforth allowed to sell her private immovable property, and that she could lawfully use it as collateral (*hypothèque*) if that served the purpose of her business.[37]

Some years later, a more general change of the existing legislation was proposed. In August 1879, the liberal Belgian government had entrusted law professor François Laurent with the project of writing a revised version of the Civil code, the original text of which had remained in force in Belgium without much change up until that time. In 1882, Laurent published a draft code (*avant-projet*), containing 2,241 sections, and which listed fundamentally new provisions with regard to the legal capacity of married women. The contemporary feminist agitation, especially in France, probably stimulated Laurent's liberal and progressive views, and most certainly he built on what was going on in the Belgian tribunals of his time. Laurent proposed the right to sell personal immovable property for both husband and wife; but he also acknowledged restrictions in the interest of the matrimonial bond. He thus took the partnership between spouses as the benchmark for the actions of both husband and wife, even with regard to their privately owned assets. Because he considered the spouses to be partners (*associés*), in his view they should restrict operations in light of their common undertakings.[38] A wife privately owning assets could thus choose to sell them, but the husband could prevent this if the sale would ruin the marriage or household.[39]

Laurent regarded the interest of the family as the crucial criterion for the validity of alienations of communal assets as well. He extended the right to oppose such transactions for both spouses. Laurent gave the management of the community property to husband and wife. Both were, according to Laurent's proposal, required to consent in how the community was run, even if the concrete act of administration was in practice only done by one of them.

See: Court of Appeal Brussels 4 August 1856, *La Belgique judiciaire*, 14 (1856), p. 1329; Court of Appeal Ghent 13 August 1856, *La Belgique judiciaire*, 16 (1858), p. 1284.

[37] Section 11 of the law of 15 December 1872, *Moniteur belge*, 22 December 1872.

[38] François Laurent, *Avant-projet de révision du Code civil* (6 vols, Brussels, 1882–85), vol. 1, p. 452 (no. 1).

[39] Ibid., p. 446 (no. 6).

If a spouse did not agree, he or she could file complaint with the tribunal. The wife could thus, according to Laurent, oppose her husband's administration of the community property. Any action of sale or hypothecation of immovable communal property should be done with authorization of both husband and wife; and in case one of them did not support the proposed act, he or she could resort to a judge. If the husband wanted to prevent the projects of his wife, he could only start proceedings and seek a judgement confirming his views. When exerting its control in such cases, the tribunal had to take the interests of the family into consideration.[40]

Neither in his *avant-projet* nor in his many other publications did Laurent refer to judgements of the Brussels Court of Appeal that supported the mentioned views. It is nonetheless most certain that he knew the decisions summarized above, that he agreed with their contents and that they determined at least some of his convictions. However, notwithstanding its corroboration of legal practice at this point, in the end Laurent's project remained without results. This was due to political reasons. The text of Laurent, who was a member of the liberal party, was met with strong opposition from Catholic politicians, and when in 1884 the Catholic party won the elections, it formed a new government that swiftly put Laurent's work aside and appointed a commission of experts to write a new draft text. This commission was warned to stick to the existing Civil code as closely as possible. As a result, in decades thereafter, legislation was not substantially changed.[41]

In a first phase after 1884, only minor legal improvements were made. In France, laws of 9 April 1881 and of 6 February 1893 relaxed the strict rules for married women to a minimal extent. The first law allowed a wife to open a savings account and to make deposits without her husband's consent. The second one provided that factual separation, even without judicial acknowledgement, brought about the end of the incapacity of the wife and thus of the requirement of authorization by the husband.[42] Some of these rules were copied into Belgian legislation. A Belgian law of 1900 granted married women the right to open a savings account irrespective of their husbands' views,[43] and another law of the

---

40 Ibid., pp. 445–6 (nos 4–5) and pp. 451–2 (no. 1). See also, with respect to the guiding principle of the interests of the family: François Laurent, *Cours élémentaire de droit civil* (4 vols, Brussels, 1878), vol. 1, pp. 275–6 (no. 213); François Laurent, *Principes de droit civil* (33 vols, Brussels, 1869–78), vol. 3, p. 163 (no. 126).

41 Dirk Heirbaut, 'L'émancipation tardive d'un pupille de la Nation française: l'histoire du droit belge aux 19e et 20e siècles', in Alain Wijffels (ed.), *Le Code civil entre* ius commune *et droit privé européen* (Brussels, 2005), pp. 614–15.

42 James F. McMillan, *France and Women, 1789–1914: Gender, Society and Politics* (London, 2000), p. 152.

43 Law of 10 February 1900, *Moniteur belge*, 12–13 February 1900.

same year acknowledged a woman's right to sign a labour contract and to receive wages, even when she was married.[44]

It was only in 1932 that, after long deliberations in parliament, fundamentally new rules were inserted into the Belgian Civil code. The limited suffrage, which in 1919 had been granted to war-struck women (predominantly widows and mothers of deceased soldiers), had engendered a *changement d'esprit*. After that time, many thought it inconsistent that married women, who were thenceforth citizens with voting rights, remained in many respects subjected to their husbands.[45] However, even in 1932 the regime of authorization by the husband did not end, even though many exceptions were acknowledged. A wife could, for example, dispose of earnings from labour without consent from her husband. It was, too, for the first time expressly provided that the revenues of the husband should compensate the debts of the household. If this obligation was violated, the wife could seek remedy in court in order to block and cash her husband's wages and rewards. The 1932 law also allowed general authorizations of husbands, for all acts.[46] However, these legal innovations were – generally speaking – limited, since the required consent of the husband was confirmed as a general principle. Still in the 1940–50s, legal scholars generally considered the husband to be 'the head of the household',[47] and it was only 10 years after general suffrage had been accorded to women in 1948 that the Belgian legislator formally abandoned the marital authority regime of the 1804 Civil code. Thereafter, it would take another 18 years, until 1976, before married women were given powers with regard to the administration of the matrimonial community property.[48]

The mentioned legislative changes did not only respond to changes of thought within legal doctrine and practice, but foremost to women's demands. The two World Wars were catalyst events, also in this respect, as in their wake voting rights were extended to women. This was implicitly meant as a reward for their patriotism and as a form of compensation for losses suffered. Even so, the reform of the legal position of women was slow, and in private law even slower than for topics of public law, to which voting rights pertained. After World War I, a few members of the Belgian parliament, among them the liberal politician Emile Jennissen, advocated a thorough revision of the Civil code's articles regarding married women. Jennissen's 1925 proposal for

---

44 Law of 10 March 1900, *Moniteur belge*, 14 March 1900.

45 Belgian Senate, *Pièces parlementaires*, 1925–26, no. 18, p. 1 (see hereafter).

46 Henri De Page, *Traité élémentaire de droit civil belge. Principes – doctrine – jurisprudence* (10 vols, Brussels, 1933–49), vol. 1, pp. 783–9.

47 Ibid., p. 781 (no. 712); René Dekkers, *Handboek van burgerlijk recht* (3 vols, Brussels, 1956–58), vol. 1, p. 169 (no. 250).

48 Section 1415 Civil code, as changed by the law of 14 July 1976, *Moniteur belge*, 18 September 1976.

inter alia the abolishment of the first part of section 213, which provided that a married woman owed obedience to her husband,[49] was blocked early on. After World War II, the first female members of parliament reanimated the debate. In May 1946 and in December 1947, the liberal senator Georgette Ciselet[50] submitted proposals of law that aimed at introducing equal rights of husbands and wives as to matrimonial and private property.[51] In March 1948 and in February 1949, a female member of the Chamber of Representatives, Isabelle Blume-Grégoire, made comparable proposals to abolish marital authority and to acknowledge full legal capacity of married women.[52] None of these proposals made it to law, but they did give cause to the creation of a legislative committee that was to prepare a reform of the system of reciprocal duties and rights within marriage. The committee's proceedings ultimately resulted in the 1958 law, of which Ciselet had been one of the most active proponents.[53] Yet the slowness of legislative reform had been a clear indication of the reluctance of a predominantly male parliament towards the necessary legal changes.[54]

---

49 Belgian Senate, *Pièces parlementaires*, 1925–26, no. 18 (*proposition de loi tendant à libérer les femmes de certaines inégalités qui les frappent au point de vue civil et pénal* [proposition of law for the liberation of women of some inequalities in civil and penal law]).

50 After World War II, Georgette Ciselet (1900–83) played an important role in opening the legal profession to women, and demanding immediate voting rights. In 1923, as the fourth woman in Belgium, she had taken the oath of advocate and she quickly specialized in divorce litigation. Based on her own experience, in the 1930s she published texts on the discrimination of married women and on the comparative study of the law relating thereto. In the meantime she became member of the women's section of the liberal party and chaired its legal commission after the war. She left Belgian politics when in 1963, as the first woman in Belgium, she was appointed to become judge in the *Conseil d'Etat*. Until then, Ciselet had tirelessly devoted herself to women's political, social and legal rights. She was also a member of the board of the National Women's Council and was active, there as well, in its legal commission. See: Georgette Ciselet, *La Femme: ses droits, ses devoirs et ses revendications* (Brussels, 1930); Eliane Gubin, Catherine Jacques, Valérie Piette and Jean Puissant (ed.), *Dictionnaire des femmes belges. XIXe et XXe siècles* (Brussels, 2006), pp. 100–103.

51 Belgian Senate, *Pièces parlementaires*, 1946 (Special Session), no. 38, and 1947–48, no. 73, in particular sections 16–23.

52 Belgian Chamber of Representatives, *Pièces parlementaires*, 1947–48, no. 299, and 1948–49, no. 207.

53 Claude Renard, 'La réforme du statut de la femme mariée en Belgique', *Revue internationale de droit comparé*, 10/1 (1958): pp. 56–64.

54 In the introduction to the 1958 law, it was said that the committee had worked 'cautiously, but in a determined fashion'. See: Belgian Senate, *Pièces parlementaires*, 1956–57, no. 69, p. 1 (*Exposé des Motifs*). Between 1921 and 1950, only very few women had seats in the Belgian parliament. See: Eliane Gubin and Leen Van Molle, *Femmes et politique en Belgique* (Brussels, 1998), p. 67. On the whole, the socialist political party was not in favour

Conclusion

The regime of marital authority, which had been written into the Civil code, took the *puissance* of the husband and the obedience of his wife as starting points, rather than the conjugal partnership. The provisions of the Civil code were strict and more severe than legislation of previous periods, but they allowed some progressive interpretation. In France, legal scholars attempted to broaden some of the exceptions of the code's harsh rules. The distinction between *mandat/procuration* and *autorisation* was expanded. Judges of tribunals in the Belgian province of Brabant followed their lead. In the first half of the nineteenth century, the Brussels Court of Appeal copied ideas of French legal authors by acknowledging autonomous actions of married women, and it was in some respects more lenient than French doctrine. The solutions that were imposed on litigants, in particular the exception to the relative nullity rule for profitable contracts, closely resembled what had been known in Brabant during the Old Regime. The local laws of that province, dating from before 1789, had taken spousal cooperation as the basis for rules regarding the position of married women. The proposed reform by François Laurent breathed the spirit of this older legislation as well, since it was based on the mentioned legal interpretations that were common in contemporary court practice. However, these ideas did not take full root until after World War II. Gender equality in private law was not an important political issue – not in the early 1900s, and not before.

The mentioned moderate relaxation of the Civil code's articles, in legal practice and doctrine of the 1800s, should therefore not be overestimated. It is surprising but true that in the course of the nineteenth century a more softened interpretation of the stubborn provisions of the 1804 Civil code with regard to married women mostly served economic goals. The interests of creditors were considered as being paramount. It was the acknowledgement of their needs that had the indirect effect of raising the contractual capacity of wives. This is clear in the interpretation of the Civil code's rule of relative nullity by the Brussels Court of Appeal. The Civil code provided that contracts signed by a married woman were in principle illegitimate if the husband had not consented in them, but also that they remained legally valid until successful judicial contestation. It was a rule of the Old Regime that a beneficial and reciprocal contract could not be attacked, even if it had been signed by a married woman without her husband's cooperation. Early nineteenth-century French legal doctrine allowed compensation for the creditors, but only to the extent of the profits made by

of general suffrage for women, which it thought to be to the advantage of the Catholic party. The success of the socialist movement in the early 1900s thus seriously hampered the claims of Belgian feminism, which after 1895 had chosen voting rights as its main goal. See: ibid., pp. 30–44.

the husband. In its judgements, the Brussels Court of Appeal went further and took the older rules as guiding principles. It decided that even without formal authorization a wife could bind the community property for contracts that were to the husband's advantage. Yet, such verdicts usually concerned cases that were situated in the sphere of business. The approach of the Brussels Court had indeed more to do with safeguarding the rights of those parties who had contracted with a woman than with a full recognition of married women's rights. Therefore, one must conclude that, all in all, the nineteenth-century changes in legal interpretation were not so much engendered by a cultural turn recognizing the role of the wife; and they were certainly not the result of a political sense of urgency as to equality between the sexes. In both the law and the legal practice, the gender bias within the Civil code remained unchallenged for the most part, and this well into the twentieth century.

Bibliography

Primary Sources

Ciselet, Georgette, *La Femme: ses droits, ses devoirs et ses revendications* (Brussels: L'Eglantine, 1930).

Dalloz, Désiré, *Répertoire méthodique et alphabétique de législation, doctrine et jurisprudence* (Paris: Bureau de la Jurisprudence Générale du Royaume, 1852).

Dekkers, René, *Handboek van burgerlijk recht* (3 vols, Brussels: Bruylant, 1956–58).

De Longé, Guillaume (ed.), *Coutumes de la seigneurie de Malines. Coutumes de la ville de Malines* (Brussels: Gobbaerts, 1879).

De Page, Henri, *Traité* élémentaire *de droit civil belge. Principes – doctrine – jurisprudence* (10 vols, Brussels: Bruylant, 1933–49).

Delvincourt, Claude-Etienne, *Cours de code civil* (3 vols, Paris: Fournier, 1819).

Demolombe, Charles, *Cours de code civil* (15 vols, Brussels: Stienon, 1847–82).

Duranton, Alexandre, *Cours de droit français suivant le code civil* ... (21 vols, Paris: Nève, 1825–37).

Duranton, Alexandre, *Cours de droit civil suivant le code français* ... (12 vols, Brussels: Wahlen and Cie, 1841).

Fenet, Pierre-Antoine, *Recueil complet des travaux préparatoires du Code civil* (15 vols, Paris: Imprimerie de Ducessois, 1827–28).

La Belgique judiciaire: gazette des tribunaux belges et étrangers (Brussels: Frameries, 1842–1938).

Laurent, François, *Principes de droit civil* (33 vols, Brussels: Bruylant, 1869–78).

Laurent, François, *Cours élémentaire de droit civil* (4 vols, Brussels: Bruylant, 1878).

Laurent, François, *Avant-projet de révision du Code civil* (6 vols, Brussels: Bruylant, 1882–85).
Laurent, François, *Supplément aux principes de droit civil* (8 vols, Paris: Maresoq, 1898–1903).
Merlin, Philippe Antoine, *Répertoire universel et raisonné de jurisprudence* (17 vols, Paris: Garnery, 1812).
Moniteur belge (Brussels: Department of Justice, since 1831).
Nougarède de Fayet, André Jean Simon, *Lois du mariage et du divorce, depuis leur origine dans le droit romain* (Paris: Le Normant, 1816).
Pasicrisie ou recueil général de la jurisprudence des cours de France et de la Belgique, en matière civile, commerciale, criminelle, de droit public et administratif: cours de France (Brussels: Bruylant, since 1832).
Pièces parlementaires (annales et documents) (Brussels: Belgian Senate and Chamber of Representatives, since 1831).
Toullier, Charles-Bonaventure-Marie, *Le droit civil français, suivant l'ordre du Code civil…* (13 vols, Paris: Warée, 1824–28).
Viaud, Jean, *De la puissance maritale considérée sous les rapports historique, philosophique et juridique…* (Paris: Durand, 1855).
Zachariae, Carl Salomé, *Le droit civil français (avec des annotations de G. Massé et CH. Vergé)* (5 vols, Paris: Durand, 1854–60).

Secondary Sources

Baeteman, Gustaaf, and Jean-Pierre Lauwers, 'Le statut de la femme dans le droit belge depuis le Code civil', in *La Femme* [Recueils de la Société Jean Bodin pour l'histoire comparative des institutions, 12] (Brussels: Librairie encyclopédique, 1962).
Beauthier, Régine, 'Construction du divorce et des relations entre époux dans les travaux préparatoires du Code Napoléon', in Anne Devillé and Olivier Paye (ed.), *Les femmes et le droit: constructions idéologiques et pratiques sociales* (Brussels: FUSL, 1999).
Beauthier, Régine, 'Le juge et le lit conjugal au XIXe siècle', in Marie-Thérèse Coenen (ed.), *Corps de femmes: sexualité et contrôle social* (Brussels: De Boeck & Larcier, 2002),
Bordeaux, Michèle, 'Le maître et l'infidèle. Des relations personnelles entre mari et femme de l'ancien droit au Code civil', in Irène Théry and Christian Biet (ed.), *La famille, la loi, l'état de la Révolution au Code civil* (Paris: Imprimerie Nationale, 1989).
Burton, June K., *Napoleon and the Women Question: Discourses of the Other Sex in French Education, Medicine and Medical Law, 1799–1815* (Austin: Texas Tech University Press, 2007).

Deroussin, David, *Histoire du droit privé (XVIe–XXIe siècle)* (Paris: Ellipses, 2010).
De ruysscher, Dave, 'The Capacity of Married Women to Engage in Contracts: Emancipation Through *Ius Commune* in the Southern Netherlands (12th–18th Centuries)', in Grethe Jacobsen and Heide Wunder (ed.), *East Meets West: A Gendered View of Legal Tradition* (forthcoming).
Desan, Suzanne, *The Family on Trial in Revolutionary France* (Berkeley: University of California Press, 2004).
Gay, Jean, 'Capacité de la femme mariée et puissance maritale dans l'élaboration du Code civil', *Revue de l'Institut Napoléon*, 161 (1993/2): 33–65, 162 (1994/1): 51–64, and 163 (1994/2): 19–43.
Godding, Philippe, 'La femme sous puissance maritale (1804–1958)', in Luc Courtois, Jean Pirotte and Françoise Rosart (ed.), *Femmes et pouvoirs. Flux et reflux de l'émancipation féminine depuis un siècle* (Louvain-la-Neuve: Collège Erasme, 1992).
Gubin, Eliane, 'Du politique au politique. Parcours du feminisme belge (1830–1914)', in Hans Moors (ed.), *Fabrics of Feminism: Comparative Analysis of Nineteenth-Century Gender Discourse in Belgium and the Netherlands* [*Revue belge de philologie et d'histoire*, 77 (1999)] (Brussels: Société pour le Progrès des Etudes Philologiques et Historiques, 1999).
Gubin, Eliane, and Leen Van Molle, *Femmes et politique en Belgique* (Brussels: Racine, 1998).
Gubin, Eliane, Catherine Jacques, Valerie Piette and Jean Puissant (ed.), *Dictionnaire des femmes belges. XIXe et XXe siècles* (Brussels: Racine, 2006).
Heirbaut, Dirk, 'The Belgian Legal Tradition: Does it Exist?', in Hubert Bocken and Walter De Bondt (ed.), *Introduction to Belgian Law* (Brussels: Bruylant, 2000).
Heirbaut, Dirk, 'L'émancipation tardive d'un pupille de la Nation française: l'histoire du droit belge aux 19e et 20e siècles', in Alain Wijffels (ed.), *Le Code civil entre* ius commune *et droit privé européen* (Brussels: Bruylant, 2005).
Heirbaut, Dirk, 'Law Reviews in Belgium (1763–2004): Instruments of Legal Practice and Linguistic Conflicts', in Michael Stolleis and Thomas Simon (ed.), *Juristische Zeitschriften in Europa* (Frankfurt am Main: Klostermann, 2006).
Heirbaut, Dirk, 'Les juges belges face au Code civil aux 19ième et 20ième siècles: l'exemple des troubles de voisinage', in Barbara Dölemeyer, Heinz Mohnhaupt and Alessandro Somma (ed.), *Richterliche Anwendung des Code civil in seinen europäischen Geltungsbereichen außerhalb Frankreichs* (Frankfurt am Main: Klostermann, 2006).
Lepointe, Gabriel, 'La femme au XIXe siècle en France et dans le monde de l'Europe occidentale', in *La Femme* [Recueils de la Société Jean Bodin pour l'histoire comparative des institutions, 12] (Brussels: Librairie encyclopédique, 1962).

Matthijs, Koen, 'Changing Patterns of Familial Sociability: Family Members as Witnesses to (Re)Marriage in Nineteenth-Century Flanders', *Journal of Family History*, 31 (2006): 115–43.

McMillan, James F., *France and Women, 1789–1914: Gender, Society and Politics* (London: Routledge, 2000).

Petot, Pierre, and André Vandenbossche, 'La femme dans les pays coutumiers français', in *La Femme* [Recueils de la Société Jean Bodin pour l'histoire comparative des institutions, 12] (Brussels: Librairie encyclopédique, 1962).

Renard, Claude, 'La réforme du statut de la femme mariée en Belgique', *Revue internationale de droit comparé*, 10/1 (1958): 56–64.

Van de Putte, Bart et al., 'The Rise of Age Homogamy in 19th Century Western Europe', *Journal of Marriage and Family*, 71 (2009): 1234–53.

Visser, Daniël, 'Das Recht der ungerechtfertigten Bereicherung', in Robert Feenstra and Reinhard Zimmermann (ed.), *Das römisch–holländische Recht. Fortschritte des Zivilrechts im 17. und 18. Jahrhundert* (Berlin: Duncker & Humblot, 1992).

Chapter 6

Women and Law in Nineteenth-century Greece: The Impact of the Modern State

Evdoxios Doxiadis

The modern state has not been always kind to women, particularly in matters of law where women in the transition from the Early Modern to the Late Modern period suffered considerable erosion over their rights, especially with respect to property. Such is the case in much of Europe, including such models of European statehood like Britain and France, with the eventual supremacy of common law and with the adoption of the Civil code respectively. The discussion, however, has focused almost exclusively on Western Europe, and the state-building efforts there, and has ignored contemporary developments in Southern or Eastern Europe, where different traditions were in place in the Early Modern period but which also experienced much of the same state-building efforts seen in France, Germany, or Britain. This chapter will discuss one such case: the emergence of the modern Greek state, which took place well before the emergence of such quintessential European states as Germany or Italy. I will attempt to examine the relationship of women, law, and property rights when Greece was still a province of the Ottoman Empire, and then look at the effects of the modern state of Greece.

Although the question of the development of law in the early modern Greek state has been examined before, much of what has been published is relatively dated, and often completely ignores questions of gender.[1] Although scholars dealing with the Byzantine and Ottoman periods have produced very insightful works on women and law,[2] the formative years of the modern Greek state have strangely been ignored. What has been published on the position of women in this period either draws its sources from early Greek feminist literature, which does not emerge until after the mid nineteenth century,[3] or when it addresses

[1] Some of these early scholars (Visvizis, Zepos, Tourtoglou) did discuss issues that involve gender aspects such as dowries, defloration, and so on but because of the time they were writing (mid twentieth century) the focus was never on the gender aspect of the issues.

[2] See Macrides, Laiou, Papagianni, Kasdagli, and others.

[3] See Eleni Varika, *I Exegersi ton Kyrion* [The Rebellion of the Ladies] (Athens, 2004).

questions of law and gender it focuses on areas that were not part of the original Greek state but were added in the course of the nineteenth century.

This examination is an attempt to introduce gender into the debates regarding legal development in the early nineteenth century in evidence of new material from the records of the notaries of the time. The source material used involves primarily notarial documents and communal records for the period from 1750 to 1850 from four areas: the islands of Naxos and Mykonos, and the cities of Athens and Leonidio, with their surrounding territory supplemented by some of the early legislative efforts of the Greek governments. The choice was made in order to include a varied sample that would include maritime as well as continental areas; regions involved in mercantile and shipping activities; areas of an agricultural and pastoral economy; urban as well as rural areas that would reflect as much as possible the composition of Ottoman Greece and the new state. Additional material included family archives from the same regions and the early Greek state government archives.

The Legal Tradition of Ottoman Greece

The Greek Ottoman legal tradition had its origins in Roman law, and in particular its Byzantine variant which was based upon Justinian's *Corpus Juris Civilis* and subsequent modifications by later emperors. Under Byzantine law men's and women's property rights were in theory clearly defined. All offspring had equal rights to the patrimony, although there was always a question whether the obligatory dowry given to a daughter constituted her full share or not. A woman's dowry had to be set in writing, belonged to her, was inalienable, and was supposed to be returned to her intact upon the dissolution of the marriage.[4] The husband managed her property and enjoyed the proceeds, but there was never a question of common conjugal property in marriage.[5] The husband assumed the obligation to protect the dowry during his management in addition to his obligation to provide for all material needs of his family.[6] These obligations were not mere formalities, as evidenced by the surviving record of Byzantine courts,[7]

4 The very act of the writing of the dowry could divide marriage from concubinage (*pallakeia*) (Eleftheria Sp. Papagianni, *I Nomologia ton Ekklisiastikon Dikastirion tis Vizantinis kai Metavizantinis Periodou se Themata Perousiakou Dikaiou, II Oikogeniako Dikaio* [The Legislation of the Ecclesiastical Courts of the Byzantine and Post-Byzantine Period in Matters of Property Law II Family Law] (Athens, 1997), p. 47).

5 According to the law, whoever carried 'the burdens of marriage' also received the fruits of the dowry (ibid., p. 16).

6 Ibid., pp. 95–7.

7 Angeliki E. Laiou, *Gender, Society and Economic Life in Byzantium* (Aldershot, 1992), p. 234.

in which women were quite active, not hesitating to file lawsuits against their husbands for mismanaging their dowry, often seeking to assume direct control of their wealth.[8]

Byzantine women also sought justice in the ecclesiastical courts since through their participation in liturgical life they gained some knowledge of Canon law.[9] Canon law has many sources (the Bible, apostolic tradition, the ecumenical and local synods, and the writings of Church Fathers) but the Orthodox Church did not seek to produce a full codification of all its canons until the early nineteenth century.[10] Besides, lay and ecclesiastical law were not seen as distinct from each other, hence the emergence of mixed civil–ecclesiastical legal collections known as the *Nomokanons*.[11] The caseload in ecclesiastical courts concerned primarily issues of marriage, dowries and inheritance,[12] and Church officials served a dual role: on the one hand instructing women of their rights, and on the other making rulings, often in their favour.[13]

Even after the final dissolution of Byzantium, the Church maintained its authority since Mehmet II found the institution a useful tool for the control of the Christian population of his expanding empire and thus elevated the Patriarch of Constantinople to head the Orthodox *millet*, and bestowed upon him significant powers, chief among them the right to oversee justice in his Orthodox flock.[14] The influence of ecclesiastical law was felt in almost every aspect of a Greek's life, and was particularly significant in family matters such as

8 Ibid., p. 237; Papagianni, *Nomologia*, p. 108.

9 Ioannis M. Konidaris, 'The Ubiquity of Canon Law', in Angeliki E. Laiou and Dieter Simon (ed.), *Law and Society in Byzantium, Ninth–Twelfth Centuries* (Washington, 1994), pp. 146–7.

10 Anastasios P. Christophilopoulos, *Ellinikon Ekklisiastikon Dikaion* [Greek Ecclesiastical Law] (Athens, 1965), pp. 47–8, 63. This was due to the principle of *oikonomia*, meaning that the Church reserved the right to refrain from applying the law for reasons of equity, limited of course by the boundaries of dogma (ibid.; Konidaris, 'Ubiquity', pp. 133–4).

11 R.J. Macrides, 'Nomos and Kanon on Paper and in Court', in *Kinship and Justice in Byzantium 11th–15th Centuries* (Aldershot, 1999), pp. VI 64–7.

12 R.J. Macrides, 'Dowry and Inheritance in the Late Period: Some Cases from the Patriarchal Register', in *Kinship and Justice*, p. V 89–90.

13 Ibid., pp. V 90, 94. Even convicted women were treated more leniently in ecclesiastical courts. St. Ioannis o Nisteftis had pronounced that a woman should never be separated from the Church and the congregation whatever her crime but should only be barred from Communion, to forestall suicides from their great shame. Valsamin added that they should even get the consecrated bread and simply be barred from receiving the Eucharist to avoid making their crime publicly known (Agapios Ieromonachos and Nikodimos Monachos, *Pidalion* [Rudder] (Athens, 2003), p. 715).

14 Nikolaos I Pantazopoulos, *Apo tis 'Logias' Paradoseos eis ton Astikon Kodika, symvoli eis tin istorian ton pigon tou neoellinikou dikaiou* [From the 'Learned' Tradition

the administration of the property of orphans, marriage licences, notarization of wills, and so on, some of which functions continued even after the emergence of the Hellenic Kingdom.[15]

The Ottomans did not seek to impose a unified legal system, but accepted a multitude of different practices applicable to different groups, usually according to their religion, that often overlapped or even competed with each other.[16] For the Orthodox population the system of justice that applied to them was not unlike what had existed towards the end of the Byzantine Empire. Local bishops presided over ecclesiastical courts, and judged according to Roman-Byzantine law, which for the period that concerns us was frequently based upon the collection of the fourteenth-century scholar Konstantinos Armenopoulos known as the *Exavivlos*.[17]

The decentralized nature of the Ottoman state led to further legal fragmentation. Local communities had to develop systems of administration that would oversee tax collection and would negotiate on behalf of the community with the regional Ottoman authorities, the tax farmer, or even with the Sublime Porte (that is the central government of the Ottoman Empire).[18] Once such bodies emerged, it was only natural that they would seek to expand

---

to the Civil Code: Contribution to the History of the Sources of Modern Greek Law] (Thessaloniki, 1965), p. 92.

[15] Papagianni, *Nomologia*, p. 202; Eleni E. Koukkou, *Diamorfosis tis Ellinikis Koinonias kata tin Tourkokratia* [Transformation of Greek Society during Ottoman Rule] (Athens, 1971), p. 55.

[16] The influence of the ecclesiastical courts has been prominent in the writings of foreigners, but the communal courts have been largely absent (D. Urquhart, *La Turquie* (Paris, 1837), pp. 52–3; Felix Beaujour, *Pinakas tou Emporiou tis Ellados stin Tourkokratia 1787–1797* [Table of the Commerce of Greece during the Period of Ottoman Rule 1787–1797] (Athens, 1974), p. 51; Gustav Karl Geib, *Parousiasi tis Katastasis tou Dikaiou stin Ellada* [Exposition of the Condition of Law in Greece] (Athens, 1990), p. 60).

[17] Urquhart, *Turquie*, p. 52; Pantazopoulos, *Logias*, p. 93. Konstantinos Armenopoulos (1320–ca. 1385) was a Byzantine jurist from Greece who held the post of 'universal judge' of Thessaloniki, one of the highest judicial offices in the Byzantine Empire. He is best known for his *Hexabiblos* (1344–45), a law book in six volumes in which he compiles a wide range of Byzantine legal sources. First printed 1540 in Paris, the *Hexabiblos* was widely adopted in the Balkans under the Ottoman Empire. In 1828, it was also adopted as the interim Civil code in the newly independent Greek state.

[18] It is a matter of some debate when customary law first emerged, some seeing it appear in Byzantine times (Aglaia E. Kasdagli, *Land and Marriage Settlements in the Aegean: A Case Study of Seventeenth-Century Naxos* (Venice, 1999), pp. 69–73). Similarly complicated is the question of the emergence of the local administrative bodies (Theod. E. Theodorou, *I Elliniki Topiki Aftodiikisi* [The Greek Local Self-Government] (vol. 1, Athens, 1996), pp. 145–58). Kasdagli also mentions the efforts of the ecclesiastical authorities to suppress the use of customary law (Kasdagli, *Land and Marriage*, p. 76).

their authority into the judicial realm. These local councils soon doubled as courts and were composed of lay notables and on occasion by religious potentates. They did try to emulate the pre-Ottoman legal practices of the Byzantine Empire, but with the lack of standardized written texts regional differences quickly emerged, especially where the locals had managed to receive formal recognition by the Ottoman state of their right to practise their own laws – as was the case with many islands in the Aegean, but also Mani and some other regions.[19] The judicial authority of these bodies was enhanced in commercial cases and slowly expanded their jurisdiction to include civil and penal matters as well.[20] On the other hand the Church retained its authority over matters that were of a religious nature, such as marriage and divorce, and bishops maintained a prominent role in their immediate surroundings, primarily the urban centres.

The communal courts were by definition local and as a result access to them was fairly easy for any member of the community, male or female. They were informal, without lawyers or even standardized codes by which to judge. Instead local customs were applied and every local inhabitant had the necessary knowledge to navigate the system and defend his or her rights. Because these local legal customs varied to a lesser or greater degree from region to region, and even from village to village, the local inhabitants had a distinct advantage over foreigners both in terms of knowledge and due to familiarity with those who judged. Finally the judgements were also more or less final and appeals incredibly rare and irregular.

In many respects they resembled the Islamic *kadi* courts that every inhabitant of the empire, despite his or her religion, could also choose to appeal to. At the time the *kadi* had achieved a near monopoly of judicial power as far as Ottoman Muslims were concerned,[21] and it has been demonstrated that Christians often sought justice in these courts even for such matters as divorce, arousing the fury of the Church which continuously demanded, and often received, imperial edicts banning *kadis* from interfering in such matters, though the repeated

---

19 N. Moschovakis, *To Dimosio Dikaio stin Ellada tin Epochi tis Tourkokratias* [Public Law in Greece at the Time of Ottoman Rule] (Athens, 1998), p. 112; Eleni E. Koukkou, *I Koinotikoi Thesmoi stis Kyklades kata tin Tourkokratia* [The Communal Institutions in the Cyclades at the Time of Ottoman Rule] (Athens, 1980), pp. 25–53, 89. In Hydra for example 'the *koinon* had as laws the customs, common sense, and the opinions of the householders' (Spyridon Trikoupis, *Istoria tis Ellinikis Epanastaseos* [History of the Greek Revolution] (vol. A, Athens, 1978), p. 145).

20 Michail B. Sakellarios, *I Peloponnisos kata tin Defterin Tourkokratian 1715–1821* [The Peloponnese during the Second Period of Ottoman Rule 1715–1821] (Athens, 1939), p. 89. See also Koukkou, *Koinotikoi*, p. 168.

21 Haim Gerber, *State, Society and Law in Islam: Ottoman Law in Comparative Perspective* (Albany, 1994), p. 70.

issues of such edicts shows that the practice never ceased.[22] One could also seek the judgement of the Ottoman executive authorities like the local *pashas*, and even of some non-Muslims who held Ottoman administrative posts such as the *Dragomans* of the Fleet who often sat in judgement when they visited the islands of the Aegean and who initiated the codification of the customary laws of those islands.[23]

Women in the Ottoman period certainly owned property,[24] but their ability to exercise any sort of control varied from region to region, often depending upon the terms of widowhood and the life stage that allowed greater agency to women.[25] Broadly speaking we can see diverging attitudes between the mainland and the islands with regards to these questions, with the former maintaining a more restrictive attitude, though with great local variation, whereas the latter seem more flexible. Women everywhere, however, were very active as litigants and their presence reveals a remarkable knowledge of their rights despite the multiplicity of legal practices available. The fact that Christian women frequently appear in the registers of the Ottoman *kadi* courts is an indication that they were quite aware of the significant benefits in doing so in certain issues, as was often the case with divorce.[26]

Women, however, usually found themselves in court regarding matters involving property. Husbands were frequently at the centre of such disputes since they managed the dowry and on occasion sold parts of it for their own use

---

[22] Mohamed Afifi has found many cases of Copts and Jews recording their marriages in front of the *kadi* and thus making them subject to Muslim law (Mohamed Afifi, 'Reflections on the personal laws of Egyptian Copts,', in Amira El Azhary Sonbol (ed.), *Women, the Family and Divorce Laws in Islamic History* (Syracuse, NY, 1996), p. 203). These are analogous with the infamous *kepinio* marriages denounced by Orthodox religious authorities (Evlogios Kourilas, *Patriarchiki Istoria* [Patriarchal History] (vol. A, Athens, 1951), p. 347; see also Leslie Peirce, *Morality Tales: Law and Gender in the Ottoman Court of Aintab* (Berkeley, 2003), p. 60; Manouil Io. Gedeon, *Vrachia Simiosis peri ton Ekklisiastikon imon Dikeon* [Brief Note about our Ecclesiastical Law] (Constantinople, 1909), pp. 59, 64, 69, 70–71).

[23] Koukkou, *Diamorfosis*, p. 148.

[24] See Evdoxios Doxiadis, *The Shackles of Modernity* (Cambridge, MA, 2012).

[25] One of the greater powers of a widow regarded her control over the property of underage children as well as her own, but this authority varied significantly throughout Greece (Papagianni, *Nomologia*, pp. 160, 173–5).

[26] See Sophia Laiou, 'Christian Women in an Ottoman World: Interpersonal and Family Cases Brought Before the Shari'a Courts during the Seventeenth and Eighteenth Centuries', in Amila Buturovic and Irvin Cemil Schick (ed.), *Women in the Ottoman Balkans* (New York, 2007); see also Nikolaos I. Pantazopoulos, *Church and Law in the Balkan Peninsula during the Ottoman Rule* (Thessaloniki, 1967), p. 102; Kourilas, *Patriarchiki*, p. 349; Dimitrios S. Ginis, *Oi Logoi Diazigiou epi Tourkokratias* [Reasons for Divorce during Ottoman Rule] (Thessaloniki, 1960), p. 244.

or needs. This was of course against the law, Byzantine or communal, and their wives did not quietly acquiesce to such actions, but demanded compensation.[27] Women as well as men also fiercely contested inheritances, and on occasion this led to bitter disputes within families. Some women felt wronged by the wills of relatives and thus lodged protests,[28] or even tried to have the wills of their husbands annulled.[29] Sons turned against their mothers,[30] women against fathers-in-law,[31] mothers against sons,[32] brothers against sisters,[33] or nieces against uncles.[34] Second marriages in particular were often at the root of serious problems regarding property allocations.

Greeks also appealed to Ottoman officials to intervene and adjudicate cases, as for example the *Kapudan Pasha* who held authority over many Aegean islands. They could also appeal on occasion to the consuls and ambassadors of various European states as a result of the 'capitulations' the Ottoman Empire had signed with the latter.[35] Thus Marino, wife of Captain Georgi Aggeli, began proceedings with the chancellery of Mykonos against the local Russian agent, and also involved the general consul of Russia in Smyrna (Izmir), all because her husband, though an Ottoman Greek, was a Russian subject.[36] This multiplicity of authorities and legal options also required litigants to be ever vigilant regarding the actions of their rivals. Since the *Kapudan Pasha* usually only visited the islands once a year, it would not have been too difficult for a litigant to arrange to be absent from the island at that time, thus avoiding a court

---

27 GAK Mykonos F18/069, 7 February 1764. Sometimes such acts appear as sales between the spouses (GAK Mykonos F96/72, 17 May 1806).

28 GAK Mykonos F16/35, 26 June 1750.

29 IEEE Naxos 4748, 19 July 1806.

30 IEEE Gizi 7486, 6 August 1773.

31 IEEE Mykonos 22581, 1811.

32 GAK Mykonos F16/50, 17 November 1768.

33 GAK Mykonos F16/96, 12 March 1818.

34 IEEE Mykonos 22551, 21 July 1817.

35 A number of Ottoman citizens had managed by the turn of the century to be under the protection of a European state, thus functioning under the principle of *sequitur forum rei* that allowed them to use consulates as courts for the settlement of their affairs. Some of the numbers that have been suggested sound fanciful (7 million under Russian protection throughout the Ottoman Empire and 200,000 under Austrian protection only in Moldavia) (Nikolaos I. Pantazopoulos, *To Dikaion tis Tourkokratias, IV, Ta 'Pronomia' os Politistikos Paragon eis tas Scheseis Christianon Mousoulmanon* [The Law of the Ottoman Rule IV: The 'Privileges' as Cultural Dimension in Christian Muslim Relations] (Thessaloniki: 1975), p. 872); but in the early 1800s the number of documents mentioning foreign agents, consuls, or ambassadors becomes significant, and on occasion we see documents bestowing foreign protection on individuals like Georgios Gizis, who received protection from the French ambassador for 'earlier services of his family' (IEEE Gizi 7507, 3 February 1790).

36 IEEE Mykonos 22540, 30 May 1817; IEEE Mykonos 22541, 31 May 1817.

decision.[37] To avoid this, litigants often filed documents to keep their opponents on their island or to ensure that their opponents did not seek redress without their presence, and women were present on both sides of such battles.[38]

Women sometimes appeared in these documents defending their husbands' interests even when their spouses were still alive. In some cases perhaps the husbands were simply unavailable and the women acted as their legal representatives, indicating great awareness not only of the financial circumstances of their families but also of those of their debtors.[39] Women were not above trying to manipulate circumstances to their benefit, and in general there can be little doubt that women were active in the financial and legal matters of their communities, with great awareness of their rights, particular circumstances, and financial transactions, not only regarding their own affairs or their husband's but also those of third parties of the island and perhaps beyond.[40]

An interesting element of the decisions of the communal courts is the fact that they were not consistent and were more concerned with maintaining a stable and peaceful community than with meting out justice in the modern concept of the word. The cases of Christodoulos Serigas and of the sons of Ioannou Ipinou are good examples of this inconsistency, since in both cases the issue revolved around the ability of a sibling to inherit based on his or her gender; but the communal court of Naxos reached very different resolutions in each case, in one dismissing differences in gender, in the other upholding them.[41] Such cases exemplify the flexibility of these courts, indicating a concern with seeking justice as opposed to legality. The courts were willing to bend the strict application of the law in order to protect people seen as particularly vulnerable: whether they had mental difficulties, were in difficult circumstances, or were simply too old and poor to provide for themselves.[42] The same attitude can be seen in the case of loans where the courts again tried to ameliorate the situations

---

[37] Eftychia D. Liata, *I Serifos kata tin Tourkokratia* [Serifos during Ottoman Rule] (Athens, 1987), p. 86.

[38] GAK Mykonos F16/39, 12 October 1752; GAK Mykonos F16/43, 20 October 1758; GAK Mykonos F16/40, 19 December 1752; GAK Mykonos F139/32, 25 May 1766.

[39] IEEE Mykonos 22537, 22 May 1817; GAK Mykonos F16/86, 21 June 1817.

[40] See Evdoxios Doxiadis, 'Legal Trickery: Men, Women, and Justice in Late Ottoman Greece', *Past and Present*, 210 (February, 2011): pp. 129–53.

[41] Naxos [Vat. Gr. 2634] 30 June 1814 from Menelaos A. Tourtoglou, 'Symvoli sti Meleti tou Metavyzantinou Ethimikou Dikaiou ton Kykladon' [Contribution to the Study of Post-Byzantine Customary Law in the Cyclades], *Epetiris Etaireias Kykladikon Meleton* [Review of the Society of Cycladic Studies], 27–8 (1980–81): p. 254; IEEE Naxos 5772, 9 November 1817; Naxos [Vat. Gr. 2634] 3 May 1811 from Tourtoglou, 'Symvoli', p. 253.

[42] IEEE Mykonos 22538, 23 May 1817; GAK Naxos F98/15, 22 October 1805 (the same document can be found at IEEE Bourgos 7994, 22 October 1805); IEEE Mykonos 22281, 24 August 1806.

and did not simply apply the terms of notarized contracts as the law demanded.[43] These attempted to maintain peace, relieve points of contention, and ensure the well-being of the community and its members. They acted as arbiters as much as courts, something that was obviously to the benefit of local individuals in cases of disputes with strangers.[44] This was what Aikaterina Martinovik from Zara discovered, leading her to denounce the rulings of the local court as being 'done based on friendly personal relations', while her opponent naturally claimed that the notables had made a fair decision.[45]

The Greek War of Independence (1821–1929)

The revolt of 1821, beyond overthrowing the executive power of the Ottoman authorities, also aimed at creating an entirely new polity with new forms of administration and justice. There was somewhat of a consensus regarding the general path that a future Greek state should follow, with two generally accepted principles, which unfortunately were not entirely compatible; and thus the attempts to reconcile them often led to bitter and, on occasion, violent conflict. The first principle was a determination that the new state would be a continuation of the past Hellenic glories, a proto-nationalist ideology that sought to eradicate whatever traces the centuries of Ottoman rule had left behind. The second idea was what we can call a modernizing principle, an eagerness for the new state to be a model European state, tailored after France or Britain.

Attempts to create 'Greek' legal codes pre-existed the revolution, especially in Moldavia and Wallachia where the Sultans, mostly based on Armenopoulos, appointed Greeks as rulers. More ground-breaking, Rigas Feraios (Velestinlis) – an eighteenth-century revolutionary influenced by the French Revolution – drafted a constitution for a Balkan federation that was to replace the Ottoman Empire, and produced his own *Rights of Man*, an adaptation of the celebrated document to the Balkan realities. Most Western-educated philhellenes or Greeks favoured the establishment of a 'modern' – that

---

43 IEEE Mykonos 22514, 1 May 1818.

44 I do not want to give the impression that the courts simply ignored the customary laws. Quite the contrary, the examples mentioned above were exceptions for extraordinary circumstances. The courts abided by the laws in the majority of cases, often even when there were reasons to act otherwise. In a decision on a dispute between a widower and his father-in-law over certain properties that the widower wanted for his orphans, the court found in favour of the grandfather, recognizing his right to allocate his property as he saw fit, but strongly urged that he assign it to his grandchildren (IEEE Naxos 5777, 5 December 1817).

45 IEEE Mykonos 22493, 16 June 1819; IEEE Mykonos 22495, 3 July 1819.

is a European – state, which necessitated the creation of uniform legal codes, and thus came into conflict with the proponents of customary law.[46]

Although in the early years of the revolution and up to the arrival of Ioannis Kapodistrias as governor in 1828 churchmen controlled the practical aspect of legal matters and were frequently appointed as religion, education, justice, and internal affairs ministers in the revolutionary governments,[47] the Church did not exercised a monopoly over law and justice. As early as July 1821, the General Organization of the Peloponnese, one of the many revolutionary bodies that emerged in Greece, recognized multiple sources for law – including natural law, the *Exavivlos* of Armenopoulos, the newly voted laws of the nation, and local customs; but other provincial authorities promoted different sources. The Legal Disposition of the Eastern Continental Hellas, for example, insisted on the exclusive use of the laws of the 'Christian Emperors' in private, public, and criminal law, while accepting the French Code for commercial law.[48] The task of combining these diverging paths to a unified whole was entrusted to the National Assemblies of Epidaurus (1822), Astros (1823), and Troizina (1827), which affirmed the primacy of the 'Imperial Laws' for private and criminal law, and the use of the French Code for commercial law.[49]

The easiest part was the adoption of the French Commercial code since it had been based on the *Statuta Mercatorum* of the Italian cities which in turn had formed the *de facto* commercial law of the Mediterranean, institutionalized by Napoleon in 1807 and already in use by the Greek merchants.[50] The persistent references to Byzantine law for civil and criminal matters may give the impression of some sort of general agreement, but there were other proposals – including the wholesale adoption of the French Civil code expressed as a 'wish'

---

[46] Pantazopoulos, *Logias*, p. 67. Notables formed a major component of those who supported customary law, as seen from a letter the notables of Tripolitsa dispatched to the government on 9 August 1823 demanding the appointment of new judges 'who know the customs of our province, know letters and laws, and [for that reason] it would make sense to appoint a local individual' (Iakovos, T. Visvizis, *I Politiki Dikaiosyni kata tin Ellinikin Epanastasin Mechri tou Kapodistriou* [Civilian Justice during the Greek Revolution and until Kapodistrias] (Athens, 1941), p. 273).

[47] Pantazopoulos, *Logias*, p. 121.

[48] Ibid., pp. 130–36.

[49] Ibid., pp. 139–47.

[50] Ibid., pp. 157–9. The Great *Dragoman* Dimitrios Mourouzis had instituted in Constantinople, and later expanded in maritime Greece, the so-called 'system of Greek merchants' with judicial authority over commercial issues. In 1807 this 'system' had accepted the French Commercial code of which two translations were published in Greek in 1817 and 1820 (Nikolaos S. Papantoniou, *To Idiotiko Dikaio ton Ellinon kata tin Epanastasi tou 1821* [The Private Law of the Greeks during the Revolution of 1821] (Thessaloniki, 1977), p. 19).

in the Third National Assembly at Troizina.[51] As early as 1824 and 1825 the Ministry of Justice had asked French and British philhellenes to provide it with the necessary legal texts as guides, and the tendency towards the incorporation of the French Code only grew stronger as time went on, especially under the governorship of Kapodistrias.[52]

We must distinguish, however, between the immediate need for a functional system of laws and ideas regarding the laws of the future Greek state. For the first there was little choice since Armenopoulos was the only widely recognizable collection of laws available.[53] The National Assemblies, however, addressed the creation of new legal codes, possibly based on the Civil code. This hope was modified under Kapodistrias, who instituted the equality of law and custom along with the supplementary use of the Civil code.[54] All Greek governments saw the variety of customary laws as incompatible with the political unity of the new state, exemplified by the surviving correspondence between the Minister of Justice Ioannis Theotokis and the *eparch* of Mykonos and Syros in 1825.[55]

Arguments regarding which statutes to implement were only one side of the issue. The second and in many respects even more crucial aspect was the effort to craft the physical components of a judicial system, a daunting task in view of the existing judicial practices, the unrelenting war, and constant political instability. In 1821, the first executive bodies set up by the rebels made provisions regarding the establishment of law courts, but no further action was taken that year. The *eforoi* of the Peloponnesian villages therefore by default assumed judicial responsibilities, although they were technically executive and not judicial officials, while in maritime Greece the pre-existing system probably continued unchanged.[56]

---

[51] Pantazopoulos, *Logias*, p. 159.

[52] Panagiotis I. Zepos, *I Neotera Elliniki Epistimi tou Astikou Dikaiou* [The Modern Greek Science of Civil Law] (Athens, 1954), pp. 10–13.

[53] The sources show repeated use of Armenopoulos in judicial decisions (Visvizis, *Politiki*, pp. 247, 310). Customary law was viewed by some 'progressive' Greeks as an expression of the interests of the elite and was thus rejected (Papantoniou, *Idiotiko*, p. 20).

[54] Nikolaos I. Pantazopoulos, 'I Entaxi tis Elladas stin Evropaiki Koinotita I Symvoli tis Antivasileias kai tou Othona 1833–1843' [The Entry of Greece in the European Community the Contribution of the Regency and Otto 1833–1843], in *I Krisi ton Thesmon tou Kratous, Symmikta pros Timin Phaidonos Th. Vegleri* [The Crisis of the Institutions of the State, Essays in Honor of Phaidonos Th. Vegleri] (Athens, 1988), p. 572.

[55] Papantoniou, *Idiotiko*, p. 21

[56] Visvizis, *Politiki*, p. 12. Law No. 12 of Epidaurus of 30 April 1821 did bestow upon the notables both administrative and judicial authority, thus giving an official seal to older practices (Michail Chouliarakis, *Geographiki, Dioikitiki kai Plithysmiaki Exelixis tis Ellados 1821–1871* [Geographical, Administrative and Demographic Development of Greece 1821–1871] (Athens, 1973), p. 90).

Thus the fragmentation of judicial responsibilities seen in Ottoman times continued, and probably grew, since in addition to the *eforoi* the higher clergy continued to play a significant role.[57] The various warlords also began to play a role through their wielding of *force majeure*, to the consternation of the notables.[58] The judicial practice of the revolutionary period was chaotic, torn between the efforts of the revolutionary governments to establish a unified system of law and the reality on the ground which saw the continuation of the fragmentation of judicial authority, now dependent upon the tides of war and the influence wielded by the warlords, notables, government officials, and the Church.

Attempts to formulate a cohesive judicial system, along with an administrative one, began in earnest in April 1822 when it was stipulated that each community should have a notary, a justice of the peace; each sub-province (*anteparchia*) a 'First Court' (*Proton Dikastirion*); and each province an appeals court (*Dikastirion* ton *Ekkliton*).[59] There was no standardization to the appointment of these officials and no formalized process, some being appointed directly by the provisional government – as was apparently the case with Tripolitsa, Mesologgi, Naxos, Paros, Serifos, and Santorini – while in Athens the Commons of the city probably elected the same individual who had functioned as a notary earlier, as was the case in many areas where the pre-revolutionary notaries continued to function without appointment from the government.[60] A Ministry of Justice was organized on 1 February 1822 but it was handicapped by instability at the very top, and as a result no court was established.[61] To complicate matters further, legislative (*Vouleftikon*) and executive (*Ektelestikon*) bodies feuded over which should function as a supreme court, a dispute enmeshed in the greater political conflict between the two bodies that would lead to violent civil strife among the Greek rebels. At the same time various ministries were becoming involved in different aspects of law, like the Ministry of Religion that took care of questions of marriage and divorce.[62] Regional executive bodies like the Peloponnesian Senate or the *Areios Pagos* in Sterea Ellada also claimed judicial functions. In Athens, as in many areas, the warlords were the effective authorities, especially under 'General' Ioannis Gouras, and for this reason the local inhabitants repeatedly demanded the formation of a regular court. Their wish was granted, but from its decisions we can see that it only operated from 20 December 1823 to 4 March 1824, possibly disbanded because of renewed Ottoman incursions.[63]

---

[57] See Visvizis, *Politiki*, p 13; and Pantazopoulos, *Logias*, p.121.

[58] Visvizis, *Politiki*, pp. 13–14.

[59] Ibid., p. 20.

[60] Ibid., pp. 24–6.

[61] Ibid., p. 26–8. Lawyers also appeared almost immediately, the so-called 'report-writers' who specialized in drafting petitions to the various ministries, courts, and executive bodies (ibid., p. 30).

[62] Ibid., p. 36.

[63] Ibid., pp. 36, 40, 42, 53, 58–9, 70, 80.

On 13 July 1824 Ioannis Theotokis was appointed Minister of Justice and began to concentrate all judicial responsibilities in his ministry, removing the judicial meddling of the Ministry of the Interior and the Ministry of Religion.[64] The authority of the ministry, however, was limited, as evidenced by the refusal of the local court of Mykonos to disband despite a clear directive issued by the ministry in 1825.[65] Ministers crippled their own efforts by trying to micromanage and concentrate nearly all power in their person, becoming directly involved even in minor property cases.[66] Officials, and even judges, were often unsure of the law and reached decisions that had no basis in any of the debated systems, as shown by the decision of the court of Paros which discovered a right of inheritance by a widow to 1/7 of the property of the husband.[67]

The presence of new legal avenues, however, allowed the evasion of local customs and traditions, as a protest from 1825 seems to imply. In this document the 'holy' *Sakelarios* of Apeiranthos (Naxos) appealed a local ruling by arbiters not in the local courts but in the 'courts of the province' (*eparchiako kritirio*), a reference to the recently instituted and only partially functioning courts of the state to be. We can already see that the people of Naxos were adjusting to the new realities and the new courts were assuming the role the Ottoman authorities used to play. There would be, however, a great difference between the two. The role of *Kapudan Pasha* and other such Ottoman dignitaries was always vague, his authority real but not well defined; and he – or rather his subordinate, the *Dragoman* of the Fleet – probably saw legal cases as an annoyance rather than an opportunity to assert control over local matters, unless there was profit in them of course. The new state courts, however, sought to assume sole responsibility for judicial decisions and their authority was undisputed, at least in the eyes of the new state authorities. To complicate things further a number of bodies vied for judicial pre-eminence. Just in Naxos decisions were taken by the *eparch*,[68] the central government appointee; the supervising-elders (*epistatogeronton*);[69] the supervisors of the

64 Ibid. pp. 96–100.

65 Ibid., p. 159.

66 Ibid., p. 232.

67 Iakovos T. Visvizis, 'To Klironomiko Dikaioma ton Syzygon epi Ateknou Gamou eis Paron kata ton 18o Aiona' [The Rights to Inheritance of Spouses in Childless Marriage in Paros in the Eighteenth Century], *Epetirida tou Archeiou tis Istorias tou Ellinikou Dikaiou tis Akadimias Athinon* [Review of the Archive of the History of Greek Law of the Academy of Athens], 8 (1958): pp. 150–51.

68 IEEE Naxos 6214, 10 July 1823.

69 IEEE Naxos 6451, 16 June 1826.

villages (*epistaton chorion*);[70] the common supervisors (*koinon epistaton*);[71] village notables (*prokriton*);[72] the council of the notables (*demogerontia*) of the island;[73] arbiters (*diaititon*);[74] the First Court of Central Cyclades (*Protoklito Dikastirio ton Kentrikon Kykladon*);[75] and the provincial council of notables of Naxos (*Eparchiaki Demogerontia Naxou*).[76] From Mykonos we can add the bishop and supervisor of the province of Mykonos (*Despoti kai topotiriti*), who sat in court with the notables;[77] the *epitropos* of the Northern Cyclades;[78] the 'commissioner (*epitropo*) of Karystos' governor-lieutenant (*archon topotiriti*) of Mykonos';[79] the 'all-holy' head priest (*Archierea*), vicar (*topotiriti*) of Mykonos;[80] and the vice-commandant (*antyparchos*) of Mykonos.[81] Although almost certainly some of these bodies were identical under different names, the documents present an administrative and judicial labyrinth in almost perpetual flux. Thus despite the efforts of the revolutionary governments to institute a modern hierarchical system there was a distinct lack of procedural clarity, reminiscent of the multiple authorities of the Ottoman period. If the locals found something confusing, it was probably not the procedures themselves but rather the constant changes, as well as the intrusion of foreigners, and perhaps foreign customs, into the system.

The majority of the court cases covered roughly the same issues of the pre-revolutionary period, although some gained more prominence than they had: as, for example, questions of inheritance due to illegitimacy, the ability of bastard children to raise property claims being a new phenomenon, not seen often in Ottoman Greece.[82] Women were still expected to know the laws, as was stated in a protest lodged by the *economos* of the village of Filotio and the chief notary (*protonotarios*) of the same village who claimed to be amazed at how a

---

70 IEEE Naxos 6459, 9 July 1823; IEEE Naxos 6472, 9 August 1826; IEEE Naxos 6481, 31 August 1826; IEEE Naxos 6484, 4 September 1826.

71 IEEE Naxos 6614, 17 July 1828.

72 IEEE Naxos 6503, 1 November 1826.

73 IEEE Naxos 6575, 21 July 1827; IEEE Naxos 6576, 27 July 1827.

74 IEEE Naxos 6572, 3 July 1827; IEEE Naxos 6577, 30 July 1827; IEEE Naxos 6396, 27 September 1825; IEEE Naxos 6397, 27 September 1825; IEEE Naxos 6620, 14 September 1828.

75 IEEE Naxos 6676, 23 October 1829.

76 IEEE Naxos 6649, 13 May 1829.

77 GAK Mykonos F139/47, 18 March 1827.

78 GAK Mykonos F117/102, 2 August 1828.

79 GAK Mykonos F117/419, 12 October 1828.

80 GAK Mykonos F117/714, 6 May 1829.

81 IEEE Mykonos 22469, 5 July 1823.

82 IEEE Naxos 6495, 13 October 1826.

widow could make the claims she did since she was of an age 'and knowledgeable of the local customs'.[83]

There was, however, a new procedural development, the frequent involvement of outside judicial authorities. Many of these cases eventually went beyond the island, particularly to the neighbouring island of Syros, which was the seat of the regional authority.[84] With the involvement of different, and remote, authorities people were able to delay or manipulate circumstances, especially in the uncertain conditions of the time, as indicated by the case of Eirini from Mykonos, who was denounced by the notables to the *epitropos* of the Northern Cyclades as 'a devious and scheming old woman who with all this deceived and is deceiving every day those who have claims upon her' because despite her claims of poverty she had two sons who owned ships.[85] Women were quite able to adapt to the new circumstances and utilize the developing institutions of the emerging state to their benefit, if not always in an honest or even lawful manner. Just as women in earlier times could threaten with appeals to the Ottoman authorities, people perceived the new government officials in the same way and tried to use them in similar fashion. After all, both the *Kapudan Pasha* and the *epitropos* were outsiders as far as they were concerned, and useful tools in their struggles with other locals.

Furthermore, in continental Greece the legislative attempts of the government were more successful than in the islands, in part because the war and the frequent Ottoman military incursions in those areas weakened the local ruling bodies. Athenian notables, for example, began to claim to take government proclamations into consideration. In a ruling over inheritance, the decision was claimed to have been reached 'according to the Royal Christian Laws established by the A' and B' National Assemblies',[86] although these 'laws' were not mentioned in detail for the simple reason that the assemblies never instituted laws but gave guidelines primarily based on Armenopoulos.

Even so, in most documents the notables throughout Greece consistently based their decision on 'old custom', that is the customs that they were using in Ottoman times and which were familiar to them and the people at large. That, however, does not seem to have been the basis for the decisions of the *eparchs* or government appointees. As early as 1823 we have a case where the notables of Naxos reversed a decision by the *eparch* Antonios Alexopoulos, stating that 'we were wholly mystified how and in what manner they misled the H[onourable] *Eparch*', indicating multiple inconsistencies and finally dismissing

---

83 IEEE Naxos 6172, 23 October 1822.

84 GAK Mykonos F97/186, 21 October 1826.

85 GAK Mykonos F117/283, 4 September 1828; GAK Mykonos F117/338, 18 September 1828.

86 GAK Athens F1/5, 20 January 1824.

the decision as illegal and 'beyond the local customs'.[87] Nor was this an isolated example. Three years later the notables reversed yet another decision by the *eparch*, who had 'irrationally' cancelled a will.[88] These cases show the tension that existed between local authorities, which at this time continued to have executive and judicial authority, and the government officials whose decisions frequently diverged from local customs. The confusion of the period is made evident by the fact that in theory the *eparchs* who made such rulings were executive, not judicial appointees. At the same time, the councils of the notables that reversed these decisions were technically a lower body than the *eparchs*. Clearly things had not been settled between these two poles of authority at this period, perhaps because the central government had a lot more important things on its mind than decisions regarding wills or dowries. Things, however, would change with the end of the hostilities when the government would be free to concentrate on creating a 'modern' and 'European' state.

Law and Gender in a Modern State

The Enlightenment and the French Revolution influenced many Greek scholars who denounced what they perceived as the lawlessness of the Ottoman Empire, in their eyes supported by the Orthodox Church, contrasting it with the European states which were seen as orderly, and where laws were observed.[89] As the anonymous author of the *Elliniki Nomarchia* (Greek Rule of Law) stated: 'Free people, my dears, can be compared to a family. The laws are like the parents to the citizens.'[90]

With the conclusion of the war these scholars could focus on creating a model European state, and one of its pillars would be a modern judicial system. However, although some consensus existed on the adoption of some statutes, as for instance regarding the adoption of the French Commercial code, on the issues of criminal and especially civil law there was no agreement, and several ill-defined groups pursued a number of contradictory policies.

---

[87] IEEE Naxos 6459, 9 July 1823.

[88] IEEE Naxos 6481, 31 August 1826.

[89] See Fotios Chrisanthakopoulos (Fotakos), *Apomnimonevmata peri tis Ellinikis Epanastaseos tou 1821* [Memoirs about the Greek Revolution of 1821] (Athens, 1996), p. 47. Also Adamantios Korais, *Adelphiki Didaskalia* [Brotherly Instruction] (Athens, 1852), p. 26; Dimitrios Fillipidis, Daniil Ieromonachos, and Grigorios Ierodiakonos ton Dimitrieon, *Geographia Neoteriki* [Modern Geography] (Athens, 2000), p. 116; and Anonymou tou Ellinos, *Elliniki Nomarchia* [Greek Rule of Law] (Athens, 1968), pp. 19, 80, 106, 110). Paschalis Kitromilidis, *Republican Aspiration in Southeastern Europe in the Age of the French Revolution* (Athens, 1980), pp. 277–81.

[90] Anonymou tou Ellinos, *Elliniki*, p. 45.

The first such grouping wanted to use Byzantine law as the basis of the system, with whatever modifications were deemed necessary. Their close association with the Orthodox Church did not endear this idea to Westernizers like Adamantios Korais who urged the rejection of Byzantine tradition.[91] Conversely, a more radical group sought a clear break with the past. They wanted to adopt the Napoleonic Civil code with some adaptations for Greek realities.[92] One difficulty with this was the fact that Greece lacked people trained in law, as the contemporary historian Spyridon Trikoupis stated.[93] On the other hand the few formally trained Greek legal experts had been mostly French educated, and were thus intimately familiar with the Napoleonic code, while the process of adopting the code seemed simply one of translation.[94] The attraction of adopting the legal system of the archetypical European state was certainly a factor, as was the case for many other European states at the time.[95] The drive towards the French model gained momentum after the recall of the Bavarian legal expert and member of the regency Georg Maurer from his post as regent,[96] supported by prominent scholars like Mavrokordatos, one of the first

[91] Adamantios Korais, *Simiosis eis to Prosorinn Politevma tis Ellados tou 1822* Etous [Note on the Temporary Polity of Greece of 1822] (Athens, 1933), p. 118.

[92] The third National Convention expressed a 'hope' for the incorporation of the Civil code, although many consider this a form of mimicry rather than a sincere attempt to establish a legal system based on French ideas (Pantazopoulos, *Logias*, p. 159). Others, however, see a strong current for the incorporation of the Civil code (Zepos, *Neotera*, p. 13).

[93] Trikoupis, *Istoria*, vol. B, p. 107.

[94] Two judges, A. Polyzoides and K. Schinas, were commissioned to supervise the translation, and in the documents of the time there were continued discussions regarding the implementation of the French Civil code as late as 1836, as can be seen from a letter of the Secretariat of Justice (GAK Othonika, Ê – Politiki Dikaiosini, á. Astiki Nomothesia etc. 1. – 1834–36, 13/25 August 1836 N. 14342).

[95] In the 'Tanzimat' period of the Ottoman Empire, following the conclusion of the Greek War of Independence, there were even suggestions that the Ottoman state adopt the 1804 code. Deniz Kandiyoti, 'End of Empire: Islam, Nationalism and Women in Turkey', in Deniz Kandiyoti (ed.), *Women, Islam and the State* (Philadelphia, 1991), p. 27. The Napoleonic code was also the model for the civil codes in Italy, the Netherlands, Belgium, Spain, Portugal, and Switzerland in addition to France. Ann Taylor Allen, *Feminism and Motherhood in Western Europe 1890–1970: The Maternal Dilemma* (New York, 2005), p. 44.

[96] Nikolaos I. Pantazopoulos, 'Georg Ludwig von Maurer – I Pros Evropaika Protypa Oloklirotiki Strofi tis Neoellinikis Nomothesias' [Georg Ludwig von Maurer: The Complete Turn of Modern Greek Legislation towards European Models], *Epistimoniki Epetiris Scholis Nomikon kai Economikon* Epistimon [Scientific Review of the School of Legal and Economic Sciences], 13 (1968), p. 1459.

professors of the Law School in 1837,[97] Palmas,[98] and Korais.[99] A third school of thought recognized that the evolution of law had not simply ended in 1453 but had continued through the evolution of local practices and customs. Maurer, who had been entrusted with the construction of the judicial system, shared these ideas and ordered a survey of the legal customs throughout Greece, to serve as the foundation for the development of an indigenous Civil code that would balance the varied customs and traditions. There were firm theoretical foundations in European legal thought regarding such a project, advocated by famed legal scholars like Friedrich Carl von Savigny, thus allowing this group to evade the accusation of opposing the Europeanization of Greece.[100] The final tendency claimed respect for customary law while elevating Roman law as the ultimate and final authority when there was need to arbitrate between conflicting traditions. In essence, however, it advanced a very different concept since it rejected the widely used Armenopoulos in favour of the original *Corpus Juris Civilis*, a text centuries older that excluded laws and modifications of later Byzantine emperors. Thus these scholars rejected both the developments of the Ottoman period and the later Byzantine tradition of jurisprudence.

This legal wrangling is beyond the scope of this examination, but the eventual outcome is significant. The decree of 23 February 1835 recognized as the law of the land the civil laws of the Byzantine emperors and the equality between custom and law,[101] but the supporters of customary law faced a significant disadvantage since the multiplicity of local practices made their compilation into a comprehensive and coherent code a near impossible task. To make matters worse, the idea of legal regional autonomy was at odds with the centralizing attitudes of the Greek governments. Furthermore, all those involved in the development of the legal system of Greece were in agreement that the country needed a unified system of justice as a prerequisite for the establishment of a modern state. As a consequence, the physical structure of a modern justice

---

97 Ibid., p. 1464.

98 Ibid., p. 1467.

99 The idea of the French code as a paragon of progress has survived even in relatively modern scholarship, especially among that of Marxist analysis (see Giannis Kordatos, *I Koinoniki Simasia tis Ellinikis Epanastasis tou 1821* [The Social Significance of the Greek Revolution of 1821] (Athens, 1977), p. 223). Kordatos on the same page blames the 'oligarchs' for the failure to implement the French code, and Kapodistrias, as an 'oligarch', imposed the Roman-Byzantine law against the wishes of many 'bourgeois'. Eventually, in his view, an alliance of bourgeois and notables led to the elimination of customary law (ibid., p. 225). I should point out, however, that many Greeks had a very suspicious attitude towards the West and Fotakos quotes a popular saying: 'God save you from the sword of the Turk and the court trials of the Venetian' (Chrisanthakopoulos, *Apomnimonevmata*, p 46).

100 Pantazopoulos, 'Entaxi', p. 547.

101 Ibid., p. 577.

system was set up with remarkable speed, and long before the state had a comprehensive system of laws.[102] Edmond About sarcastically commented that Greece had a National Council, a Supervisory Board, a Supreme Court, two Courts of Appeals, 10 courts of first instance, three commercial courts, 120 Justices of the Peace, criminal courts, juries, lawyers, notaries, court clerks – 'yet there is no justice in Greece ... [She] has a temporary Civil code borrowed from Roman Law, from the Code of Napoleon, and from German legislation.'[103] His description was not inaccurate. At the lowest level were the justices of the peace known as *eirinodikes*, who often doubled as the office of the public notary. Right above them stood the *protodikeia*, the courts of first instance in most significant towns.[104] Above those stood the courts of appeal or *efeteia*, and above them was the Supreme Court or *Areios Pagos* situated in the capital, Athens. This system required some common basis for rulings, and thus in practice it slowly turned away from the more varied aspects of customary law, especially in the higher levels of appeal.

Several other factors also influenced the outcome of the legal dispute. The formalized structure crafted favoured those who had received formal legal training, as did the familiarity of the early administrators, ministers, and functionaries, many of whom were Bavarians and other Europeans, with certain established European ideas and practices. As a result, the groups in favour of the Civil code and the German school were able to emerge as the leading contenders. The French school was seemingly getting the upper hand in 1835–36, leading to the publication of the translation of the Civil code by the noted legal scholars Vellios, Polizoidis, Pitzipios, and Schinas.[105] However, political, ideological, and even practical factors led to the eventual success of the German (or Historical) school led by the noted legal scholar Pavlos Kalligas, whose ideas set the legal future of Greece.[106]

---

[102] By 1835, when the Leonidio archive of the Justice of the Peace and Notary begins, Greece already had a fully developed four-tiered judicial system, a mere five years after the first treaty recognizing a Greek state.

[103] Edmond About, *I Ellada tou Othonos* [The Greece of Otto] (Athens 1992), p. 164. He also had a low opinion of judges who did not have life tenures or were incorruptible, and were far too full of a 'rabid patriotism', though he probably liked the difficulties the regency and the monarchy faced regarding the adoption of the death penalty, almost gleefully commenting on how carrying out death sentences had been impossible until 1847 because the people would always kill the executioners (ibid, pp. 164, 166).

[104] Vas. Vl. Sfyroeras, *Istoria tis Neoteras Ellados, I Periodos tis Vasileias tou Othonos (1832–1862)* [History of Modern Greece: The Period of the Reign of Otto 1832–1862] (Athens, 1970), p. 39.

[105] Pantazopoulos, 'Entaxi', pp. 579–80.

[106] Certainly the presence of a Bavarian administration was a factor in favour of the German school, as was the fact that many later legal experts (unlike the early ones) were

Still, in the early decades of the new Hellenic Kingdom the courts followed a mixture of customary practices, traditions stemming from Armenopoulos, and laws passed by the new governments. Although the use of Armenopoulos would become problematic quite soon after this period, and legal experts and bureaucrats continued discussing the possibility of applying 'French laws', often involving the king himself in the debates,[107] courts, ministries, and *demogeronties* regularly referred to the *Exavivlos*.[108] The significance of Armenopoulos can be seen in a report by the noted politician, judge, minister of Justice, senator, and law professor Christodoulos Klonaris regarding the translation of the *Exavivlos* of Armenopoulos, assigned to him by Governor Kapodistrias, probably to be used as a manual by judges.[109] Although customary law was recognized, its use was uncertain, as seen in the case of Marousa Filippidenas who needed, and received, from the *demogerontia* of Mykonos a statement proving that 'there is a strong custom since immemorial times in this island according to which women, whether married or single, are able to borrow and to be forced to fulfil

educated in German as opposed to French universities, and one of these, Konstanstinos Schinas, was Savigny's son-in-law (Zepos, *Neotera*, pp. 18, 22; Pantazopoulos, *Logias*, p. 236). In fact, just as Alerinos Palmas was publishing his polemic in favour of the Civil code, the noted proponents of the German school, G. Rallis and M. Renieris, translated and published Ferdinand Mackeldey's manual for the use of Roman law, which with deliberate misrepresentation transformed the entire legal theory in Greece, overcoming the equality between custom and law. Pavlos Kalligas completed what they started, supplanting the *Exavivlos* for the *Corpus Juris Civilis* of Justinian. (Pantazopoulos, 'Entaxi', p. 580; see also Caroula Argyriadis-Kervrgan, 'Byzantine Law as Practice and as History in the Nineteenth Century', in David Ricks and Paul Magdalino (ed.), *Byzantium and the Modern Greek Identity* (Aldershot, 1998), pp. 19, 32, 39, 41, 44).

107 GAK Othonika, Ypourgeio Dikaiosynis – K – Politiki Dikaiosyni, a) Astiki Nomothesia etc. No. 14342, 13/25 August 1836.

108 For ministerial decisions see GAK Othonika, Ypourgeio Dikaiosynis – K – Politiki Dikaiosyni, a) Astiki Nomothesia etc. 1834–36, No. 5308, 23 November/5 December 1838; GAK Othonika, Ypourgeio Dikaiosynis – K – Politiki Dikaiosyni, a) Astiki Nomothesia etc. 1843, No. 099, 15/27 February 1843; GAK Othonika, Ypourgeio Dikaiosynis – K – Politiki Dikaiosyni, a) Astiki Nomothesia etc. 1846, No. 102, 01/12 December 1846, among others. For *demogeronties* see GAK Othonika, Ypourgeio Dikaiosynis – K – Politiki Dikaiosyni, a) Astiki Nomothesia etc. 1834–36, No. 4379, 22 October 1834 from Ermoupolis; GAK Othonika, Ypourgeio Dikaiosynis – K – Politiki Dikaiosyni, a) Astiki Nomothesia etc. 1834–36, No. 1940, 7 March 1835 from Hydra, among others.

109 GAK Othonika, Ypourgeio Dikaiosynis – K – Politiki Dikaiosyni, a) Astiki Nomothesia 2, 1837, No. 002 (dated 18 July 1833). Of course certain parts of the centuries-old collection had to be modified as, for example, the provisions regarding *protimisis* (preference) (GAK Othonika, Ypourgeio Dikaiosynis – K – Politiki Dikaiosyni, a) Astiki Nomothesia 2 1838, No. 080; No. 18841; No. 26215; and so on.

their personal obligations'.[110] Still, as far as the rights of women to property were concerned, neither Armenopoulos nor the new laws passed at this time seriously threatened their status.

The absence of legislated change, however, did not mean that the emergence of a completely new judicial structure had no effect. Its impact on women was tremendous and in essence determined the future course of women's property rights, and eventually their legal status in Greece, much more than the laws themselves. It did so in a number of ways, most significantly by physically excluding them from the court. That resulted in making women dependent upon men – husbands, relatives, and especially professional lawyers – and reduced their incentive to know and keep up with the changes regarding the laws impacting property rights.

One of the most remarkable changes that appear in the archives compared to earlier periods is the proliferation of letters of power-of-attorney by women to men, especially lawyers. Although not an innovation of the period, such documents were rare, and certainly not gender-specific. Their purpose was usually to conduct some form of transaction in distant locations, and the person who received the authority was often someone already living in that location, or someone who was going to travel there. Such justifications did not disappear, but they became the minority.[111] A few documents were drafted for specific financial circumstances,[112] but most regarded lawsuits, a completely new phenomenon with great implication on the ability of women to be active participants in the defence of their rights.

One could perhaps expect wives to draft such documents for their husbands who managed their properties anyway, yet only 37 of 276 such documents composed by women in the town of Leonidio gave such power to husbands, a mere 7.5 per cent of the total; and even in those the husband frequently was not the sole representative of his wife. Some married women did make relatives their representatives, especially when the husband was the cause of the difficulties or when they were seeking a divorce.[113] Eleni Exarchou for instance

---

110 GAK Mykonos F111/1734, 14 February 1831.

111 GAK Leonidio 2062, 26 July 1842; see also GAK Mykonos F104/111, 27 September 1832. Of course most male letters-of-attorney fall under this category, and such letters are frequently encountered in other regions as well for men (GAK Athens F1 unnumbered, 17 May 1831) and women (GAK Athens F1 unnumbered, 20 April 1832; GAK Athens F1 unnumbered, 7 May 1832) or couples (IEEE Naxos 6741, 6 February 1832).

112 GAK Leonidio 2234, 1 November 1842; and GAK Leonidio 2171, 29 September 1842.

113 GAK Leonidio 507, 5 August 1837; GAK Leonidio 431, 19 May 1837; GAK Leonidio 2732, 14 February 1844; GAK Leonidio 211, 1 July 1848; and GAK Leonidio 475, 15 November 1848.

made her brother her representative to sue her husband at the *efeteio* of Nafplio, demanding the separation of their fields.[114] Most women who drafted such documents, however, were unmarried, often widows, who used to vigorously defend their rights in the courts.

The change can be assigned to the impact of the new judicial system. Although there were local avenues for conflict resolution, such as the justice of the peace or arbiters, the new system embodied a significant difference from the previous Ottoman system. It was hierarchically organized with a clear line of progression from the lower courts all the way to the *Areios Pagos* in Athens.[115] Thus any decision was not final but simply a stepping-stone in an elaborate process of multiple trials before appeals were exhausted. Furthermore, the physical location of the courts aggravated this complexity. From the documents of Leonidio we can see that the court of first instance that was responsible for the region of Leonidio was in Sparta, days away over formidable mountains lacking roads. The appeals court was in Tripoli and later Nafplio, even further away, although Nafplio at least was accessible by sea. The *Areios Pagos*, the Supreme Court, was in Athens, much further away, though again potentially accessible by sea.[116] Distances like this, on foot or donkey, over dangerous mountains crawling with bandits, would take days or even weeks. Adding to the difficulty and cost of finding food and lodging, the possibility of multiple trips required for the conclusion of a trial, and often the age of the individuals involved, the mere location of the courts effectively excluded the presence of women in the actual proceedings. If we add the moral considerations of women travelling for days in remote areas, the appeal of assigning a male representative is clear. Married women also needed their husbands' approval to travel, and it is doubtful that husbands would be very open to the idea.[117]

114 GAK Leonidio 2679, 5 January 1844.

115 A hierarchical system was envisioned from the very first National Assembly in 1822, which vaguely 'appointed' a Supreme Court, general courts at administrative centres, courts at the capital of every province, and justices of the peace in every community. Similar clauses were included in all constitutions except for the one of 1844, since by that date the system was functioning (Alexandros Svolos, *Ta Ellinika Syntagmata 1822–1975/1986* [The Greek Constitutions 1822–1975/1986] (Athens, 1998), pp. 118, 131, 149, 153). The early efforts, however, did not lead to the creation of the proposed systems, and as late as 1828 laws continued to mandate the creation of courts, and continued to meet the opposition of the local notables (Trikoupis, *Istoria*, vol. 4, p. 328).

116 An 1834 decree envisioned the founding of *protodikeia* at the capital of every *nomos* (Nafplio, Tripoli, Patra, Sparti, Syros, Athens, Chalkida, Amfissa, Mesologgi and Pylos); three commercial courts, *emporodikeia*, at Syros, Patra, and Nafplio; two *efeteia* at Athens and Tripoli; and the *Areios Pagos* in Athens (Sfyroeras, *Istoria*, p. 39).

117 Women were present where the court was more easily accessible, like the various

The preponderance of lawyers as beneficiaries of such aptly named documents provides further insights into the difficulties women faced in this system. By far the most common category of representative, lawyers exemplify the legal changes that had taken place in Greece. Their presence was unavoidable, not only for women but for men as well, since only they could present the case in the legal jargon necessary and in such a manner as to convince the equally professional judiciary.[118] This proliferation of lawyers is evidenced in other regions like Naxos where again most of the *epitropika* involved court cases and most of those made lawyers the representatives of women as well as men,[119] although other men such as brothers could also represent women in certain legal matters including interrogations.[120]

Women of course did not suddenly become incapable of managing their own affairs at a local level, and continued to be involved even in communal actions.[121] Women even hounded the murderers of their husbands in the courts,[122] and at least some men felt they could trust women with important decisions, like Theodoros Zimaras, who made his mother Lygeri his representative for all his disputes and financial affairs.[123] Romantic ideas may have begun to influence the attitudes of Greeks, especially regarding the abilities and frailty of women, since we encounter frequent references to 'female weakness'[124] or examples of men who would not even entrust the upbringing of their children to their wives,[125] pointing to the gradual changes in perceptions regarding the roles and capacities of women in remarkable

justices of the peace (IEEE Naxos 6717, 19 January 1831), reaffirming the difficulty of travel as a prime motivator for letters-of-attorney.

118 The repetition of the same lawyers in document after document, for example Ioannis Roussopoulos and Nikolaos Leonellos for the *protodikeio* of Sparta, indicates the emergence of a system where certain lawyers created ties with certain communities and represented them almost exclusively in the courts situated in the various towns.

119 See IEEE Naxos 8039, 20 July 1837; and IEEE Naxos 8040, 16 May 1837.

120 IEEE Naxos 6787, 19 August 1834.

121 GAK Leonidio 884, 18 January 1839; GAK Leonidio 456, 26 October 1848.

122 GAK Leonidio 1262, 14 August 1847; and GAK Leonidio 391, 7 October 1850.

123 GAK Leonidio 363, 10 September 1848. In the prominent Deligianni family it was quite common for men and women to exchange letters regarding the management of properties, the collection of debts, and other such economic matters. See EFL Nikolaos Deligiannis BIV/1, No. 16, 25 May 1836; EFL Nikolaos Deligiannis BIV/1, No. 21, 12 September 1836; EFL Nikolaos Deligiannis BIV/1, No. 23, 19 September 1836; EFL Panagos Deligiannis BII/2, No. 7, 20 September 1832.

124 GAK Leonidio 387, 27 February 1837.

125 Such arrangements by men could lead to serious conflict, as the case of Aggelina Repa indicates. Aggelina appointed a lawyer as her representative to sue the guardians of her underage daughter appointed by her husband who were apparently withholding her dowry (GAK Leonidio 418, 29 April 1837).

accordance with such changes elsewhere in Europe; but it is doubtful that such ideas had penetrated the whole society so quickly.

As in earlier times, dowry and inheritance disputes form the bulk of the cases that involved women. One interesting element that we observe regarding dowry disputes in this period is the frequent conflict between individuals who would not have been involved under the previous regime. Very often such disputes occurred after the death of a spouse, as was the case of Manoli Mpouga and his father-in-law Ioanni Hatzi over the dowry of the wife of the former. A compromise was reached with the latter receiving most of the dowry in return for a payment 4,200 drachmas to his son-in-law.[126] Assuming the spouse was indeed deceased, and the document is not clear on this point, this agreement implies that spouses had developed in this period claims upon the property of their deceased partners, a radical departure from the strictly separate properties of earlier years, and the emergence of the concept of common marital property. A similar implication is found in the agreement between Marousa Fanti and her daughter-in-law Metaxou, the widow of G. Rontaki, where the latter received her dowry and premarital gift and relinquished her rights to the property of her late husband.[127] Although again the precise circumstances are unclear and the widow's rights may be based upon a will, the existence of such rights was a rather significant departure from earlier times, and an indication that the properties of spouses were starting to be viewed if not yet as joint, then as not entirely separate.

The archive of Leonidio also contained 54 compromises that involve women, most regarding disputes over dowries and inheritance, some already in the courts.[128] What is particularly interesting, however, was the drafting of such agreements after the judicial process was well on its way and the courts of first instance had reached a decision.[129] These examples indicate the ability of wealthier individuals to outlast poorer ones and to force them to accept settlements giving them less than their full rights. Widows would be particularly vulnerable to such tactics, since most could hardly afford years of delays and mounting legal costs before they received their due and could be inclined to settle for less. Wealthy individuals could even convince a widow to abandon her lawsuit regarding the murder of her husband by offering sufficient funds for 'her dowry and premarital gift and the civil demands of her orphaned children',[130] or

---

126 GAK Leonidio 293, 18 August 1836.

127 GAK Leonidio 1986, 25 May 1842.

128 GAK Leonidio 1556, 20 March 1841; GAK Leonidio 1625, 28 May 1841; GAK Leonidio 1695, 10 August 1841; GAK Leonidio 2347, 6 April 1843, among others.

129 GAK Leonidio 488, 19 February 1846; see also GAK Leonidio 1483, 23 December 1847.

130 GAK Leonidio 1305, 1 September 1847.

even in cases like rape, indicating a very different mindset from the one of the earlier communal courts.[131]

The tradition of letters of complaint continued in the post-independence period, again often acting as a preamble to possible legal action. Many of these complaints make reference to the turmoil of the war and many of the conflicts stemmed from circumstances of the war and its aftermath.[132] Many, however, also involved the new state and especially state confiscations and the auctioning off of properties, including those of wives over the debts of their husbands.[133] The situation described in these documents should not have been possible, since the property of the wife was supposed to be in the administration of the husband and at the same time inalienable. Yet men on occasion apparently managed to put it in jeopardy while retaining their own intact.

Even more problematic were cases regarding the property of a deceased spouse and the claims of the surviving one, once again indicating that the former clear divisions between the properties of husband and wife were breaking down, or at least people were attempting to break them down, not always through legal means. Stamatis Refenes, for example, viewed his wife's property as part of his own, isolated his wife from her relatives, and even convinced a priest to write a counterfeit will to advance his claims, as the priest was forced to admit.[134] Zoitsa Tsolina, was expelled from her husband's house by her father-in-law, who also took his son's entire property, although Zoitsa was presumably the legal guardian of her daughter Eleni, the heir to her father's wealth.[135] More complicated was the case of Maroula Panagiotou, widow of Dimitriou Karamanou.[136] She stated that her son-in-law, who had married her daughter Aggelina, had died without a will, leaving behind two daughters, Pagona and Maroula, from his marriage to Aggelina, and a second wife with three other children. Maroula claimed the right to be guardian of the first two children as the 'maternal grandmother' but the second wife managed to block her and, to make matters worse, she and the mother of the deceased arranged a dowry contract for Pagona limiting her paternal inheritance to a pittance. Maroula was trying to assert her rights based on bloodlines and she would have been successful in earlier times under customary law, but in the new state her rights had been eroded. The paternal grandmother was able to exert influence in a married son's family but the maternal could not, which is consistent with the legal notions that would soon

131 GAK Leonidio 154, 11 May 1848.

132 GAK Leonidio 234, 18 May 1836; or GAK Leonidio 131, 13 January 1836, among others.

133 GAK Leonidio 102, 29 November 1835.

134 IEEE Bourgos 8030, 26 January 1830.

135 GAK Leonidio 2344, 1 April 1843.

136 GAK Leonidio 254, 20 August 1845.

prevail.[137] Conflicts over guardianship became very common, indicating that people were confused about the new circumstances and uncertain regarding the rights of parents and grandparents over guardianship.[138] Although the rights of the father were occasionally challenged, it was much more common for those of the mother to be in question, despite the fact that the law gave guardianship of children to the surviving spouse.[139]

Many court decisions seem to go against the customary practices seen in the Ottoman period. In Mykonos as early as 1832 Aikaterina, the mother of the deceased Avgousti Mastromarkou, sued her daughter-in-law Despoina regarding the property of the deceased valued at 598 *grosia*.[140] Although clearly there were no offspring from the marriage, the court proceeded to split the property into three parts: one for the spouse, one for the mother, and one for the soul of the deceased to be spent by the mother, a textbook example of Byzantine *trimoiria*. The rather significant break from most of the customary practices which did not recognize any rights to inheritance to the spouse gives credence to the increasing significance of Armenopoulos and the undermining of customary law by the courts of the new state, as well as the slow amalgamation of spouses' property.

Another example of problems stemming from the property of a deceased spouse can be seen in the case of Metaxou Trochani, whose first husband's property had been confiscated. With the permission of her second husband, Dimitriou Hatzimpakirou, she sued in the *protodikeio* of Sparta in order to recover 2,000 *drachmas* as her dowry and premarital gift, and she did eventually

---

137 Pavlos Kalligas (1814–96), perhaps the most influential Greek scholar of the nineteenth century, stated regarding the guardianship of orphans that 'the family of the father had precedence over that of the mother' (Pavlos Kalligas, *Systima Romaikou Dikaiou* [System of Roman Law] (vol. D, Athens, 1930), p.226). The precedence of the spouse over the bloodline as far as guardianship of children were concerned is also seen in the case of the widow Maroula, who had managed her late husband's property for 20 years before having to account for it to her stepson Konstantino Siora. In order to 'satisfy' the latter she gave up her claims to her husband's property (4/5 of it). This claim was based upon her right to inherit her own offspring from her marriage to the father of Siora who had died after her husband (GAK Leonidio 2720, 5 February 1844). It would have been remarkably unusual for a stepmother to assume such authority in earlier times.

138 Ioannis Sotirou Theodorou for example complained that his father-in-law, Nikolaos Georgios Makrymichalos, took by force his toddler Evgenou to his house and refused to give her back, putting the child in danger since he was not able to sustain her as he had done until then 'like a mother' since the death of his wife a month earlier. Strangely for such a conscientious father, he ended his complaint by declaring that he should be considered blameless for whatever happened to his daughter, and that he refused to recognize any expenses his father-in-law might undertake for her sustenance (GAK Leonidio 1218, 17 July 1847).

139 Georg Ludwig Maurer, *O Ellinikos Laos* [The Greek People] (Athens, 1976), p. 698.

140 GAK Mykonos F92/3, 23 August 1832.

receive 1,300 *drachmas*.[141] Significantly, the decision took over six months, and clearly the case was longer than that since she had had the time to remarry well before the case reached the courts. Nor was this an isolated case. Women frequently had to defend their property from those who sought to confiscate it because of the debts or misdeeds of their husbands, as we saw in the letters of complaint and as is evidenced in actual court cases.[142] Thus although the law was rather clear in maintaining that the spouse was to receive her dowry intact before the creditors claimed their dues, the people who enforced confiscations had a difficult time separating the two, or perhaps did not consider the two properties as separate, forcing women to seek the expensive course of legal action. Furthermore, certain aspects of the property like the dower (*progamiaia dorea*) had an unclear status since Armenopoulos and customary practices viewed them in very different ways, allowing for different interpretations and thus conflict.[143]

A final example will bring in some new institutions of the state that would become increasingly significant in the financial transactions of the nineteenth century and to this day. The legal dispute of Dionysios Chrysospathis, representing his daughter Eleni who had inherited the property of his late wife Marioris, against the National Bank, just recently established, is indicative of the fundamental changes taking place both in the way the economy functioned and the manner in which the new judicial system resolved disputes. The dispute originated because the grandparents of Eleni, Kanelos Deligiannis and his wife Anastasia, took a loan from the bank, placing a house as surety, even though this house had been assigned to the dowry contract of their daughter. The bank tried to repossess the house when the loan went unpaid, but Chrysospathis successfully defended his claim that the house, as part of his wife's dowry, could not have been set as surety, pursuing the case all the way to the *Areios Pagos*, where he was vindicated.[144] Despite this decision by the Supreme Court, however, a few months later the National Bank sent a new letter to Kanelos and his wife informing them that they were continuing their suit to recover their

141 GAK Leonidio 446, 30 December 1850.

142 GAK Leonidio 624, 5 May 1846.

143 Byzantine law saw the dower as ultimately being part of the husband's property, reverting to his heirs. Customary law bestowed it upon the woman, as did, eventually, later modern Greek law (Georgios S. Maridakis, *To Astikon Dikaion eis tais Nearais ton Byzantinon Avtokratoron* [Civil Law in the Nearais of the Byzantine Emperors] (Athens, 1922), p. 148). Armenopoulos stated that although a widow had the right to receive her dowry before any creditors, the dower was excluded from the rule (Konstantinos Armenopoulos, *Procheiron Nomon I Exavivlos* [Manual of Laws or the Six-Books] (Athens, 1971), p. 80).

144 EFL Chrysospathis BV/2, No. 78, 22 June 1853.

loan.[145] Thus Chrysospathis was dragged into the courts again in a three-way legal battle with his parents-in-law and the National Bank.[146]

Besides the obvious significance of the appearance of banks as a new source of lending that transformed the economic functions of the Greek economy, what is most striking about this case is the length of time of the dispute, a point that gives new emphasis to my earlier assertion regarding the difficulties the new courts presented. Even though the dispute had already reached the *Areios Pagos* by 1853, four years later the dispute was still unresolved. If we add to this time the time it took for this case to actually reach the *Areios Pagos*, we can clearly visualize the effort, and cost, of such endeavours. The 68 *drachmas* awarded to Chrysospathis in the 1853 decision for court expenses at the *Areios Pagos* alone are an excellent indication of such costs. Clearly the great majority of Greeks, and widows in particular, would be incapable of enduring such costs over an extended period of time, which may have acted as an additional impediment to their use of the judicial system.

Women also protested regarding certain actions by their husbands, usually involving their dowries. Two such documents from Leonidio dealt with the sale of property which, according to the women involved, was forced upon them. In the first case Aggelina Hatzi Theodori complained that an exchange of a dowered field with a house belonging to her husband was done 'by force' and never finalized and demanded the annulment of the exchange.[147] In a similar vein, Maroula Reppa claimed that she had been forced by her husband Nikolao Mpoutzela to sell a dowered field for 200 *drachmas* which she never received and wanted the reversal of the sale.[148] Although similar, these two cases help us clarify two very different aspects of the sales and exchanges regarding married women. The second case is indicative of the pressures husbands could exert on women to force them to alienate their dowries. The first, however, is more interesting because the field in question had apparently been lost to debts and auctioned off, raising the possibility that married couples could try to exploit the laws and perceptions surrounding dowered properties to their financial benefit vis-à-vis third parties, a possibility recognized by the law as far back as Armenopoulos.[149]

---

145 EFL Kanelos Deligiannis BI/F8, No. 117, 11 December 1853.

146 EFL Kanelos Deligiannis BI/F8, No. 115, 6 October 1857.

147 GAK Leonidio 1039, 21 April 1847.

148 GAK Leonidio 1380, 30 September 1847.

149 Armenopoulos, *Exavivlos*, p. 78. In a similar case Kyrana Metirtika, wife of Giannaki Oikonomou, made her uncle, Georgio Karamano, her representative to sue Dimitrio Mastrogiorgo, who had bought three fields from her husband without her permission (GAK Leonidio 2931, 7 September 1844). It is rather perplexing why people would be willing to buy properties under such uncertain circumstances unless they were already beginning to see the properties of a married couple as one and the law lagged behind the reality.

On the other hand such ambiguities also meant that widows could be held accountable for the debts and obligations of their husbands, and perhaps attempts could even be made to take advantage of them, but they frequently defended themselves against such machinations strenuously. An extraordinary example is the case of Aikaterini the wife of the late Georgiou Parotzi, who replied in a complaint by Ioani Makropoliti that:

> I, as a woman, was not aware of the transactions of my late husband, as it is not proper for women to be involved in the works and deeds of men, more so those that are external and commercial and thus I am not obliged by the Laws to give to your honour any of what you demand.

She also added that:

> According to the established laws and the civil procedure and because my late husband died without a will, I am not obliged to get involved in the exchanges of my husband but the first court (*protokliton Dikastirion*) is obliged to assign guardians for the children with the concurrence of all the relatives and then those must [illegible] the required and to all of my late husband's exchanges.

And she concluded:

> Finally, regarding all that you present that you have to receive from my late husband, for all that you can prove by his own signature, those are acceptable. Those that you present through your own signature, because the deceased is not alive to respond to those, for that reason they are unacceptable. These in reply and for your information.[150]

This remarkable document is a true treasure trove of information. First of all the language is noteworthy in the sense that it closely resembles a rather simplified form of the legalistic jargon of the time, indicating that Aikaterini probably sought some expert advice before composing her reply. She also used and appealed to concepts that were just being introduced in Greek society at the time. Those familiar with Romantic ideals would certainly recognize appeals to gendered separate spheres (female–private, male–public) that Aikaterini mentioned ('external', 'commercial'). Aikaterini even refused to automatically assume the guardianship of her husband's property, claiming that other guardians must be legally appointed, probably a delaying tactic on her part. Finally she rejected all claims not backed by documentation, again an appeal to the new legalistic and formalized legal culture that was being established. In short, Aikaterini was not

---

150 IEEE Naxos 6749, 1 January 1832.

hesitant to use all the new cultural, legal, and social innovations to combat the claims of Parotzi, even if her very own actions betrayed her words.

Until the establishment of the modern Greek state, the ecclesiastical courts heard divorce cases, with any property complications trickling down to the communal courts occasionally. The new state could not entrust such a significant part of civil society entirely to the hands of the Church, with which it was already embroiled in rather significant conflict over its links to the Patriarchate of Constantinople and over ecclesiastical property, so it assumed partial responsibility.[151] Certainly the question of divorce was given some significance in the exchanges between the responsible ministries of the new state (Justice, Religious Affairs and Education, Interior), especially regarding the acceptable causes for divorce which during the Ottoman period had proliferated compared to the rather more restrictive practices of the Byzantines.[152] Adultery was a particular concern, but so were practical matters such as whether divorces should be publicly announced like all other acts of the state.[153]

Several cases appear in the archives of Leonidio, and many were rather straightforward.[154] In these examples divorce appears as a rather casual affair, undertaken almost lightly as long as there were no complications regarding property or children. The frequency and ease of divorce and remarriage is further shown by the case of the comb-maker Georgios (Mpazinis) who gave a house, various fields, and household goods to Diamanto Rori, whom he considered as his wife, though he could not marry her ecclesiastically because he had already married three times and divorced and the Church did not allow fourth marriages.[155] This case does not simply exemplify the ease of divorce at the time but also the continuing of the practice of cohabitation. Other cases

151 Legal scholars quickly resorted to historical arguments for this intrusion by the state, claiming that the Orthodox Church had assumed authority over marriage only towards the end of Byzantine, and especially during Ottoman times (Kalligas, *Systima*, vol. D, p. 15).

152 GAK Othonika, Ypourgeio Dikaiosynis – K – Politiki Dikaiosyni, b) Politiki Dikonomia 1835–39, No. 5392, 14 October 1835. An example of this widening of the grounds of divorce in Ottoman times involves consensual divorce that had become legal under the Ottomans but was eventually abolished in the Modern Greek state (Maridakis, *Astikon*, p. 92). The new state also instituted legal separation without a divorce, possibly as a means to stem the numbers of divorce cases (Kalligas, *Systima*, vol. D, p. 145).

153 GAK Othonika, Ypourgeio Dikaiosynis – K – Politiki Dikaiosyni, b) Politiki Dikonomia 1835–39, No. 109, 24 March 1836. The final decision was for divorces to be publicly announced but for the grounds of the divorce to be kept confidential (GAK Othonika, Ypourgeio Dikaiosynis – K – Politiki Dikaiosyni, b) Politiki Dikonomia 1835–39, No. 10799, 2/14 April 1836; see also No. 5392 and No. 2751).

154 GAK Leonidio 187, 7 April 1836; GAK Leonidio 489, 21 July 1837.

155 GAK Leonidio 554, 1 December 1849. In Ottoman times this case would have led to a clandestine (*kepinio*) marriage, but such options were no longer available.

fall in between divorces and property disputes where wives sued husbands, perhaps implying separation but not necessarily stating it. One such example involved Varvara Triantinou, who was settled in Russia and who had made her mother Stamatou the manager of her property in Greece. Varvara, hearing that her husband, Nikolaos Triantinos – having abandoned Varvara and her two adolescent children since 1814 without support and thus having lost any claim to her property, as she stated – was harassing her mother, gave her mother full authority to prosecute him in the courts in order to allow the unimpeded flow of the income from her properties to her in Russia.[156]

More surprising are cases where there was an almost detached dispute over property between husband and wife that did not seem to impact the marriage itself. Eleni Exarchou and her husband Michail Arkoudaris for instance, appeared together in a document stating that Eleni had filed a lawsuit for the separation of her fields from her husband because he had spent her dower and other wealth, and, as per the clause 675 of Civil Jurisprudence, she wanted his leave to present a report to the *Protodikeio*.[157] Surprisingly, her husband did give her his permission to appear in court and repeat her lawsuit against him, as he succinctly stated. One may be tempted to admire Eleni for her persistence if this case is taken at face value, but it is quite possible that the couple engineered this process to secure part of their properties against possible debts of the husband, as the loss of the moveable dowry may indicate. It is interesting to observe the renaissance of the requirement of the husband's permission, seen in Byzantine law but rather ignored as far as I can tell in Ottoman times, as well as the legalistic attitudes of the new courts which stuck to the letter and forms of jurisprudence, as opposed to the old communal courts which were much more interested in substance over formality. The difficult conditions of the early decades of the new state in the aftermath of the terrible war and the waves of refugees offered opportunities to people to bend the rules of proper behaviour or legality; but, unlike the actual years of the war, and even earlier periods, the rapidly centralizing state and the return to some normalcy made such efforts increasingly hard and resulted on at least one occasion in the discovery of such an attempt before it was consummated.[158]

---

156 GAK Leonidio 214, 18 July 1845. I should note that although both the Russian Empire and the Hellenic Kingdom claimed Orthodox Christianity as the official state religion, there were significant differences between their attitudes towards many civil matters, including divorce, which may have led Varvara to seek a Greek rather than a Russian divorce since Russia had been tightening the practice (see Gregory L. Freeze, 'Bringing Order to the Russian Family: Marriage and Divorce in Imperial Russia 1760–1860', *Journal of Modern History*, 62/4 (December 1990): pp. 709–46.

157 GAK Leonidio 263, 28 August 1845.

158 GAK Mykonos F111/1920, 18 May 1831.

The European Influence

Before concluding this investigation, I would be remiss in not discussing the influence of European ideas and ideals which were flooding into Greece at the time. Although I have maintained that as far as this period is concerned the effects on the relationship between women and property were due to structural changes that the modern nature of the Hellenic state required, that does not mean that there were no other changes that were taking place in the cultural and social environment of Greece which would have far-reaching implications in the future. This was after all the period of Romanticism, of the emergence of nationalism, and the second Industrial Revolution, which had begun to transform Europe and of course Greece.

Much of the governmental structure of the Greek state was manned by Europeans up to 1843, especially French and Germans, whose influence was even greater than their physical presence since they shaped the institutions of the Greek bureaucracy.[159] Greece in its early, formative years was inundated with foreign troops (French and Bavarian), foreign travellers, fortune seekers, and philhellenes, many of whom chose to stay after the end of the hostilities. All these could not but affect the culture of the areas where they were present, which primarily meant the major urban centres. Furthermore, the king, his wife, and much of the court were German, although King Otto took great pains to embrace a Greek identity.

Even more pervasive, and certainly more enduring, was the influence of expatriate Greeks and foreign-educated Greeks who became the core, and perhaps the bulk as well, of the political and bureaucratic elites of the new state. The two most prominent Greek politicians of the time, Ioannis Kolettis and Alexandros Mavrokordatos, had been born beyond the confines of the then Greek state, had received 'European' education, and, in the eyes of many Greeks, represented the European influences that many of their followers tried to emulate.[160] The combination of actual foreigners and foreign-educated

[159] It is telling that the early state documents of Greece were composed in a mixture of Greek, German, and French, the last serving as a *lingua franca* (literally) between the Greek and Bavarian administrators.

[160] The role of these educated elites has been widely recognized as instrumental for the development of the state, at the time as well as in modern historiography. De Gobineau thought that without the *Phanariotes* there would have been no possibility of even minimal interaction between foreign 'experts' and Greeks (Artur de Gobineau, *Sto Vasileio ton Ellinon* [In the Kingdom of the Greeks] (Athens, 1999), p. 54), while Kitromilidis for his part sees these intellectual elites as fulfilling the crucial role in expressing the goals of the revolution in terms comprehensible to Europe (for example as an expression of political liberalism) while at the same time shaping the institutions of the new state according to Western principles (Paschalis Kitromilidis, *Neoellinikos Diafotismos* [Modern Greek

Greeks covers nearly the entirety of the administrative elites of the new state, and thus the character instilled in the institutions that were being born could not help but reflect their experiences and knowledge. Greece looked for ideas to the West, particularly for those aspects that were new to the mindset of the people. One such was the concept of nationality, which was definitively defined as male. The law regarding nationality stated among others that whereas those born abroad of a Greek father and a foreign mother had the right to seek Greek nationality, and the wives of Greek men were also considered to have the Greek nationality, Greek women who married foreigners lost theirs, which they could recover upon their widowhood.[161] The stipulations above could have been copied for all intents and purposes from Albert Fritot, who had stated that the nationalization of the man automatically implies that of the woman, since she owes her husband obedience and her fortune is irrevocably tied with his.[162] It is no coincidence that Fritot was translated into Greek a year after the law on nationality was enacted; nor that among the subscribers to the publication were some of the most significant political, academic, legal, and cultural figures of the new nation.[163]

Nationality became a crucial element in the new state as an irredentist form of nationalism took hold of Greece from the mid 1840s onwards

Enlightenment] (Athens, 2000), p. 467). The *Phanariotes* were perfectly fitted for this role as intermediaries since they had served as such between the Ottoman Empire and Europe before the Greek Revolution (K.Th. Dimaras, *Neoellinikos Diafotismos* [Modern Greek Enlightenment] (Athens, 2002), p. 7).

161 Law No. 199, Athens, 15 May 1835 (B.K. Nikolopoulos and A.I. Kakoulidis, *Syllogi Apanton ton Nomon, Diatagmaton, Egkyklion, Odigion, kai Eidopoiiseon ton Ypourgeion kai Synthikon tis Ellados meta ton Allon Ethnon* [Collection of All the Laws, Decrees, Proclamations, Directions, and Announcements of the Ministries and Treaties of Greece with Other Nations] (vol. A, Athens, 1859), p. 364). Later scholars expounded upon the law and defined a Greek as someone who was a) born to a Greek father; b) born of a Greek mother 'and no lawful father'; c) born in Greece of unknown parents; and d) born of foreign women and non-lawful Greek fathers who recognized them. A woman who married a Greek automatically became Greek, and was able to maintain that nationality if the marriage was dissolved 'because although a woman has to follow the man, it does not follow that so much authority has been given to him that he can repeal her adopted nationality at will' (Kalligas, *Systima*, vol. A. pp. 211–15).

162 Albert Fritot, *Didaskalia Peri Physikou Dikaiou* [Teachings about Natural Law] (Athens, 1836), p. 77.

163 Some of the prominent names in the list of subscribers included X. Paparigopoulos, A. Mamoukas, G. Kambouroglou, P. Soutzos, A. Rizos Ragavis, A. Mavrokordatos, N. Paparigopoulos, G. Tertsetis, G. Gryparis, P. Triantafilopoulos, N. Oikonomou, N. Renieris, D. Metaxas, D. Soutzos, I. Filimon, N. Vamvas, and the *demogerontia* of Ermoupolis (Fritot, *Didaskalia*, p. 128).

known as the Great Idea (*Megali Idea*).[164] The impact of this ideology would be unprecedented. It would transform perceptions regarding Greek history, advancing a concept of continuity from antiquity to the present, with Byzantium transformed from a period of darkness to the glorious Greek Middle Ages, superior to European states of the times.[165] Proponents of this idea sought the causes of the fall of the ancient Greeks in their civil strife, the pervasive immorality spread by ideas such as those espoused by the Sophists, and the ambition of certain men like Alexander and his successors. What Greece needed to achieve its ultimate destiny was National Unity (*Ethniki Enotis*) and a return to 'old', moral philosophy.[166] This context of unity towards a common goal – of stressing morality, obedience, and Christian values, as advanced by a simultaneous religious revival – created an environment where to challenge the accepted or promoted roles was paramount to treason. Even thinkers who rebelled against this climate, like Theofilos Kairis, urged women towards obedience, love, and support for husbands within the home, as both neo-traditional and European ideas like those of the influential jurist Robert Joseph Pothier suggested.[167]

---

[164] First formulated by the poet Alexander Soutsos in 1843 but catching the imagination of the entire country after a speech by the then prime minister Ioannis Kolettis, the Great Idea laid claim to all lands inhabited by Greeks (Paschalis Kitromilides, 'On the Intellectual Content of Greek Nationalism: Paparrigopoulos, Byzantium and the Great Idea', in David Ricks and Paul Magdalino (ed.), *Byzantium and the Modern Greek Identity* (Aldershot, 1998), p. 27).

[165] Michael Herzfeld, *Ours Once More: Folklore, Ideology and the Making of Modern Greece* (Austin, 1982), pp. 4, 40; Paschalis Kitromilidis, 'Ideologika Revmata kai Politika Aitimata: Prooptikes apo ton Elliniko 19o Aiona' [Ideological Currents and Political Demands: Views from the Greek Nineteenth Century], in G. Tsaousis (ed.), *Opseis tis Ellinikis Koinonias tou 19ou Aiona* [Facets of Greek Society of the Nineteenth Century] (Athens, 1984), p. 32; Dimaras, *Neoellinikos*, p. 115.

[166] Georgios G. Kozakis Typaldos, *Philosofikon Dokimion, peri tis proodou kai tis ptoseos tis palaias Ellados* [Philosophical Essay, Regarding the Progress and Fall of Old Greece] (Athens, 1839), p. 407.

[167] Theofilos Kairis, *Gnostiki i ton tou Anthropou Gnoseon Syntomos Ekthesis* [Gnostic or a Brief Exposition of Human Knowledge] (Athens, 1849), pp. 72–3; Sarah Hanley, 'Social Sites of Political Practice in France: Lawsuits, Civil Rights and the Separation of Powers in Domestic and State Government 1500–1800', *American Historical Review*, 102/1 (February 1997), p. 43. An example of the power of both this attraction to 'old' morality and the appeal of Europe is seen by the sudden attention of Greek scholars to authors like François Fénelon, whose text on the raising of girls was translated into Greek in 1857. Fénelon, despite writing in the late seventeenth and early eighteenth centuries, was a strong proponent of the domestication of women, their mental weakness, but also of the need to 'properly' educate them, all very appealing ideas to the intellectual Greek elites of the time (Fenelonos, *To Peri Agogis Korasion* [About the Education of Girls] (Athens, 1868), pp. 2, 58, 61, 65–6).

With the political, cultural, academic, and business elites so influenced by Europe, emerging European ideologies like Romanticism were bound to be quickly disseminated among the Greek elites.[168] Women were seen as in need of male supervision and protection, not only young women but even mature women who used to be able to function with considerable independence before. Widows like Sofia who sold a property had to be 'guided (*cheiragogoumeni*) by her son Apostoli'.[169] How much of this was rhetoric as opposed to reality is open to question, since at the same time we encounter women as witnesses in documents of prominent families.[170] Legal discrimination, however, was present throughout the newly enacted laws, which on the one hand saw the need to protect women and on the other valued them considerably less than men.[171]

Along with such ideals, we should not ignore that competing sources of authority and cultural foci had been wiped out by the revolution. Almost the entire Jewish and Muslim communities of Greece had been eradicated, making the new state one of the most homogeneous political entities in Europe. There were no longer competing cultural trends in the area, no other cultural icons, no alternative views. Greece had become a small, homogeneous European state; and, as was happening throughout Europe at the time, the cultural imperatives of the elites would soon be passed on to the rather egalitarian Greek society through the effects of education, urbanization, and later military service. When this would take place, the legal framework that had been inherited from the Byzantine and Ottoman traditions would be challenged as inadequate, backward, impure, undeveloped, and Asiatic, and would be changed, bringing it closer to a European ideal that was ironically coming under attack at that very moment by

---

168 The influence of even the early members of the Greek Romantic school (Soutsos, Neroulos, Ragkavis) is rarely in dispute, even upon the leaders of the conservative 'Christian feudalism' like the former great notable families of the Lontos, Zaimis, Notaras, Kountouriotis (Kostis Moskov, *I Ethniki kai Koinoniki Syneidisi stin Ellada 1830–1919* [The National and Social Consciousness in Greece 1830–1919] (Thessaloniki, 1972), pp. 109–10).

169 GAK Athens F1/50, 21 October 1832.

170 EFL Kanelos Deligiannis BI/F4, No. 37, 18 July 1840.

171 An excellent example of both was the law stipulating the details regarding travel and compensation of witnesses in trials. That law stipulated that 'witnesses of female gender or aged under 15 years old are to receive only half of the determined compensation [note – determined according to the profession of the witness]; but if children under 15 or women who have not completed 25 years are called to witness, they are to be accompanied on the road trip or their stay by their father, guardian mother, or legal guardian; the chaperone, assuming he presents himself as such, received the entire compensation of witnesses'. Thus women 25 years of age needed the supervision of, preferably, men, while female witnesses received only half the compensation of men; not of course because they were seen as inferior, but because their economic value was half that of men (Decree No. 181, in Nikolopoulos and Kakoulidis, *Syllogi*, vol. A. p. 239).

feminists for its inadequacies. Greece would seek to adopt a 'European' model that Europe was beginning to abandon.

Although in law women's property rights remained unchanged, the archival evidence led me to believe that a transformation was slowly taking place. Many women sought formal security for their dowries by placing their husbands' properties as surety or tried to receive compensation for the parts of their dowries that were lost.[172] It is disturbing to observe, however, how many of these women lifted previous sureties without explanation, possibly under pressure exerted by their husbands.[173] The apparent ability of husbands to influence the decisions of their wives regarding the security of their dowries, coupled with the equally disturbing trend whereby wives regularly stood surety with their properties for the commercial transactions of their husbands, is indicative that the formerly clear boundaries between the properties of a husband and a wife were being eroded, slowly leading to the concept of joint property in a marriage, under the supervision and authority of the husband of course.

In my view there are three developments that point to gathering threats which would eventually impact women's property rights in the future, undermining their ownership of their dowries, their ability to separate their property from that of their husbands, and their right to act as independent individuals. First was the merging of a husband's and a wife's properties which would eventually lead to the concept of joint properties in married couples, which was quite well known in contemporary Europe and actively promoted since keeping separate properties was seen as 'unromantic'.[174] Although by itself this concept was not necessarily detrimental to women, its effects were dependent upon the legal requirements regarding the disposition of properties within a marriage, simply stated, who managed the property. If the husband was the sole administrator and did not require the consent of his wife, obviously the move from legally separate to commonly held properties would have seriously undermined the economic standing of a woman within the marriage.

Second was the exclusion of women from the courts, which had different but equally detrimental effects. If women could not be present themselves and defend their rights by themselves, they were naturally dependent upon other, exclusively male, individuals. By removing themselves from the judicial system, women also began to lose the need to know the laws that governed their properties. This knowledge used to be necessary to them since it was common

172 GAK Leonidio 201, 10 June 1848; GAK Leonidio 515, 12 November 1849; GAK Leonidio 1757, 8 October 1841.

173 GAK Leonidio 380, 2 September 1849; GAK Leonidio 412, 18 September 1849; GAK Leonidio 583, 22 December 1849; GAK Leonidio 218, 5 July 1848.

174 Amy Louise Erickson, *Women and Property in Early Modern England* (New York, 1993), p. 107.

that at some stage in their lives women may have had to assume the management of their properties, and thus potentially be embroiled in disputes. In the post-independence period such concerns were the province of their husbands and lawyers, and, although useful, such knowledge was no longer critical. At the same time, through the lack of education, much greater in women than men, and thus their exclusion from the information dissemination process as well, women became increasingly ignorant of the details of their rights and possible changes to said rights. As a result they moved from being unable to being incapable of acting on their own, ironically fulfilling the claims of the emerging ideas regarding female duties and capacities.

The third development was the relative deterioration of women's rights, not due to erosion of the rights they had but in comparison to male rights. If women did not gain or lose rights with the establishment of the modern Greek state, that is not the case with men. The adoption of a constitution in 1843 gave nearly universal manhood suffrage to Greeks. Men could suddenly elect the various officials and political figures of the state and influence the development of society directly. Furthermore, the outcome of this universal suffrage in Greece was to have the democratic function merge with the pre-existing patronage traditions and develop into a clientelist system, which of course excluded women who had few things to offer in return for benefits.[175]

The same process can be seen in education. Although men were always on average better educated than women, in Ottoman times this mostly meant that a handful of men perhaps knew how to write. For the vast majority of the population conditions were more or less identical. The new state, on the other hand, willingly undertook the responsibility to provide education to all its citizens; but it did not have the resources to do so, and of course it chose to concentrate its efforts on the male side of the population. This discrepancy in education by definition led to the undermining of women's ability to know their rights as those were changing with new legislative acts. Such changes were naturally announced through the newly founded, and rapidly expanding, Greek press, a fact that made such laws vastly superior to customs according to the noted legal scholar Pavlos Kalligas, since 'through publication the laws become known to all, especially to the judge'.[176] Customs, lacking such dissemination, could not be as impartial or ensure proper judicial due process. What Kalligas ignored was the widespread illiteracy in Greece, as well as the existence of other means than print to disseminate information regarding customary law. And as

---

[175] The system of patron-client pre-existed the establishment of the Greek state but merged with it, influencing the political scene well into the twentieth century. It was based on institutionalized ties (marriage, godparenthood and so on) with economic benefits for all concerned (John Anthony Petropoulos, *Politics and Statecraft in the Kingdom of Greece 1833–1843* (Princeton, 1968), pp. 53–60).

[176] Kalligas, *Systima*, vol. A, p. 145.

the male illiteracy rates rapidly decreased while women's did not, knowledge of law became increasingly a male prerogative and source of influence and power.

Not only that but, in accordance with European models of the time, even when they received education, women did not receive the *same* education as men. It was not the kind of education that would enable them to assert themselves in the marketplace or society, but rather it was education that would enable them to raise upright citizens, or so the experts thought. In comparison, women in earlier times had learned, if education is defined broadly, the means to survive in every aspect of their existence, from the laws governing their wealth, as was indicated in earlier chapters, to the management of wealth.

Conclusion

It is interesting that right about the time when we can actually bring concepts of equality and universal rights into a discussion of women, law, and society there is a remarkable inequality emerging due to the fact that men forge ahead receiving a multitude of rights while women remain tied to the past, and would soon begin to see even their traditional rights eroded. While Ottoman Greek society had allowed women a place in its courts, a place that women actively used to defend their rights, the new state had difficulty even giving them the right to bestow the Hellenic nationality on their husbands, an indication of the fact that women were not seen as citizens in the same manner as men. The relative position of women compared to that of men deteriorated, and at the same time the conditions were being set in place that would undermine their standing and rights. Women silently relinquished responsibility for the defence of their rights and properties to men, whether lawyers or family members, and were excluded from the new profitable professions and from the required and now necessary education, all without the discriminatory legislation seen in much of Western Europe. Even though the new Greek state ostensibly maintained the legal framework of the previous centuries which had allowed women a remarkable degree of involvement in the courts, the necessary institutions of a modern state undermined those very rights long before new legislation attacked them directly. Perhaps when we talk about the sacrifices of the Greek nation in the struggle for independence we should mention that no other group lost as much, sacrificed as much, as women, not only then but by undermining their gender's own future in the new state.

Bibliography

Unpublished Primary Sources

General State Archives of Greece, Athens Notarial Archive (GAK Athens)
General State Archives of Greece, King Othon Archive, Ministry of Justice, Civil Law Section Archive (GAK Othonika, Politiki Dikaiosini, Astiki Nomothesia)
General State Archives of Greece, Leonidio Notarial Archive (GAK Leonidio)
General State Archives of Greece, Mykonos Notarial Archive (GAK Mykonos)
General State Archives of Greece, Naxos Notarial Archive (GAK Naxos)
Historical and Ethnological Society of Greece, Bourgos Notarial Archive (IEEE Bourgos)
Historical and Ethnological Society of Greece, Gizi Family Archive (IEEE Gizi)
Historical and Ethnological Society of Greece, Mykonos Notarial Archive (IEEE Mykonos)
Historical and Ethnological Society of Greece, Naxos Notarial Archive (IEEE Naxos)
Society of the Friends of the People, Chrysospathis Family Archive (EFL Chrysospathis)
Society of the Friends of the People, Kanelos Deligiannis Family Archive (EFL Kanelos Deligiannis)
Society of the Friends of the People, Nikolaos Deligiannis Family Archive (EFL Nikolaos Deligiannis)
Society of the Friends of the People, Panagos Deligiannis Family Archive (EFL Panagos Deligiannis)

Published Primary Sources

Agapios Ieromonachos, and Nikodimos Monachos, *Pidalion* [Rudder] (Athens, 2003).
Armenopoulos, Konstantinos, *Procheiron Nomon i Exavivlos* [Manual of Laws or the Six-Books] (Athens, 1971).
Nikolopoulos, B.K., and A.I. Kakoulidis, *Syllogi Apanton ton Nomon, Diatagmaton, Egkyklion, Odigion, kai Eidopoiiseon ton Ypourgeion kai Synthikon tis Ellados meta ton Allon Ethnon* [Collection of All the Laws, Decrees, Proclamations, Directions, and Announcements of the Ministries and Treaties of Greece with Other Nations] (vol. A, Athens, 1859).

Secondary Sources

About, Edmond, *I Ellada tou Othonos* [The Greece of Otto] (Athens: Afoi. Tolidi, 1992).

Afifi, Mohamed, 'Reflections on the personal laws of Egyptian Copts, in Amira El Azhary Sonbol (ed.), *Women, the Family and Divorce Laws in Islamic History* (Syracuse, NY: Syracuse University Press, 1996).

Allen, Ann Taylor, *Feminism and Motherhood in Western Europe 1890–1970: The Maternal Dilemma* (New York: Palgrave Macmillan, 2005).

Anonymou tou Ellinos, *Elliniki Nomarchia* [Greek Rule of Law] (Athens: Kalvos, 1968).

Argyriadis-Kervrgan, Caroula, 'Byzantine Law as Practice and as History in the Nineteenth Century', David Ricks and Paul Magdalino (ed.), *Byzantium and the Modern Greek Identity* (Aldershot: Ashgate, 1998).

Beaujour, Felix, *Pinakas tou Emporiou tis Ellados stin Tourkokratia 1787–1797* [Table of the Commerce of Greece during the period of Ottoman Rule 1787–1797] (Athens: Afoi Tolidi, 1974).

Chouliarakis, Michail, *Geographiki, Dioikitiki kai Plithysmiaki Exelixis tis Ellados 1821–1871* [Geographical, Administrative and Demographic Development of Greece 1821–1871] (Athens: Ethnikon Kentron Koinonikon Erevnon, 1973).

Chrisanthakopoulos, Fotios (Fotakos), *Apomnimonevmata peri tis Ellinikis Epanastaseos tou 1821* [Memoirs about the Greek Revolution of 1821] (Athens: Vergina, 1996).

Christophilopoulos, Anastasios P., *Ellinikon Ekklisiastikon Dikaion* [Greek Ecclesiastical Law] (Athens: Afoi Tzaka, 1965).

De Gobineau, Artur, *Sto Vasileio ton Ellinon* [In the Kingdom of the Greeks] (Athens: Periplous, 1999).

Dimaras, K. Th., *Neoellinikos Diafotismos* [Modern Greek Enlightenment] (Athens: Ermis, 2002).

Doxiadis, Evdoxios, 'Legal Trickery: Men, Women, and Justice in Late Ottoman Greece', *Past and Present*, 210 (February, 2011): 129–53.

Doxiadis, Evdoxios, *The Shackles of Modernity* (Cambridge, MA: Harvard University Press, 2012).

Erickson, Amy Louise, *Women and Property in Early Modern England* (New York: Routledge, 1993).

Fenelonos (François Fénélon), *To Peri Agogis Korasion* [About the Education of Girls] (Athens: 1868).

Fillipidis, Dimitrios, Daniil Ieromonachos, and Grigorios Ierodiakonos ton Dimitrieon, *Geographia Neoteriki* [Modern Geography] (Athens: Vivliopoleio Estias, 2000).

Freeze, Gregory L., 'Bringing Order to the Russian Family: Marriage and Divorce in Imperial Russia 1760–1860', *Journal of Modern History*, 62/4 (December 1990): pp. 709–46.

Fritot, Albert, *Didaskalia Peri Physikou Dikaiou* [Teachings about Natural Law] (Athens: Andreas Koromilis, 1836).

Gedeon, Manouil Io., *Vrachia Simiosis peri ton Ekklisiastikon imon Dikeon* [Brief Note about Our Ecclesiastical Law] (Constantinople: Patriarchiko Typografeio, 1909).

Geib, Gustav Karl, *Parousiasi tis Katastasis tou Dikaiou stin Ellada* [Exposition of the Condition of Law in Greece] (Athens: Govosti, 1990).

Gerber, Haim, *State, Society and Law in Islam: Ottoman Law in Comparative Perspective* (Albany: State University of New York Press, 1994).

Ginis, Dimitrios S., *Oi Logoi Diazigiou epi Tourkokratias* [The Reasons for Divorce during Ottoman Rule] (Thessaloniki: Aristoteleio Panepistimeio Thessalonikis, 1960).

Hanley, Sarah, 'Social Sites of Political Practice in France: Lawsuits, Civil Rights and the Separation of Powers in Domestic and State Government 1500–1800', *American Historical Review*, 102/1 (February 1997): 27–52.

Herzfeld, Michael, *Ours Once More: Folklore, Ideology and the Making of Modern Greece* (Austin: University of Texas Press, 1982).

Kairis, Theofilos, *Gnostiki i ton tou Anthropou Gnoseon Syntomos Ekthesis* [Gnostic or a Brief Exposition of Human Knowledge] (Athens: Em. Antoniadou, 1849).

Kalligas, Pavlos, *Systima Romaikou Dikaiou* [System of Roman Law] (vol. D, Athens: Georgios Fexis & Yios, 1930).

Kandiyoti, Deniz, 'End of Empire: Islam, Nationalism and Women in Turkey', in Deniz Kandiyoti (ed.), *Women, Islam and the State* (Philadelphia: Temple University Press, 1991).

Kasdagli, Aglaia E, *Land and Marriage Settlements in the Aegean: A Case Study of Seventeenth-Century Naxos* (Venice: Hellenic Institute of Byzantine and Post-Byzantine Studies, 1999).

Kitromilidis, Paschalis, *Republican Aspiration in Southeastern Europe in the Age of the French Revolution* (Athens: Consortium on Revolutionary Europe, 1980).

Kitromilidis, Paschalis, 'Ideologika Revmata kai Politika Aitimata: Prooptikes apo ton Elliniko 19o Aiona' [Ideological Currents and Political Demands: Views from the Greek Nineteenth Century], in G. Tsaousis (ed.), *Opseis tis Ellinikis Koinonias tou 19ou Aiona* [Facets of Greek Society of the Nineteenth Century] (Athens: Vivliopoleion tis Estias, 1984).

Kitromilidis, Paschalis, 'On the Intellectual Content of Greek Nationalism: Paparrigopoulos, Byzantium and the Great Idea', in David Ricks and Paul

Magdalino (ed.), *Byzantium and the Modern Greek Identity* (Aldershot: Ashgate, 1998).

Kitromilidis, Paschalis, *Neoellinikos Diafotismos* [Modern Greek Enlightenment] (Athens: Morfotiko Idryma Ethnikis Trapezis, 2000).

Konidaris, Ioannis M., 'The Ubiquity of Canon Law', in Angeliki E. Laiou and Dieter Simon (ed.), *Law and Society in Byzantium, Ninth–Twelfth Centuries* (Washington, DC: Dumbarton Oaks, 1994).

Korais, Adamantios, *Adelphiki Didaskalia* [Brotherly Instruction] (Athens: Kadmos, 1852).

Korais, Adamantios, *Simiosis eis to Prosorinn Politevma tis Ellados tou 1822 Etous* [Note on the Temporary Polity of Greece of 1822] (Athens: 1933).

Kordatos, Giannis, *I Koinoniki Simasia tis Ellinikis Epanastasis tou 1821* [The Social Significance of the Greek Revolution of 1821] (Athens: Epikairotita, 1977).

Koukkou, Eleni E., *Diamorfosis tis Ellinikis Koinonias kata tin Tourkokratia* [Transformation of Greek Society during Ottoman Rule] (Athens: Ethniko Kentro Koinonikon Erevnon, 1971).

Koukkou, Eleni E., *I Koinotikoi Thesmoi stis Kyklades kata tin Tourkokratia* [The Communal Institutions in the Cyclades at the Time of Ottoman Rule] (Athens: Istoriki kai Ethnologiki Istoria tis Ellados, 1980).

Kourilas, Evlogios, *Patriarchiki Istoria* [Patriarchal History] (vol. A, Athens: 1951).

Kozakis Typaldos, Georgios G., *Philosofikon Dokimion, peri tis proodou kai tis ptoseos tis palaias Ellados* [Philosophical Essay, Regarding the Progress and Fall of Old Greece] (Athens: P. Matzarakis, 1839).

Laiou, Angeliki E., *Gender, Society and Economic Life in Byzantium* (Aldershot: Ashgate, 1992).

Laiou, Sophia, 'Christian Women in an Ottoman World: Interpersonal and Family Cases Brought Before the Shari'a Courts During the Seventeenth and Eighteenth Centuries', in Amila Buturovic and Irvin Cemil Schick (ed.), *Women in the Ottoman Balkans* (New York: Tauris, 2007).

Liata, Eftychia D., *I Serifos kata tin Tourkokratia* [Serifos during Ottoman Rule] (Athens: Idryma Erevnas kai Paideias tis Emporikis Trapezas tis Elladas, 1987).

Macrides, R.J., *Kinship and Justice in Byzantium 11th–15th Centuries* (Aldershot: Ashgate, 1999).

Maridakis, Georgios S., *To Astikon Dikaion eis tais Nearais ton Byzantinon Avtokratoron* [Civil Law in the Nearais of the Byzantine Emperors] (Athens: Vasileiou, 1922).

Maurer, Georg Ludwig, *O Ellinikos Laos* [The Greek People] (Athens: Afoi Tolidi, 1976).

Moschovakis, N., *To Dimosio Dikaio stin Ellada tin Epochi tis Tourkokratias* [Public Law in Greece at the Time of Ottoman Rule] (Athens: 1998).

Moskov, Kostis, *I Ethniki kai Koinoniki Syneidisi stin Ellada 1830–1919* [The National and Social Consciousness in Greece 1830–1919] (Thessaloniki: Nea Poreia, 1972).

Pantazopoulos, Nikolaos I, *Apo tis 'Logias' Paradoseos eis ton Astikon Kodika, symvoli eis tin istorian ton pigon tou neoellinikou dikaiou* [From the 'Learned' Tradition to the Civil Code: Contribution to the History of the Sources of Modern Greek Law] (Thessaloniki: Aristoteleion Panepistimeion Thessalonikis, 1965).

Pantazopoulos, Nikolaos I., *Church and Law in the Balkan Peninsula during the Ottoman Rule* (Thessaloniki: Institute for Balkan Studies, 1967).

Pantazopoulos, Nikolaos I., 'Georg Ludwig von Maurer – I Pros Evropaika Protypa Oloklirotiki Strofi tis Neoellinikis Nomothesias' [The Complete Turn of Modern Greek Legislation towards European Models], *Epistimoniki Epetiris Scholis Nomikon kai Economikon Epistimon* [Scientific Review of the School of Legal and Economic Sciences], 13 (1968): 1346–506.

Pantazopoulos, Nikolaos I., *To Dikaion tis Tourkokratias, IV, Ta 'Pronomia' os Politistikos Paragon eis tas Scheseis Christianon* Mousoulmanon [The Law of the Ottoman Rule IV: The 'Privileges' as Cultural Dimension in Christian Muslim Relations] (Thessaloniki: 1975).

Pantazopoulos, Nikolaos I., 'I Entaxi tis Elladas stin Evropaiki Koinotita I Symvoli tis Antivasileias kai tou Othona 1833–1843' [The Entry of Greece in the European Community, the Contribution of the Regency and Otto 1833–1843], in *I Krisi ton Thesmon tou Kratous, Symmikta pros Timin Phaidonos Th. Vegleri* [The Crisis of the Institutions of the State: Essays in Honor of Phaidonos Th. Vegleri] (Athens: Ant. N. Sakkoulas, 1988).

Papagianni, Eleftheria Sp., *I Nomologia ton Ekklisiastikon Dikastirion tis Vizantinis kai Metavizantinis Periodou se Themata Perousiakou Dikaiou, II Oikogeniako Dikaio* [The Legislation of the Ecclesiastical Courts of the Byzantine and Post-Byzantine Period in Matters of Property Law, II Family Law] (Athens: Ant. N. Sakkoulas, 1997).

Papantoniou, Nikolaos S., *To Idiotiko Dikaio ton Ellinon kata tin Epanastasi tou 1821* [The Private Law of the Greeks during the Revolution of 1821] (Thessaloniki: Aristoteleio Panepistimeio Thessalonikis, 1977).

Peirce, Leslie, *Morality Tales: Law and Gender in the Ottoman Court of Aintab* (Berkeley: University of California Press, 2003).

Petropoulos, John Anthony, *Politics and Statecraft in the Kingdom of Greece 1833–1843* (Princeton, NJ: Princeton University Press, 1968).

Sakellarios, Michail B., *I Peloponnisos kata tin Defterin Tourkokratian 1715–1821* [The Peloponnese during the Second Period of Ottoman Rule 1715–1821] (Athens: Ermis, 1939).

Sfyroeras, Vas. Vl., *Istoria tis Neoteras Ellados, I Periodos tis Vasileias tou Othonos 1832–1862* [History of Modern Greece: The Period of the Reign of Otto 1832–1862] Athens: 1970).

Svolos, Alexandros, *Ta Ellinika Syntagmata 1822–1975/1986* [The Greek Constitutions 1822–1975/1986] (Athens: Stochastis, 1998).

Theodorou, Theod. E., *I Elliniki Topiki Aftodiikisi* [The Greek Local Self-government] (vol. 1, Athens: Tolidis, 1996).

Tourtoglou, Menelaos A., 'Symvoli sti Meleti tou Metavyzantinou Ethimikou Dikaiou ton Kykladon' [Contribution to the Study of Post-Byzantine Customary Law in the Cyclades], *Epetiris Etaireias Kykladikon Meleton* [Review of the Society of Cycladic Studies], 27–8, (1980–81): 245–56.

Trikoupis, Spyridon, *Istoria tis Ellinikis Epanastaseos* [History of the Greek Revolution] (vol. A, Athens: Christos Giovanis, 1978).

Urquhart, D., *La Turquie* (Paris: Hauman Cattors, 1837).

Varika, Eleni, *I Exegersi ton Kyrion* [The Rebellion of the Ladies] (Athens: Katarti, 2004).

Visvizis, Iakovos, T., *I Politiki Dikaiosyni kata tin Ellinikin Epanastasin Mechri tou Kapodistriou* [Civilian Justice during the Greek Revolution and until Kapodistrias] (Athens: Papanikolaou, 1941).

Visvizis, Iakovos T., 'To Klironomiko Dikaioma ton Syzygon epi Ateknou Gamou eis Paron kata ton 18o Aiona' [The Rights to Inheritance of Spouses in Childless Marriage in Paros in the Eighteenth Century], *Epetirida tou Archeiou tis Istorias tou Ellinikou Dikaiou tis Akadimias Athinon* [Review of the Archive of the History of Greek Law of the Academy of Athens], 8 (1958): 135–203.

Zepos, Panagiotis I., *I Neotera Elliniki Epistimi tou Astikou Dikaiou* [The Modern Greek Science of Civil Law] (Athens: Ioannis Zacharopoulos, 1954).

Chapter 7

Women's Rights in the Late Russian Empire: The Paradoxes of the Legislative Basis in the Family Sphere

Nadezda Belyakova and Taisiya Belyakova

Introduction

This chapter deals with the history of legislative norms and their actual impact on social life and women's status in the late Russian empire. Our main attention goes to the codification of family law in the nineteenth century, but we will also look at the Byzantine legal tradition and its influence on Christian legislation from the Middle Ages onwards.[1] Women's status is considered here in relation to their property rights and in relation to the changes in divorce procedures that occurred in the nineteenth century in a context of shifting attitudes towards the institution of civil marriage. This is a story of contradicting patriarchal norms in the family sphere and independent property principles for women in the financial sphere. It is based on numerous memoirs and articles by famous Russian jurists of the nineteenth century.[2]

One of the problems of the nineteenth-century tsarist legal system was the lack of developed family law. This area was regulated by customary law, most so in the traditional agrarian regions. In most European countries the nineteenth century brought some important changes to women's legal status as a consequence of the introduction of civil marriage and the simplification of divorce procedure, but in late imperial Russia the situation was different. There, the social rights of a woman largely depended on the stratum she belonged to, and remained strictly limited because of the low legal status of women in general and their complete dependence on husbands in the family sphere, based on the notion of paternal power and authority. Divorce procedures were also very difficult to initiate. The actual changes in nineteenth-century

---

1 D. Obolensky, *The Byzantine Commonwealth: Eastern Europe 500–1453* (London, 1971).

2 M. Zirin and C.D. Worobec (ed.), *Women and Gender in Central and Eastern Europe, Russia, and Eurasia* (vol. 2, New York, 2007).

social life – because of the general impoverishment of the population, men could often no longer manage to support their families alone – demanded an increase in women's participation in the labour market, and thus more freedom and independence in their family status. Yet the concept of sacramental marriage hampered the formation of the institution of civil marriage and the simplification of divorce procedures; it preserved and dictated patriarchal traditions in the family and in society at large. Russian contemporaries described women's living conditions as 'in servitude and submission' and their situation as one of 'constantly defying their female and human dignity'.[3]

The issue of divorces in nineteenth-century Russia and their long-term consequences on Russian society has notably been examined by American historian Gregory L. Freeze, who suggested that keeping divorce in the competence of the Church resulted in the crisis of the family as an institution. It also contributed to the growth of dissatisfaction and general distrust towards Church authorities. In other words, the inadequacy of this legal regime has led to important social and political developments in society. Eventually, it led to the revolutionary process at the beginning of the twentieth century, including the rapid radicalization of the Russian women's emancipation movement.[4]

Next to the strict rules for divorce, the property status of women was another paradox in Russian family law. In contrast to European legislation and practice, the Russian legal system fixed the principle of separate property of spouses. This tradition of separate property rights of spouses was connected with the regulations of Byzantine family law: according to Byzantine law, the dowry of the wife did not become common family property after marriage, but still belonged to the wife only; her husband was not able to sell or make any advantage out of it. Every spouse was able to dispose of their property separately, without special legal obligations.[5] This meant that women in the Russian empire had wide property rights. In the second part of this chapter, we will examine the peculiarities of the property status of women from different social strata, as well as their inheritance rights and the question of the dowry.

---

[3] S. Paschenceva, 'Pravovoye i ekonomicheskoe polozheniye zhenschin v Rossiyskoi imperii (vtoraya polovina XIX veka–nachalo XX veka)' [The legal and economic status of women in the Russian empire, second part of the nineteenth, beginning of the twentieth century], *Mir truda* (1906); GARF (State Archive of the Russian Federation). F.516. Op.1, D.6. L.349.

[4] G.L. Freeze, 'Mirskiye narrativy o svyaschennom tainstve: brak i razvod v pozdneimperskoy Rossii' [Mundane narratives about a sacrament: marriage and divorce in late imperial Russia], in *Pravoslaviye. Konfessiya, instituty, religioznost'. XVII–XX vv.* (St Petersburg, 2009), p. 165.

[5] *Svod zakonov grazhdanskih* [The Code of civil laws] (St Petersburg, 1900), ed. 1: p. 85; ed. 2, p. 117.

Changes in Women's Status in Medieval and Pre-Modern Russia (Tenth–Eighteenth Century)

Women's legal status in the family sphere was strongly influenced by Byzantine tradition and normative law regulation. The Church had always regulated the institution of marriage. At the same time, marriage was organized and controlled by the parents. Marriage and family relations were thus also strongly influenced by customary law, which was largely applied in Russian rural communities, up until the end of the nineteenth century. In these areas the Church notion of marriage was not so currently accepted.[6]

According to Russian specialist in the history of family law Marina Tsaturova, regulation in spouses' relationships underwent important changes from the sixteenth century onwards: from freedom in disposal of property for the married woman at the beginning of the sixteenth century, to complete dependence on her husband in the second half of the seventeenth century, and finally to independence and separateness of property protected by law in the eighteenth century.[7] However, the basic principle of a wife's inferior position in the family remained intact throughout all these legislative changes. Public opinion considered (married) women to be inferior to their husbands not only in a religious but also in an everyday life sense.[8]

Already in the sixteenth century, certain changes in women's family status, accompanied by the tendency to lock up women at home, can be observed in Russia. The *Domostroi* (a sixteenth-century Russian set of household rules and instructions, edited by archpriest Silvester, the influential advisor of Ivan the Terrible) fixed norms of women's family treatment.[9] This book, modelling family relationships after monastic ones, applied 'tower hermit' ideals to create

---

[6] M.F. Vladimirsky-Budanov, *Ocherki iz istorii rusko-litovskogo prava* [Notes from the history of Russian-Lithuanian law] (Kiev, 1890). This Church notion of marriage could be broken down to at least four conditions traditionally to be observed: 1. the demand of a mandatory Church wedding ceremony; 2. the prohibition of kidnapping brides; 3. the prohibition of violence; 4. the prohibition of close relatives' marriages. The fulfilment of these simple demands could lead to a general improvement of women's status, guaranteeing them at least some kind of security. A. Eck, 'La situation juridique de la femme russe au moyen âge', *Recueils de la société Jean Bodin pour l'histoire comparative des institutions*, 12 (1962): pp. 405–20; R. Hellie, 'Women and Slavery in Moscow', *Russian History*, 10/2 (1983): pp. 213–29: A. Kleimola, 'In Accordance with the Canons of the Holy Apostles': Muscovite Dowries and Women's Property Rights', *Russian Review*, 51/2 (1992): pp. 204–29.

[7] M.K. Tsaturova, *Russkoye semeynoye pravo XVI–XVIII vv.* [Russian family law in the sixteenth to eighteenth century] (Moscow, 1991), p. 45.

[8] Ibid.

[9] C.J. Pouncy (ed.), *The Domostroi: Rules for Russian Households in the Time of Ivan the Terrible* (New York, 1994); L.R. Lewitter, 'Women, Sainthood and Marriage in Muscovy',

the notion of the perfect wife. This development poses an inevitable question for Russian legal historians: was this phenomenon completely new for Russian culture, or was it just an explicit manifestation of some tendencies that had already existed before?[10] The adoption of monastic life features by Russian family culture in the sixteenth century resulted in the further exclusion of women from the sacral sphere: even church attendance was no longer obligatory for them.

It is important to notice that in pre-Peter Russia (that is, before the 1680s) the institution of divorce existed. Sources point out the following causes for divorce at that time: mutual consent (the most widespread reason for this was the wish to become a monk); barrenness; inability to perform marital relations; adultery; violence; pauperism; embezzlement of the wife's property by her husband; hard drinking and debauchery; instigation to robbery; attempts by one of the spouses on the life of the other one; crimes against the state; going missing without reason; slander; having information on threats to the husband's life and not warning him; dishonourable behaviour; contagious disease; and marriage by abduction. In this pre-Peter period divorce could be achieved only with a priest's blessing.

During the seventeenth century, the influence of West European Catholic views that had come to Russia by means of Kiev learning[11] acquired considerable importance, resulting in changing ideas about marriage from a legal point of view.[12] The Metropolitan of Kiev (that is the leader of an Orthodox ecclesiastical province), Peter Mogila,[13] used wording from the Catholic catechism about marriage that then reached the Russian printed *Kormchaya* (the in 1653 in

Journal of Russian Studies, 37 (1979): pp. 3–11; S. Levy, 'Women and the Control of Property in Sixteenth-Century Muscovy', *Russian History*, 10/2 (1983): pp. 201–12.

10 N.L. Pushkareva, 'Woman and Her Property and Legal Status: Was the XVIth Century a Turning Point?', in S. Cavaciocchi (ed.), *La donna nell'economia secc. XIII–XVIII: Atti della ventunesima Settimana di studi, 10–15 aprile 1989* (Florence, 1990).

11 In the seventeenth century, there were more Orthodox scientists in Kiev than in Moscow, where a new Orthodox high school was founded. Moreover, many Kiev scientists received their education from Western European universities and learned different foreign languages. That is why during the rule of Tsar Aleksey Mikhailovich Romanov (1645–76), the Kiev scientists were invited to translate European texts into Slavic languages, and to publish books in Moscow.

12 S.J. McNally, *From Public Person to Private Prisoner: The Changing Place of Women in Medieval Russia* (PhD diss., State University of New York at Binghamton, 1976); V.A. Kivelson, 'Through the Prism of Witchcraft: Gender and Social Change in Seventeenth-Century Muscovy', in B.E. Clements et al., *Russia's Women: Accommodation, Resistance, Transformation* (Berkeley, 1991), pp. 74–94.

13 Peter Mogila (Metropolitan 1633–46) is known for strengthening the status of the Kiev Orthodox Metropoly and for founding an Orthodox high school in Kiev and for his publications. His catechism was edited in 1645 and supported by Orthodox patriarchs.

Moscow first printed edition of the Slavic Code of Church canons),[14] thereby achieving the status of law. The new element introduced into Russia matrimonial tradition was the agreement of two parties in front of a priest, this becoming the key moment in the marriage ceremony. The idea was innovative for Russian culture, as the emphasis shifted from the process of wedding to that of betrothal and to the necessity of agreement from the couple getting married. This actually limited the absolute power of parents in the issue of marriage. From the second half of the seventeenth century on, Church hierarchs' epistles often requested that bishops investigate if marriages were concluded under parents' pressure. Another change that the *Kormchaya* had brought about was the strict definition of a circle of people who were forbidden to marry each other because of spiritual relationships or blood relationships.

All these conflicting elements – marriage as a mystic and indissoluble alliance of two persons, while preserving the necessity of parents' agreement, a woman's right to her property, and at the same time her absolute dependency from her husband in the public sphere – remained in Russian law until 1917.

'Estate enslavement' that occurred during the construction of the absolutist state with the purpose of putting the entire population to serve the state machine at any cost[15] was accompanied by a common deterioration of the legal climate in Russian society and relationships between its members. Suppression of human rights and people's servile position made family relations even more despotic. Jurist A.G. Goikhbarg wrote:

> If a husband legally assumes the role of tyrant for his wife at home, he assumes the role of an absolute despot's slave in any other relationship more easily: unlimited lord in his seraglio, his harem, in women's chambers – he is a slave deprived of any rights outside.[16]

Apparently, the worsening of social and economic conditions for all Russian classes, and first of all the peasantry, led to a general degradation of family relations. The catastrophic status of Russian peasants in the eighteenth and nineteenth centuries deteriorated spouses' conditions: ethnographers and

---

14 This is an Orthodox analogue of Corpus Juris Canonici, which included the main canons of the ecumenical and local councils, as well as polemical works and also the monuments of Byzantine legacy – Ekloga, Prochiron, Justinian's Novels and a collection of decisions about marriages.

15 B.A. Mironov, *Social'naya istoriya Rossii perioda imperii (XVIII–nachalo XX v.)* [The Social History of Imperial Russia 1700–1917] (St Petersburg, 2000).

16 A.G. Goikhbarg, 'Zamuzhnyaya zhenschina kak neravnopravnaya lichnost' v sovremennom obschestve' [A married woman as a person unequal in her rights in contemporary society], *Pravo*, 51 (1914): pp. 3540–52.

researchers point out a great number of Russian folklore proverbs about wives beaten by their drunken husbands.[17]

From the beginning of the eighteenth century, family law became a subject of systematic state regulation. Important laws were introduced under Peter I and Catherine II. Three trends can be distinguished: 1. the legal protection of a wife's property rights, reforming the dowry institution; 2. the formalization of marriage conclusion and the legal regulation of divorce; 3. the transformation of relations between parents and children.

Since Peter the Great, parental authority had been gradually restricted, but it still remained considerable until the nineteenth century. Parents were entitled, for example, to send children to jail. Laws did not directly determine the distribution of parental authority in relation to children while parents lived together, although the father was given preference. Yet in peculiar cases (when it was for the child's benefit) the upbringing could be handed over to the mother by court order. Children were obliged to provide parents' subsistence and housing till their death, if parents were in need, decrepit or in sickness.[18] The law described in detail the right of parents for respect and, among other things, determined that no action of children's offending by parents could be accepted in court.

Although by the eighteenth century marriage could be concluded without parents' consent, the latter could sue for the imprisonment of guilty children for a period of four to eight months; children could also be excluded from inheriting the estate of insulted parents. Parents' duty to support children did not expire when they attained majority in case they were still in need of care, but this duty could be annulled before the children had attained their majority, especially if the child was female; after a daughter's marriage, the duty to support her passed to her husband.

Yet, on the whole, during the second half of the eighteenth to the nineteenth century, the principle of authority in relationships between parents and children in Russian family law gradually gave place to the principle of children's benefit, depriving parents of autonomous authority.[19]

---

[17] V.I. Dal', *Poslovicy russkogo naroda* [Russian Folklore Proverbs] (Moscow, 1964); E.P. Elnett, *Historic Origin and Social Development of Family Life in Russia* (New York, 1926); V.Yu Leschenko, *Sem'ya i russkoye pravoslaviye XI–XIX vv.* [Family and Russian Orthodoxy in the Eleventh to Nineteenth Century] (St Petersburg, 1999), pp. 48–9; M.M. Gromyko, *Mir russkoy derevni* [The World of Russian Villages] (Moscow, 1991), p. 170.

[18] *Polnoye sobranije zakonov* [The Complete Code of Laws] (1900), vol. 21, part 1, article 194.

[19] L. Tumanova, 'Lichniye imushestvenniye i neimushestvenniye otnosheniya suprugov v Rossii vo vtoroy polovine 19 veka. Usynovleniye i uzakonyeniye' [Personal property and

Women's Status in Late Imperial Russia (Nineteenth–Twentieth Century)

During the nineteenth century, the legal framework regulating women's status underwent considerable changes. The Russian legal system defined norms of relations between spouses, confirming the dependent position of women. The Statute of Deanery (a legislative act regulating the work of the police, issued by Catherine II in 1782) treated the issue in the following way:

> The husband should join his wife in consent and love, respecting, protecting and excusing for her defects, simplifying her infirmity, delivering her livelihood in accordance with his status and opportunities ... The wife should live with love, respect and obedience to her husband and should please him and show affection towards him as a wife.[20]

The social status of a woman was determined by the social status of her husband. A Ukrainian marrying a serf woman, for example, made her free of serfdom and made him not lose his freedom. The residence of the spouses, however, was determined by the husband's place of living. The wife had to follow her husband and could be settled in her husband's house by force. Only the husband's exile made a woman free from this obligation. In the eighteenth century the wife acquired a right to demand judicial separation in the case of violent treatment. But in 1819 separate residence of spouses as a measure replacing divorce was abolished.

The Legal Basis for Divorce

State authorities had begun their struggle against voluntary divorces since the 1720s. Already in the Attachment to the Spiritual Order (issued in 1722 as an addition to the previous legal statute regulating the status and rights of Russian clergy and monastic communities) the taking of monastic vows by one of the spouses as a reason for divorce was forbidden.[21] At the beginning of the nineteenth century, Russian state legislation tried to reject the concept of marriage as an entirely religious institution. This was a new evolution in contrast with the previous legal tradition. Opposed, however, were the adherents of religious mysticism who propagated the establishment of a 'universal Christian Church'. Amongst others, there was the influence of pr. Aleksander Golitsyn, the

non-property relations of spouses in Russia in the second part of the nineteenth century: adoption and legitimating], *Pravo i zhizn'*, 61 (2003): pp. 248–57.

[20] *Polnoye sobranije zakonov*, 21/15379; *Ustav o blagochinii* [The Statute of Deanery], 41/8, p. 465.

[21] *Zakonodatel'stvo Petra I* [The legislation of Peter I] (Moscow, 1997), pp. 582–603.

Chief-Procurator of the Synod (1803–17), later Minister of Religious Affairs and National Education (1817–24), known for his struggle against freethinking and atheism.[22] The secular position was presented to the State Council by Michael Speransky (1772–1839), one of the most talented statesmen of the first half of the nineteenth century, author of several reform projects, and the main character of the codification of Russian laws under Nicholas I.[23] Speransky pointed out that in the early Christian Church marriage was registered by civil contract and that it depended entirely on the Christian's conscience to let their marriage be sanctified by the Church or not.[24]

In the end, the conclusion and dissolution of marriage remained in the competence of confessional structures, to which the bridal couple belonged. The state reserved for itself the regulation of only the *forms* of marriage and divorce procedures, enacting the civil and criminal consequences of incorrect process organization (such as punishing the clergy for incorrect procedure or flawed metric recording).

The rules of divorce (that could be committed solely by the Church court) were getting more and more complex in the nineteenth century. Nevertheless, the laws that regulated Church legal procedure were approved by the state. From 1805 on, only the Holy Synod (the highest institution of the Russian Orthodox Church) could allow divorce, and only cases of marriage dissolution by reason of long-term absence of one of the spouses could be dealt with at the diocesan level.

The strictness and complexity of Russian divorce legislation in the nineteenth century finally resulted in the Statute of the Religious Consistory of 1841, according to which marriage could only be dissolved by formal a Church court on demand of one of the spouses. The following reasons could be valid for divorce: 1. in case of proven adultery or non-ability to marital cohabitation; 2. in case of one of the spouses being under a sentence or exile to Siberia together with deprivation of rights and privileges; 3. in case of one spouse's obscure absence.[25] Also, divorce was permitted if both spouses were

---

22 E. Vishlenkova, *Zabotyas' o dushah poddanih: religioznaya politika v Rossii v pervoy chetverti XIX v.* [Taking care of the subjects' souls: religious policy in Russia in the first quarter of the nineteenth century] (Saratov, 2002).

23 M. Raeff, *Michael Speransky: Statesman of Imperial Russia, 1772–1839* (The Hague, 1957).

24 M. Shahmatov and M. Kostricin, O*bzor istorii kodifikacii i duhovnih pravil Pravoslavnoy Greko-Rossiyskoy Cerkvi s konca XVIII v. po nashe vremya* [The history of codification and spiritual rules of the Orthodox Greek-Russian Church from the end of the eighteenth century until the present] (Petrograd, 1917), p. 44.

25 S.O. Grigirovskiy, *O razvode. Prichiny i posledstviya razvoda i brakorazvodnoye sudoproizvodstvo. Istoriko-yuridicheskiy ocherk* [About divorce. Causes and effects of divorce

ready to take monastic vows and if they had no young children. The guilty party was deprived of the right to remarry.

The procedure for divorce became more and more bureaucratized, despite the religious and canon norms that should have served as its framework. Neither Byzantium nor pre-Peter Russia had ever known such restrictions for divorce procedures as the Russian empire in the nineteenth century. Gregory L. Freeze noticed that in comparison with continental Europe – where divorce had been quite common among Protestants, and Catholics were able to dissolute marriage as well – the prohibitive approach of the Russian Orthodox Church was absolutely unique.[26]

Even the form of investigating divorce cases in the eparchial (consistorial) court became a target of much mockery in society. The problem was that the recognition of guilt by the defendant was not sufficient proof to the court 'if it did not accord with the circumstances of the case and if not accompanied by averment, amongst which were: 1. testimony of two or three obvious witnesses; 2. the existence of children born out of wedlock, proven by metric acts'.[27] Other proof could be used, such as letters that demonstrated the illegal relationship of the demander; the testimony of witnesses who had not been eyewitnesses to the crime but had knowledge of it from trustworthy witnesses or rumours; and finally also the testimony of people who had information about the depraved life of the demander.[28] The main task was to present to the court the 'witnesses to the adultery'. If the civil court punished perjurers, the clerical court when investigating adultery, on the contrary, welcomed false witnesses.[29] The demand to present 'witnesses to adultery' remained until 1917. After reform of the Russian legal system in the 1870s, the inefficiency of the clerical court became more and more obvious to contemporaries.

Representatives of different states as well as Church institutions themselves suggested excluding divorce proceedings from the spiritual courts' competence (first of all, Orthodox). Yet weddings and divorces did remain under the jurisdiction of Church authorities. This stimulated the growth of anticlericalism and the radicalization of anti-Church attitudes in society. In reality, and despite strict legislative norms, statistics show a steady increase in the number of official divorces from the 1860s onwards, although the Holy Synod denied in more than 70 per cent of the cases the dissolution of Church marriages. The major part of divorces had long absence without reason as their legal basis, as this was the simplest procedure for getting a divorce.

---

and divorce proceedings. Historic-legal essay] (St Petersburg, 1911), p. 181; *Ustav duhovnih konsistoriy* [The code of spiritual consistories] (St Petersburg, 1841), article 223.

26 Freeze, *Mirskiye*, p. 128.

27 *Ustav duhovnih*, article 253.

28 Ibid., article 251, 252.

29 Grigirovskiy, *O razvode*, p. 45.

The tendency of divorce injunction went against the actual situation in society. The practice of non-stated divorces spread rapidly. Statistician P. Bechasnov mentioned that in Russian society of the mid nineteenth century separation without actual divorce was quite common, yet it was impossible to appraise this phenomenon as it was not properly registered.[30]

The secularization of society, as well as certain changes in its consciousness, the so-called 'revolution of feelings', contributed to conjugal infidelity as marriage itself was primarily and often solely founded on material and economical reasons ('profitable party'). The sociologist Leonid Zolotarev wrote about his contemporaries: 'speaking about men, they all break the marriage laws and oaths, enjoying a much greater freedom than their slave-wives ... Nevertheless, "the art of tender passion" has taken nowadays such deep root that a faithful wife is considered as lagging behind the life.'[31] If the fact of conjugal infidelity is well documented by literature, it is ignored by statistics.

Another increasingly new phenomenon in Russian society of the mid nineteenth century was the differentiation between the rural population and townspeople. In the intelligentsia, secular ideas were developing rapidly.[32] The majority of Russian women though lived in poverty, primarily because of land shortage.

Women in the Russian Countryside

High death rates amongst women and infants were typical in the Russian rural population. A peasant woman's reproductive history was not unusual to add up to the following picture: a woman 55 years old, of which 35 years were spent in marriage, would have 24 pregnancies; 8 would be stillbirths, with 14 of her children dying at an early age and only 2 surviving.[33] Women's and children's death rates impressively surpassed those of Western Europe.

The nineteenth century saw a worsening of women's treatment among the peasantry. Many observers of peasant life wrote that proverbs such as 'If one doesn't beat the woman, he doesn't love her' or 'I could eat my wife with porridge

---

[30] P. Bechasnov (ed.), 'O razvodah i nedeistvitel'nih brakah za 1867–1886 gg.' [About divorces and invalid marriages in 1867–86], *Vremennik CSK MVD*, 26 (St Petersburg, 1893).

[31] L.A. Zolotarev, *Supruzheskiye izmeny, ih znacheniye i prichiny* [Adultery in marriage, its meaning and reasons] (Moscow, 1895), pp. 5, 21.

[32] V. Broido, *Apostles into Terrorists: Women and the Revolutionary Movement in the Russia of Alexander II* (London, 1967); M.C. Bumet-Vigniel, 'Femmes russes dans le combat evolutionnaire. L'image et son modele à la fin du XIX siecle', *Culture et sociétés de l'Est*, 12 (Paris, 1990); A. Bobroff-Hajal, *Working Women in Russia Under the Hunger Tsars: Political Activism and Daily Life* (New York, 1994).

[33] *Trudy pervogo vserossiyskogo zhenskogo s'ezda* [Proceedings of the First All-Russian Women's Congress] (St Petersburg, 1909), pp. 211–15.

if I liked' represented existing attitudes towards women.[34] This brutality was undoubtedly inspired by the general conditions of serfdom: the economic conditions of Russian peasants in general, their total lack of basic human rights and the lack of legal consciousness in society at large contributed to this.

Cruel treatment of a wife was not considered to be a reason for divorce. Under the title *The complaints of peasant women*, the magazine *Yuridicheskiy Vestnik* [Jurisprudence Bulletin] issued a number of publications authored by city executives which addressed the rights-deprived status of women in the family. The city executives demanded broadening the number of legal reasons for divorce, aiming to protect women's life and health and prevent domestic abuse.

Jurists maintained that women were deprived of any legal protection from violence in the family. Justice of the peace Yaroslav Ludmer wrote:

> Our legal system doesn't give any means of protecting a woman from abusive and violent treatment ... And only when she can't endure it anymore, after all these terrible sufferings and abuses, she trudges to a magistrate, often with a plaint torn up by her husband, in the hope that he would save her if not formally then by his authority or influence.[35]

Judges admitted that they did not have any legal means to halt the violence of a husband against his wife. The single beating of a wife could not be used as grounds for a trial: 'the single beating according to the law is not punished; in such a treatment the wife should see only a way of admonishing ... which she should apprehend with obedience and respect'.[36] The only chance for the judge to put a husband-tyrant in prison was:

> In the case of constant, happening at different times and often repeated beating of a wife by her husband, with remaining traces and signs on her body and the use by her husband of a stick, a belt or a lash ... So it means that if the wife has not been seriously injured yet, she would not even hope that the husband would be restrained or moved away from her even for a while.[37]

After the fact that the wife had been crippled was attested to, the cruel husband would be put under arrest for several days and after that come back to his family.

---

[34] N. Dobrotvorskiy, 'Krest'yanskiye yuridicheskiye obychai v vostochnoy chasti Vladimirskoy gubernii' [Peasants' legal customs in the eastern part of the Vladimir province], *Yuridicheskiy sbornik*, 509 (1889): p. 263.

[35] Y. Ludmer, 'Bab'i stony' [Women's cries], *Yuridicheskiy vestnik* (November 1884): pp. 446–7.

[36] Ibid., p. 464.

[37] Ibid.

Judges' attempts 'to reconcile the spouses' after women's complaints about abuse often had deplorable results.

The only social organizations that could somehow influence peasants' family life were the peasants' courts.[38] However, the notion of unlimited power of husbands over their wives that was deeply rooted among peasants impeded these courts' work: in several areas the peasants thought that 'there is no judge for the relations between husband and wife'. There was the example of one husband who put out his wife's eye, and yet the court did not punish him for this. And because society treated badly those wives who made complaints about their husbands, there often were no complaints at all.[39]

In addition, as historian Lazovsky has noticed, those peasants' courts had a very patriarchal notion of the family, considering it to be something isolated:

> No one can make out if the husband is right or a wife, so they always try to finish such cases by conciliation of the parties ... The other reason for refusing investigating wives' complaints is that the peasants' courts shared the same point of view as the peasants in general: the wife was apprehended as an animal working power and her husband's property, as a slave, as a thing; so the punishment of the husband had to be delivered in a way that would not humiliate him in his wife's eyes and at the same time would not damage his economic interests.[40]

This terrible way of life in Russian villages, where beating wives was considered normal and where women could get no protection, should have been a good enough reason to pose the question of divorce. However, it would be a mistake to suggest that family violence took place only among peasants; violence in the family was characteristic of all strata of Russian society.

The legal insecurity of women was obvious to contemporaries. The laws were strongly criticized by jurists. According to the Criminal code, husbands' crimes against wives and wives' crimes against their husbands were punished in the same way, yet the de facto equalization of rights and responsibilities has never been actually true. Russia's famous jurist Michael Gernet wrote: 'The judicial practice is not aware of any cases, when a wife was taking advantage of her husband's weakness, afforded to beat him hard, torture and bedevil him.'[41]

---

[38] P. Czap Jr., '"A Large Family: The Peasant's Greatest Wealth": Serf Households in Mishino, Russia, 1814–1858', in R. Wall, J. Robin and P. Laslett (ed.), *Family Forms in Historic Europe* (Cambridge, 1982), pp. 105–51.

[39] N. Lazovsky, 'Lichnyje otnoshenija suprugov po russkomu obychnomu pravu' [Personal relations between spouses according to Russian common law], *Yuridicheskiy vestnik*, 13/6 (1883): p. 360.

[40] Ibid., pp. 382–97.

[41] M. Gernet, *Zhenskoye ravnopraviye i ugolovniy zakon* [Women's equal rights and criminal law] (St Petersburg, 1916), p. 40.

In the decisions of the Department of Criminal Appeal, only actions about husbands' crimes were registered. Gernet reported that initially the Criminal code had been different and more advantageous for women, because the law had prohibited not only 'to maim, injure and beat hard', but any 'cruel treatment' altogether. However, in 1871 a Highly Confirmed Act of the State Council was issued, erasing this definition.[42]

Women's Status in the City

From the second half of the nineteenth century, Russia's urban population increased dramatically by the inflow of former peasants. The census of 1900 registered in St Petersburg 116,400 natives of Tverskaya, 83,500 natives from Yaroslavskaya, and 50,800 natives of the Novgorodskaya provinces.[43] This process had started when seasonal work became men's regular occupation. The peasants coming into towns supplemented all ranks of the working class. In 1900 the number of factory workers in Russia reached more than 2 million, and 32 per cent of all workers were employed in the textile industry.[44] Women had also started looking for jobs in towns; the major part of workers occupied in the textile industry was female. According to Nadezhda Krupskaya's information (an active participant of the social democratic party, and Vladimir Lenin's wife), in the 1890s in the European part of Russia alone some 250,000 women worked in factories and plants.[45]

At the beginning of the twentieth century, the number of women workers in industry was increasing rapidly: from 26 per cent in 1901 it reached 31 per cent in 1913.[46] Women started to replace men even in traditionally male professions such as bench work.

Women sought jobs to survive and to feed their children. If in Western Europe most female workers were widows and unmarried girls, who ceased work after getting married, in Russia the situation was totally different. In the Vladimir province, according to the census of 1896, the age category of 30–40 years prevailed amongst female workers.[47] As the feminist Ekaterina L'vova

---

42 Ibid.

43 S. Bruk and V. Kabuzan, 'Dinamika i etnicheskiy sostav naseleniya Rossii v epohu imperializma (konec XIX veka–1917 g.)' [The dynamics and ethnic composition of the population of Russia in the period of imperialism], *Istoriya SSSR*, 3 (1980): p. 83.

44 Ibid., pp. 86, 105.

45 N.K. Krupskaya, *Zhenschina-rabotnica* [The woman worker] (Moscow/Leningrad, 1926), p. 11.

46 *Obschestvenniy vrach* [The social doctor], 9–10 (1915): p. 592.

47 Ibid., p. 597.

noted, in St Petersburg only in eight families of textile workers out of 100 did the mother not have to leave her children and go to work.[48]

The needs of city life began to change the traditional type of family: the nuclear family began to prevail; workers tried to avoid having too many children; and the practice of extramarital cohabitation and changing sexual partners became more and more widespread. Also, the number of unmarried people was increasing, not only amongst men but also amongst women. In the cities, the census of 1897 showed a strange situation: single men and unmarried women prevailed over married ones. Amongst 1,000 men, there were 582 single ones and amongst 1,000 women 560 unmarried.[49] As I. Preobrazhensky, the author of one of the first serious Church statistics, wrote:

> We could be hardly wrong when suggesting that the main reason for lessening the number of legal marriages is the rapid development of urban life to the detriment of rural life ... The answer to the question "Why do people not conclude a Church marriage?" now usually sounds like "Not to multiply beggars".[50]

The logical consequence of these social problems was the increase of female crimes in cities, rejection of legal marriages, and a growing number of abandoned children. The practice of abortion, which was unknown in the traditional family, spread in the cities. Contemporaries noted that in the workers' milieu, people began to accept abortion as something totally ordinary and easily accessible. In workers' families the doctors' and midwives' addresses passed from hand to hand.[51]

In St Petersburg in 1867 the number of children born was 19,342, amongst whom 4,305 were born out of wedlock; in 1889 there were 28,640 born, with 7,907 born out of wedlock.[52] The Central Statistics Committee officially published these figures (which were then used by Preobrazhensky) that show that almost every third child in St Petersburg was born out of wedlock.[53] In accordance with the official statistics of 1890, the number of children taken to

---

48 E. L'vova, *Russkaya rabotnica* [The Russian female worker] (St Petersburg, 1914), p. 4.

49 *Naseleniye Rossii v XX v. Istoricheskiye ocherki* [The population of Russia in the 20th century. Historical overview] (Moscow, 2000), p. 34.

50 I. Preobrazhensky, *Otechestvennaya cerkov' po statisticheskim dannim s 1840–1841 po 1890–91 gg.* [The domestic Church in accordance with statistical data, from 1840–41 to 1890–91] (St Petersburg, 1897), pp. 69–70.

51 N.A. Vigdorchik, 'Detskaya smertnost' sredi peterburgskih rabochih' [Child mortality amongst St Petersburg workers], *Obschestvenniy vrach*, 2 (1914), p. 217.

52 Preobrazhensky, *Otechestvennaya cerkov'*, p.78

53 B.C. Urlanis, *Istoriya odnogo pokoleniya* [The history of one generation] (Moscow, 1968), p 77.

the orphanage of St Petersburg was 9,578; in Moscow 16,636. In Kiev, every year the number of children who were given to the Department of Social Charity was 2,000. At the beginning of the twentieth century, the yearly number of foundlings all round Russia amounted to tens of thousands.

Legal experts noticed a clear connection between the strictness in relation to divorces and the number of children born out of wedlock.[54] Jurist A.D. Sposobin, in his book *On the Question of Divorce in Russia*, named as consequences of the unreasonably severe divorce procedure: a reduction in the number of legal marriages and an increase in the number of illegal ties; an increase in the number of bastard children, infanticides, spouse murders, and adulteries; the slow degradation of the whole society that was getting used to depravity, moral poverty, and the distortion of ethic ideals; and the fact that these evolutions were regarded as ordinary events. He concluded that it was a huge risk to conclude a marriage, and that logically lots of people did not want to take the risk, rather settling for illegal unregistered relations where it was possible to find the pleasant side of marriage without most part of its dark sides.[55]

Attempts at Reforming the Divorce Suit and the Problem of Civil Marriage

The pressing necessity to reform matrimonial law was obvious for jurists. Since the middle of the nineteenth century this need was comprehended even in the Department of Religious Affairs. Yet it took several decades before the reform was realised. After the imperial justice system was reformed in the 1860s during the reign of Alexander II, some attempts to reform the Church courts were undertaken as well. The committee for religious and judicial reform in 1870–73 considered it necessary to pass the investigation of divorce processes to the competence of civil courts,[56] preserving for the Church only the admonition to conciliation and the rendering of the final decision. However, due to resistance the project was not implemented. Notably, the archbishop of Orenburg, Mitrophan (Vitsinskiy), commented on this project: 'Extracting the matrimonial affairs of lay people from the competence of the clerical court would be an important global error of the Committee; it would be the same as taking them off the Church submission at all.'[57]

---

54 Mulhall, M.G., *Dictionary of Statistics* (London, 1892).

55 A.D. Sposobin, *O razvode v Rossii* [On the question of divorce in Russia] (Moscow, 1898), p. 173.

56 I.S. Berdnikov, *O reforme cerkovnogo suda* [About reforming the Church court] (St Petersburg, 1905), p. 46.

57 N.A. Belyakova, 'Materialy arhiva Sv. Sinoda po voprosu o reforme cerkovnogo suda (o popytke reformy cerkovnogo suda v 1870-e gg.)' [Material of the Archive of the Holy

In 1902, a project of the Civil code was published, stipulating that the civil courts should be charged with marriage procedures and the clerical courts should be able to pass judgement on the basis of the actual decision by a civil court. The project called to increase the number of legal reasons for divorce, such as violent treatment confirmed by the court.[58] The project also suggested that the court should allow separate residence or separation on the following grounds: 1. violent treatment; 2. insults; 3. contagious disease; 4. depraved life; 5. constant hard drinking; 6. wastefulness with ruinous consequences for the family; 7. wife's illness. A married woman would get permission for separate residence if her husband refused to provide necessary support for his wife and children, or impeded his wife, when short of maintenance, from working herself.[59] Cases of separate residence of spouses fell entirely within the competence of the civil courts.

Enactment of the procedure of civil marriage was inevitable and many lawyers and even canonists insisted on its necessity. An opponent to civil marriage enactment, one of the most conservative statesmen of late imperial Russia, the Chief Procurator of the Synod (in 1880–1907) and jurist Konstantin Pobedonoscev, considered that the legalization of civil marriage in Russia was 'impossible without abdicating the Church, without tempting and breaking nationwide believe in the authority of the ecumenical council dogmas'.[60] He noticed the close tie in the popular consciousness between Church and state affairs. On the other hand, he wrote that people had their own perception of marriage:

> The present economic situation makes common people consider marriage first of all as an economic act, as well as judge their wives from the perspective of economic use. The woman in the house is considered above all as a labour unit; marriages are contracted only in accordance with this reason; parents choose the brides and fiancés for their children themselves, without asking them about their will.[61]

Yet, another fact occurred. The edict of 17 April 1905 'About strengthening the basis of religious tolerance' changed the status of the Russian Orthodox Church considerably. It introduced a new problem into the marriage question,

---

Synod in relation to Church court reform], *Arkhivy russkoy pravoslavnoy cerkvi: materiali mezhdunarodnoy konferencii* (Moscow, 2004).

[58] *Proekt Grazhdanskogo Ulozheniya* [The Civil code project], vol. 2: Semeistvennoye pravo [Family law] (St Petersburg, 1902).

[59] Ibid.

[60] K.P. Pobedonoscev, *Kurs grazhdanskogo prava* [The course of civil law] (St Petersburg, 1896), p. 82.

[61] Ibid.

which was the issue of marriage to a non-Orthodox. The restrictions for marriages to Christians or followers of other confessions were abolished. And as far as the only legal form of marriage for Orthodox people was the church marriage, it became possible to demand from the priest to marry in church with sectarians or so-called old believers.[62] This situation once more made the question of the necessity for civil marriages in Russia urgent. The possibility of registering old believers' marriages from 1874 on was regarded as a precedent for the general enactment of civil marriage procedures in Russia.[63]

After 1905, even the Orthodox clergy started talking about the necessity of civil registration of marriages in order to free the Church from the burden of officiating at marriage ceremonies of atheists or old believers: 'Without insulting sacraments and even the simple dignity of the Church, it is not possible to force everyone to observe all the religious rites and sacraments. Hence it appears that it is necessary to introduce the civil-administrative registration of newborns, civil marriage, and civil funerals.'[64]

Priests pointed out that society had for a long time considered religious sacrament as an unpleasant but inevitable procedure of fixing acts of civil status:

> When you wed someone, you often see that for him it has totally no meaning, what is sung or read, it could be a funeral service, if only it lasted longer. He would for sure pay even more than he had paid for church wedding, if he could just be registered in some book, if in such a way the marriage was anyhow officially admitted by the state.[65]

In the existing situation, an Orthodox priest could not demand from his parishioners an attentive attitude towards the sacraments, while at the same time those citizens were forced to accomplish some kind of social act:

> There is no sense in reminding an unbeliever that he participates in a sacrament. For me it is a sacrament, but for him it is not. He came to me because he had to, under pressure: if he did not baptize a child, legally his child would not exist at all. Without a church wedding your wife would be regarded not as a wife but as a

---

62 In 1654, Patriarch Nikon had started reforming the Church rites and rewriting religious books on the model of the Greek ones. Those who did not accept this reform were called 'old believers'. The old believers' protest movement was widespread in the seventeenth century, but its leaders were condemned by the council of 1666–67 and repressed by state authorities until 1905.

63 M.I. Krasnozhin, *Stariye i noviye zakoni o razvode* [Old and new laws on divorce] (Yur'ev. 1904), p. 33.

64 'Svieshennik ob otdelenii cerkvi ot gosudarstva' [The priest on the question of separation between Church and State], *Cerkovnaya reforma*, 1 (1908), p. 28.

65 Ibid., p. 27.

> mistress, and children would be considered as born out of wedlock. Neither wife nor children would possess any kind of heritage or social rights of their husband and father. Without confessing or receiving communion you would not be able to marry in church. That is why the only thing which is accessible is that everyone who participates in sacraments and rites needs to dissemble as well as possible, concealing their lack of faith.[66]

Divorce proceedings did not change until the revolution of 1917. According to the statistics of 1913, only 3,791 persons were divorced (less than 1 per cent of the whole Orthodox population of 98.5 million people) in the Russian empire.[67] According to the census of 1897, among 1,000 men there was only one divorcee and among 1,000 women there were only two. The problems of family law and divorce procedures determined in many ways the large-scale cataclysms that occurred in Russian society after the October Revolution. One of the first acts of the new Soviet government would be the decree about divorces that withdrew all marriage procedures from the Church's competence. The contrast between the ease of getting a divorce in the new civil courts after 1917 and that slow, difficult Church divorce procedure (that could be initiated only according to strictly limited reasons) that had existed before the revolution influenced the demographic situation. The new easiness of divorce procedures made them so popular that the 1920s witnessed a peak of divorces and second marriages, as well as free cohabitation.

Property Rights of Women in the Russian Empire

Separate Property of Spouses

The famous Russian legal historian M.F. Vladimirsky-Budanov who examined property relations between spouses, came to the conclusion that 'Russian law has a distinctive feature: the equality of property rights for both spouses'.[68] The property status of women in the Russian empire was high and differed considerably from that in other European countries. Researchers consider that the tradition of separate property rights of spouses in Russia was connected to the regulations of Byzantine family law: according to Byzantine laws, the dowry of the wife after marriage did not become common familial property, but still belonged to the wife only. Her husband was not able to sell or take any

66 Ibid., p. 28.
67 *Naseleniye*. vol. 1, p. 50.
68 Vladimirsky-Budanov, *Ocherki*, p. 458.

advantage of his spouse's dowry.[69] The fact that women's high property rights were preserved and developed in Russian legislation seems to be a real paradox, as women did not possess any other important rights; as stated before, the patriarchal structure of the family made any woman's attempt at independence from her husband fruitless.

Several nineteenth-century historians wrote about these wide property rights of Russian women, which contrasted with those of Western European countries. A Russian lawyer at the end of the nineteenth century noticed that 'in Russia we do not really have this "women's question", thank God. Russian woman do not have anything to complain about. Their property status is in many ways more advantageous than the status of European women.'[70] Women possessed a considerable part of immovable goods. In the Siberian town of Tobol'sk women in 1848 possessed 757 items of real estate, while men had 1,159.

From the end of the seventeenth century on, one can observe a process of deliberate strengthening of separate property rights of the spouses and giving back to women the right to possess their own share of common familial property.[71] Researchers noticed that eighteenth-century laws sequentially protected the property rights of wives. A number of edicts established the separateness of the spouses' property: wives could not dispose of their husbands' patrimonial estate; and husbands could not take advantage of their wives' estates that they had inherited from their relatives or received as a gift when married. The dowry or any other property that the wife received was

---

[69] A. Laiou and D. Simon (ed.), *Law and Society in Byzantium: Ninth–Twelfth Centuries* (Washington, DC, 1994); M. Golovko, 'Vliyaniye vizantiyskogo prava na stanovleniye russkogo semeinogo prava (X–XVII vv.)' [The influence of Byzantine law on the formation of Russian family law], in *Sovremenniye problemi sovershenstvovaniya rossiyskogo zakonodatel'stva* (Barnaul, 2002), p. 33–4; A.M. Doronin and V.V. Rusinov, 'Vliyaniye vizantiyskogo prava na brachno-semeystvenniye otnosheniya i nasledstvennoye pravo na Rusi' [The influence of Byzantine law on marital family relations and inheritance law in Russia], in *XXXII Nedelya nauki SPbGU: materialy mezhvuzovskoy nauchno-tehnicheskoy konferencii* (St Petersburg, 2004); V.V. Chemerinskaya, *Vliyaniye vizantiyskogo prava na drevnerusskoye i rossiyskoye zakonodatel'stvo X–XVII vv. (Opyt sravnitel'nogo analiza)* [The influence of Byzantine law on old-Russian and Russian legislation] (PhD diss., Moscow, 2003); I.U. Sobina, 'Vliyaniye vizantiyskogo prava na razvitiye otechestvennogo prava: istoriografia voprosa' [The influence of Byzantine law on the development of domestic law: historiography of the question], *Obschestvo i pravo* (2009): pp. 61–6; Robin Bisha, *The Promise of Patriarchy: Women, Marriage, and Property in Imperial Russia* (PhD diss., Indiana University, 1994).

[70] K.A. Nevolin, *Istoriya rossiyskih grazhdanskih zakonov* [The history of Russian civil law] (vol. 1, Moscow, 2005), p. 267.

[71] P.L. Pushkareva, *Zhenschina v russkoy sem'ye: dinamika sociokulturnih izmeneniy X–XIX vv.* [The woman in the Russian family: dynamics of socio-cultural changes in the tenth to nineteenth century] (PhD diss., Moscow, 1997), pp. 23, 25.

considered her private possession. According to paragraph 115 of the Civil laws, the wife was entitled to dispose of the familial property without asking her husband's permission. The husband could get advantage on his wife's property only by power of an attorney as representative. Spouses were able to dispose of their own property separately. A wife was not able to dispose of her husband's property, or vice versa, without special legal contracts.[72] Spouses could make a contract between them to donate or sell their estates to one another. This practice led to many abuses because many landowners and merchants formally 'sold' their immovable property or landholdings to their wives to escape paying taxes; yet this right of purchase and sale between spouses was confirmed by the Senate in 1825.[73]

The spouses were not responsible for the crimes of each other, which meant that if according to law the husband was punished by confiscation, the wife's property remained inviolable, even if she had received it by her husband's donation or by contract with him. This legal norm was confirmed in different edicts of 1758, 1809 and 1824.[74] The only exception was the question of a widow's pension that should be taken out or lessened if after the husband's death facts of his criminal activity were revealed. At this point the state regarded these pensions as the husband's property, not as his wife's.[75]

Already according to the norms of Byzantine law the husband was obliged to support his wife and his children. The same notion existed in Russian family law: husbands had to care for their family's welfare.[76] However, the right to be supported by her husband was guaranteed for a wife only if she fulfilled her spousal duties. On the other hand, if she refused to follow her husband, for example to Siberia, she lost this right.[77]

The property status of women was especially important for merchants and for the nobility.[78] By their property rights, aristocratic women could achieve a degree of independence from their husbands. Often they advocated feminist

---

72 *Svod zakonov grazhdanskih*, ed. 1, p. 85; ed. 2, p. 117.

73 Nevolin, *Istoriya*, p. 267.

74 Ibid., p. 273.

75 *Svod zakonov grazhdanskih*, ed. 1, p. 82; ed. 2, p. 114.

76 Nevolin. *Istoriya*, p. 258.

77 N. Nizhnik, *Pravovoye regulirovanie semeyno-brachnih otnosheniy v russkoy istorii* [Legal regulation of family and marital relationships in Russian history] (St Petersburg, 2006), p. 143.

78 L. Bernstein, 'Women on the Verge of a New Language: Russian Salon Hostesses in the First Half of the Nineteenth Century', in H. Goscilo and B. Holmgren (ed.), *Russia, Women, Culture* (Bloomington, 1996), pp. 209–24.

progressive ideas[79] by promoting women's education[80] and the widening of women's rights in the family and in society at large.

For merchant-class women separate property rights played even a bigger role, as they often possessed a lot of immovable goods. These women sometimes joined the merchants' guilds on their own and traded under their proper names, separately from their husbands. Spouses could also make contracts and debts as independent partners.[81] In cases where the head of the family was often absent because of his trade dealings, his wife could undertake his duties and assume control over trade and shops as well as pay debts.[82] This mutual assistance was not customary for traditional patriarchal merchant milieus, but changes in the nineteenth century were dictated by the shifting economic situation.

In peasant milieus, the situation was as follows. Peasants always strived for marriage with equals.[83] They apprehended women as mere workers in the family; more important than the richness of the bride's family were her working qualities. The bride always received a dowry from her relatives, and this remained her property throughout marriage. The dowry of peasant girls usually consisted of dresses, linen, textile, tableware, instruments, and sometimes also cattle. When the woman lived with husband's family (this was common in villages as it was difficult for young men to become independent of their family, since property was difficult to acquire before the father's death), his relatives were not able to sell her property without her agreement. Yet if the couple lived separately, the husband could take advantage of his wife's property, especially if they had children. If the spouses lived together and did not have any children, and the husband wasted his wife's property, she had the right to make complaints to the authorities.[84] The property situation

---

79 L. Edmondson, 'Russian Feminists and the First All-Russian Congress of Women', Russian *History*, 3/2 (1976): pp. 123–49.

80 R. Dudgeon, 'The Forgotten Minority: Women Students in Imperial Russia, 1872–1917', *Russian History*, 9/1 (1982): pp. 1–26.

81 A.E. Zuyeva, *Russkaya kupecheskaya semya v Sibiri konca XVIII–pervoy poloviny XIX v.* [Russian merchant families in Siberia at the end of the eighteenth, beginning of the nineteenth century] (PhD diss., Novosibirsk, 1992), p. 125; Yu.M. Goncharov, *Gorodskaya semya Sibiri vtoroy poloviny XIX–nachala XX vv.* [The urban family of Siberia in the second half of the nineteenth, beginning of the twentieth century] (Barnaul, 2002), p. 283.

82 N.F. Yemelyenov, *Gorod Kurgan 1782–1917* [Kurgan city] (Kurgan, 1991), p. 101.

83 V.A. Aleksandrov, 'Semeino-imushchestvennye otnosheniia po obychnomu pravu v russkoi krepostnoi derevne XVIII–nachala XIX veka' [Family property relations in accordance with common law in Russian serf-villages in the eighteenth, beginning of the nineteenth century], *Istoriia SSSR*, 6 (November–December 1979): pp. 37–54.

84 *Russkiye krestiane: zhizn', byt, nravy* [Russian peasants: lives and customs], vol. 6 (St Petersburg, 2008), p. 360.

among peasants was regulated according to custom law, more than to family law based on Byzantine norms.

Inheritance Law

The peculiarities of inheritance law greatly influenced the legal and actual status of women in the late Russian empire.

The patrimonial principle resulted in male preference in inheritance cases. In contrast, the ties of women with their paternal kin-group diminished substantially after marriage. In fact, in descendant lines each woman received only one-eighth of the movable and one-fourteenth of the immovable property of the deceased, while her brothers shared the remaining estate equally.

Although merchants, small traders and manufacturers had to contend with the restrictiveness of patrimonial property and the system of shared inheritance, they could avoid the difficulties established by the law more easily than the landowners.[85] The necessity to change the law to avoid permanent splitting of estates and final impoverishment had always been evident for landowners, and therefore during the eighteenth and nineteenth centuries they tried to influence imperial jurists and legislative commissions to reform existing rules. Noble landowners frequently proposed reducing the number of shares in the inheritance of property by granting daughters and widows the right to a monetary payment only, or to the use and possession of patrimonial property for life.[86] Yet by trying to improve the law to their advantage, the landowners also diminished women's property rights.

It was only in 1848 that jurist I. Ilinsky proposed a project for changing existing inheritance law with the intention of guaranteeing equality between both sexes. The so-called 'Second Section of His Imperial Majesty's Chancellery' in charge of codification asserted that inheritance law must both satisfy the demands of justice and serve state interests. Defining justice as the moral obligation of an owner to provide adequately for his family, this department advocated restricting the power to dispose of acquired property in order to safeguard the spouse, children and parents of the owner from his irresponsible or capricious actions. It was proposed that the inheritance rights of women and men be made equal, yet in the end this principle was to be sacrificed in the economic interests of the state.[87] Noble landowners and

---

85 R.D. Bohac, 'Peasant Inheritance Strategies in Russia', *Journal of Interdisciplinary History*, 16 (Summer 1985): pp. 23–42; W.G. Wagner, *Marriage, Property and Law in Late Imperial Russia* (Oxford, 1994), pp. 233–4.

86 Wagner, *Marriage*, p. 236.

87 Ibid., pp. 240–41.

daughters, for example, were granted the right only for half of their brother's share of property in inheritance.[88]

Russian women were thus discriminated against in this field; a woman's share of inheritance was much less than that of the male members of her family. Still, because of the dowry and separate property rights in marriage, a woman's status could sometimes be more independent and advantageous than a man's. This was, for example, the case in peasant kinship families where men even after marriage remained absolutely dependent on their parents, while women after marriage got freedom from their parents. This was one more of the many paradoxes of law and traditions in the family sphere in late imperial Russia.

The Dowry

The tradition of a dowry to a daughter existed in Russia since ancient times. First legal norms about the bride's dowry had been determined in the first Russian legal code, *Russkaya Pravda*, from the eleventh century.[89] The closest relatives of the bride – her parents, brothers or uncles – were obliged to guarantee the bride her dowry before the wedding. This norm was closely connected with the problem of limited inheritance rights of women in Russia. The items that composed a woman's dowry could be various, depending on the stratum and financial status of the bride's relatives, from large landholdings, villages with peasants, and houses, to jewellery and clothing. The dowry constituted the main part of a woman's property in Russia. This was the basis for the relative high and independent property status of women in the Russian empire that existed in contradiction with the low legal status of Russian women in society at large and her rightless status in the family sphere.

Conclusion

Russian social life in the nineteenth century was affected by the same processes as elsewhere in Europe: there was the influence of the patriarchal family norm that increasingly existed in contradiction with women's shifting role in society; and their aspiration for emancipation, legal and financial independence from their husbands. Throughout the nineteenth century, family relations did not change from their authoritarian model to more democratic ones, although some Russian historians would not agree with this conjecture.[90] The family remained the most conservative unit of society. This can be explained not only

88 Ibid., p. 241.
89 Nevolin, *Istoriya*, pp. 274–87.
90 Mironov, *Social'naya,* p. 264.

by the patriarchal and traditional psychology of peasants – the most populous stratum in this society – but also by the peculiarities of Russian family law and the conservative religious concepts that were imposed by state and Church ideologues and that had legal force in tsarist Russia.

Imperial Russia did not create a developed system of family law. Byzantine legal norms were retained by nineteenth-century legislation. The enormous influence that Church authorities enjoyed in the sphere of marriage and divorce procedures did not suit the actual situation, where the level of secularization was growing. This secularization process in society was not reflected in the legislation. Marriage remained in the competence of the Church, which was itself part of the state system. Yet, when Church influence on society weakened and it no longer had the means to regulate family relations, the Church still could prohibit legal divorces, for which demand was peaking. The growing demand for divorce reflected the problem of gender antagonism: women's struggle against patriarchal authority and tyranny of husbands in the family matched economic changes in society, where husbands or fathers were no longer able to be the only breadwinners of the family.[91] The rejection of the civil marriage procedure contradicted those realities and social necessities of the nineteenth century. It worsened the apprehension of Church institutes and encouraged breaking with the traditional notions of religious authorities. This loss of connection with Orthodox or traditional ways of thinking – be it in religion, education or social life – may explain the fact that in Russia women's emancipation got such a radical character.[92] The women's movement that had started at the end of the 1850s widely spread throughout the country, leading to a net of women's associations struggling for legal equality and to women's organizations that in 1905 would appear with their own political programmes.[93]

Bibliography

Primary Sources

Bechasnov, P. (ed.), 'O razvodah i nedeistvitel'nih brakah za 1867–1886 gg.' [About divorces and invalid marriages in 1867–86], *Vremennik CSK MVD*, 26 (St Petersburg, 1893).

---

91 Freeze, *Mirskiye*, pp. 157–60.

92 D. Tzanaki, *Women and Nationalism in the Making of Modern Greece: The Founding of the Kingdom to the Greco-Turkish War* (Basingstoke, 2000), p. 66; V. Budnitskiy, *Zhenschini-terroristki v Rossi* [Women terrorists in Russia] (Rostov-on-Don, 1996).

93 Mironov, *Social'naya*, p. 266.

Dobrotvorskiy, N., 'Krest'yanskiye yuridicheskiye obychai v vostochnoy chasti Vladimirskoy gubernii' [Peasants' legal customs in the eastern part of the Vladimir province], *Yuridicheskiy sbornik*, 509 (1889).
Gernet, M., *Zhenskoye ravnopraviye i ugolovniy zakon* [Women's equal rights and criminal law] (St Petersburg, 1916).
Goikhbarg, A.G., 'Zamuzhnyaya zhenschina kak neravnopravnaya lichnost' v sovremennom obschestve' [A married woman as a person unequal in her rights in contemporary society], *Pravo*, 51 (1914): 3540–52.
Grigirovskiy, S.O., *O razvode: prichiny i posledstviya razvodoa I brakorazvodnoye sudoproizvodstvo. Istoriko-yuridicheskiy ocherk* (About divorce: causes and effects of divorce and divorce proceedings. Historic-legal essay] (St Petersburg, 1911).
Krasnozhin, M.I., *Stariye i noviye zakoni o* razvode [Old and new laws on divorce] (Yur'ev, 1904).
Krupskaya, N.K., *Zhenschina-rabotnica* [The woman worker] (Moscow/Leningrad, 1926).
L'vova, E., *Russkaya rabotnica* [The Russian female worker] (St Petersburg, 1914).
Ludmer, Y., 'Bab'i stony' [Women's cries], *Yuridicheskiy vestnik* (November 1884), pp. 446–67.
Mulhall, M.G., *Dictionary* of *Statistics* (London: Routledge, 1892).
Obschestvenniy vrach, [The social doctor], 9–10 (1915).
Paschenceva, S., 'Pravovoye i ekonomicheskoe polozheniye zhenschin v Rossiyskoi imperii (vtoraya polovina XIX veka–nachalo XX veka)' [The legal and economic status of women in the Russian empire, second part of the nineteenth, beginning of the twentieth century], *Mir truda* (1906), GARF (State Archive of the Russian Federation), F.516. Op.1, D.6. L.349.
Pobedonoscev, K.P., *Kurs grazhdanskogo prava* [The course of civil law] (St Petersburg, 1896).
Polnoye sobranije zakonov [The complete code of laws] (1900): vol. 21, no. 5379, *Ustav o blagochinii* [The Statute of Deanery].
Pouncy, C.J., (ed.), *The Domostroi: Rules for Russian Households in the Time of Ivan the Terrible* (New York, 1994).
Preobrazhenskiy, I., *Otechestvennaya cerkov' po statisticheskim dannim s 1840–1841 po 1890–91 gg.* [The domestic Church in accordance with statistical data, from 1840–41 to 1890–91] (St Petersburg, 1897).
Proekt Grazhdanskogo Ulozheniya [The Civil code project]: vol. 2. Semeistvennoye pravo [Family law] (St Petersburg, 1902).
Sposobin, D.A., *O razvode v Rossii* [On the question of divorce in Russia] (Moscow, 1898).
'Svieshennik ob otdelenii cerkvi ot gosudarstva' [The priest on the question of separation between Church and State], *Cerkovnaya reforma*, 1 (1908).
Svod zakonov grazhdanskih [The Code of civil laws] (St Petersburg, 1900).

Trudy Pervogo Vserossiyskogo zhenskogo s'ezda [Proceedings of the First All-Russian Women's Congress] (St Petersburg, 1909).

Ustav duhovnih konsistoriy [The Code of spiritual consistories] (St Petersburg, 1841).

Vigdorchik, N.A., 'Detskaya smertnost' sredi peterburgskih rabochih' [Child mortality amongst St Petersburg workers], *Obschestvenniy vrach*, 2 (1914).

Zakonodatel'stvo Petra I [The legislation of Peter I] (Moscow, 1997).

Zolotarev, L.A., *Supruzheskiye izmeny, ih znacheniye i prichiny* [Adultery in marriage, its meaning and reasons] (Moscow, 1895).

Secondary Sources

Aleksandrov, V.A., 'Semeino-imushchestvennye otnosheniia po obychnomu pravu v russkoi krepostnoi derevne XVIII–nachala XIX veka' [Family property relations in accordance with common law in Russian serf-villages in the eighteenth, beginning of the nineteenth century] *Istoriia SSSR*, 6 (November–December 1979): 37–54.

Belyakova, N.A., 'Materialy arhiva Sv. Sinoda po voprosu o reforme cerkovnogo suda (o popytke reformy cerkovnogo suda v 1870-e gg.) [Material of the Archive of the Holy Synod in relation to Church court reform], *Arhivy russkoy pravoslavnoy cerkvi: materiali mezhdunarodnoy konferencii* (Moscow, 2004).

Bernstein, L., 'Women on the Verge of a New Language: Russian Salon Hostesses in the First Half of the Nineteenth Century', in H. Goscilo and B. Holmgren (ed.), *Russia, Women, Culture* (Bloomington: Indiana University Press, 1996).

Berdnikov, I.S., O reforme cerkovnogo suda [About reforming the Church court] (St Petersburg, 1905).

Bisha, Robin, *The Promise of Patriarchy: Women, Marriage, and Property in Imperial Russia* (PhD diss., Indiana University, 1994).

Bobroff-Hajal, A., *Working Women in Russia under the Hunger Tsars: Political Activism and Daily Life* (New York: Carlson, 1994).

Bohac, R.D., 'Peasant Inheritance Strategies in Russia', *Journal of Interdisciplinary History*, 16 (Summer 1985): 23–42.

Broido, V., *Apostles into Terrorists: Women and the Revolutionary Movement in the Russia of Alexander II* (London: Oxford University Press, 1967).

Bruk, S., and V. Kabuzan, 'Dinamika i etnicheskiy sostav naseleniya Rossii v epohu imperializma (konec XIX veka-1917 g.)' [The dynamics and ethnic composition of the population of Russia in the period of imperialism], *Istoriya SSSR*, 3 (1980).

Budnitskiy, O.V., *Zhenschini-terroristki v Rossii* [Women terrorists in Russia] (Rostov-on-Don: Feniks, 1996).

Bumet-Vigniel, M.C., 'Femmes russes dans le combat evolutionnaire. L'image et son modele *à* la fin du XIX siecle', *Culture et sociétés de l'Est*, 12 (Paris, 1990).
Chemerinskaya, V.V., *Vliyaniye vizantiyskogo prava na drevnerusskoye i rossiyskoye zakonodatel'stvo X–XVII vv. (Opyt sravnitel'nogo analiza)* [The influence of Byzantine law on old-Russian and Russian legislation] (PhD diss., Moscow, 2003).
Czap, P., Jr, '"A Large Family. The Peasant's Greatest Wealth": Serf Households in Mishino, Russia, 1814–1858', in R. Wall, J. Robin and P. Laslett (ed.), *Family Forms in Historic Europe* (Cambridge: Cambridge University Press, 1982).
Dal', V.I., *Poslovicy russkogo naroda* [Russian folklore proverbs] (Moscow: Hudozhestvennaya literatura, 1964).
Doronin, A.M., and V.V. Rusinov, 'Vliyaniye vizantiyskogo prava na brachno-semeystvenniye otnosheniya i nasledstvennoye pravo na Rusi' [The influence of Byzantine law on marital family relations and inheritance law in Russia], *XXXII Nedelya nauki SPbGU: materialy mezhvuzovskoy nauchno-tehnicheskoy konferencii* (St Petersburg, 2004).
Dudgeon, R., 'The Forgotten Minority: Women Students in Imperial Russia, 1872–1917', *Russian History*, 9 (1982): 1–26.
Eck, A., 'La situation juridique de la femme russe au moyen âge', *Recueils de la société Jean Bodin pour l'histoire comparative des institutions*, 12 (1962): 405–20.
Edmondson, L., 'Russian Feminists and the First All-Russian Congress of Women', *Russian History*, 3 (1976): 123–49.
Elnett, E.P., *Historic Origin and Social Development of Family Life in Russia* (New York: Columbia University Press, 1926).
Freeze, G.L., 'Mirskiye narrativy o svyaschennom tainstve: brak i razvod v pozdneimperskoy Rossii' [Mundane narratives about a sacrament: marriage and divorce in late imperial Russia], in *Pravoslaviye: konfessiya, instituty, religioznost', XVII–XX vv.* (St Petersburg: European University at St Petersburg, 2009).
Golovko, M., 'Vliyaniye vizantiyskogo prava na stanovleniye russkogo semeinogo prava (X–XVII vv.)' [The influence of Byzantine law on the formation of Russian family law], in *Sovremenniye problemi sovershenstvovaniya rossiyskogo zakonodatel'stva* (Barnaul: Altaiskogo universiteta 2002).
Goncharov, Yu.M., *Gorodskaya semya Sibiri vtoroy poloviny XIX–nachala XX vv.* [The urban family of Siberia in the second half of the nineteenth, beginning of the twentieth century] (Barnaul: Altaiskogo universiteta, 2002).
Gromyko, M.M., *Mir russkoy derevni* [The world of Russian villages] (Moscow: Molodaya gvardiya, 1991).
Hellie, R., 'Women and Slavery in Moscow', *Russian History*, 10 (1983): 213–29.
Kivelson, V.A., 'Through the Prism of Witchcraft: Gender and Social Change in Seventeenth-Century Muscovy', in B.E. Clements et al. (ed.), *Russia's*

Women: Accommodation, Resistance, Transformation (Berkeley: University of California Press, 1991).

Kleimola, A., '"In Accordance with the Canons of the Holy Apostles": Muscovite Dowries and Women's Property Rights', *Russian Review*, 51 (1992): 204–29.

Laiou, A., and D. Simon (ed.), *Law and SOCIETY in Byzantium: Ninth–Twelfth Centuries* (Washington, DC: Dumbarton Oaks Research Library and Collection, 1994).

Lazovsky, N., 'Lichnyje otnoshenija suprugov po russkomu obychnomu pravu' [Personal relations between spouses according to Russian common law], *Yuridicheskiy vestnik*, 13/6 (1883): 358–414.

Leschenko, V.Yu., *Sem'ya i russkoye pravoslaviye XI–XIX vv.* [Family and Russian orthodoxy in the eleventh to nineteenth century] (Moscow: Frolovoy, 1999).

Levy, S., 'Women and the Control of Property in Sixteenth-Century Muscovy', *Russian History*, 10 (1983): 201–12.

Lewitter, L.R., Women, 'Sainthood and Marriage in Muscovy', *Journal of Russian Studies*, 37 (1979): 3–11.

McNally, S.J., *From Public Person to Private Prisoner: The Changing Place of Women in Medieval Russia* (PhD diss., State University of New York at Binghamton, 1976).

Mironov, B.A., *Social'naya istoriya Rossii perioda imperii (XVIII–nachalo XX v.)* [The social history of imperial Russia 1700–1917] (St Petersburg: Bulanin, 2000).

Naseleniye Rossii v XX v. Istoricheskiye ocherki [The population of Russia in the 20th century: historical overview] (Moscow: ROSSPEN, 2000).

Nevolin, K.A., *Istoriya rossiyskih grazhdanskih zakonov* [The history of Russian civil law] (Moscow: Statut, 2005).

Nizhnik, N.S., *Pravovoye regulirovanie semeyno-brachnih otnosheniy v russkoy istorii* [Legal regulation of family and marital relationships in Russian history] (St Petersburg: Yuridicheskiy Press, 2006)

Obolensky, D., *The Byzantine Commonwealth: Eastern Europe 500–1453* (London: Weidenfeld and Nicolson, 1971).

Pushkareva, N.L., 'The Woman and her Property and Legal Status: Was the XVIth Century a Turning Point?' in S. Cavaciocchi (ed.), *La donna nell'economia secc. XIII–XVIII: Atti della 'ventunesima Settimana di studi, 10–15 aprile 1989* (Florence: Le Monnier, 1990).

Pushkareva, P.L., *Zhenschina v russkoy sem'ye: dinamika sociokulturnih izmeneniy X–XIX vv.* [The woman in the Russian family: dynamics of socio-cultural changes in the tenth to nineteenth century] (PhD diss., Moscow, 1997).

Raeff, M., *Michael Speransky: Statesman of Imperial Russia, 1772–1839* (The Hague: Martinus Nijhoff, 1957).

Russkiye krestiane: zhizn', byt, nravy [Russian peasants: lives and customs] (St Petersburg: Delovaya poligrafiya, 2008).

Shahmatov, M., and M. Kostricin, *Obzor istorii kodifikacii i duhovnih pravil pravoslavnoy Greko- Rossiyskoy cerkvi s konca XVIII v. po nashe vremya* [The history of codification and spiritual rules of the Orthodox Greek-Russian Church from the end of the eighteenth century until the present] (Petrograd: Senatskaya tipografiya, 1917).

Sobina, I.U., 'Vliyaniye vizantiyskogo prava na razvitiye otechestvennogo prava: istoriografia voprosa' [The influence of Byzantine law on the development of domestic law: historiography of the question], *Obschestvo i pravo*, (2009): 61–6.

Tsaturova, M.K., *Russkoye semeynoye pravo XVI–XVIII vv.* [Russian family law in the sixteenth to eighteenth century] (Moscow: Jurist, 1991).

Tumanova, L., 'Lichniye imushestvenniye i neimushestvenniye otnosheniya suprugov v Rossii vo vtoroy polovine 19 veka: usynovleniye i uzakonyeniye' [Personal property and non-property relations of spouses in Russia in the second part of the nineteenth century: adoption and legitimating], *Pravo i zhizn'*, 61 (2003): 248–57.

Tzanaki, D., *Women and Nationalism in the Making of Modern Greece: The Founding of the Kingdom to the Greco-Turkish War* (Basingstoke: Palgrave Macmillan, 2000).

Urlanis, B.C., *Istoriya odnogo pokoleniya* [The history of one generation] (Moscow: Misl', 1968).

Vishlenkova, E., *Zabotyas' o dushah poddanih: religioznaya politika v Rossii v pervoy chetverti XIX v.* [Taking care of the subjects' souls: religious policy in Russia in the first quarter of the nineteenth century] (Saratov: izd-vo Saratovskogo universiteta, 2002).

Vladimirsky-Budanov, M.F., *Ocherki iz istorii rusko-litovskogo prava* [Notes from the history of Russian-Lithuanian law] (Kiev: Tipografiya Zavadskogo, 1890).

Wagner, W.G., *Marriage, Property and Law in Late Imperial Russia* (Oxford: Clarendon Press 1994).

Yemelyanov, N.F., *Gorod Kurgan, 1782–1917* [Kurgan city] (Kurgan, 1991).

Zirin, M., and C.D. Worobec (ed.), *Women and Gender in Central and Eastern Europe, Russia, and Eurasia* (New York: Armonk, 2007).

Zuyeva, E.A., *Russkaya kupecheskaya semya v Sibiri konca XVIII–pervoy poloviny XIX v.* [Russian merchant families in Siberia at the end of the eighteenth, beginning of the nineteenth century] (PhD diss., Novosibirsk, 1992).

PART III
Gendered Legal Cultures in Global Perspective

Chapter 8

Women Lawyers and Women's Equality Movements at the Turn of the Twentieth Century: Paradoxical Relationships?

Mary Jane Mossman

Women *Avocates* and Nineteenth-century Sex Equality Goals

> La question de la femme-avocat est une face du grand et complexe problème de l'affranchissement du sexe féminin. Non seulement nous souhaitons que toutes les carrières intellectuelles et libérales, y compris le barreau, soient rendues accessibles aux femmes, mais notre désir est de voir disparaître enfin les incapacités injustifiables qui frappent encore les femmes.[1]

As Louis Frank's comment reveals, the 'Woman Question' in the late nineteenth century encompassed a wide variety of progressive reforms that were designed to overcome existing practices of sexual inequality. Some of these reforms included proposals for women's access to education and professional work to enable women to attain economic independence, as well as changes in the legal status of married women in the family and recognition of women's political rights, especially in relation to female suffrage.[2] Significantly, Frank's comment, which positioned the question of women's eligibility to become *avocates* as an important part of this larger reform agenda, reflected the context of his treatise in support of Jeanne Chauvin's application to gain admission to the bar in Paris.[3] Overall, however, Frank's comment reveals how women's claims to become *avocates* were firmly

[1] Louis Frank, *La Femme-Avocat: Exposé Historique et Critique de la Question* (Paris, 1898), p. ii.

[2] For examples, see Christine Bolt, *The Women's Movements in the United States and Britain from the 1790s to the 1920s* (Amherst, 1993); Jane Rendall, *The Origins of Modern Feminism: Women in Britain, France and the United States 1780–1860* (Chicago, 1985); and Maïté Albistur and Daniel Armogathe, *Histoire du Féminisme Français* (Paris, 1977).

[3] *Chauvin v. Procureur Géneral,* Cour d'appel de Paris (1er Chambre) GP 2, 1897, p. 600. See also John Savage, 'The Problems of Wealth and Virtue: The Paris Bar and the Generation of the *Fin-de-Siècle*', in W. Wesley Pue and David Sugarman (ed.), *Lawyers and Vampires: Cultural Histories of the Legal Professions* (Oxford, 2003), p. 171.

embedded as a significant aspect of the broader movement for women's equality in the late nineteenth century. Frank was an inspirational force behind the middle-class feminism of the day; and around the turn of the century he conducted a wide correspondence with fellow supporters of more women's rights, men and women activists, suffragettes, publishers of women's journals and women lawyers all over the world.

Louis Frank was a Belgian barrister who became widely known in the 1880s and 1890s for his support of women lawyers in Italy, Belgium and France, and also for his support of the broader issues of the 'feminist' cause.[4] In relation to women lawyers, for example, an early treatise (written by Frank while he was a graduate student at the University of Bologna) had addressed the issue of women *avocates* in relation to a decision refusing Lidia Poët's application for admission to the bar in Turin in 1884.[5] A few years later, he became actively involved in Marie Popelin's application for admission to the bar in Belgium in 1888, although her application also failed before the courts.[6] Thus, Frank's comments in his 1898 treatise in support of Jeanne Chauvin's application for admission to the Paris bar revealed his longstanding interest in the cause of these aspiring *femmes-avocates*.

Yet, during this same period, Frank was also publishing a number of treatises concerning other aspects of the nineteenth-century 'Woman Question'. For example, his *Essai sur la Condition Politique de la Femme*, published in 1892, was an ambitious treatise of more than 600 pages, which comprehensively reviewed ideas about women's economic and political emancipation, as well as details about women's lives in many jurisdictions of the world, including countries in Europe, Britain and its colonies, the United States, Hawaii, Japan and parts of Latin America.[7] According to Frank, since there was evidence that the goal of sexual equality was gradually being achieved all over the world, it was necessary to amend the civil codes in Europe to reflect these new and important changes in the status of women.[8] In addition to this major treatise, Frank also authored a number of

---

[4] Françoise de Bueger-Van Lierde, 'Louis Frank, Pionnier du Mouvement Féministe Belge', *Revue Belge d'Histoire Contemporaine* 4/(3–4) (1973): p. 377. See also Mary Jane Mossman, *The First Women Lawyers: A Comparative Study of Gender, Law and the Legal Professions* (Oxford and Portland OR, 2006), pp. 246–68.

[5] Louis Frank, *De L'Exercice de la Profession d'Avocat en Italie: Exposé Sommaire des Règles* (Brussels, 1887). See also Vittorio Olgiati, 'Professional Body and Gender Difference in Court: The Case of the First (Failed) Woman Lawyer in Modern Italy', in Ulrike Schultz and Gisela Shaw (ed.), *Women in the World's Legal Professions* (Oxford, 2003), p. 419.

[6] Françoise de Bueger-Van Lierde, 'A L'Origine du Mouvement Féministe en Belgique: "L'Affaire Popelin"', *Revue Belge de Philologie et d'Histoire* 50 (1972): p. 1128.

[7] Louis Frank, *Essai sur la Condition Politique de la Femme:* Étude *de Sociologie et de Législation* (Paris, 1892).

[8] Ibid., p. 221.

publications in the early 1890s about women's higher education; marriage and married women's earnings; women doctors and pharmacists; and suffrage, as well as an important treatise about women in public employment.[9] In addition, in 1895, he presented an extension course at the Université Libre de Bruxelles about 'feminist legislation', and published the course materials.[10] Louis Frank's activities thus reveal the close connections between claims for access to the legal profession and the broader issues of the movement for women's equality. Clearly, for Frank in the late nineteenth century, these claims of aspiring *femmes-avocates* were all part of the larger 'women's question'.

This congruence between the claims of aspiring women lawyers and other reform proposals in the women's equality movements also occurred in the United States, where women had succeeded in gaining admission to the bar as early as the 1870s.[11] In this context, the American feminist historian Nancy Cott argued that the first American women to gain admission to state bars recognized their struggles as part of the greater 'cause of women' – that is, these early women lawyers in the United States understood 'the practice of law [as] ... a part of the broad movement to achieve equal rights [for women]'.[12] In this context, for example, a number of American women lawyers attended the founding conference of the International Council of Women (ICW) in Washington in 1888, and many of them were involved in nineteenth-century campaigns for suffrage and other goals of the movement for women's equality.[13] One woman lawyer, Catharine Waugh McCulloch from Chicago, even organized her honeymoon trip with her new husband around her commitments to speak in the suffrage campaign in South Dakota.[14]

Yet, by the turn of the twentieth century, it appears that some women lawyers began to focus their attention more pointedly on their professional activities

---

9 Louis Frank, 'University Opportunities for Women', *Educational Review* (1894): p. 471; Louis Frank, 'La Question du Mariage', *Revue du Belgique* (June 1890); Louis Frank, *L'Epargne de la femme Mariée* (Brussels, 1892); Louis Frank, *La Femme dans les Emplois Publics: Enquête et Rapport* (Brussels, 1893); and pamphlets written by Louis Frank for *La Ligue Belge du Droit des Femmes* as its first secretary general: 'La Femme-Médecin' (March 1893); 'Les Femmes-Pharmaciens' (October 1894); and 'Le Suffrage des Femmes en Nouvelle-Zélande' (November 1893). See also De Bueger-Van Lierde, 'Louis Frank, Pionnier'.

10 Louis Frank, *Cours sur la Législation Féministe: Notions Élémentaires* (Brussels, 1895).

11 Mossman, *The First Women Lawyers*, pp. 23–9.

12 Nancy Cott, *The Grounding of Modern Feminism* (New Haven and London, 1987), pp. 232–4.

13 Virginia G. Drachman, *Women Lawyers and the Origins of Professional Identity in America: The Letters of the Equity Club, 1887–1890* (Ann Arbor, 1993), p. 135; and Ada M. Bittenbender, 'Women in Law', in Annie Nathan Meyer (ed.), *Women's Work in America* (New York, 1891), p. 243.

14 Drachman, *Women Lawyers*, pp. 176–7: letter of Catharine Waugh, 1889.

rather than providing ongoing support to women's equality struggles, including suffrage campaigns. For these women lawyers, the priority was to succeed in being accepted within (male) professional culture, and to be recognized as *lawyers* rather than *women* lawyers. At the same time, however, other women who had completed university degrees in law continued to work hard for the cause of women's equality, thus combining their professional and gendered identities in the struggle for women's rights. In this context, this chapter examines some of these differing, and often paradoxical, approaches by these early women lawyers to the larger 'Woman Question' at the turn of the twentieth century.

The chapter begins by examining how different women lawyers, in a variety of different jurisdictions, were engaged in forging professional identities as *lawyers*, eschewing any commitment to women's equality movements. In this context, the chapter then explores briefly some of the activities of three women who remained more involved in the movement for women's equality even after becoming women in law: Myra Bradwell in the United States, Eliza Orme in Britain and Marie Popelin in Belgium. However, as will become evident, none of these women acquired formal admission to their respective legal professions; applications submitted by Bradwell and Popelin were rejected by the courts, and Orme chose not to seek formal admission to the bar or the solicitors' profession. In this context, the chapter assesses how their different circumstances may assist in understanding the paradoxical relationships of women lawyers and the movements for women's equality at the turn of the twentieth century.

Women Lawyers: The Paradox of Gender and Professional Identities

As Cott argued, the nineteenth-century congruence between the claims of women lawyers and the larger women's movement gradually revealed fissures, particularly around the turn of the twentieth century, as the magnetism of professional ideology promoted a greater sense of community of interest between women lawyers and professional men, and a gulf between women lawyers and non-professional women.[15] It is arguable that the first signs of these fissures were revealed as early as 1893, when women lawyers participated along with male lawyers and judges in the Congress on Jurisprudence and Law Reform, but did not take part in the Congress on Representative Women, both of which took place as part of the World's Columbian Exposition in Chicago.[16] Significantly, these women lawyers, who did not take part in the women's

---

15 Cott, *The Grounding of Modern Feminism*, pp. 232–4.

16 Mary Jane Mossman, '"*Le Féminisme*" and Professionalism in Law: Reflections on the History of Women Lawyers', in Martha A. Fineman (ed.), *Transcending the Boundaries of Law: Generations of Feminism and Legal Theory* (Abingdon, 2011), p. 9.

Congress, then organized their own meeting, which resulted in the creation of a National League of Women Lawyers, an organization that seemed to confirm women lawyers' identity as women *lawyers*, clearly emphasizing their professionalism.[17] Moreover, particularly after World War I, when suffrage was finally achieved in many countries (including the United States, Britain and some European jurisdictions), women lawyers increasingly embraced a professional identity. Indeed, for many of these women lawyers, there was a sense that the goals of the women's equality movement had been fully and substantially achieved.[18]

There are numerous examples of this fissure between women lawyers and the women's equality movement, as women lawyers began to accept their identity with the culture of professionalism and to downplay their gender. In the United States, for example, Mary Greene, who had been admitted to the bar in Boston in 1888, engaged in some legal practice and was also involved in legal writing and publishing. Indeed, Greene had translated Louis Frank's 1888 treatise on women lawyers for publication in the *Chicago Law Times* in 1889, and she was one of four women lawyers who were invited to participate in the Congress on Jurisprudence and Law Reform in Chicago in 1983.[19] Yet, as her correspondence with Louis Frank in 1895 revealed, Greene had no sympathy with the goals of the suffrage movement, stating:

> I do not know enough about the methods of the women suffragists in this country to tell you much about them. My views on the subject differ in so many ways from those of the leaders that I cannot work with them. I do not believe that the ballot will cure all ills, nor do I believe that women are powerless without the ballot. I prefer to teach women how to use the power and the rights they already possess (which here in America are many) in order that they may know how to ask intelligently for changes in the laws. I do not like the way in which these leaders persistently misrepresent the present laws ....[20]

---

[17] Ibid.

[18] Barbara J. Harris, *Beyond Her Sphere: Women and the Professions in American History* (Westport, CT, 1978); Anne Witz, *Professions and Patriarchy* (London and New York, 1992); and James C. Albisetti, 'Portia ante Portas: Women and the Legal Profession in Europe, ca 1870–1926', *Journal of Social History*, 33 (2000): p. 825.

[19] Lelia J. Robinson, 'Women Lawyers in the United States', *The Green Bag*, 2 (1890): p. 10. See also Mary Jane Mossman, 'Women Lawyers and Women's Legal Equality: Reflections on Women Lawyers at the 1893 World's Columbian Exposition in Chicago', *Chicago-Kent Law Review*, 87/2 (2012): p. 503.

[20] Bibliothèque Royale, Brussels, Section des Manuscrits, Papiers Louis Frank, #7791–6 (envelope 1): letter from Mary Greene to Louis Frank, May 1895.

Similarly, other women lawyers also advocated that women needed to adopt a professional identity and to disregard their gender. For example, Lelia Robinson, the first woman to gain admission to the bar in Massachusetts in 1882,[21] wrote to other women lawyers a few years later to suggest:

> *Do not take sex* into the practice. Don't be "lady lawyers." Simply be *lawyers*, and recognize no distinction – no existence of any distinction between yourselves and the other members of the bar. This will be your surest way to ... achieve success. Let no one regard you as a curiosity or a *rara avis* ....[22]

Robinson's advice to her colleagues was consistent with advice that was sometimes given to new women lawyers by male members of the profession. For example, Waugh McCulloch reported in her letter to colleagues in 1889 that she often received advice from other attorneys and from judges about the incongruity of trying to practise law and also to work for women's rights,[23] although her decision to combine her honeymoon with suffrage organizing suggests that she did not always heed such advice. For other women lawyers, moreover, the challenge of achieving economic independence by earning a living in the practice of law may have curtailed their energy and opportunities for supporting the women's movement. As Virginia Drachman concluded, 'the hard realities of life, not the romantic notions of ideal womanhood, determined the direction of their professional careers'.[24]

There is some evidence that early women lawyers in other jurisdictions faced similar pressures to conform to the culture of professionalism in law, and several of them seem to have made similar decisions to embrace a professional, rather than a gendered, identity. For example, Clara Brett Martin, who became Canada's first woman lawyer in 1897, received a good deal of support from the broader women's equality movement in her quest to gain admission to the Ontario bar.[25] However, it seems that she was not much involved in issues about women's equality after she gained admission to the bar, but instead focused

[21] Mary A. Greene, 'Mrs. Lelia Robinson Sawtelle: First Woman Lawyer of Massachusetts', *The Women Lawyers' Journal*, 7/7 (1918): p. 51.

[22] Drachman, *Women Lawyers*, p. 66: letter of Lelia Robinson, 1887 (emphasis in original).

[23] Ibid., p. 174: letter of Catharine Waugh, 1889.

[24] Virginia G. Drachman, *Sisters in Law: Women Lawyers in Modern American History* (Cambridge, MA, 1998), pp. 99–100.

[25] Martin requested support from the Dominion Women's Enfranchisement Association; and the International Council of Women also organized a 'volley of letters in the daily, weekly, and monthly journals, all recommending Miss Martin'. See Theresa Roth, 'Clara Brett Martin: Canada's Pioneer Woman Lawyer', *Law Society Gazette*, 18 (1984): p. 328.

primarily on her legal practice. Indeed, she even failed to participate in the meeting of the International Council of Women in Toronto in 1909, merely sending her 'regrets'.[26] Another Canadian woman lawyer, Mabel Penery French – who was called to the bar of New Brunswick in 1906 and then to the bar of British Columbia in 1912 (after relocating there) – did participate in the ICW meeting in Toronto, presenting a paper on the topic of child custody.[27] However, shortly after this event, French abandoned Canada and the practice of law to move to Britain, where she married and never again worked as a member of the legal profession.[28]

Significantly, Ethel Benjamin, the first woman admitted to the bar in New Zealand in 1897, created a public furore when she provided comments to the press that were critical of a convention of the National Council of Women there in 1898. Benjamin had suggested to the press that:

> [It was] really absurd for a few women, as yet political infants, to meet and in a moment "carry unanimously" motions which few of them understand, which in all probability are quite impractical, or which, if given effect to, might revolutionize society in a way that few of them thoroughly appreciate.[29]

Not surprisingly, the National Council criticized Benjamin's remarks, particularly because many women members of the Council were themselves the 'political infants' who had successfully lobbied for female suffrage, enacted in New Zealand in 1893, as well as the opening of the legal profession to women in 1896, *before* Benjamin had been called to the bar:

> [D]oes the poor child fully understand what she talks about – so "glibly"? The "political infants" – those of them, at least, who have taken a prominent part in the discussion – are grey-haired women, who for a quarter of a century or more (before Miss Benjamin was born) have been working for the emancipation of women, and, through them, of men.[30]

---

26 *Report of the International Congress of Women* (Toronto, 1910), vol. 1, pp. 173–4 and 203; and Mossman, *The First Women Lawyers*, pp. 82 and 101.

27 *Report of the International Congress of Women* (Toronto, 1910), vol. 2, p. 203.

28 Lois Yorke, 'Mabel Penery French (1881–1955): A Life Re-Created', *University of New Brunswick Law Journal*, 42 (1993): pp. 3–49; and Mossman, *The First Women Lawyers*, pp. 109–10.

29 Roberta Nicholls, *The Women's Parliament: The National Council of the Women of New Zealand 1896–1920* (Wellington, 1996), p. 35, citing the *Evening Post*, 30 April and 5 May 1898.

30 Ibid., pp. 21 and 35–6.

Even Emilie Kempin-Spyri, a committed feminist with a Swiss law degree, whose application for admission to the bar in Zurich had been rejected in 1887, and who had then become involved in law teaching in New York and Switzerland, eventually parted from the feminist movement. As she explained in a letter to Frank, she did not attend an international women's meeting in Berlin in 1896 because she did not agree with recent developments concerning women's equality.[31] Indeed, as Gisela Shaw argued, Kempin-Spyri was increasingly shunned by more radical feminists because her need to make a living and the '*habitus* of the profession she had made such sacrifices to join' compromised her ability to pursue her feminist goals.[32]

At the same time, it is important to note that Jeanne Chauvin, whose unsuccessful application for admission to the Paris bar in 1897 resulted in the enactment of legislation to permit women to become *avocates* in France in 1900, may have continued to work for reforms promoting women's equality after she gained admission to the bar. Her involvement with *L'Avant Courrière*, which had begun in the 1890s, continued at least until 1907 when the organization succeeded in its efforts to reform the law about married women's earnings.[33] According to Sara L. Kimble, Chauvin was also registered with *L'Assistance Judiciaire*, the legal aid agency of the Paris bar, and she was active in promoting legal reforms concerning paternity and in drafting provisions to enforce support payments for illegitimate children. However, Chauvin also continued to teach in several girls' *lycées*, probably to ensure her financial security, and it is unclear whether she engaged in activities promoting suffrage reform.[34]

Similarly, Lidia Poët engaged in some legal practice in a law office in Turin, where qualified members of the legal profession in Italy signed her letters.[35] She too was involved in reform efforts, but mainly in relation to prisons and penal issues, and she attended and participated in at least one International Penal Congress in Rome in 1885.[36] Unfortunately, Poët's views about women's equality, and suffrage in particular, have not survived.

Overall, these examples suggest that a number of women who gained admission to the legal profession in the last decades of the nineteenth (and

---

31 Papiers Frank, #6031 (file 5): letter from Kempin-Spyri, 27 August 1896.

32 Gisela Shaw, 'Conflicting Agendas: The First Female Jurists in Europe to be Awarded a Doctorate in Law', *International Journal of the Legal Profession*, 10/2 (2003): pp. 177–9.

33 Mossman, *The First Women Lawyers*, pp. 261 and 273–4; and Anne Boigeol, 'French Women Lawyers (*Avocates*) and the "Women's Cause" in the First Half of the Twentieth Century', *International Journal of the Legal Profession*, 10/2 (2003): p. 196.

34 Sara L. Kimble, *Justice Redressed: Women, Citizenship, and the Social Uses of the Law in Modern France, 1890–1939*, PhD diss. (University of Iowa, 2002), pp. 150–51, 161–2 and 177–9.

35 Papiers Frank, #6031 (file 4): letter to Frank, 24 January 1897.

36 Ibid.

early twentieth) centuries experienced increasingly fragile, and sometimes quite hostile, relationships with the women's equality movements in a number of different jurisdictions, including Western Europe, the United States and some British colonies. Yet, for other women lawyers, a commitment to the women's equality movements did not seem to dissipate after they gained admission to the bar, at least not to the same extent. In this context, it seems important to examine how and why some women lawyers continued to connect their achievement in gaining admission to the bar with broader goals concerning women's equality in the early twentieth century.

Paradoxical Relationships: Women Lawyers and Goals of Women's Equality

In examining relationships between gender and professionalism in the lives of some women in law in different jurisdictions at the end of the nineteenth century, there are several examples of women lawyers who continued to express significant support for these broader issues in the cause of women's equality. In the United States, for example, Phoebe Couzins, the first woman to graduate from Washington University Law School in the early 1870s, devoted much of her life to the suffrage cause, and frequently exhorted women to become lawyers in order to advance the broader goals of women's equality. As she argued, both the legal profession and the women's equality movements needed 'women's wit, women's fairness and women's sense of right and righteousness'.[37] Similarly, Ada Bittenbender, who had become attorney for the National Women's Christian Temperance Union in the United States, continued to be involved in the women's equality movement alongside her professional work. Nonetheless, Bittenbender also acknowledged that her ability to combine these activities resulted, at least in part, because she was not involved in the challenge of maintaining her own legal office.[38] Moreover, some women lawyers, like Belva Lockwood, the first woman admitted to the bar of the US Supreme Court in 1879, and Clara Foltz, the first woman admitted to the bar of California in 1878, combined the practice of law with major speaking engagements on a variety of reform issues, including issues about legal reforms and women's rights.[39] Nonetheless, the necessity of earning

---

[37] Hedda Garza, *Barred from the Bar: A History of Women in the Legal Profession* (New York, 1996), pp. 80–81.

[38] Drachman, *Women Lawyers*, p. 153: letter of Ada M. Bittenbender, 1889.

[39] See Jill Norgren, *Belva Lockwood: The Woman Who Would Be President* (New York and London, 2007); and Barbara Babcock, *Woman Lawyer: The Trials of Clara Foltz* (Stanford, 2011).

a living in the practice of law in order to support their families imposed some constraints on these reform activities for women like Lockwood and Foltz.[40]

In this context, the experiences of Myra Bradwell in the United States, Eliza Orme in Britain and Marie Popelin in Belgium, all of whom made important contributions to the women's equality movements in different ways, deserve some scrutiny to understand how they managed to achieve these accomplishments. The individual circumstances of these three women were somewhat different, since Bradwell was married, while Orme and Popelin remained unmarried. In addition, Orme's parents were relatively well off financially, while Popelin came from a respected but apparently less wealthy family; and Bradwell's husband, a judge, was both reasonably secure financially and seems to have been supported Bradwell's activities, including her efforts to promote women's rights.[41] Among these three, only Orme was engaged in legal work for clients, while Bradwell edited a legal newspaper and Popelin founded *La Ligue Belge du Droit des Femmes* to promote women's rights in Belgium. In this way, their efforts as women in law to promote broader goals about women's equality reveal both similarities in their goals and differences in the strategies they adopted to achieve them.

Unfortunately, there is no evidence that these three women ever met in person. Although Orme was invited by Bradwell to participate in the Congress on Jurisprudence and Law Reform during the Chicago Exposition in 1893, Orme sent a paper but did not attend in person.[42] And unfortunately, Bradwell had died before Popelin apparently travelled to North America to attend the ICW meeting in Toronto in 1909.[43] Yet, while their circumstances were quite different in a number of ways, all three women made important contributions, as women in law, to the cause of women's equality at the turn of the twentieth century. In this context, it appears significant that all of these women in law were excluded from their respective legal professions, a point explored later in this chapter. Before doing so, however, it is necessary to provide a brief examination of the contributions of these three women in law to the cause of women's equality.

---

[40] Norgren and Babcock both identified financial difficulties in the lives of Lockwood and Foltz. See also Mossman, *The First Women Lawyers*, p. 62.

[41] See Jane Friedman, *America's First Woman Lawyer: The Biography of Myra Bradwell* (Buffalo, 1993); Leslie Howsam, '"Sound-Minded Women": Eliza Orme and the Study and Practice of Law in Late-Victorian England', *Atlantis*, 15 (1989), p. 44; and Albisetti, 'Portia ante Portas'.

[42] *Chicago Legal News*, 12 August 1893.

[43] See Friedman, *America's First Woman Lawyer*, and *Report of the International Congress of Women* (Toronto, 1910, vol. 2, p. 248.

Myra Bradwell

Myra Bradwell had worked with her husband in his law office before the Civil War in the United States, assisting him with legal research and writing. However, she had also established the first law journal in the West in 1868, the *Chicago Legal News*, and her journal regularly provided synopses of judicial decisions as well as advocating legal reforms and supporting women lawyers and women's equality issues relating to law.[44] In 1869, Bradwell had decided to seek admission to the Illinois bar, citing the precedent of Arabella Mansfield's admission by an Iowa court earlier that year.[45] However, by contrast with the reasoning of the court in Iowa, the Illinois court rejected Bradwell's application, using arguments about women's disabilities at common law and the need to interpret statutory language narrowly.[46] Bradwell published the rejection letter in her journal, along with a scathing critique of the court's reasoning.[47]

Significantly, however, it seems that Bradwell met with Elizabeth Cady Stanton and Susan B. Anthony, leaders of the American women's movement for equality, later in 1869, as she was contemplating an appeal to the US Supreme Court.[48] In due course, she filed an appeal to the Supreme Court, adding additional arguments about equal rights pursuant to the 14th Amendment's guarantee of equal protection in the US Constitution. However, as Nancy Gilliam concluded, Bradwell's equal rights argument was 'generations ahead of her time',[49] and the appeal was dismissed with just one dissenting opinion in 1873.[50] Although Susan B. Anthony wrote to Bradwell to announce that they hoped to 'pour hot shot into that old Court' in an upcoming woman's rights convention,[51] Bradwell's unsuccessful appeal resulted in a legal ruling that women were *constitutionally* ineligible to become members of the bar, a result that required subsequent aspiring women lawyers to seek legislative amendments to gain admission to state bars.[52]

Thus, in spite of the rejection of Bradwell's application, the Illinois legislature later enacted an amending statute to permit women to become attorneys in

---

[44] Nancy T. Gilliam, 'A Professional Pioneer: Myra Bradwell's Fight to Practice Law', *Law and History Review*, 5 (1987): p. 105. See also George Gale, 'Myra Bradwell: The First Woman Lawyer', *ABA Journal*, 39/12 (1953), p. 180.

[45] Joan Hoff, *Law, Gender, and Injustice: A Legal History of US Women* (New York, 1991), p. 247.

[46] Gilliam, 'A Professional Pioneer', pp. 110–13.

[47] Hoff, *Law, Gender, and Injustice*, p. 173; and *Chicago Legal News*, 19 June 1880.

[48] Drachman, *Sisters in Law*, p. 17.

[49] Gilliam, 'A Professional Pioneer', pp. 114–15.

[50] *Bradwell v. Illinois*, 83 US 130 (1873); and Gilliam, 'A Professional Pioneer', p. 125.

[51] Friedman, *American's First Woman Lawyer*, p. 27.

[52] Mossman, *The First Women Lawyers*, pp. 46–52.

the state, and by 1900, there were just over 100 women members of the state bar.[53] Until the mid 1890s, moreover, Bradwell continued her advocacy as the editor of the *Chicago Legal News*, while also using her influence as the wife of a prominent member of the judiciary to promote a variety of reforms. Thus, for example, when she was selected to chair the women's committee in relation to the Congress on Jurisprudence and Law Reform in connection with the Chicago Exposition, it seems that she exercised her influence to arrange for women lawyers to be included in this prestigious gathering, rather than organizing a separate Congress for women lawyers. According to Mary Greene:

> Mrs. Bradwell's latest triumph was secured in 1893, when she, as the Chairman [*sic*] of the Women's Branch of the World's Congress of Jurisprudence and Law Reform, obtained recognition of women lawyers as speakers, on the same platform with the male jurists .... In this successful battle, she was ably assisted by her brilliant daughter, Bessie Bradwell Helmer [a member of the Illinois bar].[54]

As a result, two women lawyers from the United States, Mary Greene and Clara Foltz, presented papers to the Congress on Jurisprudence and Law Reform.[55] In addition, papers by Eliza Orme from Britain and Cornelia Sorabji from India were read by women members of the Illinois bar.[56] As Louis Frank concluded, their appearance at this Congress confirmed that women lawyers had received official recognition from the most eminent jurists in the world.[57]

In relation to this accomplishment, it seems that it was Bradwell's influence that resulted in this important recognition for women lawyers in 1893, but it is also important to acknowledge her crusading reform work for several decades prior to this accomplishment. Moreover, Bradwell never reapplied for admission to the bar, stating in an interview in 1889 that her business had become so significant after the Supreme Court decision that she 'had no time to give to law practice', and she did not wish to be admitted 'just for the privilege of putting "Attorney" after [her] name'.[58] However, in 1890, the

---

53 Gwen H. McNamee (ed.), *Bar None: 125 Years of Women Lawyers in Illinois* (Chicago, 1998), p. 8; and Gwen H. Jordan, *Creating a Woman's Legal Culture: Women Lawyers in Illinois, 1855–1939*, PhD diss. (University of Illinois, 2004).

54 Papiers Frank, #6031 (file 2): letter from Greene to Frank, 9 September 1896.

55 Mossman, 'Women Lawyers and Women's Legal Equality'.

56 Mossman, *The First Women Lawyers*, chapters 3 and 5.

57 Frank, *La Femme-Avocat*, p. 133.

58 Friedman, *America's First Woman Lawyer*, p. 29, citing *Chicago Tribune*, 12 May 1889.

Supreme Court of Illinois granted Bradwell a licence to practise, and the US Supreme Court also did so in 1892.[59]

Eliza Orme

Eliza Orme, who became a well-known public figure in England in the last decades of the nineteenth century, had grown up in a comfortable home in London in which visitors regularly discussed culture, science and politics. Among these visitors was John Stuart Mill, who had introduced the unsuccessful amendment to provide for women's suffrage in the British Parliament in 1867.[60] Orme's family also supported education for women, and she and her sisters attended Bedford College for Women. Thus, when University College London opened its lectures to mixed groups of men and women in 1871, Orme became a student; and when the university eventually permitted women to receive the degree of Bachelor of Laws, Orme became the first woman to graduate in law in Britain in 1888.[61]

However, by 1888, Orme had been engaged in legal work with a woman partner in an office in Chancery Lane since 1875.[62] Prior to opening her office, she had spent some time as a pupil with a sympathetic barrister at Lincoln's Inn, as well as attending lectures at the university, and it seems that she and her partner did legal work that did not require them to be members of the legal profession, including patent work and drawing wills. In addition, Orme and her partner may have engaged in some property and conveyancing work for barristers at Lincoln's Inn, for which they were paid 'half fees'.[63] As Jessie Wright, a visiting woman lawyer from Massachusetts, described Orme's situation:

> Miss Orme is fine; a first-rate kind of woman, and nobody could have been more kind and cordial than she has been to me. She tells me that she has never applied for admission to the bar, but that when four or five women are ready to ask for admission they will do so. She says that she thinks things look more hopeful now than ever, and that several of the benches are already in favour of their being admitted – not as solicitors, for which an act of parliament would have to be

---

59 Ibid., pp. 29–30. Both licences dated from Bradwell's original application in 1869. See also Carol Sanger, 'Curriculum Vitae (Femininae): Biography and Early American Women Lawyers', *Stanford Law Review*, 46 (1994): pp. 1261–2.

60 Howsam, 'Sound-Minded Women', p. 45. See also Constance Rover, *Women's Suffrage and Party Politics in Britain 1866–1914* (London, 1967), p. 218.

61 Howsam, 'Sound-Minded Women', p. 45; and 'Orme Family' in Elisabeth Crawford, *The Women's Suffrage Movement: A Reference Guide (1866–1928)* (London, 1999), p. 480.

62 'The Year "That's Awa"', *Englishwoman's Review*, 6 (1875): pp. 533–4.

63 'Orme Family', in Crawford, *The Women's Suffrage Movement*, p. 480; and Mossman, *The First Women Lawyers*, pp. 131–7.

> changed ... but as barristers. She now has a good business, working for barristers and solicitors, but getting their work as they do, she says, they only get half fees; though, of course, when they do what work they are qualified to do – drawing of wills, for instance – for private parties, it is different.[64]

In addition to her legal work, Orme was an active woman in the public sphere. For example, she participated in the Society for Promoting the Employment of Women, an organization established to promote better educational opportunities for women and employment in a number of trades; the Society also established the Victoria Press, a printing business run by women.[65] In addition, Orme was actively involved in the London National Society for Women's Suffrage and a frequent and articulate speaker at suffrage meetings. She was also an active member of the Women's Liberal Association (WLA) and became editor and manager of the *Women's Gazette*, its journal, in 1888, even though the suffrage issue had never achieved significant prominence in the Liberal Party.[66] Indeed, when some women suffragists voted to make female suffrage an objective of the WLA, Orme and other Liberal Party supporters resigned and established a rival organization. Unfortunately, the new organization failed to prosper, while the original one went from strength to strength, a situation that must have vexed Orme and others.[67] At the same time, it is likely that her support for the Liberal Party resulted in her appointment in 1892 as a Lady Assistant Commissioner for the Royal Commission on Labour. In this context, she investigated and reported on the employment of women and their conditions of work in England, Wales, Scotland and Ireland: their reports examined in meticulous detail the work of barmaids, waitresses and bookkeepers in hotels, and women working in the nail, chain and bolt and other industries.[68]

Probably as a result of her prominence in Britain, Orme was invited to participate in the Congress on Jurisprudence and Law Reform in Chicago in 1893, and although she was not able to be present in person, she sent a brief

---

64 Drachman, *Women Lawyers*, p. 144: letter of Jessie Wright, 1888.

65 'Orme Family', in Crawford, *The Women's Suffrage Movement*, p. 480; and Lee Holcombe, *Victorian Ladies at Work: Middle-Class Working Women in England and Wales 1850–1914* (Hamden, CT, 1973): pp. 5–6 and 15–16.

66 Howsam, 'Sound-Minded Women', pp. 49 and 51–2; and 'Orme Family', in Crawford, *The Women's Suffrage Movement*, p. 480.

67 Eliza Orme, 'A Commonplace Correction', *Welsh Review* 1 (1892): p. 467; and Orme, *Lady Fry of Darlington* (London, 1898), pp. 131–5. See Peter Gordon and David Doughan, *Dictionary of British Women's Organizations 1825–1960* (London, 2001), p. 173.

68 Royal Commission on Labour, *The Employment of Women: Reports by Miss Eliza Orme, et al. (Lady Assistant Commissioners) on the Condition of Work in Various Industries in England, Wales, Scotland and Ireland* (London, 1893).

but detailed report about the status of women in Britain for the Congress.[69] According to Leslie Howsam, Orme regarded herself as 'an educated person, an authoritative expert, prepared to give her opinion on subjects ranging from Home Rule in Ireland to jurisprudence in India', and a woman who was fully committed to making a contribution to public life.[70] Clearly, she combined her legal work with significant efforts to support women's equality, even though she eventually parted company with the main women's suffrage organization in Britain. Orme never sought admission to the bar, and by the time that women in Britain became eligible to apply, she was in her early seventies and had retired from legal work.[71]

Marie Popelin

Marie Popelin initially worked as a teacher in Belgium, but at the age of 37 relinquished teaching to attend the law programme in Brussels. She graduated with distinction in 1888, two years after Frank had completed the same course, and immediately announced her intention to take the oath to become an *avocate* before the Court of Appeals.[72] Her decision created great excitement in the Belgian press as *L'Affaire Popelin*, and Frank then published his 1888 treatise to confront all the legal arguments in the case.[73] In addition, Frank appeared in support of Popelin's application before the Court, alongside a distinguished member of the Belgian bar, Jules Guillery. In spite of this support, however, the Court rejected Popelin's application, and an appeal to the *Cour de Cassation* was dismissed in 1889.[74]

Popelin provided a detailed report about the case in a letter to women lawyers in the United States, explaining that the reasoning of the courts included discussion of Roman law, the customs of the Middle Ages, the decree of 1810 regarding the legal profession, and the Napoleonic Code. However, as she then lamented: '[B]ut no one discussed the progress made in ... women's condition, of

---

69 Eliza Orme, 'The Legal Status of Women in England', *Chicago Legal News*, 25 (1893): p. 431.

70 Howsam, 'Sound-Minded Women', p. 53.

71 'Women and the Bar', *The Law Journal* (12 December 1903): p. 620; and Mossman, *The First Women Lawyers*, pp. 152–3.

72 De Bueger-Van Lierde, 'A L'Origine du Movement Féministe', pp. 1128–9.

73 Ibid. Frank's 1888 publication was *La Femme-Avocat: Exposé Historique et Critique de la Question* (Brussels/Bologne).

74 De Bueger-Van Lierde, 'A L'Origine du Movement Féministe', p. 1133. See also Françoise Van Lierde, *La 'Ligue Belge du Droit des Femmes' 1892–1897*, Master diss. (Louvain-la-Neuve, 1971), pp. 35–65.

her entry [into] most of the liberal careers, and especially of the woman lawyer, and the experience, tried with success in the United States.'[75]

Although there were a number of critiques of this decision, legislative proposals to permit women to become *avocates* were defeated in 1912 and again in 1920.[76]

Frank's support for Popelin's application, along with the success of his *Essai* in 1892, resulted in the creation of a new organization, *La Ligue Belge du Droit des Femmes*, the 'first feminist organization in Belgium'.[77] As the organization's first secretary general, Frank presented a detailed report at the first meeting in November 1892 at the Université libre de Bruxelles, outlining a proposed programme and other arrangements, and concluding with a hope for '*le triomphe final du féminisme*'. However, only two years later, Frank was forced to resign in the midst of quarrels between the 'Frankistes' and the 'Popelinistes' about who was the founder of *La Ligue*. In this context, Popelin was regarded as the founder, while Frank's contributions became almost invisible.[78]

There is some evidence of Popelin's continuing involvement in women's equality projects, including those of *La Ligue*. For example, as President of Belgium's National Council of Women, she participated in the International Council of Women meeting in 1909 in Toronto, where she presented a paper about marriage and divorce laws in Belgium.[79] More significantly, the proceedings of a *Congrès Féministe Internationale*, which took place in Brussels in April 1912 to celebrate the twentieth anniversary of the founding of *La Ligue Belge*, clearly demonstrated Popelin's prominent role among women's rights activists in Belgium.[80] Indeed, the proceedings noted that Popelin represented '*l'âme du Congrès*', and included a five-stanza poem in her honour.[81] Thus, it seems that Popelin had remained fully involved in the projects of *La Ligue Belge* for 20 years, and was widely recognized for her many contributions to women's equality goals in Belgium.

---

75 Drachman, *Women Lawyers*, p. 199: letter from Marie Popelin, 1890.

76 De Bueger-Van Lierde, 'A L'Origine du Mouvement Féministe', pp. 1136–7; and Albisetti, 'Portia ante Portas', pp. 829–30.

77 De Bueger-Van Lierde, 'A L'Origine du Mouvement Féministe', p. 1137.

78 Van Lierde, *La Ligue Belge*, pp. 82–8.

79 Marie Popelin, 'Laws on Marriage and Divorce in Belgium', in *Report of the International Congress of Women, Toronto* (1910), vol. II, p. 248.

80 Ligue Belge du Droit des Femmes, *Actes du Congrès Féministe Internationale de Bruxelles 1912* (Brussels, 1912).

81 Ibid., Avant-Propos.

However, it was not until 1922 that Belgium enacted legislation that permitted women to become *avocates*.[82] Unfortunately, Popelin had died in 1913 at the age of 67, '*sans avoir pu réaliser son rêve*'.[83]

Reflections on Women Lawyers and Women's Equality Movements

By contrast with a number of other women lawyers, it seems significant that Bradwell, Orme and Popelin continued to make significant contributions to the larger women's equality movement, after their applications for formal admission were rejected (Bradwell and Popelin) or even without making an effort to attain formal admission (Orme). In this context, however, it is possible that the fact of their work 'outside the boundaries' of the legal professions provided them with more scope to engage with women's rights activities. That is, by contrast with women lawyers who were working as legal practitioners, these three women were not required to conform to the culture of the legal professions.

However, this conclusion requires some exploration of how ideas about professionalism were also changing at the turn of the twentieth century. For example, Cott argued that ideas about 'dispassionate professionalism' became increasingly magnetic for women professionals in the early twentieth century, especially after suffrage had been widely achieved after World War I:

> The professional ethos, with its own promise of freedom from sex-defined constraints, was released to flourish in aspiring women's minds .... [Women professionals assumed that] the professions' supposedly neutral and meritocratic ideology was not only their best armor but their only hope. As the scientific areas ... led the way, emphasizing that the professions' hallmarks were objectivity, empiricism, rationality, impersonality, and collegially determined standards, feminism seemed more openly to conflict with those hallmarks.[84]

Such ideas may have constrained women who had gained admission to the bar, while women who had not achieved formal admission experienced greater freedom to engage in feminist activities in pursuit of women's equality.

In this context, Eliza Orme's situation was somewhat ambiguous, since she was engaged in legal practice and needed to retain the support of barristers at Lincoln's Inn who regularly provided her with legal work. In addition, her appointments to a variety of public positions depended on the preservation of the Liberal Party's trust in her loyal commitment to its goals. As a result, she was

82 Albisetti, 'Portia ante Portas', p. 830.

83 *Vies de Femmes 1830–1980* (Brussels, 1980), pp. 24–5.

84 Cott, *The Grounding of Modern Feminism*, pp. 233–4.

not wholly 'independent' of professional and political commitments, and this insight may explain her decision to resign from the Women's Liberal Association when its members wished to adopt positions that were probably not widely accepted at Lincoln's Inn or in the Liberal Party. In this way, Orme may have experienced some of the attractiveness of professionalism even as she carved out a role outside the formal constraints of the legal profession.

In addition to the rise of new ideas about professionalism, however, the women's equality movement was also experiencing changes in the early twentieth century, changes that might well have distanced women practitioners from the leaders of the women's movement. As Sylvia Bashevkin argued, for example, issues in the women's equality movement in the early twentieth century increasingly focused on social reforms, including temperance, child welfare, and suffrage, and its leaders had become somewhat less concerned about the movement's earlier goals of access to employment and economic independence for women. Of course, these changes in the goals of the women's movement tended to reflect the interests of its twentieth-century leaders, most of whom were middle-class married women who were involved in a variety of philanthropic activities, including social feminism, and less often engaged in paid work. As a result, they had little in common with women who were seeking economic independence by engaging in professional work, and often foregoing marriage to do so. As Bashevkin explained: '[There was always] an older "hard-core" minority, which sought to challenge the discriminatory treatment of women [in employment, but they were increasingly marginalized by the] more moderate reformist mainstream of "social feminism"'.[85]

In this context, Bradwell represents some ambiguity. Clearly, she was a woman with an independent career as publisher of the *Chicago Legal News*, but she was also the wife of a member of the judiciary. To some extent at least, she seems to have combined these aspects of her life to achieve a good deal of influence in legal matters and in relation to women's equality issues, and not only in relation to her appointment to chair the women's committee of the Congress of Jurisprudence and Law Reform. In this way, it is difficult to untangle the relative usefulness of her publishing career and her social status, although it seems clear that she used them in a strategic combination to achieve women's rights goals. In this context, it is possible that, had Bradwell lived beyond the 1890s, she might well have continued to have significant influence in relation to changing goals of the women's movement in the twentieth century.

---

[85] Sylvia Bashevkin, 'Independence versus Partisanship: Dilemmas in the Political History of Women in English Canada', in Veronica Strong-Boag and Anita C. Fellman (ed.), *Rethinking Canada: The Promise of Women's History* (Toronto, 1986), p. 249.

Thus, these relationships between women lawyers and the women's equality movements at the turn of the twentieth century require a complex assessment. Not only is it necessary to examine the concrete circumstances in the lives of individual women lawyers, but it is also important to take account of the attraction of emerging ideas about professionalism as well as the evolution of different priorities within the women's equality movements in this period. As Berenice Fisher argued, we need to engage in a 'radical social analysis' which examines the objective constraints for women, as well as how they coped with, tested and challenged them.[86]

Bibliography

Manuscript Sources

Bibliothèque Royale, Brussels, Section des Manuscrits, Papiers Louis Frank.

Printed Sources

Albisetti, James C., 'Portia ante Portas: Women and the Legal Profession in Europe, ca 1870–1926', *Journal of Social History*, 33 (2000): 825–57.

Albistur, Maïté, and Daniel Armogathe, *Histoire du Féminisme Français* (Paris: Editions des Femmes, 1977).

Babcock, Barbara, *Woman Lawyer: The Trials of Clara Foltz* (Stanford: Stanford University Press, 2011).

Bashevkin, Sylvia, 'Independence versus Partisanship: Dilemmas in the Political History of Women in English Canada', in Veronica Strong-Boag and Anita Clair Fellman (ed.), *Rethinking Canada: The Promise of Women's History* (Toronto: Copp Clark Pitman, 1986).

Bittenbender, Ada M., 'Women in Law', in Annie Nathan Meyer (ed.), *Women's Work in America* (New York: Holt, 1891).

Boigeol, Anne, 'French Women Lawyers (*Avocates*) and the "Women's Cause" in the First Half of the Twentieth Century', *International Journal of the Legal Profession*, 10/2 (2003): 193–207.

Bolt, Christine, *The Women's Movements in the United States and Britain from the 1790s to the 1920s* (Amherst: University of Massachusetts Press, 1993).

Chicago Legal News, 19 June 1880, 12 August 1893.

Cott, Nancy, *The Grounding of Modern Feminism* (New Haven and London: Yale University Press, 1987).

---

86 Berenice Fisher, 'The Models Among Us: Social Authority and Political Activism', *Feminist Studies*, 7 (1981): p. 111.

Crawford, Elisabeth, *The Women's Suffrage Movement: A Reference Guide (1866–1928)* (London: University College London Press, 1999).
De Bueger-Van Lierde, Françoise, 'A L'Origine du Mouvement Féministe en Belgique: "L'Affaire Popelin"', *Revue Belge de Philologie et d'Histoire*, 50 (1972): 1128–37.
De Bueger-Van Lierde, Françoise, 'Louis Frank, Pionnier du Mouvement Féministe Belge', *Revue Belge d'Histoire Contemporaine*, 4/3–4 (1973): 377–92.
Drachman, Virginia G., *Women Lawyers and the Origins of Professional Identity in America: The Letters of the Equity Club, 1887–1890* (Ann Arbor: University of Michigan Press, 1993).
Drachman, Virginia G., *Sisters in Law: Women Lawyers in Modern American History* (Cambridge, MA: Harvard University Press, 1998).
Fisher, Berenice, 'The Models Among Us: Social Authority and Political Activism', *Feminist Studies*, 7 (1981): 100–112.
Frank, Louis, *De L'Exercice de la Profession d'Avocat en Italie: Exposé Sommaire des Règles* (Brussels: Moens & Fils, 1887).
Frank, Louis, 'La Question du Mariage', *Revue du Belgique* (June 1890).
Frank, Louis, *Essai sur la Condition Politique de la Femme: Étude de Sociologie et de Législation* (Paris: Arthur Rousseau, 1892).
Frank, Louis, *L'Epargne de la femme Mariée* (Brussels: Vromant et Cie, 1892).
Frank, Louis, *La Femme dans les Emplois Publics: Enquête et Rapport* (Brussels: Charles Rozez, 1893).
Frank, Louis, 'La Femme-Médecin' (March 1893); 'Les Femmes-Pharmaciens' (October 1894); and 'Le Suffrage des Femmes en Nouvelle-Zélande' (November 1893): pamphlets written for *La Ligue Belge du Droit des Femmes.*
Frank, Louis, 'University Opportunities for Women', *Educational Review* (1894).
Frank, Louis, *Cours sur la Législation Féministe: Notions Élémentaires* (Brussels: Moreau, 1895).
Frank, Louis, *La Femme-Avocat: Exposé Historique et Critique de la Question* (Paris: Giard et Brière, 1898).
Friedman, Jane M., *America's First Woman Lawyer: The Biography of Myra Bradwell* (Buffalo: Prometheus Books, 1993).
Gale, George, 'Myra Bradwell: The First Woman Lawyer', *ABA Journal*, 39/12 (1953): 1080–83, 1120–21.
Garza, Hedda, *Barred from the Bar: A History of Women in the Legal Profession* (New York: Franklin Watts, 1996).
Gilliam, Nancy T., 'A Professional Pioneer: Myra Bradwell's Fight to Practice Law', *Law and History Review*, 5 (1987): 105–33.
Gordon, Peter, and David Doughan, *Dictionary of British Women's Organizations 1825–1960* (London: Woburn Press, 2001).

Greene, Mary A., 'Mrs. Lelia Robinson Sawtelle: First Woman Lawyer of Massachusetts', *The Women Lawyers' Journal*, 7/7 (1918): 51.
Harris, Barbara J., *Beyond Her Sphere: Women and the Professions in American History* (Westport, CT: Greenwood Press, 1978).
Hoff, Joan, *Law, Gender, and Injustice: A Legal History of US Women* (New York: University Press, 1991).
Holcombe, Lee, *Victorian Ladies at Work: Middle-Class Working Women in England and Wales 1850–1914* (Hamden, CT: Archon Books, 1973).
Howsam, Leslie, '"Sound-Minded Women": Eliza Orme and the Study and Practice of Law in Late-Victorian England', *Atlantis*, 15 (1989): 44–55.
Jordan, Gwen H., *Creating a Woman's Legal Culture: Women Lawyers in Illinois, 1855–1939* (PhD diss., University of Illinois, 2004).
Kimble, Sara L., *Justice Redressed: Women, Citizenship, and the Social Uses of the Law in Modern France, 1890–1939* (PhD diss., University of Iowa, 2002).
Ligue Belge du Droit des Femmes, *Actes du Congrès Féministe Internationale de Bruxelles 1912* (Brussels: Imprimerie Scientifique Charles Bulens, 1912).
McNamee, Gwen H. (ed.), *Bar None: 125 Years of Women Lawyers in Illinois* (Chicago: Chicago Bar Association Alliance for Women, 1998).
Mossman, Mary Jane, *The First Women Lawyers: A Comparative Study of Gender, Law and the Legal Professions* (Oxford and Portland, OR: Hart, 2006).
Mossman, Mary Jane, '"*Le Féminisme*" and Professionalism in Law: Reflections on the History of Women Lawyers', in Martha A. Fineman (ed.), *Transcending the Boundaries of Law: Generations of Feminism and Legal Theory* (Abingdon: Routledge, 2011).
Mossman, Mary Jane, 'Women Lawyers and Women's Legal Equality: Reflections on Women Lawyers at the 1893 World's Columbian Exposition in Chicago' *Chicago-Kent Law Review*, 87/2 (2012): 503–19.
Nicholls, Roberta, *The Women's Parliament: The National Council of the Women of New Zealand 1896–1920* (Wellington: Victoria University Press, 1996).
Norgren, Jill, *Belva Lockwood: The Woman Who Would Be President* (New York and London: New York University Press, 2007).
Olgiati, Vittorio 'Professional Body and Gender Difference in Court: The Case of the First (Failed) Woman Lawyer in Modern Italy', in Ulrike Schultz and Gisela Shaw (ed.), *Women in the World's Legal Professions* (Oxford: Hart, 2003).
Orme, Eliza, 'A Commonplace Correction', *Welsh Review*, 1 (1892).
Orme, Eliza, 'The Legal Status of Women in England', *Chicago Legal News*, 25/431 (1893).
Orme, Eliza, *Lady Fry of Darlington* (London: Hodder and Stoughton, 1898).
Popelin, Marie, 'Laws on Marriage and Divorce in Belgium', in *Report of the International Congress of Women, Toronto*, vol. II (1910).

Rendall, Jane, *The Origins of Modern Feminism: Women in Britain, France and the United States 1780–1860* (Chicago: Lyceum Books, 1985).
Report of the International Congress of Women (Toronto: Parker & Sons, 1910).
Robinson, Lelia J., 'Women Lawyers in the United States', *The Green Bag*, 2 (1890).
Roth, Theresa, 'Clara Brett Martin: Canada's Pioneer Woman Lawyer', *Law Society Gazette*, 18 (1984): 323–40.
Rover, Constance, *Women's Suffrage and Party Politics in Britain 1866–1914* (London: Routledge & Kegan Paul, 1967).
Royal Commission on Labour, *The Employment of Women: Reports by Miss Eliza Orme, et al. (Lady Assistant Commissioners) on the Condition of Work in Various Industries in England, Wales, Scotland and Ireland* (London: HMSO, 1893).
Sanger, Carol, 'Curriculum Vitae (Femininae): Biography and Early American Women Lawyers', *Stanford Law Review*, 46 (1994): 1245–81.
Savage, John, 'The Problems of Wealth and Virtue: The Paris Bar and the Generation of the *Fin-de-Siècle*', in W. Wesley Pue and David Sugarman (ed.), *Lawyers and Vampires: Cultural Histories of the Legal Professions* (Oxford: Hart, 2003).
Shaw, Gisela, 'Conflicting Agendas: The First Female Jurists in Europe to be Awarded a Doctorate in Law', *International Journal of the Legal Profession*, 10/2 (2003): 177–91.
'The Year "That's Awa"', *Englishwoman's Review*, 6 (1875): 533–4.
Van Lierde, Françoise, *La 'Ligue Belge du Droit des Femmes' 1892–1897* (Master diss., Université catholique de Louvain, 1971).
Vies de Femmes 1830–1980 (Brussels: Banque Bruxelles Lambert, 1980).
Witz, Anne, *Professions and Patriarchy* (London and New York: Routledge, 1992).
'Women and the Bar', *The Law Journal* (12 December 1903).
Yorke, Lois, 'Mabel Penery French (1881–1955): A Life Re-Created', *University of New Brunswick Law School*, 42 (1993): 3–49.

Chapter 9
Legal Cultures in Transition: The Role of Italian Jurist Women

Maria Rita Bartolomei

Research Objective and Working Method

Feminist legal theory starts from the fact that laws have, until recently, been made, interpreted and enforced by men and for men.[1] Yet, over the last 30 years in the Western world we have witnessed such profound gender-related and social-economic changes that we are urged to consider the increasing importance of women's role in transforming legal practice and legal culture.[2]

Differences between men and women in cultural terms and on the labour market have drastically diminished in the last decades. In Italy, the number of qualified female lawyers has more than doubled since 1995. Today, women represent there over 50 per cent of all lawyers, while in 1982 they counted only 6 per cent.[3] In 1965, at the time of their entry in the judiciary, women judges represented less than 1 per cent. At present in Italy nearly half of all new judges are women, as almost one-third of the notaries are. Moreover, figures indicate that there are now more female students in the law faculties, and more law graduated and qualified women under the age of 45 than men.[4]

Some scholars stress that the massive entry of women into the legal profession stems less from women's increasing gender awareness and empowerment than from structural contingencies, that is from demographic and economic changes

1 Joan Brockman, *Gender in the Legal Profession: Fitting Or Breaking the Mould* (Vancouver, 2001); Virginia Drachman, *Sisters in Law: Women Lawyers in Modern American History* (Cambridge MA, 1998); Mary Jane Mossman, *The First Women Lawyers: A Comparative Study of Gender, Law and the Legal Professions* (Oxford, 2006).

2 Although 'legal culture' is not an easy concept to define, I understand it as the ideas, values and attitudes people in society share with regard to the law and the legal system; legal culture is what determines the impact of legal norms on society (Lawrence Friedman, 'Is There a Modern Legal Culture?', *Ratio Juris*, 7/2 (1994): pp. 117–31.

3 Centro Studi Investimenti Sociali, *Dopo le buone teorie, le proposte. Programma di ricerca per le donne avvocato, Census Report 2010*, http://www.aiga.it.

4 Consiglio Nazionale Forense (CNF) and Consiglio Superiore della Magistratura (CSM), *Le donne nelle professioni legali di domani* (National Meeting Rome, 11 June 2010).

transforming the productive labour system and family relations.[5] It is however beyond doubt that the increasing participation of women in the labour market has fostered the extraordinary rise of worldwide access to legal knowledge and legal professionalism. Parallel to this, a growing body developed of what might broadly be described as feminist legal scholarship.[6]

Feminist authors seek to identify the ways in which the legal system jeopardizes women, and they consequently recommend remedial legal reforms. The feminist areas of criticism in legal matters can be summarized in four categories: equal treatment; recognition of difference; dominance and subordination; anti-essentialism and intersectionality.[7]

Feminist legal theory has generated a lively debate on the necessity of legal regulation in improving women's position in society by focusing not only on discrimination covered by existing legislation, but also on forms of social behaviour which are discriminatory and unfavourable to women.[8] Yet, the deficiency should be noted of empirical research and of theoretical approaches acquiring a deep and meaningful understanding of the institutional impediments to women's success in the practice of law;[9] the challenges that jurist women face in balancing work and family;[10] and of discriminations and 'glass ceiling'[11] mechanisms.

---

5 Vittorio Olgiati, 'Donne & lavoro. L'inclusione della differenza di genere nelle attività economiche e professionali', *I Quaderni dell'Istituto di Sociologia*, 3 (Università di Urbino, 2006): pp. 1–72.

6 Nancy Levit and Robert R.M. Verchick, *Feminist Legal Theory: A Primer* (New York, 2006); Alison Young and Nina Puren, 'Signifying Justice: Law Culture and the Question of Feminism', *Australian Feminist Law Journal*, 13 (1999): pp. 3–12.

7 The anti-essentialist or intersectionality approach rejects the idea that gender issues in the law can be considered in isolation. Human differences such as race, sexual orientation, class and religion inseparably intersect with gender and should thus always be considered together in (feminist legal) theory as well as in practice. See: Ann Bartow, *Legal Theory Lexicon 061: Feminist Legal Theory*, http://lsolum.typepad.com/legal_theory_lexicon/2006/11/legal_theory_le.html.

8 Sandra Fredman, *Discrimination Law* (Oxford, 2002); John Hagan and Fiona Kay, *Gender in Practice: A Study of Lawyers' Lives* (Oxford, 1995); Mona Harrington, *Women Lawyers: Rewriting the Rules* (New York, 1994).

9 Ulrike Schultz and Gisela Shaw (ed.), *Women in the World's Legal Professions* (Oxford, 2003).

10 Deborah L. Rhode, 'Balanced Lives: Changing the Culture of Legal Practice' (Stanford, 2001).

11 Jacquelyn Slotkin and Samantha Goodman (ed.), *It's Harder in Heels: Essays by Women Lawyers Achieving Work-Life Balance* (Lake Mary, FL, 2007); Hilary Sommerland and Peter Sanderson, 'Professionalism, Discrimination, Difference and Choice in Women's Experience in Law Jobs', in Philip Thomas (ed.), *Discriminating Lawyers* (London, 2000), pp. 155–82.

In this chapter, I will examine how gendered legal expertise greatly contributes to developing new jurisdictional patterns that force us to redefine the parameters of the public and the private spheres. Some Italian jurist women's associations have indeed played an important role in the legal qualification of domestic violence against women and children as an attempt to violate their human dignity, and therefore their human rights. I will show how these jurist women, interacting with and practising in law firms, courts and other legal fields, transform themselves, their working space and the wider society of which they are part.

Based on current literature and adopting a rich mixture of qualitative methodologies as participant observation and ethnographic interviewing, this research work has been carried out in different periods of time starting from January 2008. Fieldwork included: 1. spending some periods of participant observation in 10 law courts that operate in the Central Eastern Marche region of Italy; 2. collecting quantitative data, that is a sample of 30 court cases relating to domestic violence brought to court between 2008 and 2010; 3. in-depth interviews with female lawyers (65), male lawyers (20), clients (40) and judges (15), all of them living in the Marche region; 4. a life history collection, that is 30 life stories of abused wives and daughters.

The interviewed lawyers, either women or men, have been selected from those living and practising in the Marche region within seven legal associations corresponding to the courts of Ancona, Ascoli Piceno, Camerino, Fermo, Macerata, Pesaro and Urbino. Most of the female lawyers are members of women lawyers associations such as Associazione Donne Avvocato di Fermo (ADAF) and Associazione Donne Avvocato del Piceno (ADAP), the former at Fermo Law Court, the latter at Ascoli Piceno Law Court. The selection of lawyers has been quite easy: I initially found knowledgeable informants through friends and colleagues, then through contacts given by other interviewees by means of so-called 'snowball sampling'. Access to the abused women has been a little more difficult. In order to explore their ideas on the law, I assembled a life history collection and sometimes, when I felt it relevant, I offered my thoughts and experiences for comparison.

The interviewees were encouraged to provide elaborate answers and to produce 'thick descriptions' of their views on the topic. According to the 'narrative of non-neutral interviewing' – that is dominant in contemporary methodology texts, and assumes that face-to-face interviews are locally and collaboratively produced[12] – it is important for the interviewer to be able to

[12] Tim Rapley, 'Interviews', in Clive Seale et al. (ed.), *Qualitative Research Practice* (Thousand Oaks, 2004), pp. 15–33.

try to 'communicate trust, reassurance and even likeableness'.[13] For this reason, I always arranged interviews with abused women in private spaces without too much outside interaction.

Provisional findings appear to confirm some interesting trends. First of all, I witnessed an unquestionable widening of law and legality horizons in two different concurring ways. On the one hand, jurist women reshape the meaning of legality as they deploy legal meanings in new settings. On the other hand, legal knowledge provides cultural schemes that women use not only at work but also to understand their everyday experience.

To analyse the first aspect, I have relied on the framework elaborated by Patricia Ewick and Susan Silbey to explore legal consciousness.[14] Their study identifies three common narratives about law in people's thinking: the idea of the law being magisterial and remote – what they call 'before the law'; the view of the law as a game with rules that can be manipulated to one's advantage – what they call 'with the law'; the description of law as an arbitrary power that is actively resisted – what they call 'against the law'.[15] As far as the second aspect is concerned, I will discuss women's empowerment through law and how this entails different social outcomes.

Presenting individual experiences and case studies, this study aims to give a glimpse of women lawyers' attitudes such as they emerge from talks, accounts and statements of judges, clients and abused women.

Without of course settling all debates on the subject, this chapter offers, from an anthropological perspective, a better understanding of the multiple ways in which gender and law can interact.[16]

Domestic Violence in Italy

In recent years, there has been a greater understanding of the problem of domestic violence, its causes and consequences, and an international consensus has developed on the need to deal with the issue. The Convention on the Elimination of All Forms of Discrimination against Women adopted

---

13 Stephen Ackroyd and John Hughes, *Data Collection in Context* (Harlow, 1992), p. 108. To have some level of control on the interaction as a whole, I decided to use an interview guide in dealing with the various topics. The content of the list of questions varies in relation to the different categories of interviewees.

14 Patricia Ewick and Susan Silbey, *The Common Place of Law* (Chicago, 1998). The authors collected accounts from hundreds of people from diverse backgrounds in order to investigate the different ways in which people use and experience the law.

15 Ibid., pp. 47–9.

16 Patricia Frazier and Jennifer Hunt, 'Research on Gender and the Law: Where Are We Going, Where Have We Been?', *Law and Human Behaviour*, 22/1 (1998): pp. 1–16.

by the United Nations General Assembly in 1979, the Convention on the Rights of the Child in 1989, and the Platform for Action adopted at the Fourth International Conference on Women in Beijing in 1995 all reflect this historically grown consensus. Yet, progress has been slow and effective strategies to address domestic violence are still being defined. As a result, women worldwide continue to suffer, with estimates varying from 20 to 50 per cent from country to country.[17]

Although in developing countries women are more susceptible to abuse of all kinds, domestic violence is very common and an important cause of mortality for women in every country. While from the outside Italy looks like a highly civilized country, the problem has been a major concern here, where attacks by jealous husbands – passionate, hot-blooded and possessive – are rarely regarded as crimes. Yet the latest figures suggest that in 2006 almost 7 million women were victims of violence and that in Italy at least one in four women experiences domestic abuse over their lifetime.[18]

In Italy, the Osservatorio Nazionale sulla Violenza Domestica (ONVD) adopts the definition of domestic violence given by the World Health Organization (WHO) in 1996: any act of 'gender-based violence that results in, or is likely to result in, physical, sexual or mental harm or suffering to women, including threats of such acts, coercion or arbitrary deprivation of liberty, whether occurring in public or in private life'.[19] Domestic violence – also known as domestic abuse, spousal abuse, battering, family violence[20] and intimate partner violence (IPV) – is defined by the ONVD as a pattern of abusive behaviour by one partner against another in an intimate relationship such as marriage, dating, family or cohabitation. Partners may be married or not, heterosexual, gay or lesbian. Although both men and women can be abused, most victims are women. Children in homes where there is domestic violence are more likely to be abused and/or neglected. Even if a child is not physically harmed, they may have emotional and behaviour problems.

All forms of domestic violence come from the abuser's desire for power and control over other family members or intimate partners. Although every situation is unique, there are common factors involved. Research shows that domestic violence can affect any woman, regardless of race, age, sexual orientation, religion, social class, disability or lifestyle. It can take many forms,

---

17 Unicef/Innocenti Research Centre, *Innocenti Digest 6*, June 2000, http://www.unicef-irc.org/publications/pdf/digest6e.pdf.

18 Italian National Institute of Statistics, *Report 2007*, http://www3.istat.it.

19 http://www.onvd.org; World Health Organization, *Violence against Women Act* (FRH/WHD/96.27) (Geneva, 1996).

20 Family violence is a broader definition, often used to include child abuse, elder abuse and other violent acts between family members.

including physical aggression or assault,[21] sexual abuse,[22] economic deprivation,[23] emotional and psychological abuse.[24]

According to the Italian National Institute of Statistics (ISTAT)[25] report of 2007, partners are responsible for the largest part of physical abuse: partners or former partners have committed 70 per cent of the rapes that have been reported. All kinds of abuses are serious, but only 18 per cent of women in the ISTAT sample regard it as a crime, 44 of the interviewed women think of it as something wrong and 36 as something that 'simply happened'.[26] In 68 per cent of the cases, violence is perpetrated at home, but aggression and abuse also occur in the street and in cars. Figures show that only 7 per cent of incidents are reported to the police, and that more than one woman out of three remains silent on

---

21 Such as hitting, kicking, biting, shoving, restraining, slapping, throwing objects, punching, choking, pushing, pinching, pulling hair out, burning, strangling and other types of contact that result in physical injury to the victim. Physical abuse can also include denying the victim medical care when needed, depriving the victim of sleep or other functions necessary to live, or forcing the victim to engage in drug/alcohol use against his/her will.

22 Sexual abuse is any situation in which force or threat is used to obtain participation in unwanted sexual activity. Coercing a person to engage in sexual activity against their will, even if that person is a spouse or intimate partner with whom consensual sex has occurred, is an act of aggression and violence. Categories of sexual abuse include also attempted or completed sex acts involving a person who is unable to understand the nature or condition of the act, unable to decline participation, or unable to communicate unwillingness to engage in the sexual act, because of underage immaturity, illness, disability, or the influence of alcohol or other drugs, or because of intimidation or pressure.

23 Denying the victim access to money or other basic resources and necessities. The motive behind preventing a spouse from acquiring resources is to diminish the victim's capacity to support him/herself, thus forcing him/her to depend on the perpetrator financially, which includes preventing the victim from obtaining education, finding employment, maintaining or advancing their careers and acquiring assets.

24 Emotional abuse can include verbal abuse and is defined as any behaviour that threatens, intimidates, undermines the victim's self-worth or self-esteem, or controls the victim's freedom: controlling behaviour, intimidation, humiliation, harassment, domineering, damage to property, threats, social isolation, stalking, constant criticism, name-calling, blaming, ridicule, falsely accusing, disrespect, denial and any other conflicting actions or statements which are designed to confuse and create insecurity in the victim. Degradation in any form can be considered psychological abuse. Such behaviour leads the victims to question themselves, causing them to believe that the abuse is their fault, leaving them feeling helpless and unable to escape the situation. Women or men undergoing emotional abuse often suffer from depression, which puts them at increased risk of suicide, eating disorders, and drug and alcohol abuse.

25 ISTAT is a public research organisation. It has been present in Italy since 1926, and is the main producer of official statistics in the service of citizens and policy-makers.

26 The sample size was of 25,000 women aged between 16 and 70.

being wronged. As a consequence of missing reported abuse, of the complexity of gathering meaningful information on case numbers, case outcomes and compilation of statistics with challenges mostly due to issues of confidentiality, the dark number is estimated to be around 92 per cent of cases.

Although domestic violence accounts for between 16 per cent and one-quarter of all recorded violent crime, not all forms of domestic violence are illegal. For example, harassment, assault, criminal damage, attempted murder, rape and false imprisonment are crimes, whereas some forms of emotional abuse are not defined as crimes. Nevertheless, these types of violence can also have a serious and lasting impact on a woman's or a child's sense of wellbeing and autonomy.

Alcohol consumption and mental illness can be co-morbid with abuse, and present additional challenges in eliminating domestic violence. Awareness, perception, definition and documentation of domestic violence differ widely from country to country, and from era to era. In this regard the director of one of the visited antiviolence centres argues that in Italy violence is a cultural problem. Until 1996, there did not exist a law against sexual violence, and men were not punished if they were sexually abusing women. Court hearings for custody of their children are still under way in the majority of the cases, and as a result many women prefer not to show their faces.

In sum, violence against women is globally acknowledged as a basic human rights violation and a development issue with severe consequences to economic growth. Indeed, the estimated direct and indirect, human and monetary total cost[27] of domestic violence to individuals, households, the Italian government and society is enormous.[28]

Domestic violence is a complex problem, which may take place within very different societal contexts. There is no one strategy that will work in all situations, since the degree to which a community sanctions it will naturally influence the kind of strategy needed. Besides, considering the interconnections between the factors responsible for domestic violence – gender dynamics of power, culture and economics – strategies and interventions should be designed within a comprehensive and integrated framework.[29]

---

27 This is the cost to the criminal justice system, to social services, housing costs, the cost of physical healthcare treatment, of treating mental illness and distress, and of civil legal services.

28 ISTAT, *Report 2007*; Unicef/Innocenti Research Centre, *Innocenti Digest*.

29 On a global understanding of domestic violence and barriers to legal aid services, and access to justice for discrimination complainants, see Rosemary Hunter's work, notably *Domestic Violence Law Reform and Women's Experience in Court: The Implementation of Feminist Reforms in Civil Proceedings* (New York, 2008).

Reshaping the Meaning of Legality

Findings suggest that jurist women often deploy legal meanings in new settings, more so in cases of domestic violence. As domestic violence may comprise a number of different behaviours and consequences, it is not included in the Italian Penal code as an explicit crime on its own. Consequently, to persecute the behaviour labelled as domestic violence, lawyers need to make use of other types of crime; they have to appeal and refer to a set of legal paradigms and rules both general and specifically enacted to fight gender violence.[30]

To illustrate the different processes of 'creating legality' by jurist women, I selected as analytical tools the three key dimensions mentioned above: before the law, with the law and against the law. I will limit myself to reporting only one example of each narrative.

Before the Law

According to this pattern the law is perceived, represented and depicted as something magisterial and remote, hardly available to common people.

This pattern refers for example to all cases of intimate partner violence in which women do not want to report the crime to the authorities. Especially when there are minor children, women face many challenges that stop them from doing so. In general, abused women do not find the courage to proceed against their abusers and/or enforce their rights, because of their lack of legal consciousness and trust in the law with its slow procedures.[31] In the Marche region, furthermore, there are no institutional facilities to really protect women: in this region counting more than 1,560,000 inhabitants, there is only one so-called secure-house situated in Ancona, the regional capital, to keep women and children safe from further abuses and violence. This contributes to the fact that many of these women think they have neither the chance nor the ability to utilize the legal system and structures to their advantage. Consequently, abusive behaviour, which takes place within the private sphere of the home, often

---

30 Art. 29 of the Italian Constitution (family protection and safeguard), Title XI (Articles 556 to 574 – crimes against family) and XII (Articles 575 to 623 bis – crimes against individuals) of the Italian Penal code; Art. 283 of the Italian Code of Civil Procedure. Regarding the latter kind of rules, I refer to the Law n.66/1996 on sexual abuse and violence, the Law n.154/2001 concerning abusive relationships, Art. 612 bis of the Italian Penal code (introduced by the Law 38/2009) that punishes the crime of stalking.

31 About the variability in women's legal consciousness in matters of sexual harassment as well as in their belief that law can help them, see: Sandy Welsh and Jayne Baker, 'To Report or Not? Legal Consciousness and Women's Decisions to Report Sexual Harassment' (American Sociological Association Annual Meeting, Montreal, 2006), www.allacademic.com/meta/p103411_index.html.

remains 'invisible', underreported and underestimated in the official statistics. That is why social scientists time and again fight against the 'dark number' of domestic crimes of all sorts. In this regard, both lawyers and laywomen agree in affirming: 'As a general rule, abuses and violence rarely emerge and, in any case, only when judicial separation or divorce have occurred' (A.E., 50-year-old female lawyer).

Since, as I explained before, Italian legislation is quite silent on rules or provisions on domestic violence, this pattern also refers to cases in which informal means of social control, either community or neighbour related, get activated 'before the law', or in cases in which lawyers make innovative use of existing legal paradigms in order to persecute abusive behaviour in particular circumstances. Let me give an illustration of both cases in the following one example.

The husband of a Tunisian woman living near Fermo had for a long time been beating and insulting his wife (he forced her to work illegally at home for a local shoe factory without giving her money), leaving her without healthcare (though she was in need of gynaecological treatment) and locking her up in the house. After continually hearing screams, cries and moans, yet never seeing or meeting the woman, the neighbours called the local social services. When they arrived, the woman could not open the door because she was locked up inside and had no key. In order to get the husband convicted, according to the statement of the Sentence of the Penal Court of Cassazione (Supreme Penal Court) n. 3368/2005, the lawyer successfully used the crime of 'reducing somebody to servitude' as defined in Art. 600 of the Italian Penal code (Riduzione o mantenimento in schiavitù o servitù – enslaving or reducing somebody in servitude).[32]

With the Law

According to the 'with the law' pattern, the law is perceived, represented and depicted as a game with rules that can be manipulated to one's advantage. This is the case whenever laypeople or legal professionals defend interests and rights by using existing law and legal procedures.

Most lawyers in the sample declared that they often had strategically used abuse complaints to achieve major legal outcomes.

One enlightening example goes as follows: after five years of marriage, a man began beating his wife, insulting and harassing her, even during pregnancy. At first, she minimized the importance and significance of her husband's conduct and limited herself to confiding it to two intimate friends.

---

[32] This article has been modified by the Law n. 228/2003 (Misure contro la tratta di persone), which has added to the original topic of 'enslaving' a similar yet less serious course of action, that of 'reducing somebody to servitude'.

But following subsequent episodes of humiliation and violent behaviour in front of friends, her parents and their underage children, the woman decided to make a complaint against her husband and to leave the family home with the children, taking refuge at her parents'. In order to get a consensual legal separation – her husband promised to never do it again – she decided to withdraw her complaint against him. Yet shortly after the separation decree, her now ex-husband not only continued his intimidation and verbal abuse in person and on the phone, but he even applied to modify the terms of the legal separation – Art.710 of the Italian Code of Civil Procedure (Modificabilita' dei provvedimenti relativi alla separazione dei coniugi) – in order to obtain joint custody of their children. Consequently, the woman was compelled to complain again and to request a restraining order against this man who also did not respect the separation agreements: he neither paid the children's maintenance nor returned his wife's personal belongings and furniture.

At that point the lawyer used the complaints presented by the wife before as well as after their legal separation to show how the man's petition was only a way not to pay alimony and, therefore, how he was absolutely inadequate to properly care for, educate and raise the children. His violent, harmful and persistent conduct was considered not only as prejudicial to the mother's health, safety and dignity, but also to that of the children.

The mother won the case and the judge – applying the interest of the minors as per Art. 155 bis of the Italian Civil code as amended by Law 54/2006 (Affidamento condiviso) – assigned her their sole custody.

Against the Law

According to this pattern the law is perceived, represented and depicted as an ideological and arbitrary power, which is employed as a medium for unfairness, persecution and discrimination. As such, the law should be actively resisted.

In relation to this, I would like to present an interesting case referred to by an aged female lawyer. It shows how, even when the law seems to protect them, women are often disregarded and devalued.

The story is that of a battered woman who killed her abusive male partner. For more than 10 years the woman had been beaten time after time when her husband returned home drunk. She was often experiencing severe injuries, together with mental, emotional and verbal abuse. The woman made repeated but failed attempts to enlist the help of law enforcement agencies against this situation. She did obtain a protection order that temporarily excluded the man from their home, but as violation of such orders are not punished severely, the man returned home to intimidate and assault his partner once more. This woman and her two sons (who were trying to defend their mother) had just been beaten when the violence escalated and the homicide occurred. The woman stated she had the impression that their lives were in danger and that her killing was unplanned yet reasonable because in self-defence. After the event the woman was arrested, jailed and ordered by jail staff to take mood-regulators, sedatives and anti-depressants. These drugs, inhibiting clear thinking, directly interfered with her ability to make reasoned decisions and to participate and follow the course of her own trial.[33] Her lawyer appealed on the grounds of self-defence, and provocation was effectively accepted as an extenuating factor; but the extenuating factor came in a form that pathologized the defendant: rather than explaining the homicide as this woman's necessary choice to save her own life and that of her sons, she was labelled as 'helpless' and affected by 'battered woman syndrome'.[34] Women offenders following abuse are almost always treated as having a mental disorder, even if this is not the case. If it is true that such a 'syndrome' provides a commonly used framework granting a fair trial, its judicial and public perception as a form of incapacity nevertheless reveals that, despite the purpose for which this legal strategy was conceived, old stereotypes are reproduced in a new form.[35]

Although Battered Woman Syndrome (BWS) is intended to describe the experience of women who have been battered and abused by their intimate partner and their response to such violence, the use of 'syndrome' language, defined essentially as a mental disorder, helps to create an image of pathology that can stigmatize the defendant unnecessarily and inaccurately. Diagnosis is often used as a justification in support of self-defence when the defendant in a criminal case is a woman who has experienced domestic violence, to negate the specific intent element of a crime. But, as far as it is based on an analysis of the

---

[33] In accordance with the feminist scholar Dermody Leonard, the interviewee thinks that the overuse of mood-altering drugs is a form of institutional victimization that continues the silencing of abused women (S.B., 68-year-old female lawyer). See: Elizabeth Dermody Leonard, *Convicted Survivors: The Imprisonment of Battered Women Who Kill* (New York, 2002).

[34] Battered Woman Syndrome is a notion introduced in the 1970s by psychologist Lenore E. Walker ('Battered Women and Learned Helplessness', *Victimology*, 2/3–4 (1977): pp. 525–34). It has evolved from a term used to describe a broad range of victims' (such as learned helplessness) and abusers' (such a violence cycles) reactions, to a mental health disorder. It is often used to explain experience and reaction patterns of women who have been battered and abused by their intimate partners. Although individual women respond to domestic violence differently, a number of reactions are common among those who have been exposed to these traumatic events (see Leonore E. Walker, 'Battered Woman Syndrome: Empirical Findings', *Annals of the New York Academy of Sciences*, 1087 (2006): pp. 142–57). It can explain behaviour that might be difficult for judges to understand, such as why survivors do not leave; why they act emotionally unaffected after shootings; why a woman returns to an abuser after separation or fails to call the police and so on.

[35] Lenore E. Walker, 'Battered Women Syndrome and Self-Defense', *Notre Dame Journal of Law, Ethics & Public Policy*, 6/2 (1992): pp. 321–34.

victimization dynamic only, excluding information about women's strengths – including responsibility (such as taking care of her children, providing economic resources to her family), agency (making decisions to protect herself and her children from violence and abuse) and capacity (competence to act independently and endurance to continue functioning in the face of great adversity) – it can be both misleading and potentially harmful. In fact, when the expert focuses his or her evaluation on this question, the result is an analysis of those factors that support or fail to support the reasonableness of the defendant's perception of immediate danger, given the circumstances. The focus is on the woman's internal psychological state, not on external events to explain the perception of threat posed by the abuser's behaviour. If a woman's behaviour is not understood in the full context of her life, important decisions in a legal case can be incorrectly influenced by stereotypes or assumptions about how or why women who are battered behave the way they do. Indeed, even when mental health problems and depression result from violence and abuse and influence a woman's decisions, they are usually only a part of it; how an individual woman experiences or reacts to being battered will vary depending on her psychological, social, cognitive profile and on practical circumstances.

It has been argued that battered women who kill their abusers represent a special class of defendants being unfairly treated in the legal system: criminal justice often fails to respond to abused wives, in many cases leaving women without protection, while punishing them for protecting themselves and their children.[36] Yet, it is now increasingly recognized that BWS often evokes a stigmatizing image of pathology, which may affect the whole decision-making process. This image runs counter to the self-defence argument that the defendant's perception of immediate danger was reasonable for someone in her circumstances, and therefore that her actions were justifiable under the law. It is difficult to argue that a defendant who is viewed as flawed, damaged, disordered or abnormal by virtue of a mental health diagnosis should be justified in her actions based on the reasonableness of her perceptions.[37]

To sum up, in the courtroom the use of BWS by those with scientific knowledge and specialized experience with domestic violence fails to serve those who demand and deserve the very best: judges and, ultimately, women who have endured domestic violence. Its use persists, in part, because it conveniently packages in a single phrase a far more complex issue,[38] but obviously fails to treat the female defendant as a self-respecting person.

---

[36] Dermody Leonard, *Convicted Survivors*.

[37] Mary Ann Dutton, Sue Osthoff and Melissa Dichter, *Update of the 'Battered Woman Syndrome' Critique* (2011), http://www.vawnet.org.

[38] Bess Rothenberg, 'The Success of the Battered Woman Syndrome: An Analysis of How Cultural Arguments Succeed', *Sociological Forum*, 17/1 (2002): pp. 81–103; Bess

The Impact of Legal Knowledge and Practice on Jurist Women's Personal Lives

As far as the impact of legal knowledge on jurist women's personal lives is concerned, outcomes indeed suggest that legality deeply contributes to building these women's social and professional identities. According to many female jurists, their access to the legal profession and their consciousness about legal norms have changed their ways of thinking about situations, behaviours and relationships: 'Legal knowledge is like a filter, that is, a *forma mentis* through which meanings, speeches, social and cultural practices, happenings, and so on, are read, understood and managed in the light of legal categories and concepts' (C.P., 45-year-old female lawyer).

In accordance with the theories and findings of many authors – such as Patricia Ewick and Susan Silbey, Austin Sarat and Thomas Kearns[39] – some of the jurist women I interviewed, and lawyers in particular, agreed in affirming that: 'In everyday locations, I make sense of my experiences by relying on legal categories and concepts, even though these may not be in accordance with the details of formal rules and regulations' (E.S., 60-year-old female lawyer).

The awareness of the legal consequences – sometimes really serious ones – of any kind of behaviour makes them more fearful and constantly on their guard, more so than other mothers are with their children, mostly when they are teenagers:

> I always advise and urge my husband, parents and relatives, especially my teenage sons, to be cautious in making decisions, to reflect on the legal consequences before acting ... to be compliant with the legal system every time. This is the only way to prevent damage and harm to oneself and others. (M.T., 50-year-old female lawyer)

An interesting matter is the fact that jurist women seem to be well aware of the difference between risk and danger, more so than other women.[40] And they agree in considering the law as a powerful means of control and reduction of

Rothenberg, 'We Don't Have Time for Social Change: Cultural Compromise and the Battered Woman Syndrome', *Gender & Society*, 17/5 (2003): pp. 771–87.

[39] Ewick and Silbey, *The Common Place of Law*; Austin Sarat and Thomas R. Kearns (ed.), *Law in Everyday Life* (Ann Arbor, 1995); Anna Maria Marshall and Scott Barclay, 'In Their Own Words: How Ordinary People Construct the Legal World,' *Law & Social Inquiry*, 28/3 (2003): pp. 617–28.

[40] According to Luhmann's 'risk theory', we can use the concept of danger when we think that damage, losses and unsuccessful events come from the environment or have some external reasons. The concept of risk can be used when we assume that problems, damage or unsuccessful events are due (brought about) to our inadequate decision-making processes. Niklas Luhmann, *Risk: A Sociological Theory* (New Brunswick, NJ, 2002).

risks: 'As a general rule, to prevent risk and danger, I seek to follow, in both my private and in my working life the three Rs principle: Responsibility for one's own behaviour, self-Respect and Respect of other people' (58-year-old female judge).[41]

Moreover, legal practice and culture helps them to understand the common sense notions of legal justice: 'Act within the law and you are never wrong! – this is my motto' (52-year-old female judge).

Paradoxically, they think it is precisely their legal knowledge which helps them to criticize what can be seen as the selfishness of the legal profession, and develop a thoughtful set of suggestions as to how the legal order and lawyers might redirect their thinking to be more in line with public interest. Most of the interviewees stated their inability (in the sense of unwillingness) to ask poor clients for money, and the following belief: 'A litigation strategy can be successful even if it fails to win the case, when it contributes to building awareness on issues of gender discrimination and violence against women and children' (P.C., 51-year-old female lawyer).

Women Lawyers' Attitudes and Difficulties

Women's access to the legal profession has been accompanied by an increasing gender specialization, either in family and juvenile or migration law.[42] This is called 'horizontal discrimination' and comes from the stereotyped image of women as more suited to emotional relations and affection. At the same time, women are generally excluded from important financial and political cases. Yet male lawyers often attribute this situation more to women's will and aptitude rather than to real professional segregation: 'I think women lawyers are effectively more willing to deal with family matters: they are more attentive, more patient and more intuitive than men' (S.G., 55-year-old male lawyer).

Our findings indeed show that female lawyers are keener than their male colleagues to specialize and acquire appropriate qualifications and training in juvenile law; to pay attention to psychological issues and factors; to participate in meetings; and to gather information and understanding about their underage clients.

Most female lawyers interviewed did not seem to live this situation as a case of discrimination. In fact, most of them thought they were 'more inclined and ready to bring the right arguments in the name and voice of those who are outsiders to the system of male privilege' (P.D., 67-year-old female lawyer).

---

[41] As the judges have agreed to grant interviews provided they could retain their anonymity, their quoted statements are not supported by reference to the interviewees' initials.

[42] Centro Studi Investimenti Sociali, *Dopo le buone teorie*, p. 34.

But I also collected accounts from jurist women stating: 'We are always cut off from the top management, from the upper spheres, from wealthy and profitable disputes' (M.T., 50-year-old female lawyer) and: 'Throughout my entire life I have witnessed that whenever you find a woman in leadership and in prestigious roles you can bet she is tied to a successful and powerful man: father, husband, brother, partner or colleague' (F.P., 70-year-old female lawyer).

When speaking about women's understanding of their profession and its requirements – their representation of the ideal lawyer, their motivation to become a lawyer, the way they experience the power they wield, the existing gender differences and similarities in values and attitudes – my research outcomes suggest that women lawyers consider themselves to be more patient than their male colleagues, more willing to listen to clients when they want to show their feelings and open their hearts. Consequently, they think they are more able than men to understand their clients' needs, hopes and wishes. Besides, even after litigation is concluded, their relationships with clients often continue:

> We [women lawyers] are more tolerant and empathetic, more willing to listen and to explain … (L.C., 37-year-old female lawyer)
>
> Women – you know – are generally very good at making people feel comfortable. And feeling at ease is very important for all kinds of clients, especially abused women. They must feel you understand and share pity and sorrow, their request for dignity and justice, their wish to obtain protection and safeguard. (L.B., 40-year-old female lawyer)
>
> I strongly believe that in family matters the lawyer's commitment should be not to worsen and deepen the conflict, but to dim and settle the dispute as quickly as possible, in order to protect minors from an increase of ongoing hostility, aggression and violence between parents. (G.C., 51-year-old female lawyer)
>
> Devoting oneself to family law and disputes allows for a conciliation of professionalism and social commitment. That means acting in conflict resolution always looking at the interests of the minors. (S.B., 52-year-old female lawyer)

Members of the judiciary do recognize that domestic violence exists and has to be prevented through law. In this regard, the judges that I interviewed also stated: 'In general female lawyers – at any level – are more careful than their male counterparts to attend to all the details of an ongoing case with detailed descriptions, clarity of exposition and fine psychological observations' (50-year-old male judge).

The clients interviewed – whether plaintiff or defendant – agreed in stating: 'Women are better than men at understanding the fine psychological aspects of any question, particularly in the case of family or personal matters' (F.B., 55-year-old male plaintiff).

The abused and raped women in the sample seemed to hold the same opinion, too:

> Female lawyers with their empathetic attitude and their sharp minds have given me moral support and legal ground to find the courage to report the crime. (V.B., 43-year-old battered woman)
>
> Only another woman can understand my feelings, emotions, humiliation and suffering ... I never should have gone to see a male lawyer! (M.V.S., 35-year-old raped woman)

In the struggle to balance their work and family,[43] career and affections, jurist women complain about the lack of family-friendly policies in the legal profession, about institutional impediments, economic discrimination, unsuitable court schedules and 'glass ceiling' mechanisms:

> Women lawyers have increased ... that's right! ... Yet, it's not a secret that women still face daunting obstacles to succeed in the legal profession! (M.M., 50-year-old female lawyer)
>
> I suffered adverse career consequences in my struggle to meet work and family needs. (S.B., 40-year-old female lawyer)
>
> I wish for a working life that allows me to have a satisfying home life as well. But often we [women] don't have the power and skill to negotiate that. For example to compel male colleagues to rethink the long-hours culture.[44] (M.T., 34-year-old female lawyer)
>
> To resolve competing notions of appropriate social roles and to balance the demands of work and family, women are more inclined towards the care of children and, in general, the quality of life. (50-year-old female judge)

In this regard, I can report the experience of Fernanda Contri (the first Italian woman to preside over a public session of the Constitutional Court in 2005), constitutional judge from 1996 to 2005. During an interview, she said: 'As far back as the 70s, I asked a chief judge to use a room inside the court for childcare and baby-sitting. But I was silenced with this answer: "courts are sacred places, and the law is something serious!"'

Actually, not much seems to have changed. Today in the whole of Italy there exist only five nurseries and day-care centres in law courts (in Rome, Florence, Pescara and Syracuse).

---

43 Rhode, 'Balanced Lives'.

44 See Michael Moller, 'Exploiting Patterns: A Critique of Hegemonic Masculinity', *Journal of Gender Studies*, 16/3 (2007): pp. 263–76.

Fortunately, many law firms are beginning to recognize these difficulties and are now offering a variety of employment options, including flexible and part-time, as a valuable tool in the fight for talent and skills, without jeopardizing career paths. At the same time, equal opportunity commissions as well as national and local jurist women associations work to break through institutional impediments. Yet, to fit happily and successfully into the legal profession, women face additional challenges: 'When we work in firms, we have to show all the time that we are dedicated and willing to work hard' (P.C., 37-year-old female lawyer).

Despite the fact that jurist women often graduate with better marks than men or pass their professional qualifying examinations more easily, they still earn less.[45] Furthermore, law schools often do not prepare graduates enough for practice; firms, for their part, often fail to mentor young lawyers, forcing them into a hourly billing system[46] that undermines home and family lives, encourages fraud and emphasizes marketing over legal expertise.[47] Although hourly billing was originally justified in part because of its simplicity and objectivity, it has received its share of criticism from within and without the profession.[48] Interviewees using this computational method affirmed to be very tired and uneasy about taking vacations for fear of not meeting billing expectations. According to my findings, a high percentage of women in private practices are dissatisfied with the legal profession. In part this dissatisfaction arises from spending too many hours in the office. This eventually takes its toll, both physically and mentally, and inevitably has an impact on other aspects of an attorney's life, especially the little time available for non-professional

---

45 CNF and CSM, *Le donne nelle professioni legali di domani.*

46 Hourly billing, as the term suggests, simply compensates the lawyer or the law firm for the number of hours expended on legal services for a client, multiplied by a fixed hourly rate. The widespread use of hourly billing is a relatively recent development in Western countries. Before, Italian lawyers utilized a sort of flat fee schedule approved by court or bar associations, as well as contingency and percentage fees. Yet nowadays, many large firms demand of their new associates to bill for up to around 2,200 hours each year. In order to reach that number, it has been calculated that an associate needs to spend 3,300 hours at the office, in other words over nine hours a day, including weekends and holidays. See William G. Ross, *The Honest Hour: The Ethics of Time-Based Billing by Attorneys* (Durham, NC, 1996).

47 Sol M. Linowitz and Martin Mayer, *The Betrayed Profession: Lawyering at the End of the Twentieth Century* (New York, 1994).

48 This system allows clients to compare the rates of various attorneys and to know in advance how much they will be charged for time expended, yet it does not recognize extraordinary, priority or emergency services; moreover, the lawyer is not adequately compensated in high-value and high-responsibility matters. Both advantages and disadvantages are developed in Richard C. Reed, *Billing Innovation: New Win-Win Ways to End Hourly Billing* (Chicago, 1996).

pursuits.[49] Thus, the untenable choice seems to be to work long hours and achieve professional success only at the cost of being uninvolved in one's community and a stranger to one's children and spouse.

Concluding Remarks

Gender-neutral theories presume equality of power in male–female relationships and tend to ignore centuries of male-dominated social systems. Yet in the course of history, the law, as well as the economy, traditional family structures and other social institutions, has systematically supported the authority of men over women, sometimes legitimizing and perpetuating violence against women.

Over the last decades, in turn, major social, legal and cultural changes have improved the feminine condition in the sense of decreasing direct discrimination between men and women. Notwithstanding the fact that the general normative European framework is calling for such a transformation, especially in the light of the general principles of 'equal opportunity' and 'non-discrimination', both informal and indirect discrimination seem to be still deeply entrenched in (Italian) society and in its legal system.

After more than 30 years of feminist legal theory and jurisprudence,[50] socio-legal scholars and researchers continue to debate the impact of women's presence in legal practice and scenarios for a prospective gender-oriented professional agenda, enabling European women lawyers' voice to be heard.[51]

As the extracts of interviews and narratives quoted above clearly show, jurist women often experience discrimination twice, both inside and outside the courtroom.[52] Although sometimes they find some key supporters among male colleagues and a few of them do experience success stories, jurist women suffer from an invisible closure preventing them from upward professional mobility.[53] Most of the women in this research sample felt they had, more and better than men, to prove that they were serious, professional and trustworthy. Moreover, balancing the demands of work and family, they experience the stress of combining multiple tasks and responsibilities. My findings suggest that in their professional lives, the law provides cultural patterns that jurist women use

---

49 Jeremy Holmes, *Hourly Billing: A Guide for Law Students*, htpp://www.uiowa.edu.

50 Nicola Lacey, 'Feminist Legal Theory', *Oxford Journal of Legal Studies*, 9/3 (1989): pp. 383–94.

51 Vittorio Olgiati, 'On the Women Lawyers' Voice in Europe: Scenarios for a Legal Education Agenda', in Josef Langer (ed.), *Analysis and Visions for Europe* (Frankfurt, 2011), pp. 127–48.

52 Slotkin and Goodman, *It's Harder in Heels*.

53 Celia Davies, 'The Sociology of Profession and the Profession of Gender', *Sociology*, 30/4 (1996): pp. 661–78.

not only at work but also to understand their everyday life and that of other women, especially when dealing with women victims of gender violence and domestic abuse. Dealing with such problems and crimes, women's legal strategies reveal the aim and effort to challenge the prevailing gender bias, stereotypes and discrimination.

As we have seen, female lawyers do tend to think that a litigation strategy is successful whenever it contributes to building awareness of gender issues: for example, by highlighting how women offenders are still pathologized, or by contributing to the legal qualification of domestic violence against women and children as a violation of human dignity and human rights.

Gendered legal expertise produces material and symbolic effects in the overall functioning of the socio-legal field. Just as jurist women play a fundamental role in the global understanding of domestic violence, they also have an important part in the demand for appointing women in leadership roles, and in supporting gender mainstreaming policy: all issues granted in theory, but not often enforced in practice.[54]

In this chapter I summarized the main findings of individual experiences and viewpoints gathered in the field. They show how the law often fails to protect women and how the empowerment of women through the law is still a long way from freedom, dignity and social justice.

Yet, in their attempts to spread awareness of legal rights among women, children and immigrant people, jurist women transform themselves, their working space and the wider society of which they are part. Women's access to the legal profession has indeed affected legal scholarship and jurisprudence. Thus, according to Hanne Petersen's theory about the so-called 'home knitted law',[55] we effectively witness the rise of intuitive-unofficial legal practices, where values like bargaining, sympathy, sharing and solidarity are more and more widespread. Legality, however, does not reside exclusively in the individual's ideas and attitudes, and legal consciousness is not a static set of opinions and thoughts; it is instead contingent and changeable, insofar as it is the result of the individual's 'participation in the process of constructing legality'.[56]

For this reason, the jurist women interviewed in this chapter believe it is important to explore and practise new ways of incorporating human rights awareness and values into people's daily life, even through the creative use of media, art and culture. As one member of an Italian jurist women's association said: 'Our true plan is to build a better world for all women, not just for ourselves!'

---

[54] Lauren S. Rikleen, *Ending the Gauntlet: Removing Barriers to Women's Success in the Law* (New York, 2006).

[55] Hanne Petersen, *Home Knitted Law: Norms and Values in Gendered Rule-Making* (Aldershot, 1996).

[56] Ewick and Silbey, *The Common Place of Law*, p. 45.

Bibliography

Ackroyd, Stephen, and John Hughes, *Data Collection in Context* (Harlow: Longman, 1992).

Bartolomei, M. Rita, 'Gender and Judging in Traditional and Modern Societies: A Comparison of two Case Studies (Ivory Coast and Italy)', in Ulrike Shultz and Gisela Shaw (ed.), *Gender and Judging* (Oxford: Hart, 2013).

Bartow, Ann, *Legal Theory Lexicon 061: Feminist Legal Theory*, http://lsolum.typepad.com/legal_theory_lexicon/2006/11/legal_theory_le.html.

Brockman Joan, *Gender in the Legal Profession: Fitting or Breaking the Mould* (Vancouver: UBC Press, 2001).

Centro Studi Investimenti Sociali, *Dopo le buone teorie, le proposte. Programma di ricerca per le donne avvocato*, *Census Report 2010*, http://www.aiga.it.

Consiglio Nazionale Forense and Consiglio Superiore della Magistratura, *Le donne nelle professioni legali di domani* (National Meeting Rome, 11 June 2010).

Davies, Celia, 'The Sociology of Profession and the Profession of Gender', *Sociology*, 30/4 (1996): 661–78.

Dermody Leonard, Elizabeth, *Convicted Survivors: The Imprisonment of Battered Women Who Kill* (New York: SUNY Press, 2002).

Drachman, Virginia, *Sisters in Law: Women Lawyers in Modern American History* (Cambridge, MA: Harvard University Press, 1998).

Dutton, Mary Ann, Sue Osthoff and Melissa Dichter, *Update of the 'Battered Woman Syndrome' Critique* (2011), http://www.vawnet.org.

Ewick, Patricia, and Susan Silbey, *The Common Place of Law* (Chicago: University of Chicago Press, 1998).

Frazier, Patricia, and Jennifer Hunt, 'Research on Gender and the Law: Where Are We Going, Where Have We Been?', *Law and Human Behavior*, 22/1 (1998): 1–16.

Fredman, Sandra, *Discrimination Law* (Oxford: Oxford University Press, 2002).

Friedman, Lawrence, 'Is There a Modern Legal Culture?', *Ratio Juris*, 7/2 (1994): 117–31.

Hagan, John, and Fiona Kay, *Gender in Practice: A Study of Lawyers' Lives* (Oxford: Oxford University Press, 1995).

Harrington, Mona, *Women Lawyers: Rewriting the Rules* (New York: Knopf, 1994).

Holmes, Jeremy, *Hourly Billing: A Guide for Law Students*, http://www.uiowa.edu.

Hunter, Rosemary, *Domestic Violence Law Reform and Women's Experience in Court: The Implementation of Feminist Reforms in Civil Proceedings* (New York: Cambria, 2008).

Italian National Institute of Statistics, *Report 2007*, http://www3.istat.it.

Lacey, Nicola, 'Feminist Legal Theory', *Oxford Journal of Legal Studies*, 9/3 (1989): 383–94.

Levit, Nancy, and Robert R. M. Verchick, *Feminist Legal Theory: A Primer* (New York: NYU Press, 2006).

Linowitz, Sol M., and Martin Mayer, *The Betrayed Profession: Lawyering at the End of the Twentieth Century* (New York: Charles Scribner's Sons, 1994).

Luhmann, Niklas, *Risk: A Sociological Theory* (New Brunswick, NJ: Transaction, 2002).

Marshall, Anna Maria, and Scott Barclay, 'In Their Own Words: How Ordinary People Construct the Legal World,' *Law & Social Inquiry*, 28/3 (2003): 617–28.

Moller, Michael, 'Exploiting Patterns: A Critique of Hegemonic Masculinity', *Journal of Gender Studies*, 16/3 (2007): 263–76.

Mossman, Mary Jane, *The First Women Lawyers: A Comparative Study of Gender, Law and the Legal Professions* (Oxford: Hart, 2006).

Olgiati, Vittorio, 'Donne & lavoro. L'inclusione della differenza di genere nelle attività economiche e professionali', *I Quaderni dell'Istituto di Sociologia*, 3 (Università di Urbino, 2006).

Olgiati, Vittorio, 'On the Women Lawyers' Voice in Europe: Scenarios for a Legal Education Agenda', in Josef Langer (ed.), *Analysis and Visions for Europe* (Frankfurt –am Main: Lang, 2011).

Petersen, Hanne, *Home Knitted Law: Norms and Values in Gendered Rule-Making* (Aldershot: Dartmouth, 1996).

Rapley, Tim, 'Interviews', in Clive Seale, David Silverman, Jaber F. Gubrium and Giampietro Gobo (ed.), *Qualitative Research Practice* (Thousand Oaks, CA: Sage, 2004).

Reed, Richard C., *Billing Innovation: New Win-Win Ways To End Hourly Billing* (Chicago: ABA Section of Law Practice Management, 1996).

Rhode, Deborah L., 'Balanced Lives: Changing the Culture of Legal Practice' (Stanford: ABA Commission on Women in the Profession, 2001).

Rikleen, Lauren S., *Ending the Gauntlet: Removing Barriers to Women's Success in the Law* (New York: Thompson Legal Works, 2006).

Ross, William G., *The Honest Hour: The Ethics of Time-Based Billing by Attorneys* (Durham, NC: Carolina Academic Press, 1996).

Rothenberg, Bess, 'The Success of the Battered Woman Syndrome: An Analysis of How Cultural Arguments Succeed', *Sociological Forum*, 17/1 (2002): 81–103.

Rothenberg, Bess, 'We Don't Have Time for Social Change: Cultural Compromise and the Battered Woman Syndrome', *Gender & Society*, 17/5 (2003): 771–87.

Sarat, Austin, and Thomas R. Kearns (ed.), *Law in Everyday Life* (Ann Arbor: University of Michigan Press, 1995).

Schultz, Ulrike, and Gisela Shaw (ed.), *Women in the World's Legal Profession* (Oxford: Hart, 2003).

Slotkin, Jacquelyn, and Samantha Goodman (ed.), *It's Harder in Heels: Essays by Women Lawyers Achieving Work-Life Balance* (Lake Mary, FL: Vandeplas, 2007).

Sommerland, Hilary, and Peter Sanderson, 'Professionalism, Discrimination, Difference and Choice in Women's Experience in Law Jobs', in Philip Thomas (ed.), *Discriminating Lawyers* (London: Cavendish, 2000).

Unicef/Innocenti Research Centre, *Innocenti Digest 6*, June 2000, http://www.unicef-irc.org/publications/pdf/digest6e.pdf.

Walker, Lenore E., 'Battered Women and Learned Helplessness', *Victimology*, 2/3–4 (1977): 525–34.

Walker, Lenore E., 'Battered Women Syndrome and Self-Defense', *Notre Dame Journal of Law, Ethics & Public Policy*, 6/2 (1992): 321–34.

Walker, Lenore E., 'Battered Woman Syndrome: Empirical Findings', *Annals of the New York Academy of Sciences*, 1087 (2006): 142–57.

Welsh, Sandy, and Jayne Baker, 'To Report or Not? Legal Consciousness and Women's Decisions to Report Sexual Harassment' (American Sociological Association Annual Meeting, Montreal, 2006), www.allacademic.com/meta/p103411_index.html.

World Health Organization, *Violence against Women Act* (FRH/WHD/96.27) (Geneva: WHO, 1996).

Young, Alison, and Nina Puren, 'Signifying Justice: Law Culture and the Question of Feminism', *Australian Feminist Law Journal*, 13 (1999): 3–12.

Index

Note: Entries in **bold** refer to tables.

For Product Safety Concerns and Information please contact our EU
representative GPSR@taylorandfrancis.com
Taylor & Francis Verlag GmbH, Kaufingerstraße 24, 80331 München, Germany

www.ingramcontent.com/pod-product-compliance
Ingram Content Group UK Ltd.
Pitfield, Milton Keynes, MK11 3LW, UK
UKHW020015200926
475702UK00014B/1898

* 9 7 8 1 1 3 8 7 1 0 9 7 9 *